Display and Analysis

of Spatial Data

Display

and

Analysis

Co-sponsored by

Scientific Affairs Division, North Atlantic Treaty Organization

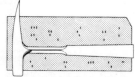

Kansas Geological Survey,
University of Kansas

Department of Geography,
University of Nottingham

of Spatial Data

NATO Advanced Study Institute

Edited by

JOHN C. DAVIS
Kansas Geological Survey,
University of Kansas

and

MICHAEL J. McCULLAGH
Department of Geography,
University of Nottingham

A Wiley–Interscience Publication

JOHN WILEY & SONS

London · New York · Sydney · Toronto

Library of Congress Cataloging in Publication Data:

NATO Advanced Study Institute on Display and Analysis
of Spatial Data, Nottingham, Eng., 1973.
Display and analysis of spatial data.

"A Wiley–Interscience publication."
Sponsored by Scientific Affairs Division, North
Atlantic Treaty Organization; Kansas Geological Survey,
University of Kansas; and the Dept. of Geography,
University of Nottingham.

1. Electronic data processing—Cartography—
Congresses. I. Davis, John C., ed. II. McCullagh,
Michael J., ed. III. North Atlantic Treaty Organization.
Division of Scientific Affairs. IV. Kansas State
Geological Survey. V. Nottingham, Eng. University.
Dept. of Geography. VI. Title.

GA106.3.N18 1973   526'.028'54   74–3449
ISBN 0 471 19915 X

Printed in Great Britain by
J. W. Arrowsmith Ltd., Bristol BS3 2NT

List of Contributors

D. P. Bickmore	*Experimental Cartography Unit, Royal College of Art, London, England.*
A. D. Cliff	*Department of Geography, University of Cambridge, Cambridge, England.*
J. T. Coppock	*Department of Geography, University of Edinburgh, Edinburgh, Scotland.*
P. Delfiner	*Centre de Morphologie Mathématique, Fontainebleau, France.*
J. P. Delhomme	*Centre de Morphologie Mathématique, Fontainebleau, France.*
G. M. Gaits	*Department of the Environment, London, England.*
M. L. Hsu	*Department of Geography, University of Minnesota, Minneapolis, Minnesota, U.S.A.*
C. J. Huijbregts	*Centre de Morphologie Mathématique, Fontainebleau, France.*
G. F. Jenks	*Department of Geography and Meteorology, The University of Kansas, Lawrence, Kansas, U.S.A.*
K. Kozar	*Minnesota Land Management Information System, University of Minnesota, Minneapolis, Minnesota, U.S.A.*
J. K. Ord	*Department of Statistics, University of Warwick, Warwick, England.*
G. W. Orning	*Minnesota Land Management Information System, University of Minnesota, Minneapolis, Minnesota, U.S.A.*
J. A. B. Palmer	*Division of Computing Research, Commonwealth Scientific and Industrial Research Organization, Canberra City, Australia.*
T. K. Peucker	*Department of Geography, Simon Fraser University, Burnaby, B.C., Canada.*
J. L. Pfaltz	*Department of Applied Mathematics and Computer Science, University of Virginia, Charlottesville, Virginia, U.S.A.*
W. D. Rase	*Department of Geography, Simon Fraser University, Burnaby, B.C., Canada.*

J. E. Robinson   *Union Oil Company of Canada Limited, Calgary, Canada.*

R. J. Sampson   *Kansas Geological Survey, The University of Kansas, Lawrence, Kansas, U.S.A.*

A. H. Schmidt   *Laboratory for Computer Graphics and Spatial Analysis, Harvard University, Cambridge, Massachusetts, U.S.A.*

B. F. Sprunt   *Department of Geography, Portsmouth Polytechnic, Portsmouth, England.*

P. G. Streed   *Minnesota Land Management Information System, University of Minnesota, Minneapolis, Minnesota, U.S.A.*

P. Switzer   *Departments of Statistics and Geology, Stanford University, Stanford, California, U.S.A.*

M. Tichenor   *Department of Geography, Simon Fraser University, Burnaby, B.C., Canada.*

W. R. Tobler   *Department of Geography, University of Michigan, Ann Arbor, Michigan, U.S.A.*

E. H. T. Whitten   *Department of Geological Sciences, Northwestern University, Evanston, Illinois, U.S.A.*

P. Yoeli   *Department of Geography, Tel-Aviv University, Tel-Aviv, Israel.*

W. A. Zafft   *Laboratory for Computer Graphics and Spatial Analysis, Harvard University, Cambridge, Massachusetts, U.S.A.*

Foreword

By H.R.H. The Duke of Edinburgh

Human civilization was made possible by communication and all further technological development is completely dependent on better and more accurate communication.

At one time it consisted of spoken language only, then pictures and writing were developed to increase the means of communication between people. A new dimension was added when it became necessary to communicate with computers designed to handle and process vast quantities of information. At this point the display and analysis of spatial data became a problem for specialists.

I hope that the international exchange of information and ideas which the N.A.T.O. Advanced Study Institute sponsored at the meeting at Nottingham in 1973 will encourage further improvement in advanced communication techniques. Every science, every technology, as well as all industry, commerce and international trade, will benefit from the results.

Preface

How can a variable that assumes different values at different locations be described and analyzed? This is a critical question in the fields of geography, geology, meteorology, and oceanography. Efficient answers have great potential importance, not only in these scientific fields, but also in the technological areas of navigation, transportation, reconnaissance, and planning, to name but a few. A specific, but classic example is the efficient creation of maps which depict the form of the Earth's surface. This is achieved conventionally by drawing lines or contours on a map, representing levels of equal elevation on the ground. A finished contour map is an effective expression of an extremely complex form; equivalent depictions are equally effective for expressing global patterns of barometric pressure, the density of people in a region, or the variations in thickness of a manufactured part.

Many algorithms have been proposed for the digital calculation of contour-type maps and for spatial display of surfaces. The production of such maps is an important aspect of computer graphics. Nevertheless, comparatively little research has been published on the statistical properties of spatially distributed variables, on the relative efficiency and effectiveness of existing and proposed contouring systems, and on the drawing of inferences from the displays created by the systems. The published literature is widely scattered, primarily through the fields of geography, geology, and computer science, although important theoretical contributions have been made by statisticians and biological scientists. A major purpose of this volume is to bring together the products of these researchers from their disparate disciplines, focusing on the common problem of display and analysis of spatial data.

The subject matter of this volume may be conveniently considered as falling into three parts. The first of these is concerned with the theoretical nature of spatially distributed variables. Included are such topics as statistical properties, including stationarity, homogeneity, and spatial autocorrelation of spatial variables. A related set of topics is concerned with sampling of spatially distributed variables and includes estimates of sample variance, relative effectiveness of sampling designs or grids, and evaluation of the reliability of map estimates.

The second part of the volume is concerned with the practical implementation of spatial displays. This includes the calculation and creation of models or maps of spatial variables. The subject area may be broken into two parts, concerned on one hand with algorithmic or computational considerations and on the other with perceptual considerations. Although literally millions of dollars are annually devoted to the automated creation of maps for such purposes as mineral exploration, highway planning, military use, and weather forecasting, almost nothing has been published on the relative merits of the algorithms used. These will be considered from the viewpoints of computational efficiency, statistical reliability, and special characteristics. Contributions in the volume include those from many of the authors of contouring algorithms now in the public domain. These scientists discuss such questions as global versus local fit techniques, ways of minimizing running time, the expected errors inherent in various algorithms, contour searching methods, hidden line problems, alternative methods of display, and many other topics of vital concern in the practical implementation of automatic methods.

Perceptual considerations include such topics as the most effective and unambiguous ways to present spatial data to an observer, the influence of contour spacing on the ability to visualize form, and physiologic factors that affect the interpretation of displayed data. These contributions acknowledge that the products of spatial analyses are created for the benefit of people; the most elegant interpretation scheme is of no use if results are not effectively communicated to the human audience. Statistics, computer science, and esthetics must be combined to produce pleasing as well as accurate and efficient spatial displays.

The third type of contribution in this volume includes the analysis and interpretation of displays of spatial data. A great variety of topics fall into this category, ranging from the application of pattern recognition techniques to mapped features, the separation of maps into constituent parts by spatial Fourier techniques, to the determination and measurement of directed features within the mapped surface. Some of the approaches are statistical, thus bringing the contributions full circle from consideration of the statistical properties of the spatial variate, to consideration of the statistical properties of the map.

The papers in this volume were written by participants at the NATO Advanced Study Institute on Display and Analysis of Spatial Data. Held in Nottingham, England, in July of 1973, the Institute was attended by approximately 140 members and associates from 19 countries. During the two weeks of the Institute, the participants engaged in a lively exchange of views and extensive discussions, often extending late into the night over a friendly glass, about the problems of computer mapping. Unfortunately, this informal exchange cannot be preserved for posterity, but its influence will be recorded in many of the activities of the participants in the years to come. Hopefully, this volume will form a record of the more formal aspects of the Institute, a reminder to the participants, and a glimpse of Institute activities to those who could not attend.

The Advanced Study Institute was sponsored by the Scientific Affairs Division of the North Atlantic Treaty Organization, who provided the bulk of the funds for the participants and for the meeting itself. The Kansas Geological Survey, University of Kansas, and the Department of Geography, University of Nottingham, were co-sponsors of the Institute, which was held in Sherwood Hall on the campus of the University of Nottingham.

The list of persons who contributed to the success of the Institute is too long for inclusion here, but a few individuals gave so unstintingly of their time that they must be personally acknowledged. These include Professor Richard Osborne of the Department of Geography and Mr George Eltringham, Deputy Registrar of the University of Nottingham. Mrs Kathy Remark assumed a major responsibility for the smooth functioning of the Institute and the production of this volume. Mr Jim Campbell was responsible for logistics and arrangement of activities that contributed much to the enjoyment of the Institute by the participants. Mr Roy Bradshaw and other members of the faculty, staff, and student body of the Geography Department at Nottingham provided invaluable help.

Dr William W. Hambleton, Director of the Kansas Geological Survey, provided financial and staff support for the editing and typing of the manuscript for this volume. Mrs Jo Anne Kellogg assumed the herculean task of typing the authors' and editors' cryptic scribblings into a legible manuscript.

JCD & MJM   1974

Contents

SECTION III: PRACTICAL APPLICATIONS OF
COMPUTER MAPPING

Estimation of the Accuracy of Qualitative Maps

P. Switzer

The question of map precision arises when a map has been constructed from data which do not cover the entire domain of the map, are subject to observation, measurement, recording, location, or ground-truth errors, or some combination of these. In such instances it is convenient to refer to the map at hand as an *estimated* map as opposed to the underlying error-free *true* map.

Typically the true map is unknown, unknowable, or difficult to obtain especially when data must be collected in the field. However, even when true maps are available, we may deliberately generate estimated maps, as when photo-imagery is digitized for computer analysis or when thin sections are point-counted for modal or textural analyses.

Precision will then be some measure of the discrepancy between the estimated and true maps. Precision measures are useful not only because they serve as indices of quality for particular maps, but also because they enable comparisons to be made between estimated maps constructed from different densities and configurations of data. Indeed, it is even possible to predict the gain in precision that would be achieved by augmenting the data in an estimated map whose precision we have already calculated.

At first it may seem that calculation of map precision is implausible because it involves comparison with the true map which is either unknown or unavailable for calculation. However, it turns out that many reasonable precision measures depend on the true map only through certain summary characteristics which can be approximated by reference to the estimated map. Thus, the estimated map itself can be used to estimate the degree of its discrepancy from the true map, making the objective of this paper attainable.

The preceding encouraging remarks presume that data underlying the estimated map are fairly dense. When the data are sparse there is not too much that can or should be said about the precision of the map. Data sparseness, however, is relative and depends on the basic complexity of the map; fortunately, the data themselves can tell you if they are relatively sparse.

1

For reasons of conciseness, we do not deal here with observation or location errors. The only error which we assume is that generated by interpolating between punctual sample data.

Formally we consider a map to be a partition of a domain R into k subdomains, where k is the number of colors used in the map. The subdomains are denoted $R_1, R_2, \ldots, R_k$ in the true map, and are denoted $\hat{R}_1, \hat{R}_2, \ldots, \hat{R}_k$ in the estimated map. The symbol μ is used to denote length, area, or volume according to whether the map is one-, two-, or three-dimensional; generically, we will refer to μ as area. *Throughout this paper we assume that the map domain has been scaled so that* $\mu(R) = 1$. The n data points underlying the estimated map are at locations denoted $s_1, s_2, \ldots, s_n$ which may or may not be at the centers of basic sampling cells denoted by $S_1, S_2, \ldots, S_n$. (The n basic sampling cells are themselves a relatively fine partition of the domain R.) The estimated map is constructed by assigning a cell to the ith subdomain $\hat{R}_i$ if the data point inside that cell is observed to fall in R_i.

As an example, consider the two-dimensional, three-color (k = 3) map of Figure 1. Taking this as the true map, we sampled it as an exercise to obtain

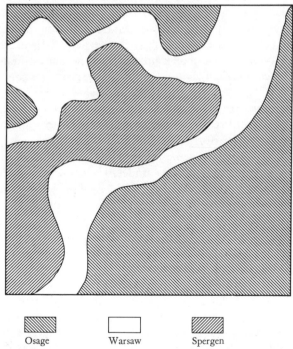

Osage   Warsaw   Spergen

Figure 1   Portion of Pre-Pennsylvanian geologic map of Kansas (true map). Subcropping units are Lower Mississippian (Osage) and Upper Mississippian (Warsaw, Spergen).

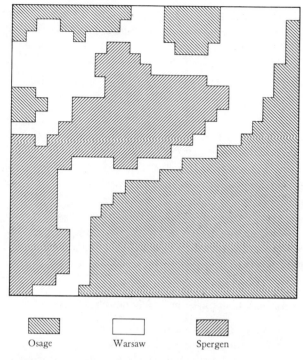

Osage   Warsaw   Spergen

Figure 2 Estimated map of Pre-Pennsylvanian geology in part of Kansas, formed by sampling Figure 1 with square net of 625 cells.

an estimated map. The basic sampling cells form a square net with n = 625 cells and a data point at the center of each cell. The resulting estimated map is shown in Figure 2.

As an index of precision we look at the discrepancy between the true and estimated maps as measured by the mismatch areas. Specifically, let

$$L_{ij} = \mu(R_i \cap \hat{R}_j) \qquad i \neq j. \tag{1}$$

Then L_{ij} is the area of that region which belongs to true subdomain i but is represented as subdomain j on the estimated map. Similarly, the total area of the incorrectly mapped portion of subdomain i is given by

$$L_i = \sum_{j \neq i} L_{ij} \qquad (i \text{ fixed}) \tag{2}$$

and the total mismatch area for the whole domain is

$$L = \sum_{i=1}^{k} L_i. \tag{3}$$

By overlaying the two maps in Figures 1 and 2 we can calculate by plani-metric methods the following mismatch areas:

$$
\begin{array}{lll}
L_{13} = 0.000 & L_{21} = 0.013 & L_{31} = 0.000 \\
L_{12} = 0.014 & L_{23} = 0.015 & L_{32} = 0.009 \\
L_1 = 0.014 & L_2 = 0.028 & L_3 = 0.009.
\end{array}
\tag{4}
$$

The total mismatch area is $L = 0.051$ or 5.1 percent. (Recall that the total domain area is scaled to be unity.)

Of course, in this example we had the "true" map available and were willing to perform an arduous calculation. Later we will show how mismatch areas can be estimated without the true map, using only the data of the estimated map and without involved measurements. First, however, we will examine the relationship of the mismatch areas to the size and shape of the basic sampling cells and the locations of data points. We will also examine the effect of randomness in the selection of data points.

Characterizations and Comparisons of Mismatch Areas

For simplicity of analysis we assume that the domain R is first divided into n basic sampling cells with a single punctual observation in each. The estimated map is constructed by coloring each sampling cell with the color representative of its datum point. We can express L_{ij} as a sum of Legesgue integrals:

$$
L_{ij} = \sum_{h=1}^{n} \delta_j(s_h) \int_{S_h} \delta_i(s)\, d\mu(s),
\tag{5}
$$

where δ_i is the indicator function for the true subdomain i, S_h are the sampling cells, and s_h are the data points.

It is possible to rewrite Equation (5) in a more revealing form. Suppose a point is chosen randomly in the domain R. Given that this random point is at a distance d from the datum point of the sampling cell into which it fell, let

$$
\begin{aligned}
P_{ij}(d) = \ &\text{probability that the random} \\
&\text{point is in true substratum} \\
&\text{i and the datum point is in} \\
&\text{true substratum j.}
\end{aligned}
\tag{5a}
$$

Then an equivalent expression for L_{ij} is

$$
L_{ij} = \sum_{h=1}^{n} \int_{S_h} P_{ij}(|s - s_h|)\, d\mu(s),
\tag{6}
$$

where $|s - s_h|$ denotes the length of the vector **v**. It is important to note that no randomness has been assumed in choosing the data points and no random process is assumed to have generated the true map. Equation (5) and (6) hold for maps in any number of dimensions.

The representation in Equation (6) provides the clue to how L_{ij} might be estimated. In general, $P_{ij}(0) = 0$, and it is known that the derivative P'_{ij} of $P_{ij}(d)$ at $d = 0$ is strictly positive. When n is large and the sampling cells are small, then $|s - s_h|$ never becomes very large. We might therefore approximate $P_{ij}(|s - s_h|)$ by the first-order Taylor expansion $|s - s_h|P'_{ij}$. Substitution of this approximation into Equation (6) gives

$$L_{ij} \doteq P'_{ij} \sum_{h=1}^{n} \mu(S_h)D_h, \tag{7}$$

where D_h is mean distance between a random point in the sampling cell S_h and the datum point s_h in that cell.

The above approximation assumes that $P_{ij}(d)$ is a nearly linear function of d near $d = 0$. It expresses the mismatch area L_{ij} as a product of two factors: the first, P'_{ij}, is a numerical property of the true map and is independent of the sampling; the second factor $\sum\mu(S_h)D_h$, is a numerical property of the geometric arrangement of sampling cells and sample point locations and is independent of the true map. Hence, L_{ij} comparisons between different sampling arrangements and densities will involve only comparisons of the geometric factor $\sum\mu(S_h)D_h$ when the approximate Equation (7) is used. (This approximation (Equation (7)) overestimates the true mismatch area since it is known that the second derivative P''_{ij} is negative at $d = 0$. However, the necessary correction is of smaller order in n. Hence, (7) is adequate for large sample comparisons of sampling designs.)

Examples will illustrate the comparisons. If the sampling cells have the same area, then $\mu(S_h) = 1/n$. Furthermore, if they are congruent and the data points are located within them in a congruent manner, the D_h value for every sampling cell will be the same, say D. In this case, Equation (7) can be simplified to

$$L_{ij} \doteq P'_{ij} \cdot D \tag{8}$$

To further specialize suppose the map domain is two-dimensional and the sampling cells form a congruent rectangular net with sides in the ratio $r:1$. If the data points are located at the centers of the rectangular cells, then

$$D(\text{rectangular net}) = \tfrac{1}{12}n^{-\frac{1}{2}}\{2\sqrt{r + r^{-1}}$$
$$+ r^{-\frac{3}{2}}ln(r + \sqrt{1 - r^2}) \tag{9}$$
$$+ r^{\frac{3}{2}}ln(r^{-1} + \sqrt{1 + r^{-2}})\}.$$

For example, the mismatch area L_{ij} as approximated in Equation (8) for $4:1$ rectangular sample cells is about 39 percent higher than it would be for a square sampling net. When the net is very elongated, then Equation (9) is very nearly D(rectangular) = $(r/16n)^{\frac{1}{2}}$. If we specialize (Equation (9)) to a square sampling net, $r = 1$, we get

$$D(\text{square net}) = 0.383n^{-\frac{1}{2}}. \qquad (10)$$

Indeed, the expression (9) is minimized when $r = 1$, indicating that a square net is better than any elongated net for a given number of data points n. However, when sampling along traverses in the field, the economies of an elongated grid may permit n to be increased for a given total budget.

Our next comparison is between the fixed square sampling grid and the optimum hexagonal grid. Here the basic sampling cells form a net of congruent regular hexagons and the data points are located at the centers of the sampling cells. Once again expression (8) for the mismatch area applies, but now with

$$D(\text{hexagonal net}) = 0.377n^{-\frac{1}{2}}. \qquad (10a)$$

Hence for the same sampling density n, the linearly approximated mismatch area for the square net is only 1.6 percent larger than that obtained using the hexagonal net.

In these examples we note that the mismatch area L_{ij} is of order $n^{-\frac{1}{2}}$. This indicates that approximately four times as many data points would be needed to reduce the mismatch by half (assuming that data is already dense enough for the linear approximation). It is true in general that mismatch shrinks at the same rate that the maximum diameters of the basic sampling cells are shrinking. In the case of a regular net of sampling cells with data points at the centers, this rate will always be $n^{-\frac{1}{2}}$ for two-dimensional domains.

If the data points are chosen independently and at random within their respective sampling cells, this will usually result in a somewhat higher mismatch area compared with data points chosen at the cell centers. In particular the geometric factors D_h will be larger because the average distance between the datum point and other points in the sampling cell is increased. For example, if the n sampling cells form a square net in two dimensions, then random sampling (one datum per cell) gives

$$D = \frac{n^{-\frac{1}{2}}}{15}\{2 + \sqrt{2} + 5ln(1 + \sqrt{2})\} = 0.520n^{-\frac{1}{2}}. \qquad (11)$$

This represents an increase of more than 35 percent over strict mid-point sampling, comparing with Equation (10). However, the order of D (the order of the mismatch) is the same whether the datum point in a cell is fixed or randomly chosen.

A related question arises when there are possible location or "ground-truth" errors; that is, when the actual datum point location may be different from where we believe it to be. Such location errors may be modeled as in Switzer (1971). However, the important point to note is that while the geometric factors D_h will decrease with increasing sampling density n, they do not decrease to zero. Therefore, the mismatch area cannot be made arbitrarily small by increasing n. In other words the order of the mismatch is a constant; this argues that the linear expansion given in Equation (7) should not be used in this case.

Specifically, suppose location errors are spherically distributed and independent and the distance u of the target point from the datum point has probability density function g(u). As the sampling density increases and the sampling cells shrink down to a point the mismatch area will tend to the positive constant

$$L_{ij}(\text{location errors}) \rightarrow \int P_{ij}(u)g(u)\,du \qquad (12)$$

for two-dimensional domains. It is clear that the rewards of additional data when there are location errors are much less than if such errors are absent.

We now look briefly at how the dimension d of the map domain affects the rate at which mismatch areas decrease with increasing sampling density. For two dimensions we have seen that this rate is $n^{-\frac{1}{2}}$. Similar arguments will show that in d dimensions, the diameters of basic sampling cells will shrink at a rate $n^{-1/d}$, hence the mismatch areas shrink at the same rate. Specifically, for three dimensions it will take eight times as many data points to reduce mismatch areas in half, whereas in one dimension we need only twice as many data points.

A locally linear approximation for $P_{ij}(d)$ was used to obtain the approximate expression (7) for the mismatch area L_{ij}. This was sufficient for asymptotic comparison of sampling designs and for establishing rates of convergence to zero. However, for actual estimation of mismatch areas this approximation would be improved by an expansion to terms of order d^2. It is known that the second derivative P_{ij}'' at d = 0 is strictly negative when the map domain R is two-dimensional or higher. Hence, the linear approximation we have been using can never be exact, whereas a quadratic approximation with a negative d^2 coefficient could be. This also demonstrates that the linear approximation tends to overestimate the mismatch area.

Writing $P_{ij}(|s - s_h|) \doteq |s - s_h|P_{ij}' + \frac{1}{2}|s - s_h|^2 P_{ij}''$, and substituting into Equation (6) gives

$$L_{ij} \doteq P_{ij}' \sum_{h=1}^{n} \mu(S_h)D_h + \frac{1}{2}P_{ij}'' \sum_{h=1}^{n} \mu(S_h)D_h^*, \qquad (13)$$

where D_h^* is the mean *squared* distance between a random point in the sampling cell S_h and the datum point s_h in that cell. If we take a limiting view as $n \to \infty$, then the ratio of the second term to the first term will tend to zero at the same rate at which the maximum sampling-cell diameter is tending to zero. As an approximation, n should be large enough so that the second term is small compared to the first term of (13). For a completely congruent sampling pattern, expression (13) simplifies to

$$L_{ij} \doteq P'_{ij} \cdot D + \tfrac{1}{2} p''_{ij} \cdot D^*. \tag{14}$$

The quadratic approximation involves two parameters of the true map, P'_{ij} and P''_{ij} in such a way that ratios of mismatch areas for different sampling patterns depend not only on the sampling patterns but also on the ratio

$$-f_{ij} = P''_{ij}/P'_{ij}. \tag{15}$$

Likewise, the ratio between the quadratic and linear approximations for L_{ij} depends on f_{ij}.

For example, if the n sampling cells form a rectangular net in two dimensions with sides in the ratio $r:1$, then for centrally located data points

$$D^*(\text{rectangular net}) = \tfrac{1}{12}n^{-1}\{1 + r^2\}. \tag{15a}$$

If the expressions (9) and (15a) are now substituted into (14), we obtain the required quadratic approximation for mismatch areas using a rectangular sampling net. In the case of a square sampling net, $r = 1$, these substitutions give

$$L_{ij}(\text{square net}) \doteq 0.383n^{-\frac{1}{2}}P'_{ij} + 0.083n^{-1}P''_{ij}. \tag{16}$$

The effect of adding the quadratic term D^* to the approximation becomes more substantial as the sampling cells become more elongated. For example, if $n^{-\frac{1}{2}}f_{ij} = 0.10$, then the mismatch area with a $4:1$ sampling grid is about 35 percent greater than the mismatch area with a square grid using quadratic approximations. This compares with 39 percent if the linear rather than the quadratic approximation is used.

The optimal hexagonal sampling net gives $D^* = 0.192n^{-1}$. Using expressions (10a) and (14), we obtain a refined approximation for the mismatch area L_{ij}, namely, $L_{ij} \doteq 0.377n^{-\frac{1}{2}}P'_{ij} + 0.096n^{-1}P''_{ij}$. It can easily be shown that this quantity is always less than the corresponding mismatch area for the square net; however, the difference is always slight.

Estimation of Mismatch Areas

In the preceding section we saw that the mismatch area could be characterized in terms of $P_{ij}(d)$ and the geometry of the basic sampling cells and data points. While the geometry is known, the $P_{ij}(d)$ functions are unknown, being properties of the true underlying map. Hence, in order to estimate mismatch areas L_{ij} without knowing the true map, we must be able to estimate $P_{ij}(d)$ without knowing the true map.

Recall the definition of $P_{ij}(d)$ given in Equation (5a). This was the probability that a pair of points distance d apart will have one point in R_i and the other in R_j, under the restriction that both points are in the same sampling cell and the first point is a datum location. If we remove this restriction we would obtain a different probability function which, we assume, differs very little from $P_{ij}(d)$. (There would be no distinction whatever if the true map were regarded as a realization of a stationary process and we were averaging over the process.) From this point of view there is no distinction between $P_{ij}(d)$ and $P_{ji}(d)$; therefore, our estimates of the mismatch areas L_{ij} and L_{ji} will be the same. That is, the area which is truly subdomain i but is mapped as j is taken to be the same as the area which is truly j but mapped as i. While this is quite reasonable, the distinction disappears completely if we want to estimate the total mismatch area $L_{ij} + L_{ji}$.

To estimate $P_{ij}(d)$ parametrically we may proceed in the following manner: for every pair of data points s_h, s_ℓ, calculate the distance $|s_h - s_\ell|$ and the quantity

$$\delta_i(s_h) \cdot \delta_j(s_\ell) \tag{17}$$

where δ_i, δ_j are the subdomain indicator functions defined in Equation (5). Now plot $|s_h - s_\ell|$ against $\delta_i(s_h)\delta_j(s_\ell)$ for every ordered pair of sample points. Having chosen some parametric family of $P_{ij}(d)$ functions, the parameters can be estimated by least-squares fitting to the plotted data. The estimated function $\hat{P}_{ij}(d)$ may now be substituted into Equation (6) to obtain a data-based estimate $\hat{L}_{ij}$ of the mismatch area.

However, in order to estimate the mismatch area L_{ij} we must estimate $P_{ij}(d)$ only for small values of d. Typically the distances $|s_h - s_\ell|$ between data points are larger than the distances d between points within a basic sampling cell, while the latter points are necessary in the L_{ij} calculation. For example, with a square sampling net in two dimensions and data points at the center of each square, the minimum distance between samples is already beyond the range of d needed in the L_{ij} calculation. Typically we will need to extrapolate the estimated $P_{ij}(d)$ down to zero; this argues that only the closest data pairs should be used in the estimation.

When the data points form a regular grid there will be many data pairs with a common distance between them. For example, if the n data points are on a plane rectangular grid with sides a, b, then approximately n data pairs will be separated by distance a, the same number by distance b, and twice as many pairs at distance $(a^2 + b^2)^{\frac{1}{2}}$. In such regular cases we can estimate $P_{ij}(a)$, $P_{ij}(b)$, etc. non-parametrically by the frequency ratios

$$\hat{P}_{ij}(d) = \sum_{|s_h - s_\ell| = d} \delta_i(s_h)\,\delta_j(s_\ell) / \sum_{|s_h - s_\ell| = d} 1 \ . \tag{18}$$

In particular, for a square grid of n data points in d dimensions we can obtain the estimates $\hat{P}_{ij}(n^{-1/d})$, $\hat{P}_{ij}(2n^{-1/d})$, etc. non-parametrically using the frequency ratios shown in (18). Of course, if the data points are irregular or if they are located with a random component, then we must use a parametric approach to estimate $P_{ij}(d)$.

Figure 3 is a digitized map of Britain and Ireland. There are only two subdomains, land and water, and the estimated map was constructed from a

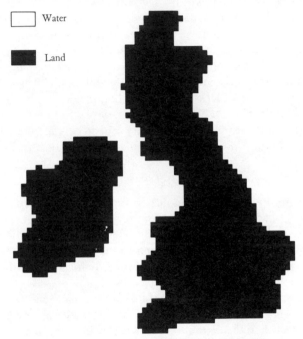

☐ Water

■ Land

Figure 3   Digitized map of Britain and Ireland, formed from a square sampling net.

square sampling net with centrally located data points. The function $P_{12}(d)$ has been estimated using the frequency ratios given by Equation (18) for values of d which are multiples of the grid spacing. The results appear in Table 1. We should note that even when the sampling design permits non-parametric estimation for certain distances d, we will still need to use a

Table 1.   Values of $\hat{P}_{12}(d)$ for the digitized map of Britain and Ireland (n = 5600). $\hat{R}_1 = 1 - \hat{R}_2 = 0.704$. Refer to Figure 3

$dn^{\frac{1}{2}}$	1	2	3	4	5	6	7	8	9	10
$\hat{P}_{12}(d)$	0.022	0.038	0.055	0.070	0.085	0.095	0.108	0.117	0.128	0.138

parametric model for extrapolation downward to $d = 0$. However, since the mismatch area L_{ij} is essentially an integral of the $P_{ij}(d)$ function, the particular choice of a parametric model for P will not greatly influence the estimate $\hat{L}$.

If we use the linear approximation of Equation (7) for the mismatch L_{ij}, then all that must be estimated is P'_{ij} (the derivative at $d = 0$). Hence the relevance of the parametric model is focused on a single number. If we have a non-parametric frequency estimate $\hat{P}_{ij}(d_0)$ for a small value d_0, then

$$\hat{P}'_{ij} = \hat{P}_{ij}(d_0)/d_0 \tag{19}$$

is the divided difference estimate of P'_{ij}. For example, for n data points on a square grid, a reasonable estimate when n is large would be $\hat{P}'_{ij} = n^{\frac{1}{2}}\hat{P}_{ij}(n^{-\frac{1}{2}})$. In general the divided difference estimate will underestimate the true P'_{ij} since the function is necessarily concave in the neighborhood of $d = 0$. Therefore, the corresponding estimate

$$\hat{L}_{ij}(\text{linear}) = 0.383\hat{P}_{ij}(n^{-\frac{1}{2}}) = \hat{L}_{ji} \tag{20}$$

will tend to underestimate the true L_{ij} slightly when n is large, whereas the original expression (Equations (8) and (10)) tends to overestimate L_{ij}.

If we use the quadratic approximation (Equation (13)) for the mismatch L_{ij}, we need to estimate the two derivatives P'_{ij} and P''_{ij} at $d = 0$ from the estimated $\hat{P}_{ij}(d)$ function. If we have frequency estimates $\hat{P}_{ij}(d_0)$ and $\hat{P}_{ij}(d_1)$ for two small values $d_0 < d_1$, then the divided difference estimates of P'_{ij} and P''_{ij} are

$$\hat{P}'_{ij} = \{d_0^{-2}\hat{P}_{ij}(d_0) - d_1^{-2}\hat{P}_{ij}(d_1)\}/\{d_0^{-1} - d_1^{-1}\},$$
$$\hat{P}''_{ij} = -2\{d_1\hat{P}_{ij}(d_0) - d_0\hat{P}_{ij}(d_1)\}/\{d_1^2 - d_0^2\}. \tag{21}$$

For example, when the n data points are on a square grid we could take $d_0 = n^{-\frac{1}{2}}, d_1 = 2n^{-\frac{1}{2}}$, giving

$$\hat{P}'_{ij} = \tfrac{1}{2}n^{\frac{1}{2}}\{4\hat{P}_{ij}(n^{-\frac{1}{2}}) - \hat{P}_{ij}(2n^{-\frac{1}{2}})\},$$
$$\hat{P}''_{ij} = \tfrac{2}{3}n^{\frac{1}{2}}\{2\hat{P}_{ij}(n^{-\frac{1}{2}}) - \hat{P}_{ij}(2n^{-\frac{1}{2}})\}. \tag{22}$$

Substitution in Equation (16) provides the data-based mismatch estimate

$$\hat{L}_{ij}(\text{quadratic}) = \hat{P}_{ij}(n^{-\frac{1}{2}}) \cdot \{0.768 - 0.110n^{-\frac{1}{2}}\}$$
$$- \hat{P}_{ij}(2n^{-\frac{1}{2}}) \cdot \{0.192 - 0.055n^{-\frac{1}{2}}\} \tag{23}$$
$$\doteq 0.76\hat{P}_{ij}(n^{-\frac{1}{2}}) - 0.19\hat{P}_{ij}(2n^{-\frac{1}{2}}),$$

provided the estimate is not negative. If it is negative it should be set to zero.

In the example of Figure 2 with $n = 625$ sampling cells we have, by Equation (18), $\hat{P}_{12}(0.04) = \hat{P}_{21}(0.04) = 82/2400$, $\hat{P}_{12}(0.08) = \hat{P}_{21}(0.08) = 146/2300$, $\hat{P}_{13}(0.04) = \hat{P}_{31}(0.04) = 0$, $\hat{P}_{13}(0.08) = \hat{P}_{31}(0.08) = 6/2300$, $\hat{P}_{23}(0.04) = \hat{P}_{32}(0.04) = 74/2400$, $\hat{P}_{23}(0.08) = \hat{P}_{32}(0.08) = 138/2300$. Hence, estimates of the mismatch areas, obtained with Equation (23) and without benefit of the underlying true map, are

$$\hat{L}_{13} = 0.000 \qquad \hat{L}_{21} = 0.014 \qquad \hat{L}_{31} = 0.000$$

$$\hat{L}_{12} = 0.014 \qquad \hat{L}_{23} = 0.012 \qquad \hat{L}_{32} = 0.012 \qquad (23a)$$

$$\hat{L}_{1} = 0.014 \qquad \hat{L}_{2} = 0.026 \qquad \hat{L}_{3} = 0.012$$

The total estimated mismatch area is therefore $\hat{L} = 0.052$ or 5.2 percent of the total area. These estimates should be compared with the actual mismatch area given by (4) and computed using both the true and estimated maps.

In earlier papers, Switzer (1965, 1972) used a parametric approach to estimate L_{ij}. There it was assumed that the $P_{ij}(d)$ functions could be approximated by the parametric model

$$P_{ij}(d) = \mu(R_i)\mu(R_j)\{1 - e^{-cd}\}, \qquad (24)$$

at least for small values of d. This model has $P_{ij}(0) = 0$, $P'_{ij} > 0$, and $P''_{ij} < 0$ as required. It decays to $\mu(R_i)\mu(R_j)$ for large values of d, corresponding to independence between distant points. The data points are used to estimate the subdomain areas and the decay parameter c. When the parameter estimates are substituted into the model and the model is substituted into Equation (6), we obtain another data-based estimate of the mismatch area L_{ij}. For a two-dimensional rectangular grid of n data points we would get

$$\hat{L}_{ij} = \mu(\hat{R}_i)\mu(\hat{R}_j)\left\{1 - n \int_{-\frac{1}{2}b}^{\frac{1}{2}b} \int_{-\frac{1}{2}a}^{\frac{1}{2}a} \exp[-\hat{c}(u^2 + v^2)^{\frac{1}{2}}]\,du\,dv\right\}. \qquad (25)$$

Since $ab = n^{-1}$, it can be determined that the integral depends only on a/b and $\hat{c}n^{-\frac{1}{2}}$. A table of this integral for purposes of estimating mismatch areas appears in Switzer (1965). Again using the example of Figure 2 with n = 625 data points on a square grid (a = b = $n^{-\frac{1}{2}}$), we get $\mu(\hat{R}_1) = 0.437$, $\mu(\hat{R}_2) = 0.318$ and $\mu(R_3) = 0.245$. An estimate $\hat{c}n^{-\frac{1}{2}}$ is obtained using the following formula from Switzer (1971, equation 11):

$$\hat{c}n^{-\frac{1}{2}} = ln\hat{T} - ln(\hat{T} - \hat{Q}), \text{ where}$$

$$\hat{T} = \sum_{i \neq j} \mu(\hat{R}_i)\mu(\hat{R}_j) \text{ and} \qquad (26)$$

$$\hat{Q} = \sum_{i \neq j} \hat{P}_{ij}(n^{-\frac{1}{2}}).$$

For these data we get $\hat{c}n^{\frac{1}{2}} = 0.22$. Substituting into (Equation (25)) and summing over i and j gives $\hat{L} = 0.052$ which agrees with the estimate obtained using Equation (23).

Experience with this and other examples strongly indicates that the type of model used to extrapolate $P_{ij}(d)$ down to d = 0 is of no great importance (when $P'_{ij} > 0$ and $P''_{ij} < 0$) in the estimation of mismatch areas. Estimation of model parameters is of greater importance. For regular grids we will have estimates $\hat{P}_{ij}(d_0)$, where d_0 is the grid spacing, constructed as frequency ratios in Equation (18). These frequency estimates do not obey the binomial law, but it is clear that when the numerators are small (less than 20) they may be unstable. This is likely to occur for small subdomains.

However, if we do not need to estimate every possible type of mismatch area, but rather obtain overall mismatch totals, our estimates will be more stable. For example, the sum L_2 is the area of true subdomain 2 which is incorrectly mapped. To estimate this quantity we do not need the L_{2j} separately, and the estimate of the sum will have better stability properties. If we want only the overall total mismatch area $L = \Sigma_{j \neq i} L_{ij}$, then the estimation is even easier. For example, if the quadratic model (Equation (23)) is used with square grid data points,

$$\hat{L}(\text{quadratic}) = 0.76\hat{P}(n^{-\frac{1}{2}}) - 0.19\hat{P}(2n^{-\frac{1}{2}}), \tag{27}$$

where $\hat{P}(d_0) = \Sigma_{i \neq j} \hat{P}_{ij}(d_0)$ = the proportion of data pairs at distance d_0 which fall in different subdomains. In a similar vein, if the exponential model given in Equation (24) is used, the overall estimated mismatch area $\hat{L}$ is the sum for $i \neq j$ of expression (25).

It is possible for the number of data points to be large even though they are sparse relative to the complexity of the map. This phenomenon is revealed when $\hat{P}_{ij}(d)$ appears flat over the range of d for which there is data or when $\hat{P}_{ij}(d) \approx \mu(\hat{R}_i)\mu(\hat{R}_j)$ even for the smallest d value for which there is data. In such cases the extrapolation down to $d = 0$ is problematic as is the estimation of mismatch areas. This would have been apparent for example if Figure 1 had been sampled on a grid with only 25 data points.

References

Matérn, B., 1960, Spatial variation: *Medd. Statens Bkogsforskningsinstitut*, v. 49, 144 p.

Matheron, G., 1965, *Les variables regionalises et leur estimation*: Masson et Cie, Editeurs, Paris, 305 p.

Switzer, P., 1965, Reconstructing patterns from sample data: *Annals of Mathematical Statistics*, v. 36, p. 138–154.

Switzer, P., 1971, Mapping a geographically correlated environment, *in* G. P. Patil, E. C. Pielou, and W. E. Waters, eds., *Statistical ecology*, volume 1: Pennsylvania State Univ. Press, p. 235–269.

Switzer, P., 1972, Applications of random process models to the description of spatial distributions of qualitative geologic variables: *24th Inter. Geological Congress*, Montreal, in press.

Linear Operators Applied to Areal Data

W. R. Tobler

Regional forecasting, spatial filtering, and map generalization have been treated advantageously by linear analytical methods. In general these methods have been applied to data assembled on a regular lattice. The objective of this study is the extension of these techniques to the case in which the data are assembled by geographical areas with irregular boundaries such as countries, counties, parishes, census tracts, or school districts. These curiously shaped regions are usually the domains of substantive interest and cannot be discarded by subdividing the world into kilometer or centimeter squares. At the same time one would like to retain the analytical power that is available when working with geographical data in gridded form. To simulate the geographical spread of ideas using Hägerstrand's model of the diffusion of innovations, for example, generally requires the use of geographical data in the form of square cells superimposed on some part of the Earth (Hägerstrand, 1968). One concern of this study is to explore how this model might be implemented using data on political units. As a second example, it would be desirable to be able to apply the same enhancement techniques to arbitrary areal data (choropleth maps to the cartographer) as are used to filter contour maps (Holloway, 1958; Tobler, 1966).

To review briefly, assume that geographical data have been collected at regular spatial intervals in two independent directions in a region small enough to allow neglect of the Earth's curvature. These data will be arranged in the form of a geographical matrix Z, with states z_{ij}, using the conventional positional notation. Entries in the matrix will now be changed in some manner to become new entries z_{ij}^*. The modification might be, for example, completely random, or could depend on the state itself, and could be deterministic or stochastic. The concern here is with processes which are such that the modification of a state z_{ij} depends only on its own state *and* on the states of the other observations. Symbolically, Z^* is a function of its own state and the collection of remaining states, $Z^* = f(Z)$. Generally, it is convenient to assume closure so that the mapping $Z \to Z^*$ has as its result objects of the same type. Such a general function has as many arguments as there are elements in the geographical matrix. The function is now restricted to be a local or neighborhood operator, a function which defines the modification of each z_{ij} in terms of its spatial neighbors only. Such an operation might be defined using a neighborhood which consists of the given element and its eight immediate neighbors. In this case the function has only nine elements and is of the form:

$$z_{ij}^* = f(z_{i-1,j-1}, z_{i-1,j}, z_{i-1,j+1}, z_{i,j-1},$$

$$z_{i,j}, z_{i,j+1}, z_{i+1,j-1}, z_{i+1,j}, z_{i+1,j+1}).$$

Neighborhoods which are larger or of a different shape can be defined in an analogous manner. It is implicit in the notation that every cell has the same definition for its neighborhood, a type of spatial stationarity generally found only in board games (Clowes, 1970) and mathematics. If the number of states is S and the number of entries in the neighborhood is N, there are obviously S^N situations which the function must cover.

From a substantive, geographical point of view the algebra of the technique also is of concern. For example, if $Z^* = f(Z)$ then in symbolic notation one might write $Z^{**} = f(Z^*) = ff(Z)$ or $Z^k = f^k(Z)$, a logical product, repeating the function k times if this is meaningful. An obvious question is what happens as k becomes very large:

$$\lim_{k=\infty} f^k(Z) = ?$$

Can the procedure be run backwards, $Z = f^{-1}(Z^*)$; or again symbolically, given Z and Z^* find $f = Z^*/Z$ in which we ask whether the *process* can be inferred from empirical instances. Alternatively, and from a planning point of view, given a current set of states Z and a desired set Z^* what are the requirements on f that Z^* be realizable in k iterations?

To give this substance, suppose that the states are land-use types. The geographical matrix Z might be a land-use map at time t and Z^* might be a land-use map at some earlier or later time period $t + \Delta t$. Alternatively, Z^* might be a generalization of the map Z and $(Z^*)^{-1}$ might represent "ungeneralization" or deconvolution. If there are five land-use categories and a neighborhood consists of a cell and its north, east, south, and west adjacent cells, then a deterministic transition rule would have to cover 3,125 cases. It is standard procedure to assume spatial isotropy, which reduces the number of cases considerably. There are several models of this type which might be used in geography and cartography (Burks, 1970; Codd, 1968; Feldt, 1968; Gardner, 1970; Harbaugh and Bonham-Carter, 1970; MacDougall, 1972; Minsky and Pappert, 1969; Ratliff, Hartline, and Miller, 1964; Smith, 1971; Switzer, 1969).

In special cases the states can be represented by numbers, with the usual arithmetic properties. Integers might be used for numbers of people by kilometer squares. Real numbers could represent elevations taken from a topographic map or grey tones measured on an aerial photograph. Complex numbers at each grid position can be used to define a two-dimensional vector field. Triplets of numbers at each point might define the tristimulus values for a colored map, or the dimensions of ellipsoids. A wind rose at each point requires a complete function at every point, and so on. The methods described below can be used for all of these examples, even if the number of states is essentially unbounded. The infinity of states does not cause serious problems because the system is closed. Of all possible ways of converting one set of numbers into another, only linear or log linear functions are considered here. In the spatially continuous case one such function can be written as

$$z^*(x, y) = \int\int\limits_{-\infty}^{+\infty} w(x, y, u, v)\, z(x, y)\, du\, dv$$

If one invokes translational invariance this becomes

$$z^*(x, y) = \int\int\limits_{-\infty}^{+\infty} w(u, v)\, z(x - u, y - v)\, du\, dv$$

and in the discrete case

$$z^*_{ij} = \sum_p \sum_q w_{pq} z_{i+p, j+q}$$

where the summation and weighting are taken over the p, q neighborhood.

One interpretation (Tobler, 1970) which can be given to this equation is that it is a finite difference approximation to the partial differential equation

$$\frac{\partial z}{\partial t} = M\left(\frac{\partial^2 z}{\partial x^2} + \frac{\partial^2 z}{\partial y^2}\right) + (\beta - \delta)z$$

describing spatial diffusion with sources and sinks. An alternate point of view (Tobler, 1969) is to assume that the data z_{ij} have been approximated by a Fourier series, that z^*_{ij} has been similarly represented, and that the difference between the two can be interpreted as the effect of a filter whose two-dimensional response function can be calculated from the weights. This is nothing but a change of basis in a linear vector space (Andrews, 1970; Rosenfeld, 1969; Tobler, 1967) and can also be treated as a Markov process (Howard, 1971; Woods, 1972).

The foregoing concepts have wide application in map generalization, geographical forecasting, spatial modeling, and picture processing. In virtually all of the literature it has been assumed that data are taken at regular spatial intervals. This is a rare event in geographical practice. Data are either taken at an irregularly distributed set of points in two or more dimensions, or they are aggregated within a set of irregularly shaped regions such as census tracts. Two strategies are used to handle these cases. The more common is to convert the data to a lattice and to proceed from there. The second strategy is to attempt to devise generalized operations which when specialized to regularly spaced observations are equivalent to those normally used.

A simple example should illustrate these two procedures. Suppose topographic elevations are known at randomly distributed locations and we wish to obtain an estimate of the slope at each of these locations. One procedure is to interpolate elevations to a lattice of points and to use standard finite difference methods to obtain derivatives. In the other instance we would attempt to use the observations directly to obtain an estimate of the slope. In principle these two approaches should give the same results (both are linear); in practice only the former strategy is used.

There are basically two problems. The first is to decide on the neighborhood. Given a random scatter of points in two dimensions, which points are neighbors of which other points? The second problem is that of choosing weights for particular purposes.

More formally, assume n observations at points $P_i, i = 1 \ldots n$, in a two-dimensional Euclidean space and label the positions with coordinates x_i, y_i. At each P_i we have a numerical observation z_i and the set of all of these observations can be called S. In a manner comparable to that given earlier, the objective is controlled modification of the values z_i at each of the observation points. The modification at a point P_i can depend on the value z_i at that point and on the values at all of the other points. Symbolically, we can say that z_i^* is some function of the value at i and of the collection of remaining values

$$z_i^* = f(z_k), \qquad z_k \text{ in } S.$$

As before it is required that the function be linear

$$z_i^* = \sum_k w_k z_k$$

with as yet undetermined weights. The next restriction is to require that the function be a neighborhood operator. Denote the set of all points which are neighbors of P_i by N_i. With this geographical restriction the modification process can be written as

$$z_i^* = \sum_k w_k z_k, \qquad z_k \text{ in } N_i.$$

In cartography a slightly different version of this problem frequently occurs. This is the interpolation problem of estimating a value z_0^* at a point P_0 of known location x_0, y_0 at which there is no observed value. It is required that this value be estimated from the known values,

$$z_0^* = F(z_k), \qquad z_k \text{ in } S$$

which is immediately specialized to a linear form

$$z_0^* = \sum_k w_k z_k, \qquad z_k \text{ in } S,$$

and is often restricted to be a neighborhood function

$$z_0^* = \sum_k w_k z_k, \qquad z_k \text{ in } N_0.$$

The value of z_0^* is usually chosen so that its departure from the true unknown value z_0 is minimized, generally in the averaged least-squares sense

$$\frac{1}{m} \sum (z_0^* - z_0)^2$$

where the summation is over all locations for which an estimate is desired. Typically the z_0^* form a lattice and these estimated values are then used for subsequent operations in place of the original scattered observations, which are now ignored. One such operation is the drawing of a contour map, usually by linear interpolation within the lattice. The similarity of the interpolation problem to the problem of modifying values at points for which values are already known should be apparent. Mathematically the two problems have virtually identical structures. Both are linear weightings of the given observations. The one operation is called prediction and the other is called filtering, but they are almost indistinguishable mathematically.

Consider first the neighborhood question. An adjacency or contiguity table can be constructed by listing all of the points in n rows and n columns, and placing a one in the ith row and jth column when points i and j are considered neighbors, inserting a zero otherwise. Clearly there are 2^{n^2} ways of doing this. The number of possibilities is reduced if the relation is symmetric and if a point is considered to be its own neighbor.

Neighbors are usually chosen by one of the following rules:

(1)   All points within distance D of the point in question are taken to be neighbors, using some agreed definition of distance.

(2)   The degree of neighborliness is defined by the distance from the point in question. Typically this results in weights being a function of distance and these approach zero at the distance D. If this bounding distance is larger than the field of observations then the neighborhood includes the complete set of points.

(3)   Thiessen neighbors (Rhynsburger, 1973). A second-order neighbor is the neighbor of a neighbor; this can be extended to higher orders. Normally all neighbors of the same order receive the same weight.

(4) Sokal neighbors (Sokal and Gabriel, 1969, p. 266–270).

(5) The nearest k points, using some agreed definition of distance, are take to be neighbors.

(6) Triangulation; each point has associated with it three neighbors and the area is partitioned into triangles. The number of topologically distinct triangulations is given by Brown (1965) to be

$$\frac{2(2m + 3)!(4n + 2m + 1)!}{(m + 2)!\,m!\,n!\,(3n + 2m + 3)!}$$

where m is three less than the number of points in the convex hull making up the outer boundary of the region, and n is the number of interior points. The number of geometrically distinct triangulations is somewhat less than this topological value. Among these there will be some whose cumulative edge lengths are minimal.

(7) Quadrangulation; each point has associated with it four neighbors and the area is partitioned into quadrangles (Brown, 1965).

(8) An assignment of neighbors using additional knowledge; *a posteriori* empirical or *a priori* theoretical knowledge is used.

Several of these definitions can be made to coincide for a lattice, which is clearly a special case. The important property is that each lattice point or cell always has the same number of neighbors; this lends considerable homogeneity to the processing operations. The concept of spatial stationarity is especially easy to visualize in this context. Try inventing a chess-like game in which the cells have variable numbers of neighbors. In the ensuing discussion it will be assumed that the second neighbor definition is used. In this case the controlled modification of data pertaining to irregularly spaced observations is fairly simple.

Suppose first that the filter kernel is known to be $K(u, v)$. This kernel is centered on the position P_i at which the observation $z(x, y) = z_i$ to be modified is located, which assumes spatial stationarity. The weights to be applied to the individual observations are now given by the value of this kernel at those points:

$$w_k = K(u - x, v - y)$$

where point k is located at (u, v). This value is then normalized so that

$$\sum_k w_k = \int\int_{-\infty}^{+\infty} k(u, v)\,du\,dv.$$

The modified value z_i^* of z_i is then given as a linear combination of these weights and the observations

$$z_i^* = \sum_k w_k z_k.$$

The kernel will vary for different types of linear operations. Two common types are differentiation and smoothing (low-pass filtering). Most important is "optimal" filtering wherein it is assumed that the observations themselves may be contaminated by measurement errors. Moritz (1962, 1963, 1967, 1970) has shown that the Wiener–Hopf equation leads to a kernel which involves covariance functions. Identical optimal filters have been derived for use in oceanography, in astronomy, in meteorology, in photogrammetry, and in mining geology (Bracewell, 1955; Burr, 1955; Kraus, 1971; Krige, 1966; Switzer, Mohr, and Heitman, 1964; Thompson, 1956). The same theory also leads to "optimal" least-squares prediction (interpolation), where it can be shown that the best predictor, when the observations are given as deviations from the mean, when there is no trend, and when the process has a stationary covariance, is

$$Z^* = AB^{-1}Z.$$

Z^* is the k by 1 vector of values to be predicted, Z is the i by 1 vector of known observations, B is the covariance matrix relating the observations, and A is the covariance between the values at the locations to be predicted and the known values. Thus the optimum prediction requires that something (the covariances) be known about the phenomena being studied. It is usually assumed that the covariances are functions only of the distances between the observations. Interestingly this theory also shows that the expected error of the prediction is

$$\text{error} = \frac{1}{k}\sum_k (Z^* - Z)^2 = \sigma^2 - AB^{-1}A^t$$

where σ^2 is the variance of the observations (Moritz, 1967). Thus it is possible to provide confidence and consequence maps which can be used to estimate the value of additional observations (Epstein, 1969; Rapp, 1964).

The next step is to extend these methods to areal data given, for example, by census tracts. Here contiguous units are usually recognized as neighbors and only the question of weights remains. In several cases the data, z_i are simply assumed to be concentrated at some point within the area; usually the centroid is taken (Pitts, 1967). From then on we can proceed as if the data were initially observed at points thus falling back on the case discussed above. The result of any operation is assumed to apply without change to the entire area with which the point is associated.

A second obvious approach is to use a set of weights proportional to the length of the common boundary (Cliff and Ord, 1969). Call this L_{ij} and use for L_{ii} the total length of the boundary of area i. Clearly $L_{ij} \equiv L_{ji}$, a theoretically desirable feature since assymmetry is prohibited. The weights can now be normalized

$$L'_{ij} = L_{ij}\Big/ \sum_j L_{ij}$$

and the n by 1 vector of modified areal values is obtained from the n by 1 vector of observed values by the multiplication

$$Z^* = LZ$$

where **L** is the n-square matrix of weights. Another attempt has been made to combine both boundary lengths and centroid distances (Cliff and Ord, 1970). The reason is obvious. Irregularly shaped regions may consist of long narrow countries, with long boundary contact, or of countries of large size making boundary contact only through narrow necks or corridors. But both size and border contact would seem to be important.

One procedure which captures these two effects is to assume that the kernel K(u, v) is given by a continuous function. Next assume that the geographical data are given by an at least piecewise continuous function z(x, y). This function is of the form $z(x, y) = z_i$ if (x, y) is in region i. Figure 1

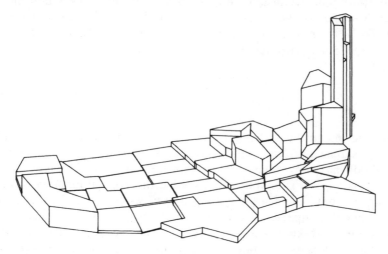

Figure 1   A piecewise continuous function z = f(x, y); 1970 population density by states

shows an important example. Until about 1820 it was thought that it was impossible to deal with such "pathological" graphs. But we now know better. As an example the equation and its derivation for a one-dimensional histogram are given by Lanczos (1966, p. 37). Suppose we write our geographical data as a continuous function, using the notation z(x, y), expandable as an infinite Fourier series in two dimensions,

$$z(x, y) = \int\limits_{-\infty}^{+\infty}\!\!\int A(\alpha, \beta) \exp[i\pi x + i\pi y]\, d\alpha\, d\beta.$$

The linear weighting procedure would then be written as the spatial convolution

$$z^*(x, y) = \int\limits_{-\infty}^{+\infty} \int k(u, v) z(x - u, y - v) \, du \, dv.$$

It is perhaps clearer in the Fourier domain where the weights induce a filter.

An approximation to this theory can be developed numerically in a direct fashion. Figure 2 shows a population profile through a latitudinal (43°N) tier of counties in Michigan from Lake Michigan to Lake Huron (87°W to 82°W longitude). To this we have fitted a high-order (100 harmonics) Fourier series, which does quite well except for the Gibbs phenomena. The sharp edges of the function would in fact require the entire infinity of Fourier coefficients. Walsh's (1923) functions probably would be more appropriate but the particular expansion is not of concern here. Finally we show the low-order expansion of the series (5 harmonics) which might correspond to the results of a low-pass filter. But this is no longer a step function. Clearly to obtain the appropriate step function we must set the new value for region i equal to

$$z_i^* = \frac{1}{b - a} \int\limits_a^b z^*(x) \, dx$$

where the integration extends from one edge of the county to the other. In this instance it is clear from Figure 2 that regional values are diminished if neighbors have low values, and the converse is also true. This is expected of a low-pass filter. It is tempting to ask what the original function was from which the county aggregation presented to us was derived. This question is of fundamental importance and suggests the use of a type of geographical enhancement. Making patterns in census data stand out more clearly is addressed in this paper only indirectly. (See Harmon and Julesz, 1973; Nordbeck and Rystedt, 1970; Tobler, 1969.)

Analogously, in two dimensions the original function $z(x, y)$ is sampled by multiplying it by a Dirac brush, the two-dimensional equivalent of the comb function. This yields values on a lattice. They are weighted and summed in the usual manner in the spatial domain

$$g_{ij}^* = \sum_p \sum_q w_{pq} g_{i+p, j+q}$$

or multiplied in the frequency domain. All values falling within region k are now integrated over the irregular shape and averaged

$$z_k^* = \frac{1}{A_k} \sum_{R_k} \sum g_{ij}^*.$$

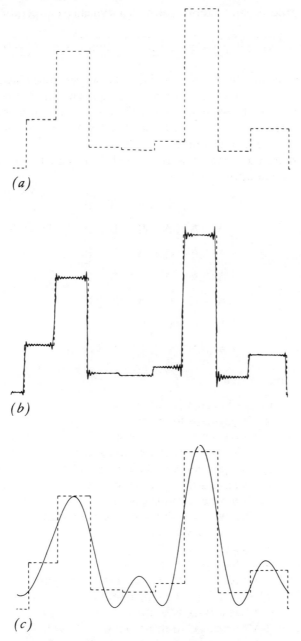

(a)

(b)

(c)

Figure 2   Latitudinal (43°N) profile (87°W to 82°W) of population density using Michigan county data, and its representation by Fourier series; 100 and 5 harmonics, respectively. Computed by J. Dozier.

This entire process can be represented as a sequence of operations

$$z_k \rightarrow z(x, y) \rightarrow \boxed{\text{sampling}} \rightarrow g_{ij} \rightarrow \boxed{\text{convolution}} \rightarrow g_{ij}^* \rightarrow \boxed{\text{summing}} \rightarrow z_k^*.$$

This is the procedure to be used for data such as per capita income by areal units. However, if the data are number of persons within an areal unit, then the averaging should take place before the convolution, thus working with density data. This is the case treated here. It is worth examining these steps in greater detail with an example.

Suppose there are three regions, labeled A, B, and C, in the following discretized configuration:

A	A	B	B	B	B
A	A	A	B	B	B
A	A	A	A	B	B
A	A	A	A	B	B
A	C	C	B	B	B
A	A	C	C	C	B
A	A	A	A	A	A

We quickly tabulate that

> 15 A's have an A to their east
> 4 A's have a B to their east
> 2 A's have a C to their east
> 1 A has an external area to its east
> 15 A's have an A to their west
> 0 A's have a B to their west
> 0 A's have a C to their west
> 7 A's have an external area to their west
> 13 A's have an A to their north
> 3 A's have a B to their north
> 4 A's have a C to their north
> 2 A's have an external area to their north
> 13 A's have an A to their south
> 1 A has a B to its south
> 2 A's have a C to their south
> 6 A's have an external area to the south
>
> 0 B's have an A to their east
> 9 B's have a B to their east

0 B's have a C to their east
6 B's have an external area to the east
4 B's have an A to their west
9 B's have a B to their west
2 B's have a C to their west
0 B's have an external area to the west
1 B has an A to the north
10 B's have a B to the north
0 B's have a C to the north
4 B's have an external area to the north
3 B's have an A to their south
10 B's have a B to their south
2 B's have a C to their south
0 B's have an external area to the south

0 C's have an A to their east
2 C's have a B to their east
3 C's have a C to their east
0 C's have an external area to the east
2 C's have an A to their west
0 C's have a B to their west
3 C's have a C to their west
0 C's have an external area to their west
2 C's have an A to their north
2 C's have a B to their north
1 C has a C to the north
0 C's have an external area to the north
4 C's have an A to the south
0 C's have a B to the south
1 C has a C to the south
0 C's have an external area to the south

There are 22 A's, 15 B's, and 5 C's in all. Suppose that the value in each region is to be modified by weighting using a neighborhood of five cells. Let these weights be labeled E, W, N, S, and X. First convert the values to densities, using an overbar to denote a value obtained after this operation. Then the modified value A′ for area A is given by

$$A' = (22X + 15E + 15W + 13N + 13S)\overline{A}$$
$$+(\qquad 4E + \qquad\quad 3N + \quad 1S)\overline{B}$$
$$+(\qquad 2E + \qquad\quad 4N + \quad 2S)\overline{C}$$
$$+(\qquad 1E + \ 7W + \ 2N + \ 6S)\overline{O}$$

and similarly,

$$
\begin{aligned}
\text{B}' = (& & 4\text{W} + & 1\text{N} + & 3\text{S})\overline{\text{A}} \\
+ (15\text{X} + & 9\text{E} + 9\text{W} + & 10\text{N} + & 10\text{S})\overline{\text{B}} \\
+ (& & 2\text{W} + & & 2\text{S})\overline{\text{C}} \\
+ (& 6\text{E} + & & 4\text{N} &)\overline{\text{O}} \\
\text{C}' = (& & 2\text{W} + & 2\text{N} & + 4\text{S})\overline{\text{A}} \\
+ (& 2\text{E} + & & 2\text{N} &)\overline{\text{B}} \\
+ (5\text{X} + & 3\text{E} + 3\text{W} + & 1\text{N} & + 1\text{S})\overline{\text{C}}
\end{aligned}
$$

or, with U^{t} given by

$$
\begin{bmatrix}
22 & 0 & 0 \\
15 & 0 & 0 \\
15 & 4 & 2 \\
13 & 1 & 2 \\
13 & 3 & 4 \\
0 & 15 & 0 \\
4 & 9 & 2 \\
0 & 9 & 0 \\
3 & 10 & 2 \\
1 & 10 & 0 \\
0 & 0 & 5 \\
2 & 0 & 3 \\
0 & 2 & 3 \\
4 & 0 & 1 \\
2 & 2 & 1 \\
0 & 0 & 0 \\
1 & 6 & 0 \\
7 & 0 & 0 \\
2 & 4 & 0 \\
6 & 0 & 0
\end{bmatrix}
$$

and **V** given by

$$
\begin{bmatrix}
X & 0 & 0 & 0 \\
E & 0 & 0 & 0 \\
W & 0 & 0 & 0 \\
N & 0 & 0 & 0 \\
S & 0 & 0 & 0 \\
0 & X & 0 & 0 \\
0 & E & 0 & 0 \\
0 & W & 0 & 0 \\
0 & N & 0 & 0 \\
0 & S & 0 & 0 \\
0 & 0 & X & 0 \\
0 & 0 & E & 0 \\
0 & 0 & W & 0 \\
0 & 0 & N & 0 \\
0 & 0 & S & 0 \\
0 & 0 & 0 & X \\
0 & 0 & 0 & E \\
0 & 0 & 0 & W \\
0 & 0 & 0 & N \\
0 & 0 & 0 & S
\end{bmatrix}
$$

then

$$
\begin{bmatrix} A' \\ B' \\ C' \end{bmatrix} = \mathbf{UV} \begin{bmatrix} \overline{A} \\ \overline{B} \\ \overline{C} \\ \overline{O} \end{bmatrix}
$$

If the conversion to density values is explicitly included in this, dividing by the area of each region, then

$$
\begin{bmatrix} A' \\ B' \\ C' \end{bmatrix} = \mathbf{UVS} \begin{bmatrix} A \\ B \\ C \\ O \end{bmatrix}
$$

where

$$
S = \begin{bmatrix} \frac{1}{22} & 0 & 0 & 0 \\ 0 & \frac{1}{15} & 0 & 0 \\ 0 & 0 & \frac{1}{5} & 0 \\ 0 & 0 & 0 & \frac{1}{26} \end{bmatrix}
$$

This is conveniently written, using $T = UV$, as

$$Z^* = TSZ.$$

If the weight field is given specific values then T is completely determined by the interaction of the weight field, the sampling density, and the shapes and adjacencies of the regions. For example, if

$$
\begin{array}{cccc}
 & N & & \frac{1}{8} \\
W = W & X & E = \frac{1}{8} & \frac{1}{2} & \frac{1}{8} \\
 & S & & \frac{1}{8}
\end{array}
$$

then

$$
T = \tfrac{1}{8} \begin{bmatrix} 144 & 8 & 8 & 16 \\ 8 & 98 & 4 & 10 \\ 8 & 4 & 28 & 0 \end{bmatrix}.
$$

This is clearly dependent on the external cells. If in-migration had been allowed,

$$
\hat{T} = \tfrac{1}{8} \begin{bmatrix} 144 & 8 & 8 & 16 \\ 8 & 98 & 4 & 10 \\ 8 & 4 & 28 & 0 \\ 16 & 10 & 0 & 182 \end{bmatrix}
$$

would have been obtained. Since a symmetrical kernel has been used the transformation rule is also symmetrical. Suppose that the values for the external area are not known. Then the weights in the last column of T cannot be applied. A boundary rule or condition must be supplied, which can be of several types. One rule is to assume all external values to be zero. Then T can be taken to be square and, if the weight field is symmetric, then T is also symmetric. T is usually diagonally dominant, which increases the likelihood of T^{-1} being uniquely determined. It may also be desirable to normalize the weights to take into account the "power" leaking through the boundary. Alternatively, a boundary condition may be chosen which is reflexive by modifying the weight field near the edges of the domain of interest. In the NE corner of this simple example, the weight field might be modified as follows,

$$
\begin{array}{cccc}
& \frac{1}{8} & & 0 \\
\overline{\frac{1}{8} \quad \frac{1}{2}} \Big| \frac{1}{8} & & \overline{\frac{1}{4} \quad \frac{1}{2}} \Big| \quad 0 \\
\frac{1}{8} \Big| & & \frac{1}{4} \Big|
\end{array}
$$

so **T** now becomes

$$
\frac{1}{8}
\begin{bmatrix}
155 & 9 & 12 \\
9 & 106 & 5 \\
8 & 4 & 28
\end{bmatrix}.
$$

An alternative would be to use

$$
\begin{array}{c}
0 \\
\overline{\frac{1}{8} \quad \frac{1}{2}} \Big| \quad 0. \\
\frac{1}{8} \Big|
\end{array}
$$

Clearly different boundary conditions lead to different results.

The operation

$$
\mathbf{Z}^* = \mathbf{TSZ}
$$

can be applied sequentially. This repeated convolution can be written as

$$
\mathbf{Z}^k = \mathbf{TSZ}^{k-1} = (\mathbf{TS})^k \mathbf{Z}.
$$

If the substantive interpretation is such that densities are not used then

$$
\mathbf{Z}^k = (\mathbf{ST})^k \mathbf{Z}
$$

in which the regional averaging is applied after each convolution. These two interpretations yield somewhat different results. The one-dimensional matrix multiplication is usually much quicker than the two-dimensional convolution because the number of areal units is generally much smaller than the number of points in a spatial lattice of data.

The important result in this discussion is that even when the data of interest are given by irregular spatial regions an equivalent to spatial filtering can be derived. Furthermore this filtering takes a simple linear form. To apply this result to Hägerstrand's model, it is only necessary to perform one computation convolving the mean information field with a discretized map of the area. This yields the weights which convert the two-dimensional contact field into the transformation rule for the irregularly shaped regions.

The method can similarly be applied to migration studies, using a mean migration field, or other types of interaction fields. The same result holds for any problem in which weights are applied to spatial data taken on a lattice, whether this be deterministic or stochastic. Map generalization and regional forecasting are two realizations of such processes. These are illustrated using Ann Arbor as the empirical instance in Figure 3 and Tables 1, 2,

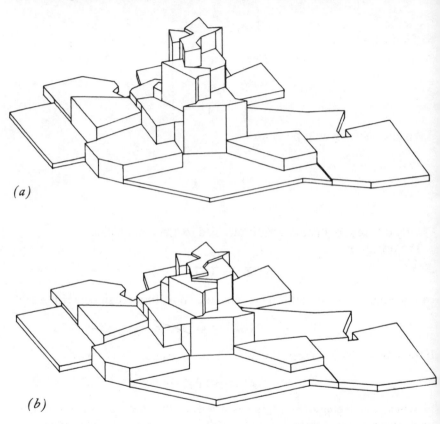

(a)

(b)

Figure 3   Ann Arbor 1960 population density by census tracts shown in perspective as a piecewise continuous function. Original and linearly modified values.

and 3. It is worth noting that the transformation matrix **T** is also an aggregation operator. For example, conversion from census tracts to school districts, or grouping into larger regions can be seen as a type of spatial filtering with particularly simple kernels.

Conversely, given a matrix equation relating spatial units, this equation may be interpreted as two-dimensional spatial filtering with an unknown spatial kernel, although this kernel is not necessarily spatially invariant.

Table 1   Ann Arbor Population by
Census Tracts

Tract No.	1960 Population
1	1250
2	8003
3	5474
4	4042
5	4827
6	4993
7	3209
8	2736
9	2498
10	4087
11	4673
12	3596
13	3005
14	6393
15	6496
16	2075
17	4445
18	2898

This second important result provides a direct connection between spatial
filtering techniques and linear analytical regional models of recognized
importance. These include demographic and exchange models and regional
input–output models (Gould, 1967; Isard, 1960; Jutila, 1971; Masser, 1972;
Rogers, 1971; Stone, 1968; Tinline, 1970). All of these suggest investigation
of the ultimate stability of the systems, their modifiability for planning
purposes, and empirical estimation procedures. Suppose that $\mathbf{Z}$ and $\mathbf{Z^*}$
are known. For example, we will take the population of Ann Arbor as given
by census tracts for 1960 and 1970 (Table 4). The model is

$$\mathbf{Z^*} = \mathbf{TSZ}$$

with inverse

$$\mathbf{Z} = \mathbf{S^{-1}T^{-1}Z^*}$$

assuming that $\mathbf{T^{-1}}$ exists. The problem is to obtain an estimate of $\mathbf{T}$ given
$\mathbf{Z^*}$ and $\mathbf{Z}$, taking $\mathbf{S}$ and $\mathbf{S^{-1}}$ as knowns. The formal least-squares solution is
immediately

$$\mathbf{T} = \mathbf{Z^*Z^t(ZZ^t)^{-1}S^{-1}}.$$

But $\mathbf{T} = \mathbf{U \cdot V}$ where $\mathbf{U}$ is determined by the spatial configuration and $\mathbf{V}$
consists of neighborhood weights. Formally, using the least-squares principle

Table 2.   Transformation Matrix

14.1	1.2	0.0	0.0	0.0	2.5	1.5	2.7	1.0	0.0	0.0	0.0	0.0	0.0	0.0	0.0	0.0	0.0	0.0	0.0
1.2	64.9	6.9	0.0	0.0	2.5	0.0	0.0	4.3	4.2	1.5	0.0	0.0	0.0	0.0	0.0	0.0	0.0	3.4	0.0
0.0	6.9	54.2	2.2	0.0	2.9	0.0	0.0	0.0	0.0	4.7	4.3	0.0	0.0	0.0	0.0	0.0	0.0	0.0	0.0
0.0	0.0	2.2	55.8	3.9	1.1	0.0	0.0	0.0	0.0	0.0	0.0	0.0	0.0	0.0	0.0	0.0	0.0	0.0	0.0
0.0	0.0	0.0	3.9	44.7	6.4	0.0	0.0	0.0	0.0	0.0	0.0	0.0	0.0	2.5	0.0	0.0	0.0	0.0	0.0
2.5	2.5	2.9	1.1	6.4	107.9	2.1	0.0	0.0	0.0	0.0	0.0	0.0	0.0	0.0	0.0	0.0	0.0	0.0	0.0
1.5	0.0	0.0	0.0	0.0	2.1	69.6	3.1	0.0	0.0	0.0	0.0	0.0	0.0	0.0	0.0	0.0	0.0	0.0	0.0
2.7	0.0	0.0	0.0	0.0	0.0	3.1	19.7	0.0	0.0	0.0	0.0	0.0	0.0	0.0	0.0	0.0	0.0	0.0	0.0
1.0	4.3	0.0	0.0	0.0	0.0	0.0	0.0	287.8	2.0	0.0	0.0	0.0	0.0	0.0	0.0	0.0	0.0	2.1	0.0
0.0	4.2	0.0	0.0	0.0	0.0	0.0	0.0	2.0	524.0	5.3	7.9	0.0	0.0	0.0	0.0	0.0	0.0	1.9	22.2
0.0	1.5	4.7	0.0	0.0	0.0	0.0	0.0	0.0	5.3	726.0	5.9	4.6	0.0	0.0	0.0	0.0	0.0	10.7	21.7
0.0	0.0	4.3	0.0	0.0	0.0	0.0	0.0	0.0	7.9	5.9	200.6	14.0	0.0	0.0	0.0	0.0	0.0	0.0	38.4
0.0	0.0	0.0	0.0	0.0	0.0	0.0	0.0	0.0	0.0	4.6	14.0	693.2	10.8	0.0	0.0	0.0	0.0	0.0	0.0
0.0	0.0	0.0	0.0	0.0	0.0	0.0	0.0	0.0	0.0	0.0	0.0	10.8	305.3	7.1	2.2	0.0	0.0	0.0	29.4
0.0	0.0	0.0	0.0	2.5	0.0	0.0	0.0	0.0	0.0	0.0	0.0	0.0	7.1	184.1	8.7	0.0	0.0	0.0	8.7
0.0	0.0	0.0	0.0	0.0	0.0	0.0	0.0	0.0	0.0	0.0	0.0	0.0	2.2	8.7	405.2	5.8	7.8	0.0	0.0
0.0	0.0	0.0	0.0	0.0	0.0	0.0	0.0	0.0	0.0	0.0	0.0	0.0	0.0	0.0	5.8	468.3	5.8	0.0	21.6
0.0	0.0	0.0	0.0	0.0	0.0	0.0	0.0	0.0	0.0	0.0	0.0	0.0	0.0	0.0	7.8	5.8	506.0	5.8	22.0
0.0	3.4	0.0	0.0	0.0	0.0	0.0	0.0	2.1	1.9	10.7	0.0	0.0	0.0	0.0	0.0	0.0	5.8	506.0	24.4
0.0	0.0	0.0	0.0	0.0	0.0	0.0	0.0	0.0	22.2	21.7	38.4	0.0	29.4	8.7	0.0	21.6	22.0	24.4	3817.5

Transformation matrix for Ann Arbor using a separable symmetric Gaussian field of 49 weights obtained as the two-dimensional product of (0.016, 0.094, 0.234, 0.312, 0.234, 0.094, 0.016) with itself. The last row and column of the transformation matrix apply to the area external to the 18 census tracts. The area of each tract is proportional to the row (or column) sum for that tract since the kernel is of unit value.

Table 3.   Ann Arbor 1960 Population by Census Tracts, after Filtering

Tract No.	Smoothing No. 1	Smoothing No. 2	Smoothing No. 3
1	1313	1313	1280
2	7031	6326	5700
3	5180	4861	4539
4	3611	3267	2989
5	4467	4160	3890
6	5040	5041	5005
7	3209	3179	3125
8	2364	2079	1856
9	2838	3128	3377
10	4831	5474	6029
11	4729	4790	4856
12	3406	3250	3123
13	3679	4279	4818
14	6459	6520	6572
15	6039	5655	5331
16	2369	2637	2880
17	4720	4975	5211
18	3491	4011	4470

Smoothed using the transformation $\mathbf{Z}^* = \mathbf{TSZ}$ as described in the text, with $\mathbf{T}$ given in Table 2, but normalized to adjust for the leakage to the external area. $\mathbf{S}$ is also implicit in Table 2.

again

$$\mathbf{V} = (\mathbf{U}^t\mathbf{U})^{-1}\mathbf{U}^t\mathbf{T}$$
$$= (\mathbf{U}^t\mathbf{U})^{-1}\mathbf{U}^t\mathbf{Z}^*\mathbf{Z}^t(\mathbf{ZZ}^t)^{-1}\mathbf{S}^{-1}.$$

For estimation purposes it may be convenient to rewrite $\mathbf{T}$ as a column vector $\dot{\mathbf{T}} = \dot{\mathbf{U}}\dot{\mathbf{V}}$,

$$T_{ij} \rightarrow \dot{T}_k$$

with $k = (i - 1)c + j$, where c is the number of columns of T_{ij}, and (for example)

$$\dot{\mathbf{V}} = \begin{bmatrix} X \\ E \\ W \\ N \\ S \end{bmatrix}$$

and

$$\dot{U} = \begin{bmatrix} 22 & 15 & 15 & 13 & 13 \\ 0 & 0 & 0 & 3 & 1 \\ 0 & 2 & 0 & 4 & 2 \\ 0 & 1 & 7 & 2 & 6 \\ 0 & 0 & 4 & 1 & 3 \\ 15 & 9 & 9 & 10 & 10 \\ 0 & 0 & 2 & 0 & 2 \\ 0 & 6 & 0 & 4 & 0 \\ 0 & 0 & 2 & 2 & 4 \\ 0 & 2 & 0 & 2 & 0 \\ 5 & 3 & 3 & 1 & 1 \\ 0 & 0 & 0 & 0 & 0 \end{bmatrix}$$

using the present simple illustrative case. Then, by least squares,

$$\dot{V} = (\dot{U}^t\dot{U})^{-1}U^t\dot{T}.$$

In this form the (assumed) spatial stationarity of the kernel is made more explicit. The matrix $\dot{U}$ is obtained as a direct count of adjacencies in the geographical data matrix. In this illustrative system there are six observations and five unknowns so that a solution is possible in principle. (Table 4 tentatively suggests that the 1970 arrangement of the Ann Arbor population might have derived from the 1960 arrangement by a neighborhood diffusion process. The kernel would not be of unit weight, however, since the 1960 population totaled 74,700 people and the 1970 value was 102,451. A rotationally invariant model would be more appropriate for city growth than a translationally invariant one [Tobler, 1970, p. 239].)

The suggestion is that it may be possible to determine the filter kernel from aggregated before and after data, which was not entirely obvious *a priori*. A spatial interpretation can thus be given to models which deal with areal units in a superficially aspatial manner. Hypotheses can also be tested concerning spatial neighborhoods and spatial invariances of various types from aggregated data. It should also be possible to use these procedures to filter categorical data given by irregularly shaped spatial regions. Changing a geological map, land-use map, or agricultural crop map into a smoothed version of the same map might proceed as follows. The new category to be assigned to an area is selected by noting the amount of ground in various

Table 4. Percentage Arrangement of Population by Ann Arbor Census Tracts

Tract No.	1960	1960 thrice smoothed	1970
1	1.67	1.71	1.23
2	10.71	7.59	6.85
3	7.33	6.05	6.82
4	5.41	3.98	3.83
5	6.46	5.18	5.87
6	6.68	6.67	5.07
7	4.30	4.16	2.83
8	3.66	2.47	2.63
9	3.34	4.50	6.47
10	5.47	8.03	4.88
11	6.26	6.47	9.69
12	4.81	4.16	5.25
13	4.02	6.42	7.06
14	8.56	8.76	8.75
15	8.70	7.10	7.28
16	2.78	3.84	3.74
17	5.95	6.94	4.91
18	3.88	5.96	6.83

categories at the neighbors of every place in the region. Next, weight these amounts by a function of the degree of neighborliness and choose the dominant weighted category to represent the region on the generalized map. The general methods discussed here can thus be extended to non-numerical situations. Extension to the multivariate spatio-temporal case also seems feasible.

Acknowledgment

Support for this study was provided in part by NSF grant GS 34070X and by a grant from the Institute of Environmental Quality, University of Michigan.

References

Andrews, H., 1970, *Computer techniques in image processing*: Academic Press, New York, 187 p.

Bracewell, R., 1955, Simple graphical method of correcting for instrumental broadening: *Jour. Optical Soc. America*, v. 45, p. 873–876.

Brown, W., 1965, Historical note on a recurrent combinational problem: *American Mathematical Monthly*, v. 72, no. 9, p. 973–977.

Burks, A., ed., 1970, *Essays on cellular automata*: Univ. Illinois Press, Urbana, 375 p.

Burr, E., 1955, Sharpening of observational data in two dimensions: *Australian Jour. Physics*, v. 8, p. 30–53.

Cliff, A., and J. Ord, 1969, The problem of spatial autocorrelation, *in* A. Scott, ed., *Studies in regional science*: Pion, London, p. 25–55.

Cliff, A., and J. Ord, 1970, A regression approach to univariate spatial forecasting, *in* M. Chisholm, ed., *Regional forecasting*: Butterworths, London, p. 47–70.

Clowes, M., 1970, On the description of board games, *in* S. Kaneff, ed., *Picture language machines*: Academic Press, New York, p. 397–420.

Codd, E., 1968, *Cellular automata*: Academic Press, New York, 226 p.

Epstein, E., 1969, Stochastic dynamic prediction: *Tellus*, v. 21, no. 6, p. 739–759, figures 8 and 10, p. 753.

Feldt, A., 1968, *The community land use game*: Cornell Univ. Press, Ithaca, 125 p.

Gardner, M., 1970, Mathematical games: *Scientific American*, Oct., p. 120–123.

Gould, P., 1967, On the geographic interpretation of eigenvalues: *Trans. Inst. British Geographers*, v. 42, p. 53–86.

Hägerstrand, T., 1968, A Monte Carlo approach to diffusion, *in* B. Berry, and D. Marble, eds., *Spatial analysis*: Prentice-Hall, Englewood Cliffs, New Jersey, p. 368–384.

Harbaugh, J., and G. Bonham-Carter, 1970, *Computer simulation in geology*: Wiley Interscience, New York, p. 435–457.

Harmon, L., and B. Julesz, 1973, Masking in visual recognition: *Science*, v. 180, no. 4091, p. 1194–1197.

Holloway, J. L., 1958, Smoothing and filtering of time series and space fields: *Advances in Geophysics*, v. 4, p. 351–389.

Howard, R., 1971, *Dynamic probabilistic systems*: John Wiley and Sons, Inc., New York, 576 p.

Isard, W., 1960, *Methods of regional analysis*: John Wiley and Sons, Inc., New York, 784 p.

Jutila, S., 1971, A linear model for agglomeration, diffusion, and growth of regional economic activity: *Regional Science Perspectives*, v. 1, no. 1, p. 83–108.

Kraus, K., 1971, Automatische Berechnung digitalen Höhenlinien: *Zeitschrift für Vermessungswesen*, v. 96, no. 6, p. 234–293.

Kraus, K., and E. Mikhail, 1972, Linear least-squares interpolation: *Photogrammetric Engineering*, v. 38, no. 10, p. 1016–1029.

Krige, D., 1966, Two dimensional weighted moving average trend surfaces for ore valuation: *Symp. on mathematical statistics and computer applications in ore valuation*, Johannesburg, p. 13–38.

Lanczos, C., 1966, *Discourse on Fourier series*: Oliver and Boyd, Edinburgh, 286 p.

MacDougall, E., 1972, Optimal generalization of mosaic maps: *Geographical Analysis*, v. 4, no. 4, p. 417–423.

Masser, I., 1972, *Analytical models for urban and regional planning*: David and Charles, Newton Abbot, 164 p.

Minsky, M., and H. Pappert, 1969, *Perceptrons*: MIT Press, Cambridge, Massachusetts, 258 p.

Moritz, H., 1962, Interpolation and prediction of gravity anomalies and their accuracy: Inst. Geodesy, Photogrammetry, and Cartography, Ohio State Univ., Columbus, *Rept. No. 24*, 69 p.

Moritz, H., 1963, Interpolation and prediction of point gravity anomalies: *Annals Academiae Scientiarum Fennicae*, v. 69 III A, p. 1–32.

Moritz, H., 1967, Optimum smoothing of aerial gravity measurements: Ohio State Univ., Columbus, *Rept. No. 81*, 51 p. Available from NTIS as AD654008.

Moritz, H., 1970, Eine allgemeine Theorie der Verarbeitung von Schweremessungen nach kleinsten Quadraten: *Deutsche Geodätische Kommission*, München, Heft Nr. 67A, 56 p.

Moritz, H., and W. Heiskanen, 1967, *Physical geodesy*: W. Freeman, San Francisco, chapter 7.

Nordbeck, S., and B. Rystedt, 1970, Isarithmic maps and the continuity of reference interval functions: *Geografiska Annaler*, B. 2, p. 92–123.

Pitts, F., 1967, MIFCAL and NONCEL: Two computer programs for the generalization of the Hägerstrand model to an irregular lattice: Office Naval Research, Geography Branch, *Tech. Rept. No. 7*, ONR Task No. 389–140, Contract Nonr-1228(33), 23 p.

Rapp, R., 1964, The prediction of point and mean gravity anomalies through the use of a digital computer: Inst. Geodesy, Photogrammetry, and Cartography, Ohio State Univ., Columbus, *Rept. No. 43*, 135 p.

Ratliff, F., H. Hartline, and W. Miller, 1964, Spatial and temporal aspects of retinal inhibitory interaction: *Jour. Optical Soc. America*, v. 53, no. 1, p. 110–120.

Rhynsburger, D., 1973, Analytic delineation of Thiessen polygons: *Geographical Analysis*, v. 2, p. 133–144.

Rogers, A., 1971, *Matrix methods in urban and regional analysis*: Holden Day, San Francisco, 508 p.

Rosenfeld, A., 1969, *Picture processing by computer*: Academic Press, New York, 196 p.

Smith, A., 1971, Two dimensional formal languages and pattern recognition by cellular automata: *12th Annual Symp. on Switching and Automata Theory*, I.E.E.E., Michigan State Univ., Ann Arbor, p. 114–152.

Sokal, R., and K. Gabriel, 1969, A new statistical approach to geographic variation analysis: *Systematic Zoology*, v. 18, no. 3, p. 259–278.

Stone, L., 1968, Stable migration rates from the multiregional growth matrix operator: *Demography*, v. 5, p. 439–442.

Switzer, P., 1969, Mapping a geographically correlated environment: Stanford Univ., *Tech. Rept. 145*, Contract Nonr-225(52), (NR-342-022), 38 p. Available from NTIS as AD693982.

Switzer, P., C. Mohr, and R. Heitman, 1964, Statistical analyses of ocean terrain and contour plotting procedures: Dept. Navy, Bureau of Ships, NObsr-81564, SS-050, *Rept. No. 1440464*, 85 p. Available from NTIS as AD601538.

Thompson, P., 1956, Optimum smoothing of two-dimensional fields: *Tellus*, v. 8, p. 384–393.

Tinline, R., 1970, Linear operators in diffusion research, *in* M. Chisholm, ed., *Regional forecasting*: Butterworths, London, p. 71–91.

Tobler, W., 1966, Numerical map generalization: Michigan Inter–Univ. Community of Mathematical Geographers, Ann Arbor, *Discussion Paper No. 8*, p. 1–24. Available from University Microfilms as OP-33067.

Tobler, W., 1967, Of maps and matrices: *Jour. Regional Science Assoc.*, v. 7, no. 2, p. 275–280.

Tobler, W., 1969, Geographical filters and their inverses: *Geographical Analysis*, v. 1, no. 3, p. 234–253.

Tobler, W., 1970, A computer movie simulating urban growth in the Detroit region: *Economic Geography*, v. 26, no. 2, p. 234–240.

Tobler, W., 1973, Regional analysis: time series extended to two dimensions: *Geographic Polonica*, v. 25, p. 103–106.

Walsh, J., 1923, A closed set of orthogonal functions: *American Jour. Mathematics*, v. 45, p. 5–24.

Woods, J., 1972, Two dimensional discrete Markovian fields: *I.E.E.E. Trans. on Information Theory*, v. IT-18, no. 2, p. 232–240.

Regionalized Variables and Quantitative Analysis of Spatial Data

C. J. Huijbregts

Variables that characterize a spatial phenomenon usually have a behavior much too complex to be studied by standard mathematical methods. Their variations in space are erratic and often unpredictable from one point to another. However, their behavior is not completely random; values taken at neighboring points are related by a complex set of correlations reflecting the structure of the underlying phenomenon. The term *regionalized variables* was chosen by Matheron (1965) to emphasize the particular features of these variables. Numerous examples of regionalized variables can be found, such as ore grade and thickness in mineral deposits, piezometric height in hydrology, gravity, geochemical contents, density of trees in a forest, density of population in a geographic area, and the quantity of gas or dust in atmosphere. These variables characterize phenomena which spread through space and possess a certain structure, called *regionalized phenomena* (or regionalizations).

When analyzing natural phenomena in practice, we have at our disposal only fragmentary sampling data of a regionalized variable: values measured at given locations, at drill-holes, or along profiles. We must be able to extract from the apparent disorder of available data the major structural characteristics of the phenomenon and a measure of the correlation between values at neighboring points throughout space. This is the aim of *structural analysis*. We also must be able to measure the accuracy of any prediction or evaluation made with the help of fragmentary data. In other words, we also need a theory of estimation. These two objectives are related: in contouring problems, for instance, the accuracy of a map based on gridded data depends on the spatial structure of the phenomenon.

The aim of the *theory of regionalized variables* is to provide a comprehensive and coherent theoretical approach to the problems of structural analysis and estimation. It analyzes and expresses the structural properties of regionalized variables in an adequate form. It takes this information into

38

account to provide quantitative tools of investigation and estimation. Since 1957, this theory (under the name of geostatistics) has been extensively applied to ore reserve estimation, a domain where optimum use of available information and appropriate methods are essential. The scope of this method has been widely extended in several other fields of application such as forest evaluation, hydrogeology, gravimetry, bathymetry, and automatic contouring.

Conceptual Background

The theory of regionalized variables is based on the theory of random functions. Indeed, this theory provides us with a conceptual tool able to take into account simultaneously the structured and random character of regionalized variables, as well as the mathematical tools necessary for application. Justification for this approach has been given elsewhere (Matheron, 1965, 1971, p. 6, 39). Our aim here is not to go deeply into mathematical developments but to show how this approach enables us to reach our objectives, which are the characterization of structure and processing of data.

A regionalized variable can be considered a particular realization of a random function. We know that the result of a particular experiment on an ordinary random variable Z is a numerical value z. That is, z is a particular realization of Z. Similarly, we can consider the value y(x) taken by a regionalized variable at a given point x to be a particular realization of a certain random variable Y(x). If we now consider all the values y(x) taken at all points x, the regionalized variable can be interpreted as a particular realization of an infinite set of random variables Y(x). This set is called a random function, as it associates a random variable Y(x) with any point x.

The utility of this point of view is that, Y(x) being a random function, the spatial correlation between the two random variables Y(x) and Y(x + h) has a precise significance. However, such a point of view would remain purely theoretical if we could not infer from a single realization some of the properties of the random function itself. In particular, for practical applications, we need to know the expectation

$$m(x) = E[Y(x)]$$

and the covariance $C(x, y) = E[Y(x)Y(y)] - m(x)m(y)$ [of the random variables Y(x) and Y(y)]. In order to make statistical inference possible, some hypotheses are necessary. The most common assumption encountered in literature is that of *weak stationarity*. That is, the expectation $E[Y(x)] = m$ is a constant. The covariance does not depend on x and y separately but only on the difference $|x - y|$,

$$C(|x - y|) = E[Y(x)Y(y)] - m^2.$$

We can also define the well known correlogram function

$$\rho(x - y) = \frac{C(x - y)}{C(0)}.$$

In this instance, we assume the phenomenon is repeating itself in space; this provides an opportunity for statistical inference. This assumption is widely used in time-series analysis and in spectral analysis.

In practice, these assumptions are too restrictive, and we may change to the weaker *intrinsic hypothesis*. Instead of $Y(x)$, only its increments $[Y(x + h) - Y(x)]$ are weakly stationary. The second moment of the increments is

$$2\gamma(h) = E[(Y(x + h) - Y(x))^2]$$

which is called the *variogram*. The basic hypothesis of the theory is that $\gamma(h)$ does not depend on x nor on the domain where it is estimated (the latter is equivalent to an assumption of stationarity). If the form of $\gamma(h)$ changes, it is assumed that its variations are slow with respect to the working scale, a condition of quasi or local stationarity. This quasi-stationarity assumption, which is specified on theoretical grounds, corresponds in practice to a postulate of local homogeneity of the physical phenomenon. The theory can take progressive variations of physical conditions into account, provided that they occur on a large scale.

When $Y(x)$ is weakly stationary, it also obeys the intrinsic hypothesis, its variogram being given by $\gamma(h) = C(0) - C(h)$. As the intrinsic hypothesis is the weaker, it will be preferred in applications. These hypotheses provide a correct and simple formulation of the problems of quantitative analysis of regionalized variables. Knowledge of the variogram is adequate for global estimation problems and in many instances for local estimation problems. However, in some situations which often arise in contouring problems, even the last assumption is too strong and not supported by experimental evidence. In this case, the expectation $E[Y(x)] = m(x)$, called the *drift*, is no longer constant. The variogram of the residuals $2\gamma(x, y) = E[(Y(x) - m(x) - Y(y) + m(y))^2]$ may then be approximated locally by an intrinsic variogram. We shall deal with this non-stationary case later.

The Basic Tool—the Variogram

The basic tool that will enable us to quantitatively describe the variation in space of a regionalized phenomenon is the variogram. The structure of a set (in this instance, the set of values taken by a regionalized variable) can be defined as the system of relationships existing between elements of this set. Therefore, we will obtain information of a structural nature from our set only by comparing values taken simultaneously at two points. The variogram is nothing but the average quadratic deviation between values at two points x and x + h of the space.

$$2\gamma(h) = E[(Y(x + h) - Y(x))^2]$$

Note that $2\gamma(h)$ is a function of the *vector* **h** and that the condensed notation $2\gamma(h)$ represents in, for example, three-dimensional space $2\gamma(h_1, h_2, h_3)$ where h_1, h_2, h_3 are the three spatial coordinates. The *semi-variogram* $\gamma(h)$, or half the variogram, is used in practice.

This function has properties closely linked to the structural features of the phenomenon and enables these features to be quantified. The study of the behavior of $\gamma(h)$ with respect to the modulus and direction of the vector **h** is the basis of structural analysis. In this sense, the semi-variogram is the minimum structural tool.

Moreover, the definition of the variogram as being the average quadratic deviation between Y(x) and Y(x + h) shows that this function is an estimation variance. It gives the simplest estimation variance; the variance of the error made when estimating Y(x + h) by Y(x). In this sense, it is also the minimum statistical tool and will allow any estimation problem to be solved.

Theory shows that the variogram is not any positive function but is a conditionally positive definite function. This condition is necessary to provide positive variances. Therefore, only a limited amount of theoretical models can be used in practice but this is in general sufficient for applications. Experimentally, the variogram can be estimated from fragmentary sampling data with good precision for small values of h. A mathematical model is then fitted to values of the experimental variogram, taking particular care near the origin. The following models are referred to in the literature:

(1) Variograms with a sill. These include spherical and exponential variograms.
(2) Variograms without a sill. Models include the linear and logarithmic (de Wijsian) variograms.

Structural Analysis

In this section, some of the properties of the variogram are briefly discussed in relation to the structural features of the regionalized variable. Figure 1 summarizes these interrelationships.

Support

A regionalized variable is localized. Its variations occur in a certain domain of space or *geometrical field*. Moreover, such a variable is in general defined on a *geometrical support* which specifies the volume, shape, and orientation of samples in space. If this support is changed, a new regionalized variable

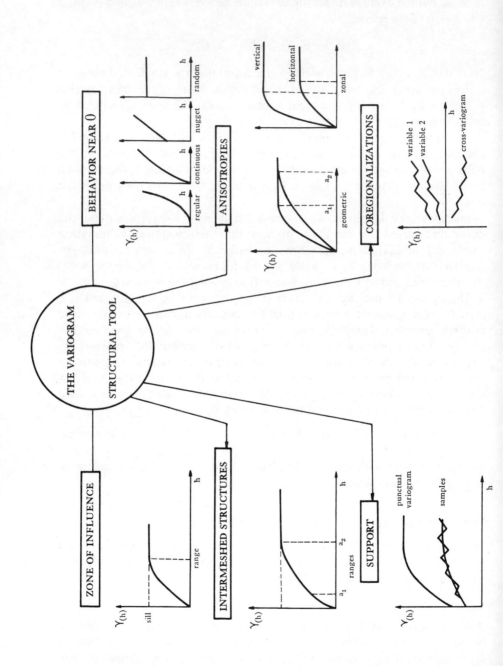

is defined, related to the initial support but with different characteristics and a different variogram. For example, a variable defined as the density of trees per $20m^2$ will have different characteristics than if it were defined as the density of trees per $100m^2$ area.

The change of support corresponds to a simple formalism that allows the punctual variogram γ to be deduced from the variogram γ_s of samples. Similarly, the variogram of larger volumes γ_V can be deduced from γ_s. Therefore, the structural properties of the target population can be deduced from that of the sampled population. The practical importance of the concept of support is readily apparent.

Zone of Influence

The variogram is in general an increasing function of the modulus of vector **h**. Values taken at two separate points differ more as these points become more distant from each other. The way in which $\gamma(h)$ increases gives a precise meaning to the traditional notion of the *influence zone* of a sample. It often happens that beyond a certain distance a, called the *range*, $\gamma(h)$ becomes constant. That is, the average variation of values of $Y(x)$ and $Y(x + h)$ no longer depends on their distance. $Y(x)$ and $Y(x + h)$ are then uncorrelated. The range measures the zone of influence.

Intermeshed Structures

Transition phenomena are characterized by variograms with a range and a sill. Often, these phenomena exhibit a superposition of different scales of variation, or *intermeshed (gigogne) structures*. Each of these scales of variation adds its own contribution to the variogram, which is then the sum of several variograms with different ranges (Serra, 1968).

Anisotropy

As the argument h is a vector, the variogram must be calculated along several directions through space. The change in behavior of $\gamma(h)$ with the bearing of **h** brings to light possible anisotropies. When the variogram has the same shape for different orientations but the ranges are distributed on an ellipse (elliptical influence zone), we speak of *geometrical anisotropy*. In other cases, the variogram may be very different in different directions, as in the model described by Huijbregts and Segovia (1973):

$$\gamma(h_1, h_2, h_3) = \gamma_1(\sqrt{h_1^2 + h_2^2 + h_3^2}) + \gamma_2(h_3)$$

This is called *zonal anisotropy*, and may be related to stratification effects, or mineral zonation.

Behavior Near the Origin

The continuity of a regionalization is closely related to the behavior of the variogram near the origin. A *parabolic behavior* is associated with a differentiable (in the sense of the mean square) regionalized variable which is thus highly regular. Examples include certain geophysical and geochemical variables. If this parabolic behavior is associated with complex zonalities, it may be a clue to the presence of a drift. When the regionalized variable is only continuous in the mean square, and thus less regular, the variogram has a *linear behavior*. Variation in most mineral grades and piezometric heights are variables which exhibit this form of variogram. Some highly irregular variables are not even continuous in the mean square, so $\gamma(h)$ is discontinuous at the origin. This discontinuity, called the *nugget effect*, may have a real physical meaning. For example, it may reflect high discontinuities or micro-regionalizations at a scale smaller than that of the sampling grid. More often, it represents an integration of the errors of measurement. Finally, a flat variogram corresponds to the case of completely random variation.

Coregionalizations

Often, several regionalized variables are defined on the same geometric field, as is the case with assays of polymetallic deposits or geochemical analyses. The cross-variogram allows *coregionalizations* (regionalized correlations) between two regionalized variables to be studied and models to be established. Several estimation methods, as for example *cokriging*, are derived from knowledge of this function.

Variance of Dispersion

Consider the idealized situation shown in Figure 2. To provide information about an area of interest A, a certain number of samples have been collected (set S of data). In addition to the experimental variogram, the mean and statistical variance of the data set S are also computed. The statistical variance of the samples is a rough measure of the spread of the local variability of the

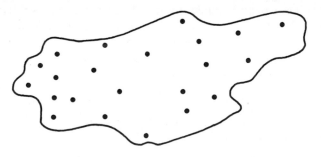

● Data location

Figure 2   Simplified example of sampled area.

regionalized variable within the area A. Because of the spatial properties of a regionalized variable, this variability depends closely on the definition of area A.

The statistical or experimental variance of the samples is not a good estimate of the true variability within the area. It is possible to give a better definition and to compute the variability more precisely. The *variance of dispersion* of a sample of volume v within a large volume V is defined as the average quadratic deviation between the value of the sample and the average value of V when the sample takes any location inside V. Our probabilistic interpretation leads to the following formula for the variance of dispersion of v within V:

$$D^2(v/V) = \bar{\gamma}(V, V) - \bar{\gamma}(v, v)$$

where $\gamma(V, V)$ indicates the mean value of the punctual variogram $\gamma(\mathbf{MM'})$, where $\mathbf{MM'}$ is the vector joining M to M' and the two points M and M' describe separately the volume V. In relation to the important notion of support, we see that this formula allows computation of the variance of any volume within a larger field.

The variance of a punctual value within any volume G is given by

$$D^2(0/G) = \bar{\gamma}(G, G).$$

The linearity of the equation leads to an important additivity relationship,

$$D^2(v/W) = D^2(v/V) + D^2(V/W),$$

which states that the variance of a sample v within a domain W is the sum of the variance of v within the volume V and the variance of the volume V within the domain W. The relationship between the within-field variance and the between-field variance is thus expressed.

The notation of variance of dispersion has many applications in analyzing the relationships between the statistical distributions of samples and that of larger domains, and in studying the overall variability of the regionalized variable. In the mining industry, it has important applications in ore selection and grade–tonnage curves (Journel, 1973a). However, it must be emphasized that this variance is clearly distinct from the variance of estimation that will now be introduced.

Variance of Estimation

Consider again the case shown in Figure 2. The mean of the observations (set S of data) is an estimator of the average value of the regionalized variable inside the area A. Determining the accuracy of this estimation is a very practical problem. When estimating the unknown average value of the area A by the known average value of our observations, we make an (unknown) error. We shall determine the possible range of this error by an estimation variance.

Let y_V be the (unknown) average value of the regionalized variable $y(x)$ inside a volume V of given shape, size, and orientation. We want to estimate the quantity y_V with the help of the known average value y_S^* of our set S of observations. In our probabilistic interpretation, the error $y_V - y_S^*$ appears as a realization of a random variable $Y_V - Y_S^*$, having a variance given by

$$\sigma_E^2 = \text{var}[Y_V - Y_S^*] = 2\bar{\gamma}(V, S) - \bar{\gamma}(S, S) - \bar{\gamma}(V, V)$$

where $\bar{\gamma}(V, S)$ is a symbolic notation for the mean value of the punctual variogram $\gamma(MM')$ when the two points M and M' describe the sets V and S separately. Hence, the estimation variance appears as the variance of the error of estimation.

This fundamental equation requires the following comments:

(1)   The equation integrates all the geometrical features of the problem: the geometry of the volume to be estimated in term $\bar{\gamma}(V, V)$, the geometry and relative location of observations S in term $\bar{\gamma}(S, S)$, and the relationships between the two sets. In the case shown in Figure 3, the different sampling arrangements will produce different estimation variances. The estimation variance decreases when the data are more representative of V and when they are more numerous.

(2)   The estimation variance also depends on the degree of regularity of the regionalized variable (in other words, on its structure as summarized by the variogram γ). The estimation variance will be less when the regionalized variable is more regular through space.

The equation for the error variance is absolutely general. In the example shown in Figure 2, we may want to estimate the average value of the area A

$$y_A = \frac{1}{A} \int_A y(x)\, dx$$

by the average value of our observations

$$y_S^* = \frac{1}{N} \sum_i y(x_i).$$

In this case, each of the samples has the same weight $1/N$. However, the locations of our samples, being far from regular, are not very good for this purpose. We may try to find a better estimator and to weight our observed values, perhaps by their areas of influence. Then

$$y_S^* = \sum_i \lambda_i y(x_i) \quad \text{with} \sum_i \lambda_i = 1.$$

The general formula gives

$$\sigma_E^2 = \frac{2}{A} \sum_i \lambda_i \int_A \gamma(x - x_i)\, dx - \sum_i \sum_j \lambda_i \lambda_j \gamma(x_i - x_j) - \frac{1}{A^2} \int_A \int_A \gamma(x - x')\, dx\, dx'.$$

Therefore, knowledge of the variogram is adequate to compute explicitly the accuracy of any linear estimator. In practice, several approximation formulae and graphs can be used to reduce computations for the most common sampling patterns (Figure 3).

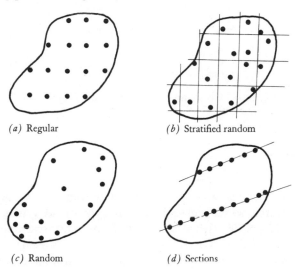

(a) Regular   (b) Stratified random

(c) Random   (d) Sections

Figure 3   Common sampling patterns

Giving a precise measure of both the quality of available information and the accuracy of the estimator in the form of an estimation variance, we have quantitative means for the solution of various practical problems. As the estimation variance does not depend on the actual values of the regionalized variable at data points, the amount and location of supplementary information necessary to attain a given precision can be calculated beforehand. This property is very useful for decision-making in the search for economical optima in exploration or in mining production (Formery and Matheron, 1963). Another important application is the optimum location of new points of measurements (Delhomme and Delfiner, 1973). Figure 4 shows the optimum location of such a point after the improvement in precision has been contoured. Estimation variances play a great role in the discussion and interpretation of quantitative results. Isovariance curves are fundamental in analyzing the representative ability of contour maps (Huijbregts, 1971). Finally Kriging is one of the most powerful applications of the notion of estimation variance, and will now be introduced.

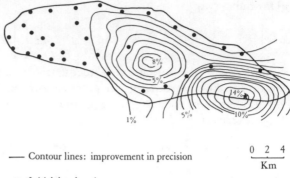

——— Contour lines: improvement in precision

• Initial data locations

★ Optimum location

Figure 4 Optimum location of an additional point of measurement.

Local Estimation

Kriging

Consider again the idealized example shown in Figure 2. As the data points are not well located, we have already seen that we should weight the observed values to obtain a better estimator than their straightforward average value. Many different types of weighting factors can be chosen; we will select weights which provide the best estimator possible. More precisely, among all estimators y*, derived from the known values of S, that can be used to estimate an unknown quantity y (in the present case, the average value inside the area), we will choose:

(1) An *unbiased* estimator. Its error of estimation must be equal to zero on the average, whatever the prevailing conditions may be.

(2) An *optimum* estimator. We look for the estimator with the smallest error; that is, one whose estimation variance is a minimum.

(3) A *linear* estimator. Our choice must be a linear combination of the known values

$$y^* = \sum_i \lambda_i y(x_i) \qquad (x_i \in S).$$

Kriging determines the weights λ_i in order to satisfy these requirements. In particular, this leads to the condition $\Sigma \lambda_i = 1$. These weights are the solution of a linear system of equations. The λ_i are related to the geometric features of the problem, as well as to the structural properties of the regionalized variable.

The Kriging estimator is the best linear unbiased estimator of an intrinsic regionalized variable. Kriging can solve the following two problems:

a. estimate the true value $y(x_0)$ at a given point x_0.

b. estimate a weighted average $y = \int y(x)p(x) \, dx$ $(\int p(x) \, dx = 1)$, or a mean value inside any domain of space.

Problem *a* is typical of contouring problems, as Kriging can be used to estimate a regular grid of points across a map area. Moreover, punctual Kriging is an exact interpolator and provides an estimation variance. Problem *b* has great importance in the estimation of mining blocks and in hydrology. Kriging has the property of conditional unbiasedness which is particularly important in mining problems associated with the selection and definition of reserves (Journel, 1973*b*). It also has orthogonality properties that are useful in the conditionalization of simulations (Journel, 1973*c*).

Local Estimation of Non-Stationary Phenomena

In many phenomena, the assumptions of the intrinsic theory do not hold, as reality often is non-stationary. We may cite, for instance, the existence of zonal drifts:

(1) in geochemical phenomena and in geologic data in general;

(2) in bathymetry, gravimetry, and hydrogeology, where drifts often are present;

(3) in other classes of problems where trends or drifts are present.

The following model (Matheron, 1971, p. 139 *ff.*; Huijbregts and Matheron, 1970) may be chosen to represent a non-stationary random function:

$$Y(x) = m(x) + R(x).$$

The term $m(x) = E[Y(x)]$ is called the *drift* or regular component of $Y(x)$. The second term, $R(x)$, is the *residual* or random component of $Y(x)$. Although random, it nevertheless has a structure which can be expressed in a variogram of the residuals.

It is also assumed that the drift can be approximated locally over a certain neighborhood by known functions of the form

$$m(x) = \sum_{\ell=0}^{k} a_\ell f^\ell(x),$$

where the a_ℓ are unknown coefficients. The variogram of the residuals may also be approximated, at least locally.

With these assumptions, *universal Kriging* procedures allow the following problems to be solved, given a set S of information:

(1) Estimation of the drift $m(x_0)$ at a point x_0. This estimation is related to the well known problem of trend-surface analysis.

(2) Estimation of the real, unknown value taken by y(x) at point x_0. This is done by punctual Kriging, which is an exact interpolation procedure, yielding an optimum linear unbiased estimate of the point in question. Punctual Kriging has obvious relevance to contouring and gridding problems.

(3) Estimation of a moving average on a support different than $S : \int p(x)y(x)\,dx$.

An estimation variance is associated with all of these estimators. The practical importance of the estimation variance has already been emphasized.

Certain problems of statistical inference, such as estimation of the underlying variogram $\gamma_0(h)$ of the residuals, may be solved by a general formalism concerned with order-k intrinsic random functions (Matheron, 1973). The model variogram and the optimum estimators may be calculated on a computer without structural interpretation (Delfiner, 1973b). However, this approach sacrifices some of the insight provided by structural analysis and interpretation.

Conditional Simulations of a Regionalized Variable

In some practical applications, as in economics or operations research, it is interesting to obtain an overall picture of the fluctuation of a regionalized variable. These fluctuations may be summarized by means of dispersion variances. However, we might wish to see how this variability affects values assumed by the regionalized variable. Previously, we have estimated these values. However, even an optimum estimator is not reality; in particular, its spatial behavior is very different from that of the regionalized variable it estimates. The variability of the estimator in space is a smoothed version of the true variability and does not reflect exactly the actual fluctuations.

Therefore, tools have been devised to simulate realizations of the initial phenomenon. These simulated realizations have the same model of variogram as the one experimentally deduced from the known data. Hence, the simulation shows the same characteristics of dispersion as the original regionalized variable. The simulation can even have the same histogram. Finally, the simulation coincides with the observed values at data locations. These models are related to the original phenomenon as far as spatial structure is concerned, and this is sufficient in practice. These models do not pretend to estimate (that is, to approach the real values in the best possible way) but try to identify all the variability of reality.

Figure 5 (Journel, 1973b) shows the relationship between reality, representing in this example total lateritic ore thickness at Prony, New Caledonia, and a conditional simulation. Reality was first known at a 100m sample spacing. The simulation was computed to coincide with the known values every 100m. Although Kriging produces the best estimate of

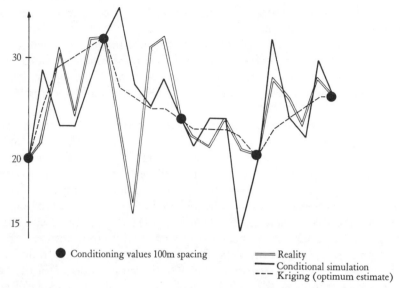

Figure 5 Relationship between reality, conditional simulation, and Kriging.

reality, and is an exact interpolator in this case, it does not give a good picture of the true variability. Both values could later be compared to reality measured at a 20m spacing.

The simulated versions can be used for many purposes; to obtain a range of forecasts in relation to mining projects (Journel, 1973c), in optimization, and in simulation of exploration. In the case of non-stationary regionalized variables, similar methods can be used to simulate contour maps and to obtain a large set of different variants of the initial phenomenon.

Examples of Practical Applications

In this section, we will make a rapid review of some of the fields of application of the theory of regionalized variables. These include the mining industry, where this theory has been extensively developed. Geostatistics is a very powerful tool in ore reserve estimation and grade control, and is used for global and local estimation, and the calculation of grade–tonnage curves. It constitutes an essential aid in ore selection, in long and short range planning, and in production control. Simulations are used for the optimization of mining operations.

The theory of regionalized variables provides tools for structural analysis and interpretation of electric well logs in the petroleum industry. Here, universal Kriging techniques are well suited, as they make optimum use of available information. The methods have been applied in geophysical calculations and contouring, reservoir calculations, simulations, and modeling of permeability patterns.

The techniques are again well suited for structural analysis and quantitative problems in hydrology. Applications include optimization of piezometric grids, water reserve calculations, contouring and simulations, hydrochemical calculations, establishment of transmissivity patterns, and in water pollution problems.

Many applications of regionalized variable theory can be found in geophysics, especially in magnetism, in the study of water turbulence, and in bathymetry. In gravimetry, for instance, the intrinsic correlation between altitude and free air anomaly can be studied; the correlation of gravity with geologic structure can be assessed through the variogram. Universal Kriging procedures are applied in the detection of ore bodies by inverse methods.

Outside the Earth sciences, the structure of forestation has been studied and stochastic models established. The theory provides tools for the difficult problems of sampling, optimization, and the estimation of the number of trees. In meteorology the theory provides optimum procedures for the contouring of geopotential, the estimation of gradients, determination of geostrophic winds, in error filtering, and all problems concerning the location of measurement stations.

Other quantitative applications can be found in geology, geochemistry, atmospheric pollution problems, and geography. Hopefully, these brief remarks and the list of references will encourage other workers in these areas to investigate the theory of regionalized variables.

References

Boletin de Geostatistica, 1972, Departamento de Minas, Universidad de Chile, Santiago, v. 1–4.

Bordet, J. P., and J. Monget, 1972, *Le variogramme révélateur de structure d'un champ bi-dimensionel*: Centre d'Informatique Géologique, Fontainebleau, 17 p.

David, M., 1972, Geostatistical ore reserve estimation: *10th Inter. Applications of Computer Methods in the Mineral Industry Symp.*, Johannesburg, p. 27–34.

Delfiner, P., 1973*a*, Analyse du géopotentiel et du vent géostrophique par krigeage universel: *Revue de la Météorologie No. 25*, 50 p.

Delfiner, P., 1973*b*, Presentation du programme BLUEPACK: Centre de Morphologie Mathématique de Fontainebleau, *Internal Note*, 32 p.

Delhomme, J. P., 1971, *Traitement géostatistique des données piézométriques: le krigeage en hydrogéologie (recyclage en hydrogéologie mathématique)*: Centre d'Informatique Géologique, Fontainebleau, France, 28 p.

Delhomme, J. P., and P. Delfiner, 1973, Application du krigeage à l'optimisation d'une campagne pluviométrique en zone aride: *Symposium on the Design of Water Resources Projects with Inadequate Data*, UNESCO-WHO-IAHS, Madrid, Spain, June 1973, p. 191–210.

Formery, P., and G. Matheron, 1963, Recherche d'optima dans la reconnaissance et la mise en exploitation des gisements miniers: *Annales des Mines*, v. 5, p. 23–42, v. 6, p. 11–30.

Guibal, D., 1973, *L'estimation des okoumés du Gabon*: *Problèmes méthodologiques*: Centre de Morphologie Mathématique de Fontainebleau, unpublished.

Huijbregts, C., 1971, Courbes d'isovariance en cartographie automatique: *Study meeting on the relationship between automatic treatment and visualization of geological information*: Centre de Recherches Petrographiques et Géochimiques, Nancy, France, 12 p.

Huijbregts, C., 1972, *Analyse structurale du gisement d'Exotica*: Centre de Morphologie Mathématique de Fontainebleau, N-258, 22 p.

Huijbregts, C., and A. Journel, 1972, Estimation of lateritic-type ore bodies: *10th Inter. Applications of Computer Methods in the Mineral Industry Symp.*, Johannesburg, p. 207–212.

Huijbregts, C., and G. Matheron, 1970, Universal Kriging: an optimal method for contouring and trend surface analysis: *Canadian Inst. Mining & Metallurgy*, Special v. 12, p. 159–169.

Huijbregts, C., and R. Segovia, 1973, Geostatistics for the valuation of a copper deposit: *11th Inter. Applications of Computer Methods in the Mineral Industry Symp.*, Tucson, Arizona, p. D24–D43.

Journel, A., 1969, *Rapport d'etudes sur l'estimation d'une variable régionalisée*: *application à la cartographie automatique*: Service Hydrographique de la Marine, Paris, 110 p.

Journel, A., 1973a, From geological reconnaissance to exploitation: a decade of applied geostatistics: Centre de Morphologie Mathématique de Fontainebleau, *Note*, 38 p.

Journel, A., 1973b, Geostatistics and sequential exploration: *Mining Engineering*, in press.

Journel, A., 1973c, Geostatistics for conditional simulation of ore bodies: Centre de Morphologie Mathématique de Fontainebleau, *Note*, 40 p.

Matheron, G., 1963, Principles of geostatistics: *Economic Geology*, v. 58, p. 1246–1266.

Matheron, G., 1965, *Les variables régionalisées et leur estimation*: Masson et Cie, Editeurs, Paris, 305 p.

Matheron, G., 1967, Kriging or polynomial interpolation procedures: *Canadian Inst. Mining & Metallurgy*, v. 70, p. 240–244.

Matheron, G., 1969, Le Krigeage universel: *Les Cahiers du Centre de Morphologie Mathématique de Fontainebleau*, v. 1, 83 p.

Matheron, G., 1970a, Random functions and their application in geology, *in* D. F. Merriam, ed., *Geostatistics*: Plenum Press, New York, p. 79–87.

Matheron, G., 1970b, Structures aléatoires et géologie mathématique: *Revue de l'Institut Inter. de Statistique*, v. 38, no. 1, p. 1–10.

Matheron, G., 1971, The theory of regionalized variables and its applications: *Les Cahiers du Centre de Morphologie Mathématique de Fontainebleau*, v. 5, 211 p.

Matheron, G., 1973, The intrinsic random functions and their applications: *Advances in Applied Probability*, London, in press.

Monget, J., 1971, A new statistical treatment of gravity data: *Jour. Inter. Assoc. of Geodesy*, v. 102, p. 451–466.

Poissonnet, M., C. Millier, and J. Serra, 1970, Morphologie mathématique et sylviculture: *3ème Conférence du groupe des Statisticiens Forestiers*, Paris, p. 287–307.

Serra, J., 1967a, Thèse: echantillonnage et estimation des phénomènes de transition miniers: *Ph.D. dissertation*, School of Mines, Univ. Nancy, France, 690 p.

Serra, J., 1967b, Un critère nouveau de découvertes de structures: le variogramme: *Sciences de la Terre*, Tome XII, no. 4, p. 275–299.

Serra, J., 1968, Les structures gigognes: Morphologie mathématique et interprétation métallogénique: *Mineralium Deposita*, v. 3, p. 135–154.

The Choice of a Test for Spatial Autocorrelation

A. D. Cliff and J. K. Ord

Consider a study region which has been exhaustively partitioned into n non-overlapping subareas. Examples include states of the United States and counties of England and Wales. Suppose the value of a variate, X, has been measured in each of the subareas, and that the value of X in a typical subarea, i, is x_i. A basic geographical principle for such areally distributed data is that the $\{x_i\}$ are likely to be related over space. This idea underlies the concept of the region in geography. More forcefully, Gould (1970) has stated that

> All our [that is, geographers'] efforts to understand spatial pattern, structure, and process have indicated that it is precisely the *lack* of independence—the *interdependence* of spatial phenomena—that allows us to substitute pattern, and therefore predictability and order, for chaos and apparent lack of interdependence of things in time and space. The drive towards the structuring of systems of events and the relationships that bind them together, and the construction and use of process models simply emphasizes that virtually all phenomena of interest to the geographer are never independent in the fundamental dimensions of his enquiry.

In the same vein, Tobler (1970*a*) suggests "the first law of geography" is that "everything is related to everything else, but near things are more related than distant things". Tobler (1970*b*) reaffirms this view with the remark that "the central dogma in geography asserts that what happens at one place is not independent of what happens at another".

A measure of the degree of interdependence among the $\{x_i\}$ in the plane is the level of spatial autocorrelation in the data. A plausible model of the spatial interdependence among the $\{x_i\}$ is the Markovian scheme,

$$x_i = \rho \sum_j d_{ij} x_j + u_i, \qquad i = 1, 2, \ldots, n. \tag{1}$$

54

Here, the $\{u_i\}$ are independent and identically distributed variates with common variance, σ^2. The $\{d_{ij}\}$ are a set of non-negative constants that specify which j subareas in the region have variate values directly related spatially with $x_i, i = 1, 2, \ldots, n$. We assume the $\{d_{ij}\}$ are scaled so $\Sigma_{(2)}d_{ij} = n$, where $\Sigma_{(2)}$ represents

$$\sum_{\substack{i=1 \\ i \neq j}}^{n} \sum_{j=1}^{n},$$

a notation we shall use throughout this paper. The parameter ρ is a measure of the overall level or strength of spatial autocorrelation among the $\{x_i x_j\}$ pairs for which $d_{ij} > 0$. For example, suppose observations are made on a regular grid and there is a north–south pattern of spatial autocorrelation present in the data. Then a first-order scheme using the model given in Equation (1) would have $d_{ij} = \frac{1}{2}$ is subarea j is due north or due south of subarea i and contiguous to it, and $d_{ij} = 0$ otherwise (Figure 1). For simplicity, all subareas are taken to have due north and due south neighboring

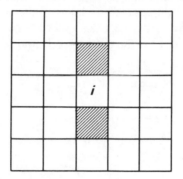

cells postulated to be
spatially autocorrelated
to the typical cell *i*

Figure 1   A north–south pattern of spatial autocorrelation.

subareas so there is no boundary problem. Clearly $\Sigma_j d_{ij} = 1$ for all i, while Equation (1) for subarea i will include terms on the right-hand side for the two shaded subareas in Figure 1. The overall level of spatial autocorrelation between north–south contiguous pairs is represented by the parameter ρ. When $\rho > 0$, we say there is positive spatial autocorrelation among the $\{x_i\}$, while $\rho < 0$ implies negative spatial autocorrelation. If $\rho = 0$, there is said to be no spatial autocorrelation in the region on X.

Several statistics have been proposed in the literature to test $H_0 : \rho = 0$ against general alternatives of the form $H_1 : \rho \neq 0$ in the model given in

Equation (1). The first purpose of this paper is to review the proposed measures. The second objective is to study these coefficients with a view to recommending which coefficient should be used in given circumstances, and what precise form the $\{d_{ij}\}$ in the model should take. We will also examine the asymptotic relative efficiency (ARE) of various statistics in discriminating between null and alternative hypotheses of the type outlined above, and will discuss use of Monte Carlo techniques to construct power curves of the statistics for some typical study areas.

Measures of Autocorrelation in the Plane

We assume in this paper that the $\{x_i\}$ are raw data rather than residuals calculated from a regression or trend-surface analysis. Testing for spatial autocorrelation among such residuals presents special problems which are discussed in Cliff and Ord (1972, 1973, ch. 5). The simplest way in which the $\{x_i\}$ can be measured is on a binary scale. Here we put $x_i = 1$ if an event has happened in a subarea and $x_i = 0$ otherwise. Following Moran (1948), we color code as black (B) those subareas for which $x_i = 1$, and color subareas with $x_i = 0$ as white (W), creating a two-color choropleth map. We can test for spatial autocorrelation in the pattern of B and W subareas in the map using the statistics,

$$BB = \tfrac{1}{2}\textstyle\sum_{(2)} w_{ij}x_ix_j, \tag{2}$$

and

$$BW = \tfrac{1}{2}\textstyle\sum_{(2)}w_{ij}(x_i - x_j)^2. \tag{3}$$

BB and BW are the weighted numbers of BB and BW links in the study region. The $\{w_{ij}\}$ are non-negative constants or weights specified by the researcher; the restriction $\Sigma_{(2)}w_{ij} = n$ serves to remove an arbitrary scale factor. If the researcher believes the variate values of the ith and jth subareas are autocorrelated, then $w_{ij} > 0$, and $w_{ij} = 0$ otherwise. We therefore make the important distinction between $\mathbf{W} \equiv \{w_{ij}\}$ and $\mathbf{D} \equiv \{d_{ij}\}$. $\mathbf{W}$ is the matrix of weights used in the test statistic and represents the researcher's belief as to which subareas are likely to be related to each other. $\mathbf{D}$ is the matrix of weights which represents the true or actual pattern of dependencies between subareas. In the ideal case, the researcher will have *a priori* knowledge as to which subareas may be spatially autocorrelated, and he will put $\mathbf{W} = \mathbf{D}$. The test statistic then provides a guide as to the value of ρ in the model (Equation (1)), conditional upon the form of $\mathbf{W}$ used. The reason for making this distinction between $\mathbf{W}$ and $\mathbf{D}$ is that we often know very little about spatial processes, and therfore have only a limited idea of which subareas are related to other subareas. Often $\mathbf{W} \neq \mathbf{D}$. Later, we will examine the effect upon the power of various test statistics of evaluating the level of spatial autocorrelation among a set of subareas whose pattern of dependencies we have specified as **W** when in fact the true pattern is $\mathbf{D} \neq \mathbf{W}$.

Equations (2) and (3) suggest that if $\rho > 0$ in the model (Equation (1)), "many" BB and "few" BW links will be recorded compared with the values of BB and BW when $\rho = 0$. That is, the B and W subareas will appear as groups or clusters on the map. If $\rho < 0$, then few BB and many BW links will be observed compared with the quantities expected when $\rho = 0$; the B and W subareas will appear to have a uniform spacing like the rows and columns of a chessboard. Krishna Iyer (1949) and Cliff (1969) have generalized Equations (2) and (3) for the case when X has $k > 2$ classes.

Suppose now that X comprises ranks or is interval scaled. Cliff and Ord (1973) have extended findings given in Moran (1950) and Geary (1954) and have defined the spatial autocorrelation coefficients,

$$I = \frac{n \sum_{(2)} w_{ij} z_i z_j}{W \sum_{i=1}^{n} z_i^2}, \tag{4}$$

and

$$c = \left(\frac{n-1}{2W}\right) \frac{\sum_{(2)} w_{ij}(x_i - x_j)^2}{\sum_{i=1}^{n} z_i^2}, \tag{5}$$

where $z_i = x_i - \bar{x}$ and $W = \sum_{(2)} w_{ij}$ in addition to previously used terms. Note that I is analogous to a serial correlation coefficient, while c corresponds in form to the Durbin and Watson d statistic (Durbin and Watson, 1950, 1951, 1971) used in time-series studies, and to the von Neumann ratio.

Under fairly relaxed conditions, coefficients BB, BW, I, and c are asymptotically normally distributed as $n \to \infty$ when $\rho = 0$ in the model (Equation (1)). For a formal statement of the conditions, see Cliff and Ord (1973, section 2.4). Informally, we require that no definite set of subareas should dominate the study region as, for example, does the articulation point in a star lattice. To test $H_0 : \rho = 0$ against $H_1 : \rho \neq 0$, we may treat

$$z = (t - \mu_1')/\sigma(t) \tag{6}$$

as (approximately) a standard normal deviate. Here, $\mu_1'(t)$ and $\sigma(t)$ denote the mean and standard deviation under H_0 of the statistic, t, which might be any of those given in Equations (2)–(5). The null hypothesis is rejected whenever the observed value of z falls in the critical region. For a two-sided test, H_0 is rejected if $|z| \geqslant z_\alpha$, where $P(|z| \geqslant z_\alpha | H_0) = \alpha$.

Moments of the Coefficients
The first two moments of BB and BW under H_0 have been evaluated for two assumptions:

(1) free sampling (or sampling with replacement), where the individual counties are independently coded B or W with probabilities p and $q = 1 - p$, respectively;

(2) non-free sampling (or exhaustive sampling without replacement), where each county has the same probability, *a priori*, of being B or W. The coding is subject to the overall constraint that there are n_1 counties coded B and n_2 coded W, and $n_1 + n_2 = n$. We obtain the following results.

Free sampling:

BB links

$$\mu_1' = \tfrac{1}{2}Wp^2, \tag{7}$$

$$\mu_2 = \tfrac{1}{4}p^2q(S_1q + S_2p). \tag{8}$$

BW links

$$\mu_1' = Wpq, \tag{9}$$

$$\mu_2 = \tfrac{1}{4}[S_2pq + 4(S_1 - S_2)p^2q^2]. \tag{10}$$

Non-free sampling:

BB links

$$\mu_1' = \frac{Wn_1^{(2)}}{2n^{(2)}}, \tag{11}$$

$$\mu_2 = \frac{1}{4}\left[\frac{S_1n_1^{(2)}}{n^{(2)}} + \frac{(S_2 - 2S_1)n_1^{(3)}}{n^{(3)}} + \frac{(W^2 + S_1 - S_2)n_1^{(4)}}{n^{(4)}} - W^2\left(\frac{n_1^{(2)}}{n^{(2)}}\right)^2\right]. \tag{12}$$

BW links

$$\mu_1' = \frac{Wn_1n_2}{n^{(2)}}, \tag{13}$$

$$\mu_2 = \frac{1}{4}\left[\frac{2S_1n_1n_2}{n^{(2)}} + \frac{(S_2 - 2S_1)n_1n_2(n_1 + n_2 - 2)}{n^{(3)}}\right.$$
$$\left. + \frac{4(W^2 + S_1 - S_2)n_1^{(2)}n_2^{(2)}}{n^{(4)}} - 4W^2\left(\frac{n_1n_2}{n^{(2)}}\right)^2\right]. \tag{14}$$

In these equations, the following new terms are defined:

$$S_1 = \tfrac{1}{2}\sum_{(2)}(w_{ij} + w_{ji})^2, \tag{15}$$

$$S_2 = \sum_{i=1}^{n}(w_{i.} + w_{.i})^2, \tag{16}$$

$$w_{i.} = \sum_{j=1}^{n}w_{ij}, \qquad w_{.j} = \sum_{i=1}^{n}w_{ij}, \qquad n^{(x)} = n(n-1)\ldots(n-x+1). \tag{17}$$

The moments of I and c can be evaluated under either of two assumptions:

(1) normality. The $\{x_i\}$ are taken to be the result of n independent drawings from a normal population (or populations); or
(2) randomization. Whatever the underlying distribution of the populations, the position of the observed value of I or c in the set of all values of I and c is considered to be obtained if I and c are evaluated for each of the n! random permutations of the $\{x_i\}$ in the study region.

Using the subscripts N and R to denote the assumptions of normality and randomization respectively, it can be shown that

$$E_N(I) = E_R(I) = -(n - 1)^{-1}, \tag{18}$$

$$E_N(I^2) = \frac{n^2 S_1 - n S_2 + 3W^2}{W^2(n^2 - 1)}, \tag{19}$$

$$E_R(I^2) = \frac{n[(n^2 - 3n + 3)S_1 - nS_2 + 3W^2] - b_2[(n^2 - n)S_1 - 2nS_2 + 6W^2]}{(n - 1)^{(3)}W^2}. \tag{20}$$

For c,

$$E_N(c) = E_R(c) = 1, \tag{21}$$

$$var_N(c) = \frac{(2S_1 + S_2)(n - 1) - 4W^2}{2(n + 1)W^2}, \tag{22}$$

$$var_R(c) = \{(n - 1)S_1[n^2 - 3n + 3 - (n - 1)b_2]$$
$$\tfrac{1}{4}(n - 1)S_2[n^2 + 3n - 6 - (n^2 - n + 2)b_2]$$
$$+ W^2[n^2 - 3 - (n - 1)^2 b_2]\}/n(n - 2)^{(2)}W^2. \tag{23}$$

These equations contain the new term b_2, the sample kurtosis coefficient, defined as $b_2 = m_4/m_2^2$. In this definition, m_j is the jth sample moment of the $\{x_i\}$ about the sample mean.

Two General Questions

We have defined four measures of autocorrelation in the plane. It appears that I or c can be used if X is binary scaled by putting $x_i = 1$ or 0. However, c is equivalent to BW under non-free sampling, apart from a constant factor. This is almost true of I as well (it is exactly true when $n = 2n_1$). Therefore, the choice really lies between BB and BW. If X is ratio or interval scaled, we are faced with a choice between I and c. Which test should be used in any given situation? We might ask further if a combination of tests is better than one test used alone in discriminating between H_0 and H_1.

A second general question relates to the non-negative constants, $\{w_{ij}\}$. These constants may be used to specify which subareas in the region are believed to have variate values spatially autocorrelated with x_i. Can anything more precise be said about the structure of these constants or weights? The remainder of this paper tries to provide some answer to these two general questions.

Choice of Test Statistic

The Criteria

The first broad question posed above, namely "which test or combination of tests is best?", implies some criterion by which "best" can be assessed. The standard Neyman–Pearson approach is to consider the *power* of a test, defined as the probability of rejecting the null hypothesis, H_0, when it is false. That is,

$$\text{power} = 1 - \text{probability (type II error)}.$$

The power is examined at given levels of the *size* of the test, where size is defined as the probability of rejecting the null hypothesis, H_0, when it is true. That is,

$$\text{size} = \text{probability (type I error)}.$$

Unfortunately, for the problem at hand, small sample results cannot be obtained by analytical methods. Therefore two alternative approaches are used in this paper.

(1) Asymptotic relative efficiency (ARE). Instead of computing the complete power curve, the local efficiency of the test is assessed as the parameter values, under the alternative hypothesis H_1, approach those specified under H_0, and the sample size n goes to infinity. This measure is discussed in Kendall and Stuart (1967, ch. 25).

(2) Monte Carlo studies. Power functions of the test statistics may be evaluated for several lattices, allowing small sample comparisons to be made.

Asymptotic Relative Efficiency

Suppose that we wish to test the null hypothesis, $H_0 : \psi = 0$, against the alternative hypothesis, $H_1 : \psi \neq 0$, where ψ is some parameter. Let h denote any test statistic under consideration and suppose that, without loss of generality, the expected value of h under H_0 is zero; that is

$$E(h|H_0) = 0. \tag{24}$$

Further, assume the variance of h exists, defined as

$$\text{var}(h|H_0) = \omega^2, \tag{25}$$

and that h is asymptotically normally distributed. Given certain conditions, which are satisfied in all cases considered here (Kendall and Stuart, 1967,

p. 265), we may examine alternative hypotheses for which h is asymptotically normally distributed and

$$E(h|H_1) = \psi b + O(\psi^{1+\delta}). \tag{26}$$

Here, $\delta > 0$, O denotes terms of this order or higher in ψ, and b is some function independent of ψ. If we consider alternatives of the form $\psi \propto n^{-\frac{1}{2}}$ as $n \to \infty$, the asymptotic *efficacy* of a test based on h is defined as

$$\Gamma(h) = \frac{b^2}{\omega^2}. \tag{27}$$

From Equation (27), the *asymptotic relative efficiency* (ARE) of a test based on h_1 to one based on h_2 is defined as

$$ARE(h_1, h_2) = \frac{F(h_1)}{F(h_2)}. \tag{28}$$

The ARE is a useful measure because it is related to power in the following way.

Let $P(h, \psi)$ be the power of a test based on h when the parameter has the value ψ under H_1. Then

$$ARE(h_1, h_2) = \lim_{n \to \infty} \left[\frac{P(h_1, \psi)}{P(h_2, \psi)} \right]^{\frac{1}{2}}, \tag{29}$$

where $\psi \propto n^{-\frac{1}{2}}$.

Thus the ARE is a measure of the comparative asymptotic local power of a test. This may seem to be a measure of strictly limited value but, in practice, the ARE of two tests often gives a fair guide to their relative power for alternatives not too far from the null hypothesis.

The ARE of Tests for Spatial Autocorrelation

Throughout this section it is assumed that the data are drawn from normal populations. In model (Equation (1)), we specify a first-order Markov scheme as the alternative hypothesis, H_1; that is, when $\rho \neq 0$. We may express Equation (1) in vector notation as

$$x = \rho Dx + u \tag{30}$$

where $x' = (x_1, \ldots, x_n)$, $u' = (u_1, \ldots, u_n)$ and $D = \{d_{ij}\}$, but $d_{ii} = 0$. For simplicity we assume the means of the X variates are known, and the variables have been adjusted to have zero mean. That is,

$$E(X) = E(u) = 0, \tag{31}$$

where X is the variate vector corresponding to the observed values x. This assumption does not affect the *asymptotic* results, but makes the analysis simpler. From the assumption

$$E(\mathbf{uu'}) = \sigma^2 \mathbf{I_n}, \tag{32}$$

and Equation (31), it follows that

$$\text{var}(\mathbf{X}) = E(\mathbf{XX'}) = \sigma^2(\mathbf{I_n} - \rho\mathbf{D})^{-1}(\mathbf{I_n} - \rho\mathbf{D'})^{-1} \tag{33}$$

which we set equal to $\sigma^2 \mathbf{V}(\rho)$.

Comparison of I *and* c. Let us consider the statistic

$$h = \frac{\mathbf{x'Tx}}{\mathbf{x'x}}, \tag{34}$$

where $\mathbf{T}$ is a matrix of constant coefficients $\{t_{ij}\}$. Both I and c given in Equations (4) and (5) can be expressed in the form of Equation (34) when the population mean is set to zero. If we assume $\Sigma_{(2)} w_{ij} = W = n$, we have for I that $\mathbf{T} = \mathbf{W}$, and for c that $\mathbf{T} = \mathbf{\Omega} - \mathbf{W}$, where $\mathbf{\Omega}$ is a diagonal matrix with elements $\Omega_{ii} = \frac{1}{2}\Sigma_j(w_{ij} + w_{ji})$. It can be shown (Cliff and Ord, 1973, ch. 7) that the efficacy of h as defined in Equation (27) is

$$F(h) = \frac{(n + 1)^2[\text{tr}(\mathbf{D'T} + \mathbf{TD})]^2}{n(n + 2)\{\text{tr}[\mathbf{T(T} + \mathbf{T')}] - (2/n)[\text{tr}(\mathbf{T})]^2\}}. \tag{35}$$

Here, tr is the trace operator which sums elements on the leading diagonal of the matrix, $\mathbf{T}$. In particular, if $\mathbf{W} = \mathbf{D}$,

$$F(I) = \frac{(n + 1)^2}{n(n + 2)} \frac{[\text{tr}(\mathbf{DD'} + \mathbf{D}^2)]^2}{\text{tr}(\mathbf{DD'} + \mathbf{D}^2)}, \tag{36}$$

while

$$F(c) = \frac{(n + 1)^2[\text{tr}(\mathbf{DD'} + \mathbf{D}^2)]^2}{n(n + 2)[\text{tr}(\mathbf{DD'} + \mathbf{D}^2) + 2\text{tr}(\mathbf{\Omega}^2) - 2n]}. \tag{37}$$

From the definition, it follows that

$$\text{tr}(\mathbf{\Omega}^2) = \tfrac{1}{4}\Sigma(w_{i.} + w_{.i})^2 = \tfrac{1}{4}S_2. \tag{38}$$

Thus, from Equations (36) and (37),

$$\text{ARE}(c, I) = \frac{1}{1 + \theta}, \tag{39}$$

where $\theta = (nS_2 - 4W^2)/2nS_1$. The equation reduces, when $n = W$, to

$$\theta = \frac{S_2 - 4n}{2S_1}. \tag{40}$$

It can be shown that $S_2 \geqslant 4n$, with equality only when $w_{i.} = w_{.i} = 1$, for all $i = 1, \ldots, n$. Therefore, for regular lattices (including time series), θ is near to or equal to zero for all n, and always converges to zero as n increases. However, this need not happen for a lattice with irregular weights. (In this context, a regular lattice is one which has the same pattern of weights for every subarea, except possibly at the boundary.)

Examples.

1. Consider a lattice broken into blocks of size three as in Figure 2. In each block of three define the weights $w_{12} = 1$, $w_{21} = w_{23} = \frac{1}{2}$, $w_{32} = 1$, and $w_{ij} = 0$ for all other pairs. If there are m ($= \frac{1}{3}n$) blocks, it follows that $W = 3m$, $S_1 = 4.5m$, and $S_2 = 13.5m$. Therefore $\theta = \frac{1}{6}$ and ARE(c, I) $= \frac{6}{7}$ for any m.

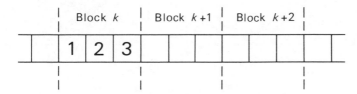

Figure 2   Lattice broken into blocks of size three.

2. For the Eire county system shown in Figure 3, it can be demonstrated that similar calculations yield ARE(c, I) $= 0.897$.

While such comparisons can only be justified for $n \to \infty$, the following conclusion appears reasonable on the basis of ARE results. The I test is generally *better* than the c test, although the margin of advantage may be slight.

Comparison of BB *and* BW. Instead of using the I or c statistics, we could use BB or BW. Two major questions arise. What is the best choice of p, where p = prob(subarea coded black)? Should the BB or BW test be used? We assume first that p is known, so the free sampling model is appropriate. If the researcher uses the matrix of weights, **W**, in the test statistic, while the true pattern of dependencies is given by **D**, it can be established that the efficacies are

$$F(BB) = \frac{[f(a)]^4 \{\mathrm{tr}(\mathbf{WD} + \mathbf{WD'})\}^2}{(S_1 p^2 q^2 + S_2 p^3 q)}, \tag{41}$$

and

$$F(BW) = \frac{[f(a)]^4 \{\mathrm{tr}(\mathbf{WD} + \mathbf{WD'})\}^2}{S_1 p^2 q^2 + S_2 pq(\frac{1}{4} - pq)}. \tag{42}$$

Figure 3　The Eire county system.

Here

$$f(a) = (2\pi)^{-\frac{1}{2}} \exp(-\tfrac{1}{2}a^2). \tag{43}$$

If $\mathbf{W} = \mathbf{D}$, then maximizing $F(BW)$ with respect to p will show that the best value for p is 0.5, for any lattice. For BB the results are more involved, as the best value of p varies with $\tau = S_2/4S_1$. At the minimum value of $\tau = 1$ as in a circular time series, $p \approx 0.25$ is best. This slowly falls to $p \approx 0.20$ at $\tau = 4$, which is the queen's case mapped onto a torus (by analogy with chess, the "queen's case" is defined for a regular lattice as $w_{ij} = 1$ if two cells have a common edge or vertex, and $w_{ij} = 0$ otherwise). As $1 \leqslant \tau \leqslant 4$ for almost all lattices of practical interest, $p = 0.20$ or 0.25 is recommended as a simple choice.

When $w_{ij} = d_{ij}$, the result given in Equation (41) reduces to

$$F(BB) = \frac{[f(a)]^4 S_1}{p^2 q(q + 4\tau p)}, \tag{44}$$

from which the best value for p can be found, given τ. Likewise when $w_{ij} = d_{ij}$ and $p = 0.5$, since $f(0) = (2\pi)^{-\frac{1}{2}}$ we have

$$F(BW) = \frac{4S_1}{\pi^2}. \tag{45}$$

Thus,

$$ARE(BB, BW) = \frac{F(BB)}{F(BW)} \tag{46}$$

can be computed from results expressed in Equations (44) and (45). Since the maximum value of this ARE, for any p and all $\tau \geqslant 1$ is only 0.307, the BW test is clearly superior to the BB test.

However, when non-free sampling is considered, a different picture emerges. Using the approach already given for free sampling, we find that $p = 0.5$ is the best value for both the BW and the BB tests, and $F(BW) = 4S_1/\pi^2$ as before, while

$$F(BB) = \frac{4S_1}{\pi^2(1 + 2\theta)}, \tag{47}$$

where θ is defined as in Equation (40). Thus, for non-free sampling,

$$ARE(BB, BW) = \frac{1}{1 + 2\theta}, \tag{48}$$

which is equal to one for regular lattices, but is less than one for irregular lattices. Thus we recommend that BW be used in preference to BB, although the margin of advantage may be slight.

Finally, from Equations (36) and (45),

$$ARE(BW, I) = \frac{4}{\pi^2}, \tag{49}$$

representing the loss of power when the BW test is used for interval scaled data. This compares with an ARE figure of $2/\pi$ for the sign test against Student's t, when testing for a difference between population means. We now show why expression (Equation (49)) is lower than the ARE for the test of means.

An Alternative Derivation of Choropleth Map Results. Let $\{x_i\}$ denote original observations drawn from a normal population, and let $\{x_i'\}$ denote coded values (0 or 1 for example). Daniels (1944) has shown that a test for correlation based on $\{x_i', y_i'\}$ instead of $\{x_i, y_i\}$, where y_i' is the coded value for y_i, has an ARE equal to $[\rho(x, x')\rho(y, y')]^2$. Here, ρ denotes the correlation between the two sets of values. When testing for autocorrelation, it can be shown that the ARE reduces to

$$\text{ARE} = [\rho(x, x')]^4. \tag{50}$$

For two-color coding, $\rho(x, x') = (2/\pi)^{\frac{1}{2}}$ and so

$$\text{ARE(BW, I)} = (2/\pi)^2, \tag{51}$$

as given in Equation (49). For the sign test comparison with Student's t, the ARE is $[\rho(x, x')]^2$, giving the value $2/\pi$ already noted. The BB and c tests represent less efficient variants of BW and I respectively, and are not covered by result (Equation (51)).

Geary (1954) observed that using three classes (0, 1, and 2) rather than two improved the efficiency of the test procedure. The logical conclusion of such an increase in the number of classes is to use ranks, $\{x' = 1, 2, \ldots, n\}$. It is known that $\rho(x, x') = (3/\pi)^{\frac{1}{2}}$ for ranks, so their use in I yields an ARE of $(3/\pi)^2 \approx 0.91$. Thus, a test based on ranks appears to provide a nonparametric procedure of high asymptotic efficiency, although a study of nonnormal populations would be required to confirm this result. The first two moments, under H_0, for the I statistic using rank data are

$$E(I) = -\frac{1}{n-1}, \tag{52}$$

and

$$E(I^2) = \frac{1}{5W^2(n-1)^2(n+1)}[n(n-1)(5n+6)S_1 - (5n+7)(nS_2 - 3W^2)]. \tag{53}$$

An absolute Benchmark: the Likelihood Ratio Test. So far, we have compared measures of spatial autocorrelation. We also need some absolute benchmark against which to judge performance of various coefficients. An obvious candidate is the likelihood ratio (LR) statistic. Under $H_1 : \rho = \rho_1 > 0$, and σ^2 known in model (Equation (1)), the log-likelihood function is

$$L_1 \propto -n \, ln\sigma - \tfrac{1}{2} ln|\mathbf{V}_1| - \tfrac{1}{2}\mathbf{x}'\mathbf{V}_1^{-1}\mathbf{x}/\sigma^2, \tag{54}$$

where $V_1 = V(\rho_1)$, as given in Equation (33). Likewise, under $H_0 : \rho = 0, \sigma^2$ known,

$$L_0 \propto -n \ln \sigma - \tfrac{1}{2} x'x/\sigma^2. \tag{55}$$

The likelihood ratio test then rejects H_0 in favor of H_1 if

$$L_1 - L_0 > k, \tag{56}$$

where k is some suitable constant. This suggests a test statistic of the form

$$\frac{x'V_1^{-1}x}{x'x}. \tag{57}$$

If we ignore constants and terms of order ρ_1^2, this reduces to the statistic

$$\frac{x'(D + D')x}{x'x} \equiv \frac{\Sigma_{(2)}(d_{ij} + d_{ji})x_i x_j}{\Sigma x_i^2} \tag{58}$$

which is equivalent to

$$\frac{\Sigma_{(2)} d_{ij} x_i x_j}{\Sigma x_i^2}, \tag{59}$$

since $x'Dx = x'D'x$. Equation (59) is the form of the I statistic defined in Equation (4). Thus Equation (59) approaches the LR statistic as $\rho_1 \to 0$. As no uniformly most powerful test is available (Anderson ,1948), we suggest that I be used, with $W = D$, since this is a locally most powerful test. This argument parallels that of Durbin and Watson (1950, p. 423–424) for the analysis of time series, although they used the statistic

$$\frac{\Sigma_{(2)} d_{ij}(x_i - x_j)^2}{\Sigma x_i^2}, \tag{60}$$

which is equally satisfactory in that particular instance.

Combinations of Tests

Given the variety of different tests, it is of interest to ask whether or not some combination of tests would be more efficient than a single test. Since the I statistic is derived from the ratio of the likelihoods (albeit as a local asymptotic test), the ARE of any procedure combined with I will not yield an improvement, although finite sampling results might show possible gains in power. For join count statistics, however, the possibilities of gain through a combined procedure seem more tangible. To explore this, we evaluate the correlation between BB and BW statistics, and then compare the best combined test with BW.

Correlation between BB *and* BW *Join Count Statistics.* Recall the definitions of the BB and BW statistics given in Equations (2) and (3). The correlation between BB and BW is given by the standard formula

$$\rho(BB, BW) = \frac{E(BB\ BW) - E(BB)E(BW)}{\sigma(BB)\sigma(BW)}. \tag{61}$$

Means and variances were given in Equations (7) through (14), so it is necessary only to compute the cross-product term. We have

$$E(BB\ BW) = E\{(\tfrac{1}{2}\Sigma_{(2)}\ w_{ij}x_i x_j)[\tfrac{1}{2}\Sigma_{(2)}\ w_{ij}(x_i - x_j)^2]\}. \tag{62}$$

For free sampling, it can be shown that

$$E(BB\ BW) = \tfrac{1}{4}p^2 q[S_2(1 - 2p) - 2S_1 q + 2W^2 p], \tag{63}$$

while under non-free sampling

$$E(BB\ BW) = \frac{(n - n_1)n_1^{(2)}}{4n^{(4)}}[S_2(n - 2n_1 + 1) - 2S_1(n - n_1 - 1)$$

$$+ 2W^2(n_1 - 2)]. \tag{64}$$

Relative Efficiency of Combined Tests. Using the results given in Equations (63) and (64), the variance of the combined statistic,

$$u = \alpha BB + (1 - \alpha)BW, \tag{65}$$

where α is an arbitrary constant, is given by

$$var(u) = \alpha^2\sigma^2(BB) + (1 - \alpha)^2\sigma^2(BW) + 2\alpha(1 - \alpha)\sigma(BB)\sigma(BW)\rho(BB, BW). \tag{66}$$

When $p = \tfrac{1}{2}$ for the free sampling models, the efficacy of u is

$$F(u) = \frac{4S_1(2 - 3\alpha)^2}{\pi^2[(2 - 3\alpha)^2 + 4\alpha^2\tau]}, \tag{67}$$

so that $\alpha = 0$ is the best choice and corresponds to use of the BW test alone. For the non-free sampling case, with $p = \tfrac{1}{2}$,

$$F(u) = \frac{4S_1(2 - 3\alpha)^2}{\pi^2[(2 - 3\alpha)^2 + 2\alpha^2\theta]}. \tag{68}$$

Thus, for $\theta > 0$, the best choice is again $\alpha = 0$ (the BW test alone). For $\theta = 0$, any linear combination of the two tests is equally efficient. Therefore *we cannot improve upon the use of the BW test alone.* If the BB test is used with a value of p different from that used for the BW test, a gain in efficiency could result. This is expected, since more information has been used.

Monte Carlo Studies

In this section we use Monte Carlo methods to construct the power curves of the BB, BW, I, and c statistics for several small lattices. As before, we assume under H_1 that the dependence between $\{x_i\}$ values in a county system is specified by a spatial Markov process of the type given in Equation (1), or, in matrix notation, in Equation (30). In the studies described below, each u_i was taken to be normally distributed with zero mean and variance σ^2. That is, u_i is $N(0, \sigma^2)$.

The Simulation Experiment. The simulation experiment had the following steps.

Step 1: choose a lattice and specify $\mathbf{D}^*$ for that lattice, where the $\{d_{ij}\}$ are obtained from $\{d_{ij}^*\}$ by the scaling

$$d_{ij} = \frac{d_{ij}}{\sum\limits_j d_{ij}^*},$$

so that, in all cases $\Sigma_j\, d_{ij} = 1$. Also $d_{ij}^* = 1$ or 0 in all cases and we define $2A = \Sigma_{(2)}\, d_{ij}^*$.

The following lattices were examined.

Lattice	Value of A/n	$\mathbf{D}^*$
4 by 3	1.42	rook's case
25 cell circle	1.00	$d_{ij}^* = 1$ if counties i and j have a common boundary, and $d_{ij}^* = 0$ otherwise
5 by 5	1.6	rook's case
5 by 5	2.88	queen's case
5 by 5	4.0	queen's case mapped onto a torus
Eire (excluding County Dublin)	2.2	$d_{ij}^* = 1$ if counties i and j have a common boundary, and $d_{ij}^* = 0$ otherwise
7 by 7	1.71	rook's case

In all cases, it is assumed that the value of X in county i is affected only by contiguous counties.

For each lattice:

Step 2: specify a value for ρ. We took $\rho = 0.0(0.1)0.9$.

Step 3: from Equation (30) it is evident that

$$\mathbf{x} = (\mathbf{I} - \rho\mathbf{D})^{-1}\mathbf{u}. \tag{69}$$

Compute $(\mathbf{I} - \rho\mathbf{D})^{-1}$ by the following steps:

Step 4: generate the vector $\mathbf{u}$ by random sampling from an $N(0, 1)$ population, and compute $\mathbf{x}$ from Equation (69).

Step 5: calculate I and c.

Step 6: code counties having the n_1 largest x values as $1 \equiv B$ and the remainder $0 \equiv W$. For n = 12, 25, 49, we took $n_1 = 6, 12, 24$ respectively.

Step 7: calculate BB and BW. (Because of step 6, the results obtained are for non-free sampling.)

Step 8: repeat steps 4 to 7 t times for each value of ρ. We took t = 200. Note that when $\rho = 0$, the sample relates to the test statistic given H_0.

Step 9: having obtained t = 200 values of the I, c, BB, and BW statistics for $\rho = 0 \cdot 0(0.1)0.9$ in each lattice, we took the results for $\rho = 0.0$ and determined the $\alpha = 0.05$ cutoff point for a one-tailed test of positive spatial autocorrelation in each set. In the case of I and c, this cutoff point was given by the tenth largest (I) or smallest (c) generated value. For BB and BW, determination of the $\alpha = 0.05$ cutoff point was made more complicated by the lumpy nature of the probability distributions. In the 5 by 5 rook's case, for example, we observed the following frequencies of joins:

BB	11	12	13
frequency	12	4	2

The decision rule was

reject H_0 with probability 1 if $BB \geqslant 12$,

with probability $\frac{4}{15}$ if $BB = 11$,

with probability 0 if $BB \leqslant 10$.

This randomized decision rule gives $\alpha = 0.05$ for the size of the test, based on the distribution function for BB under H_0 estimated from the 200 generated values of BB. The procedure is used so a value of $\alpha = 0.05$ can be achieved and is not recommended as a practical testing method.

Step 10: recall that for I and BB, positive spatial autocorrelation corresponds to the positive tails of the probability distributions for these statistics, while for c and BW, positive spatial autocorrelation corresponds to the negative tails. For each value of $[\rho = 0.1(0.1)0.9]$ and for each lattice, count the number of generated values of each statistic which are more extreme than, or equal to, the 0.05 cutoff value. The frequencies obtained, when expressed as a fraction of 200, represent the estimated power of the test statistic for that value of ρ.

The same random number sequences were used for each lattice (two separate runs of length 100) so the power curves are directly comparable for (a) different statistics (same lattice, same ρ); (b) different statistics, different value of ρ (same lattice); (c) different statistics, different value of ρ, different lattices of the same size.

Interpretation of Results. Table 1 contains results for I and c with each value of ρ for the two separate runs of length 100 in the 4 by 3 rook's case lattice. Steps 9 and 10 were performed for each set of 100 and for the combined set of 200, to obtain some idea of the different results arising from sampling variation in the Monte Carlo procedure. For sets of 100, the $\alpha = 0.05$ cutoff points for I and c were computed separately, using the fifth most extreme

Table 1. Power curves, expressed in percent, for I and c in the 4 by 3 rook's case, $\alpha = 0.05$ (one-tailed test)

ρ	1st hundred		2nd hundred		All two hundred	
	I	c	I	c	I	c
0.0	5	5	5	5	5	5
0.1	7	6	3	5	4	7
0.2	9	8	11	11	9.5	9
0.3	12	6	8	12	10.5	12.5
0.4	16	11	15	17	15.5	16.5
0.5	24	16	16	22	21.5	24.0
0.6	29	24	32	34	31	32.5
0.7	36	24	32	45	36	37.5
0.8	57	48	51	56	55.5	57.5
0.9	56	52	58	65	57.5	62

value when $\rho = 0$. This lattice has considerable sampling variation but was much less for the larger lattices and when the cutoff point was found from all 200 values. In retrospect, perhaps a larger value of t at $\rho = 0$ (about t = 600) should have been taken to determine the cutoff point more accurately. However, we have no reason to believe sampling variations have materially affected our conclusions. As lattice size increases, power curves are smoother and more stable.

Figure 4 gives power curves for the I, c, BB, and BW statistics in the various n = 25 lattices. It shows the effect of shape, as measured by A/n upon the power curves. For non-binary weights the ratio n/S_1 may be interpreted in the same way ($n/S_1 = 1$ for the circle lattice, but 4 for the queen's torus. If the weights are not scaled so W = n, the ratio W^2/nS_1 should be used). Figure 5 gives power curves for various test lattices with the lattice structure fixed (square lattice, rook's case), but different values of n.

From Figure 4 it is evident that the power of each of the statistics decreases as A/n increases. For a given test statistic and value of ρ, power is highest in the 25 cell circle (equivalent to a circular time series) and decreases

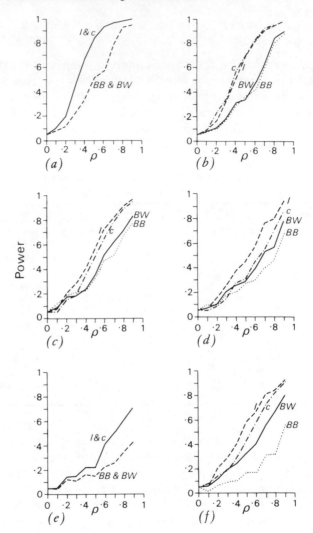

Figure 4 Power curves for BB, BW, I, and c for various
n = 25 lattices. (a) 25 cell circle, (b) (12 by 12) + 1 rook's
case, (c) 5 by 5 rook's case, (d) 5 by 5 queen's case, (e) 5 by 5
queen's case on a torus, (f) Eire excluding County Dublin.

monotonically as A/n increases, to the queen's case on a torus. In a totally
connected lattice with $d_{ij}^* = 1$ for all $i \neq j$, the power of all spatial autocorrelation test statistics is equal to α for all ρ. In other words, power is inversely
related to the degree of connectedness of the lattice.

There is clearly a conflict between a choice of d_{ij}^* which (a) maximizes
power and (b) increases the "coverage" of possible patterns of spatial auto-

correlation. For example, to maximize power, the rook's case might be preferred, but to increase coverage, the queen's case is superior. The researcher must think carefully about the choice of weights.

Figure 5 shows, as expected, that power increases as n increases. Using Figures 4 and 5 together, we find that I and c, and BW and BB, have identical power curves when $w_{i.}$ and $w_{.i}$ are the same for each subarea. See, for example, the 25 cell circle and the 5 by 5 queen's case mapped onto a torus. In the case of the (12 by 12) + 1 rook's case where 22 of the 25 subareas each have links to three other subareas, I and c, and BB and BW differ only slightly.

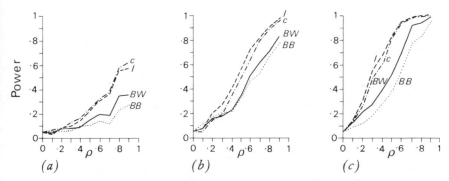

Figure 5   Power curves for BB, BW, I, and c for three lattices with fixed W but varying n. (a) 4 by 3 rook's case, (b) 5 by 5 rook's case, (c) 7 by 7 rook's case.

When the t (= 200) values are split into two separate groups of one hundred for this lattice, I was more powerful than c for one set, and c more powerful than I for the other. Similar results were obtained for BB and BW.

When most subareas do not have the same $w_{i.}$ and $w_{.i}$ values, we find, in confirmation of results in Equations (39), (48), and (49), that

$$power(I) > power(c) > power(BW) > power(BB). \qquad (70)$$

Use of the same random number stream precludes testing differences between power curves because of the dependence between results, but comparison of the separate hundreds for each statistic and between statistics allows us to assess sampling variation in the results. Equation (70) is supported by these results, given differences between the $w_{i.}$ and $w_{.i}$.

From Figures 4 and 5 it is evident that, when ρ is small, there is little to choose between the various coefficients and the relationship is obscured by sampling fluctuations.

Figure 6 shows power curves of I in the 5 by 5 rook's case for various values of α and β, the probabilities of type I and type II errors. It is evident that the risk of a type II error is high when ρ is low, whatever the value of α.

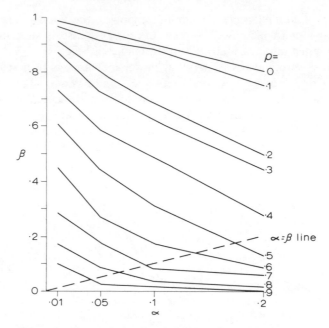

Figure 6   Comparison of probabilities of type I and type II errors for I in 5 by 5 rook's case lattice.

The graph demonstrates well the severe risk of a type II error when extreme values of α are used, and argues for the use of less stringent significant levels in inferential work. Finally, if we look at the position of the "breakeven" line, $\alpha = \beta$, it is clear that a considerable amount of spatial autocorrelation must be present in the subarea system before it can be detected without undue risk of either a type I or a type II error. For lattices with the same value of n, but higher W^2/nS_1 values, diagrams like Figure 6 give an even bleaker impression. Fortunately in empirical work spatial autocorrelation is usually marked when it is present (that is, ρ is high).

Structure of the Matrices D and W

In previous sections, we have assumed that the researcher has known enough about the pattern of dependencies among the subareas in the study region to be able to put **W** in the test statistic equal to **D**, the matrix of constants reflecting the true pattern of dependencies in the model of Equation (1). We now wish to explore the effect upon the AREs of the test statistics if **W** $\neq$ **D**.

Consider first the effect of two different weighting matrices, $\mathbf{W}_1$ and $\mathbf{W}_2$, upon the ARE of the I statistic. Suppose $\mathbf{I}_1$ has the weighting matrix $\mathbf{T}_1 =$

$\mathbf{W}_1 = \mathbf{D}$, and I_2 has the weighting matrix $\mathbf{T}_2 = \mathbf{W}_2 \neq \mathbf{D}$. Equation (36) gives the efficacy for I_1 as

$$F(I_1) = \frac{(n + 1)^2[\text{tr}(\mathbf{DD'} + \mathbf{D}^2)]^2}{n(n + 2)\,\text{tr}(\mathbf{DD'} + \mathbf{D}^2)}, \tag{71}$$

while for I_2, the efficacy is

$$F(I_2) = \frac{(n + 1)^2[\text{tr}(\mathbf{D'W}_2 + \mathbf{W}_2\mathbf{D})]^2}{n(n + 2)\,\text{tr}(\mathbf{W}_2\mathbf{W}'_2 + \mathbf{W}^2_2)}. \tag{72}$$

Thus, the ARE is given by:

$$
\begin{aligned}
\text{ARE}(I_1, I_2) &= \frac{F(I_1)}{F(I_2)} \\[2mm]
&= \frac{\text{tr}(\mathbf{DD'} + \mathbf{D}^2)\,\text{tr}(\mathbf{W}_2\mathbf{W}'_2 + \mathbf{W}^2_2)}{\{\text{tr}(\mathbf{D'W}_2 + \mathbf{W}_2\mathbf{D})\}^2}.
\end{aligned}
\tag{73}
$$

This is equivalent to

$$\frac{\Sigma_{(2)}\,[w_{ij}(1)]^2\,\Sigma_{(2)}\,[w_{ij}(2)]^2}{\{\Sigma_{(2)}\,w_{ij}(1)w_{ij}(2)\}^2}, \tag{74}$$

where $w_{ij}(k)$ is the (i, j)th element of $\mathbf{W}_k$ ($k = 1, 2$). By the Cauchy-Schwartz inequality, expression (73) cannot be less than one, that is,

$$\text{ARE}(I_1, I_2) \geqslant 1. \tag{75}$$

We conclude, therefore, that the best I statistic uses the weighting matrix $\mathbf{W} = \mathbf{D}$ to test H_0 against the alternative hypothesis specified by Equation (1). Thus the investigator should choose, *a priori*, $\mathbf{W}$ to represent the auto-correlation pattern that would exist if H_1 were true (that is, so $\mathbf{W} = \mathbf{D}$). Result (73) measures the penalty paid if some other $\mathbf{W}$ matrix is specified. Exactly the same argument holds for the c statistic.

Example. If we return to Figure 1, an appropriate choice of weights was $w_{ij}(1) = d_{ij} = \frac{1}{2}$ if county j was a due north or south neighbor of county i, and $w_{ij}(1) = d_{ij} = 0$ otherwise. However, suppose that the researcher decided to use the weights

$$w_{ij}(2) = \begin{cases} \frac{1}{2}(1 - \alpha), & \text{if county j is a due north or south} \\ & \text{neighbor of i,} \\ \frac{1}{2}\alpha, & \text{if county j is a due east or west neighbor} \\ & \text{of i,} \\ 0 & \text{otherwise.} \end{cases}$$

Then the ARE of a test based on I using the second set of weights, compared to a test based on the first set is

$$ARE(I_2, I_1) = \frac{1}{ARE(I_1, I_2)}$$

$$= \frac{(1 - \alpha)^2}{(1 - \alpha)^2 + \alpha^2},$$

since $\Sigma_{(2)}[w_{ij}(1)]^2 = \frac{1}{2}n$, $\Sigma_{(2)}[w_{ij}(2)]^2 = \frac{1}{2}n[(1 - \alpha)^2 + \alpha^2]$, and $\Sigma_{(2)}w_{ij}(1)w_{ij}(2) = \frac{1}{2}n(1 - \alpha)$. Clearly ARE (I_2, I_1) has a maximum value of one when $\alpha = 0$, and falls from one to zero as α increases from zero to one. If the so-called rook's case ($\alpha = \frac{1}{2}$) is used, then ARE $= \frac{1}{2}$. In this case the pattern of weights appears "half-correct" and the ARE result is intuitively reasonable. Using the same methods for BB and BW, we can establish that the best choice of weights in the test statistic is again $w_{ij} = d_{ij}$ [or $w_{ij} = \frac{1}{2}(d_{ij} + d_{ji})$].

Conclusions

A series of recommendations and conclusions can be summarized for this study.

(1)   Given interval scaled data, use I in preference to c, BB, or BW. This conclusion has been validated only for normal data, but the shape of lattice seems to be more important than the type of data.

(2)   For rank data, use the rank version of I.

(3)   Given binary data, use BW in preference to BB or any combination of BW and BB, particularly if the free sampling model is assumed. Code the subareas so P (subarea colored B) is as near as possible to one half in both free and non-free sampling.

(4)   Weights used in the test statistic should correspond to weights postulated in the alternative hypothesis.

(5)   The choice of weights will depend upon the tradeoff between power and "coverage" of possible patterns of spatial autocorrelation.

Acknowledgments

This work was carried out as part of a project titled, "Contiguity Constraints in Region Building Programmes", funded by the Social Science Research Council. The authors wish to thank the SSRC for their support. Pion Press Limited of London granted permission to reproduce figures from the authors' monograph, *Spatial Autocorrelation*, which gives a complete report of the authors' work. Mr. E. Sheppard, currently a graduate student at the University of Toronto, computed some of the Monte Carlo results. Finally, our thanks are due to Mrs. Anne Kempson for producing an excellent typescript.

References

Anderson, T. W., 1948, On the theory of testing serial correlation: *Skandinavisk Aktuarietidskrift*, v. 31, p. 88–116.

Cliff, A. D., 1969, Some measures of spatial association in areal data: *unpublished Ph.D. thesis*, Dept. Geography, Univ. Bristol, 295 p.

Cliff, A. D., and J. K. Ord, 1972, Testing for spatial autocorrelation among regression residuals: *Geographical Analysis*, v. 4, p. 267–284.

Cliff, A. D., and J. K. Ord, 1973, *Spatial autocorrelation*: Pion Press Ltd., London, 178 p.

Daniels, H. E., 1944, The relation between measures of correlation in the inverse of sample permutations: *Biometrika*, v. 33, p. 129–135.

Durbin, J., and G. S. Watson, 1950, Testing for serial correlation in least squares regression, I: *Biometrika*, v. 37, p. 409–428.

Durbin, J., and G. S. Watson, 1951, Testing for serial correlation in least squares regression, II: *Biometrika*, v. 38, p. 159–178.

Durbin, J., and G. S. Watson, 1971, Testing for serial correlation in least squares regression, III: *Biometrika*, v. 58, p. 1–19.

Geary, R. C., 1954, The contiguity ratio and statistical mapping: *The Incorporated Statistician*, v. 5, p. 115–145.

Gould, P. R., 1970, Is Statistix Inferens the geographical name for a wild goose?: *Economic Geography*, v. 46, p. 439–448.

Kendall, M. G., and A. Stuart, 1967, *The advanced theory of statistics*. Volume 2, Inference and relationship: Charles Griffin & Co. Ltd., London, 690 p.

Krishna Iyer, P. V. A., 1949, The first and second moments of some probability distributions arising from points on a lattice and their applications: *Biometrika*, v. 36, p. 135–141.

Moran, P. A. P., 1948, The interpretation of statistical maps: *Jour. Royal Statistical Soc.*, Series B, v. 10, p. 243–251.

Moran, P. A. P., 1950, Notes on continuous stochastic phenomena: *Biometrika*, v. 37, p. 17–23.

Tobler, W. R., 1970a, A computer movie simulating urban growth in the Detroit region: *Economic Geography*, v. 46, p. 234–240.

Tobler, W. R., 1970b, Regional analysis or time series extended to two dimensions: *Mathematical Social Sciences Board Conference on the Mathematics of Population*, Univ. Chicago, 7 p.

Frequency Analysis, Sampling, and Errors in Spatial Data

J. E. Robinson

Contour maps are a universal media for the display of spatial information. Earth scientists produce maps of everything from structural or topographic surfaces to mineral content and factor weightings. Nearly every measurable parameter that can be given coordinate positions and plotted has been contoured and displayed as a map. Contour maps form the basis for many forms of interpretative and decision-making analysis where the credibility of mapped features must be accurately determined. Effective map analysis therefore first requires an analysis of exactly what constitutes the map and of the accuracy with which contained features can be described.

Most contour maps represent some single-valued finite function of distance. They are derived from information measured or calculated at discrete sample locations. They display a variety of overlapping trends and features and contain an appreciable amount of error. The sum total of the contained errors limits the useful information that can be extracted from maps. Both the sampling interval and the variation in the individual sample measurements generate errors that contribute to this total. Repeated measurements at individual sample locations are rare in data used to produce maps, yet statistical probability suggests that errors in measurement will have a normal distribution about the true value so that confidence limits can be computed for sample locations. Error generated from the use of discrete samples is a function of the sample interval and the amplitude of the smallest features. Errors in maps can sometimes be estimated but it is difficult to compensate for them in the interpretation since they do not affect all trends and features in the same way. The contoured surface reflects the sum of all superimposed trends, features, and errors so that, along with the problem of extracting individual features for analysis, there is the question of apportioning errors so that each feature receives its correct share. Errors are real. They are present in all mapped data and error consideration should play an important part in every map analysis. Mapping errors have been

78

largely neglected in classical map analysis because solutions are difficult. Evaluation of errors and their effect on contoured maps is not intuitive and one would have to be very astute to be able to examine a map and estimate the real effect of even known errors on a map analysis.

Fortunately the analysis of maps need not be restricted to spatial domain displays. Fourier transforms permit maps or sections of maps to be considered in terms of their amplitude and phase spectra in the frequency domain. Trend analysis and error analysis are not only simpler in the frequency domain but, in many cases, procedures can be designed and visualized without the necessity for complex calculations.

The concept that functions of time or distance can be decomposed into a series of sinusoids with definite wavelengths and phase angles has been accepted and applied to time-series analysis for more than one and a half centuries. However, methods of easily transforming large data sets, such as map arrays, have only recently become available. Map transforms have only really been feasible since the advent of the high speed digital computer and the computation algorithm known as the Fast Fourier Transform. Digital transforms are widely used. Frequency analysis is an integral part of information theory and is the basis for the present state of high resolution seismic recording and interpretation. There are many good publications available on Fourier transforms and their use in analysis. Earth scientists should have at least a basic background knowledge of frequency analytical methods in order to make effective interpretations of mapped data. Selected references, ranging from non-technical to rigorous and in some cases containing algorithms and programs, include Anstey (1965), Blackman and Tukey (1958), Bendat and Piersol (1966), Cooley and Tukey (1965), Gentleman and Sande (1966), Jenkins and Watts (1969), Lee (1960), Otnes and Enochson (1972), Peterson and Dobrin (1966), Robinson (1967), and Robinson, Charlesworth, and Ellis (1969).

Frequency Analysis of Maps

Fourier transform theory considers distance functions and their frequency spectra to be mutually convertible. For every distance domain feature there is a frequency equivalent which consists of one or more sinusoidal frequency components having distinctive wavelengths, phase leads or lags, and directions. Both domains contain exactly the same information. The frequency display does not have positional definition of mapped features but has enhanced discrimination between features of various sizes and amplitudes. The transform pair in Figure 1 illustrates many of the relationships between distance and frequency. Each function can represent either distance or frequency. Phase can be neglected since both presentations are axially symmetric and all phases are zero. If the long narrow box is considered to be

DISTANCE OR FREQUENCY   FREQUENCY OR DISTANCE

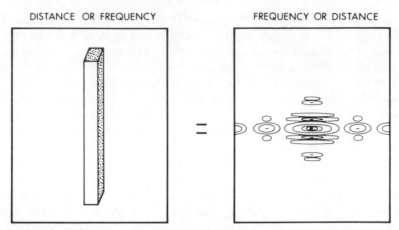

Figure 1   The Fourier transform of a long, narrow box is an axially symmetric function with maximum amplitude at the origin.

in the distance domain, the long dimension contributes mainly to the low frequency components in the transform while the short dimension or width has more definition in the higher frequencies. The zero frequency amplitude is the sum of the distance domain input values. Lengths of functions are generally inversely proportional to the lengths of their transforms.

Natural functions, such as the geological description of folds, are more often described in terms of their widths and cross sections than in terms of their lengths. Similarly it is easier and generally more useful to consider the frequency spectrum of their widths as being more definitive than that of the long dimensions. Figure 2 illustrates the relationship between a section through the box of Figure 1 and its one-dimensional transform. The box-like feature is often termed a box car function, and its transform, which is mathematically a $\frac{\sin x}{x}$ function, is familiar from Fraunhofer diffraction patterns and is sometimes termed a dif function. These are very useful transforms because a dif function in the distance domain can be used as an ideal Weiner

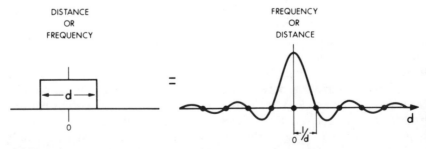

Figure 2   One-dimensional Fourier transform pairs. The box car function on the left is equivalent to the sin x/x function on the right.

interpolator for sampled data (Neidell, 1969). The box car is then considered to represent a spectrum of unit amplitude frequencies which range symmetrically about zero to a maximum frequency having a wavelength equal to twice the digital interval. This interpolator does not contain any undefined high frequencies and can be used to generate additional values between sample points without increasing the map error.

A comparison of transform pairs indicates that their lengths form an inverse relationship. If the box car is short, the dif function is rather long with prominent side lobes. However, if the corners of the box are rounded so that it appears more like a bell-shaped Gaussian curve, then the transform has a broader central peak, the side lobes become less prominent, and the amplitude quickly dies to negligible values. The rounded functions are more like natural features. Even the occasional natural vertical interface cannot be accurately described with spaced samples and will appear rounded or sloped. Since maps and their transforms must be described within a limited number of digital values, the shorter, more natural, rounded transforms are more useful than those that attempt to continue well beyond the map boundaries.

The transforms of digital maps usually display a variety of amplitude maxima and minima due to conflicting features and trends. Figure 3 illustrates a 150 by 140 mile (240 by 224km) area in northwestern Canada where

Figure 3   Index map of Western Canada showing location of topographic data.

the topography displays a variety of features ranging from folds in the foothills to deeply incised stream valleys. Figure 4 is a computer contoured replica of the original photogrammetric topographic map that has been digitized on a two mile (3.2km) interval. The amplitude spectrum of this map is displayed in Figure 5. Positive peaks in the spectrum relate to topographic highs while negative troughs are valleys. Frequency range is from zero in the center to a maximum at the edge where the highest defined frequency has a wavelength of twice the sampling interval. The spectrum has symmetry

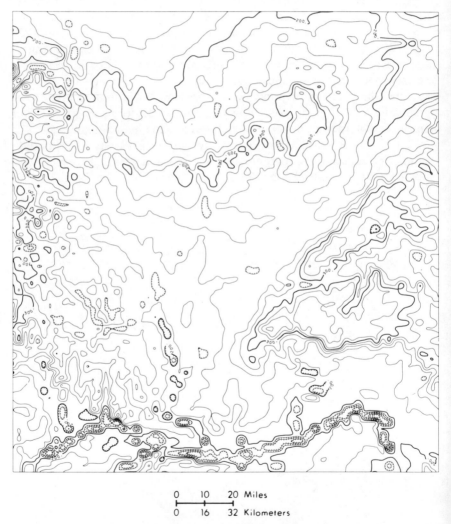

Figure 4   Computer contoured topographic map prepared from a grid of elevations on a uniform two mile (3.2km) spacing. Contour interval is 20 units of 10 feet (3 meters).

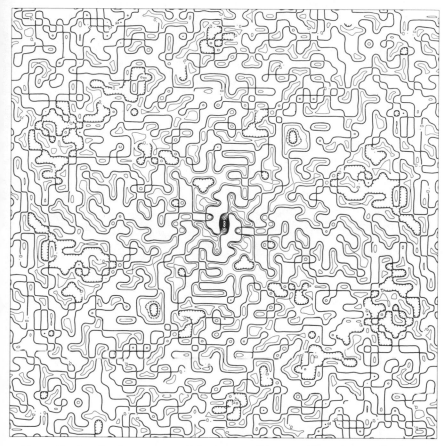

Figure 5 Amplitude spectrum of the topographic map. Since the amplitude range covers several orders of magnitude, the cube root of the actual values has been contoured to display the high frequency variations.

about the origin. Two-dimensional transforms of complex maps are difficult to work with, but sectional displays of map spectra can be useful, especially where the relative amplitudes of trends and errors are to be compared. Figure 6 is a one-dimensional transform of a typical section through the topographic map. It was digitized on a one mile (1.6km) interval to enhance the definition of any high frequency components. The absolute amplitude spectrum (Fig. 6a) exhibits considerable variation with a range of four magnitudes from the low to high frequencies. Amplitude peaks indicate strong trends that may be either highs or valleys and the frequency range indicates their size. The phase spectrum (Fig. 6b) is erratic and is usually neglected. Sectional transforms are useful in error evaluation since error amplitudes can be plotted directly and their effect on the various trends determined.

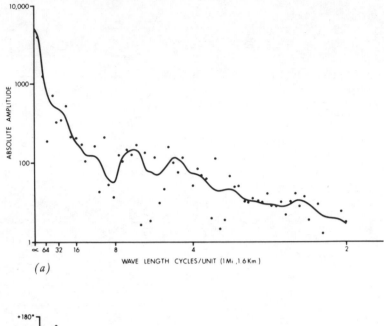

(a)

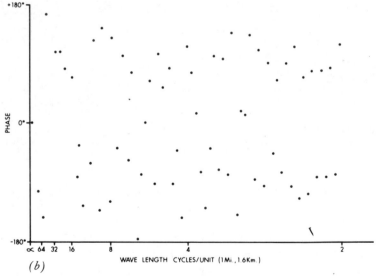

(b)

Figure 6   One-dimensional spectra of a representative section through the topographic map. Elevations were measured on one mile (1.6km) intervals and only positive frequencies are displayed. (a) Amplitude spectrum with both measured and averaged valued. (b) Phase spectrum.

Errors in Maps

There are two main sources of error in maps. One is caused by inaccuracies in the measurements at the sample locations and the second results from the use of values measured at discrete sample locations. The effect of both forms of error can be estimated statistically and displayed as amplitude functions in the frequency domain. Other errors, such as those due to the use of non-uniform sampling intervals and to irregularities generated by interpolation between sample locations, can be considered special cases in terms of sampling and measurement errors.

Unbiased measurements are usually considered to have normal distributions about the true value. This assumption is still acceptable even though the measurements are of values on a surface and the samples are taken at different locations. This normal distribution of measurement errors makes it possible to compute the amplitude spectrum for any set of samples by taking the transform of a series of random normal numbers with a mean of zero and a standard deviation calculated from the probable error in individual measurements. Figure 7 illustrates the spectra of the measurement error function

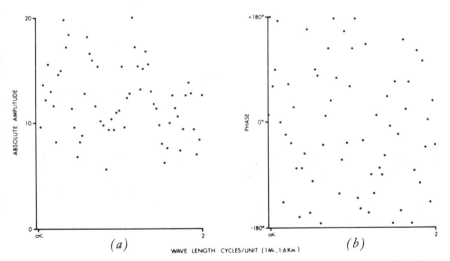

Figure 7 Amplitude and phase spectra of a random normal sequence of numbers scaled to represent measurement errors in the topographic section.

from the topographic section. Values were taken from a table of random normal numbers (Dixon and Massey, 1957, p. 371) with a mean of zero and scaled to a standard deviation of 10 feet (3m). This standard deviation was optimistically determined from the topographic map with its original contour interval of 100 feet (30.4m). The absolute amplitude varies about an average value that can be considered statistically constant for any data set. Phase

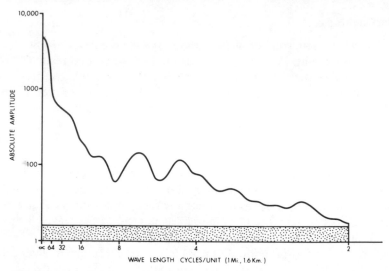

Figure 8 Amplitude spectrum of the topographic section showing contribution of error in measurements at sample locations.

again appears to be random. The statistically average amplitude value can then be plotted against the map amplitude spectrum as the contribution of measurement error (Figure 8).

Aliasing error is inherent in all maps which are constructed from sampled data. The distance between sample points limits the range of frequencies that can be determined in the map. The highest detectable frequency, the "Nyquist", has a wavelength of twice the sampling interval. Sampling theory (Blackman and Tukey, 1958) shows that frequencies higher than this limit may be present in the data set but they cannot be detected or measured. Their amplitudes, however, appear as aliased additions to the amplitudes of lower and presumably more accurately measured frequencies. Even the amplitude of the Nyquist frequency is usually in error for, unless the samples are taken exactly at peaks and troughs, the measured amplitude will be too small. A general rule (Otnes and Enochson, 1972) is that there must be at least 2.5 samples per wavelength for good amplitude definition.

The error due to aliasing can be evaluated, but it cannot be reduced without taking more samples. If there is a section through the map where samples are closely spaced then the aliasing effect can be quite accurately measured and taken into consideration in the map analysis and interpretation. Figure 9 illustrates the amplitude spectrum of the topographic section on a one mile (1.6km) digital interval, and the aliasing error that would occur if the section had been digitized on (a) a two (3.2km) and (b) a four mile (6.4km) interval. The errors are appreciable and would constitute a large proportion of some of the low amplitude, high frequency components. The aliasing error for the

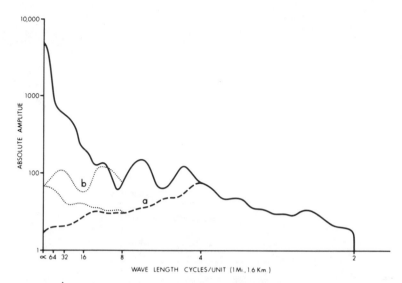

Figure 9 Amplitude spectrum of the topographic section displaying aliasing error. (*a*) Error that would be added if the section had been sampled on a two mile (3.2km) interval. (*b*) Error for a four mile (6.4km) interval.

two mile (3.2km) interval is a good approximation of its value in the topographic map. Errors are additive and Figure 10 shows the estimated total error against the measured absolute amplitudes of the component frequencies. Since this section is based on the same two mile (3.2km) digital interval as the map, additional aliasing error increases the amplitudes from that of Figure 9. Error is only a small percentage of the amplitude of the low frequency components, but may completely destroy the credibility of some of the smaller, essentially high frequency features. Error analysis points out the futility of attempting to interpret small low amplitude features in maps compiled from only a few scattered samples.

Additional values for intermediate points can be generated from the original samples by application of the Weiner interpolator but this will not decrease the basic aliasing error. If interpolation is incorrectly carried out, the total error may be increased by the unwanted generation of additional high frequency components. Aliasing error must be lived with and allowed for in map interpretation.

Where maps are generated from random samples there is always some error introduced by converting to the uniform digital intervals that are a necessary part of most computer contouring programs. It is quite possible to compute Fourier series transforms from random data (James, 1966) but computations are slow and in most cases it is easier, faster, and cheaper to convert the data to a uniform grid by the application of standard programs. Most contour packages will do a reasonably smooth job of gridding. Where

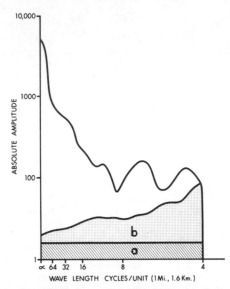

Figure 10 Amplitude spectrum of the topographic section sampled on the same two mile (3.2 km) interval as the map. The sum of (*a*) measurement error and (*b*) aliasing error is the estimated error contained in the map.

a small grid interval is necessary to justify sample values, most of the unwanted, computer-generated frequencies can be reduced by convolving the grid with a Weiner interpolator which acts as a high cut or aliasing filter. A good grid conversion will minimize the generation of any frequencies that were not contained in the original data set.

Errors in maps can only be considered in terms of statistical averages. Fortunately most mapped features are composed of a sufficient range of frequency components that the statistics are reasonably accurate. Amplitude error can be expressed as a percentage of the amplitude of the feature based on the signal to noise ratio in the frequency components. Positional validity of mapped features is dependent on the phase of their components and will also have some distortion due to measurement and aliasing errors.

Phase shifts due to error are not true normal distributions. The phase spectrum of measurement error is erratic, approaching randomness within the 360 degree range limits. Phases of aliased error are not necessarily random and may have some correlation. However, a general rule can be formulated if it is assumed that (*a*) the positional error is approximately normal, and (*b*) the maximum positional shift of the central frequency comprising the spectrum of an individual feature is approximately 1.5 percent of its wavelength for each 10 percentile increase in the error to signal ratio. It is unlikely that measurement and aliasing errors in a map will cause a positional error in any mapped feature greater than 1.5 percent of the width of the feature for each 10 percent increase in total error to signal ratio.

Trend Analysis and Error

Conflicting and often superimposed trends in maps make analysis difficult and complex. Trend analysis simplifies interpretation by splitting the original map into two or more subsidiary maps, each displaying distinctive sets of trends. All forms of trend analysis, whether by polynomial surfaces, Fourier series, or spatial filtering, can be described and their operations portrayed in the frequency domain. The observance of the effects that trend analysis has on the frequency spectra of a map often leads to a better understanding of what to expect in the spatial domain. Although many trend analysis operations can be easily carried out in the frequency domain, the final analysis and interpretation is in the spatial domain where the features and trends have positional validity.

The first and most popular trend analysis method generates regionals by the fitting of polynomial surfaces (Harbaugh and Merriam, 1968). A low order, least mean squares, best fit polynomial surface is computed for the map. This surface is the trend or regional, and when subtracted from the original map leaves the residual. If the map has been constructed from a reasonably uniform sample distribution and does not contain coherent high amplitude features, the polynomial surface will contain only low frequency components. These will correspond closely to the low frequency content of the map and exactly fit the zero frequency which is its average elevation. Subtraction is operationally the same in both the distance and frequency domains, so the residual is the map with the low frequencies deleted. The method works very well when the functions are well behaved. Unfortunately there are circumstances, particularly when higher order polynomials are used, where the computed trend will contain frequencies which have higher amplitudes than their equivalents in the map, or which do not appear in the map. Subtraction then produces erroneous frequencies in the residual as an added error.

Polynomial trend analysis is an excellent and useful method of map interpretation. It acts somewhat like a filter in separating the map into low frequency and high frequency parts. However, the action is controlled both by the map and by the order of the applied polynomial. Prediction of the relative size of features to appear in either the trend or the residual is difficult to make in advance and the usual procedure is to run several surfaces and see what happens. The most accurate method of determining what has happened is to take Fourier transforms of both map and surfaces. This permits an evaluation of errors in the original map, sizes of features in both the trend and residual, and a determination of whether or not the process has generated any additional error.

Fourier series fitting also uses the map data to compute a best-fit series of low frequency components (Harbaugh and Merriam, 1968). The sum of these components forms the trend that is subtracted from the original map to produce a residual. The low frequency components are the same as those computed in the Fourier transform and are as accurate as permitted by the data and map size. Usually only a few components are generated so that high frequencies are not determined. The wavelengths of the computed low frequencies depend on map dimensions and do not necessarily reflect components. Series frequency components actually represent a portion of a continuous spectrum rather than separate frequencies. Trends therefore require the inclusion of several components to present a smooth appearance and to prevent a cyclicity from being superimposed on both the trend and the residual. The low frequency components in maps are usually of high amplitude and real cyclicities are obvious.

Fourier series analysis divides the map into two parts. Since the trend is in terms of low frequencies that are determined from the map, it is usually a good regional representation. However, errors can be created by the inclusion of too few low frequency components, and unless the full spectrum is known there is no quantitative estimate of error. Even with Fourier series analysis, a full frequency display is very useful and can be obtained by continuing the series calculations up to the Nyquist frequency or by a separate transform.

Spatial filtering (Robinson, Charlesworth, and Kanasewich, 1968) is another trend technique which, since it does not produce a trend and residual by subtraction, has some advantages over the other methods. It can be used to extract a limited band of frequencies from a map so that trends of a designated size can be displayed on a new map relatively free from the conflicting effects of larger and smaller trends. Filtering is accomplished by multiplying the amplitudes of the frequency components by some value. Usually the multiplier is zero for frequencies that are to be deleted and unity for those that are to be retained unchanged. Since multiplication only affects frequencies that are already in the map and does not add new ones, error generation is minimal providing no alteration is made to the phase spectrum.

Filters can be constructed to extract and display features on the basis of both size and direction so that it is possible to apply a large variety of filters to any map. It is therefore very important to analyze the map components so that only the most effective filters are used. This preliminary analysis is easiest in the frequency domain where peaks in the amplitude spectrum denote strong trends that can be extracted for analysis. Filters pass frequency components without regard to any contained error so that knowledge of the complete spectrum is necessary to determine the level of error in the extracted features.

Smoothing and averaging techniques are forms of filtering. Their effect on maps can be determined from Fourier transforms of the various averaging operators. Simple running averages are equivalent to box car shaped filter operators composed of a series of ones. Their frequency domain transforms (Figure 2) are dif functions. A running average is therefore a low pass or regional filter. However, the side lobes on the dif function frequency spectrum, show that it passes certain high frequency components with a phase inversion. Weighted or tapered averaging operators are better smoothing functions as all high frequencies are eliminated. Smoothing operators can be designed as regional filters in the distance domain (Lavin and Devane, 1970), but the degree of smoothing is most readily apparent in the frequency domain. Frequency transforms are very useful for the evaluation of all smoothing and trend analysis operations.

Interpretation and Conclusions

All maps contain some error. It affects the interpretation of all contained features and varies according to the amplitudes of the errors and the amplitudes and sizes of the trends or features. The application of band pass filters to extract and display specific sets of features in the presence of error illustrates how the errors can be apportioned to the various features and shows their effect on interpretation.

Figure 11 displays the amplitude and error spectrum from the topographic section with pass bands of two spatial filters superimposed. Both filters

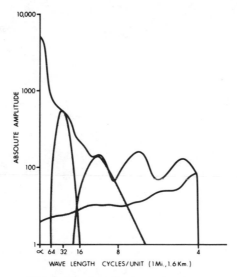

Figure 11 Amplitude and error spectrum of the map showing those frequencies that will be retained by two band-pass spatial filters. Each filter passes one octave on either side of central frequencies which have wavelengths of 12 miles (19km) for the high frequency filter and 32 miles (51km) for the low.

have peaks at central frequencies and taper smoothly to zero over approximately one octave on either side of the peak frequency. They pass a range of features but give optimum results for features or trends with widths exactly half the wavelength of the central frequency (Robinson and Ellis, 1971). The lowest pass filter gives optimum display of features with a width of 16 miles (25km) while the high pass filter best displays those with a width of 6 miles (9.5km). The high cut in the latter filter excludes all frequencies with wavelengths shorter than three miles (5km) as these contain a very high percentage of error distortion.

Figure 12   Filtered topographic map displaying features that have an average width of 16 miles (32km). Contour interval is in units of 10 feet (3 meters).

A comparison of the amplitude to error values over the filter pass bands indicate that the lower band has an average amplitude of approximately 550 units while the error is only 20 units or less than 4 percent of the total signal. Amplitude error in the filtered map (Figure 12) is therefore small and positional error is restricted to less than 1 percent of the feature widths. Thus, assuming the filter is well designed so that the features are truly displayed, aliasing and measurement errors would have very little effect and the mapped features are accurately displayed.

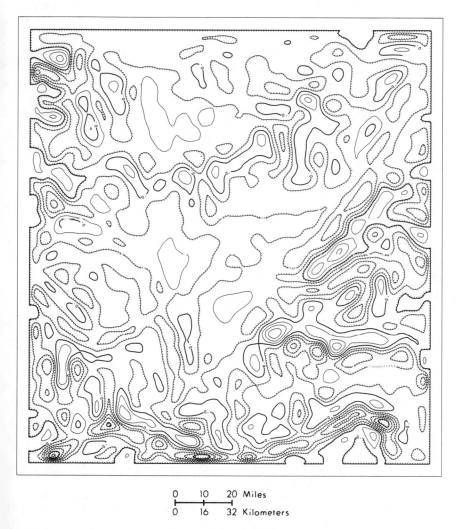

```
0      10     20  Miles
|------+------|
0      16     32  Kilometers
```

Figure 13   Filtered topographic map displaying features that have an average width of 6 miles (9.6km). Contour interval is in units of 10 feet (3 meters).

The situation is different for the second filtered map (Figure 13). In this case the average spectral amplitude is only 140 units while the error is 32 units or 23 percent of the total signal. This error is relatively large and can have a significant effect on the displayed features. Most trends appearing in the map have a relatively large amplitude so that they are real but their displayed amplitude may be as much as 23 percent in error due entirely to aliasing and measurement inaccuracies. Similarly, these errors may result in a positional shift of more than 3 percent of the feature widths. Since some of the trends are more than 4 miles (6.4km) in width, the positional error can make a difference of several hundreds of feet, an amount that is very significant in ore evaluation or oil prospecting.

Many exploration maps are compiled from control that is very sparse when compared to that for topographic maps and errors are proportionately large. Errors are significant in maps; the fewer the samples the greater the error. In most cases the number of samples cannot be increased without a great deal of effort and expense. The errors cannot be decreased but their magnitude can be estimated from the amplitude spectra and allowed for in the map interpretation. Unfortunately map errors tend to make the small features look larger and more attractive than they really are so that the ever present optimism of explorationists will continue to result in a high percentage of dry holes and abandoned prospects.

Acknowledgments

Lillian B. Kerr, John E. Hogg, and Jack M. Park critically read the manuscript and gave many helpful suggestions. Union Oil Company of Canada Limited made available the computer time necessary for the illustrations and Elaine Curley typed the manuscript.

References

Anstey, N. A., 1965, Wiggles: *Jour. Canadian Soc. Exploration Geophysicists*, v. 1, p. 13–43.

Bendat, J. S., and A. G. Piersol, 1966, *Measurement and analysis of random data*: John Wiley and Sons, Inc., New York, 390 p.

Blackman, R. B., and J. W. Tukey, 1958, *The measurement of power spectra*: Dover Publications, New York, 190 p.

Cooley, J. W., and J. W. Tukey, 1965, An algorithm for the machine calculation of complex Fourier series: *Mathematics of Computation*, v. 19, no. 90, p. 297–301.

Dixon, W. J., and F. J. Massey, 1957, *Introduction to statistical analysis*: McGraw-Hill Book Co., Inc., New York, 488 p.

Gentleman, W. M., and G. Sande, 1966, Fast Fourier transforms for fun and profit: American Federation of Information Processing Societies, *Proc.*, *Fall Joint Computer Conference*, v. 29, p. 563–578.

Harbaugh, J. W., and D. F. Merriam, 1968, *Computer applications in stratigraphic analysis*: John Wiley and Sons, Inc., New York, 282 p.

James, W. R., 1966, FORTRAN IV program using double Fourier series for surface fitting of irregularly spaced data: *Kansas Geological Survey Computer Contribution 5*, 19 p.

Jenkins, M. J., and D. G. Watts, 1969, *Spectral analysis and its applications*: Holden-Day Inc., San Francisco, 525 p.

Lavin, P. M., and J. J. Devane, 1970, Direct design of two-dimensional digital wave number filters: *Geophysics*, v. 35, no. 6, p. 1073–1078.

Lee, Y. W., 1960, *Statistical theory of communication*: John Wiley and Sons, Inc., New York, 509 p.

Neidell, N. S., 1969, Ambiguity functions and the concept of geological correlation, *in* D. F. Merriam, ed., Symposium on computer applications in petroleum exploration: *Kansas Geological Survey Computer Contribution 40*, p. 19–32.

Otnes, R. K., and L. Enochson, 1972, *Digital time series analysis*: John Wiley and Sons, Inc., New York, 467 p.

Peterson, R. A., and M. B. Dobrin, 1966, *A pictorial digital atlas*: United Geophysical Corp., Houston, Texas, 53 p.

Robinson, E. A., 1967, *Multichannel time series analysis with digital computer programs*: Holden-Day Inc., San Francisco, 298 p.

Robinson, J. E., and M. J. Ellis, 1971, Spatial filters and FORTRAN IV program for filtering geologic maps: *Geocom Programs No. 1*, 21 p.

Robinson, J. E., H. A. K. Charlesworth, and M. J. Ellis, 1969, Structural analysis using spatial filtering in interior plains of south-central Alberta: *Bull. American Assoc. Petroleum Geologists*, v. 53, no. 11, p. 2341–2367.

Robinson, J. E., H. A. K. Charlesworth, and E. R. Kanasewich, 1968, Spatial filtering of structural contour maps: *23rd Inter. Geological Congress Proc.*, Sec. 13, p. 163–173.

Optimum Interpolation by Kriging

P. Delfiner and J. P. Delhomme

In automatic contouring, there are two very distinct problems: gridding and plotting. By gridding, we mean interpolating values of the surface to be contoured at the nodes of a regular grid. Apart from contouring procedures using successive triangles or polygons, gridding is required whenever data points are not on a regular mesh. Even if the surface is already sampled at regular intervals, a grid with a smaller mesh may be necessary. Plotting consists of finding points along lines of constant Z-values, and generation of the instructions to be given to the plotter for the drawing itself. It includes smoothing, labeling, and line annotation.

The final aspect of a map depends largely on the plotting program. However, esthetics are not necessarily on a par with accuracy. Smoothing and skillful drawing cannot make up for the erroneous values produced by an incorrect interpolation procedure. Here, we shall be concerned only with the critical step of gridding. Our purpose will be to find the optimal interpolation procedure for specific objectives and to assess the goodness-of-fit. A related problem will be to visualize the variability in the results.

Kriging and simulation techniques are a general approach that can deal with different cases using the same theoretical principles. The whole theory cannot be presented intelligibly in a few pages, but the references include articles that develop the theory in full. However, Matheron's group has been accused of being rather hermetic (Watson, 1971), so to make amends, we shall not dwell too long on theory but place emphasis on practical aspects of Kriging and simulations. The results will be discussed and compared with those of some classical interpolation techniques.

Linear Estimators

Most interpolation procedures use a linear combination of the data. The major difficulty with non-linear estimators is that they involve parameters or characteristics that cannot be inferred from the data. (In the notation used

96

in this article, sample points in p-dimensional space are denoted by x_i. Known values are $z_i = z(x_i)$: $\hat{Z}$ is an *estimator* while $\hat{z}$ is an *estimate*, that is, the value taken by $\hat{Z}$.) We will indicate summation by the following notation:

$$z = \sum_i \lambda^i z_i.$$

Linear estimators are of the form:

$$\hat{Z} = \sum_i \lambda^i Z_i. \tag{1}$$

The λ^i are coefficients, or weights, for the measured values z_i. The wellknown least-squares estimator itself is of type (1). We recall here a simple proof. Let

$$E[Z(x)] = m(x) = \sum_\ell a_\ell f^\ell(x) \tag{2}$$

be the regression equation with unknown coefficients a_ℓ and given functions f^ℓ (monomials or trigonometric functions for example). The estimated $\hat{a}_\ell$ are solutions of the set of linear equations

$$\sum_\ell \hat{a}_\ell T^{\ell s} = \sum_i f^s(x_i)z_i,$$

where the coefficients $T^{\ell s} = \Sigma_i\, f^\ell(x_i)f^s(x_i)$ do not depend on the z_i. Denoting by $U_{\ell s}$ the inverse of $T^{\ell s}$, we obtain $\hat{a}_\ell = \Sigma_s\, U_{\ell s} \Sigma_i\, f^s(x_i)z_i$ which can be rearranged as $\hat{a}_\ell = \Sigma_i\, [\Sigma_s\, U_{\ell s} f^s(x_i)]z_i$. The $\hat{a}_\ell$ are linear combinations of the z_i. Substituting in Equation (2) yields

$$\hat{m}(x) = \sum_i \left[\sum_{\ell,s} U_{\ell s} f^s(x_i) f^\ell(x) \right] z_i$$

and writing:

$$\lambda^i = \sum_{\ell,s} U_{\ell s} f^s(x_i) f^\ell(x) \tag{3}$$

we obtain

$$\hat{m}(x) = \sum_i \lambda^i z_i.$$

Equation (3) shows that the λ^i are functions of the point x to be estimated. The fact that they can be expressed as linear combinations of the basic $f^\ell(x)$ themselves derives from the use of linear regression (Equation (2)). However, there is no reason to confine the $\lambda^i(x)$ to such simple analytical forms.

Distance Weighting Functions

A sensible and easy scheme for weighting data points used in an estimating procedure is to ascribe higher weights to closer points. In mining, for example, some authors recommend inverse distance weighting while others advocate inverse squared distance weighting. Meteorologists (Cressman, 1959) use as a weighting function

$$\lambda = \frac{R^2 - d^2}{R^2 + d^2} \qquad d \leqslant R \qquad d: \quad \text{distance of sample to estimated point}$$

$$\lambda = 0 \qquad\qquad d > R \qquad R: \quad \text{radius of the neighborhood centered at estimated point.}$$

Negative exponential influence functions can also be found in the literature.

Clearly, no general rule can be derived from experiments on particular data and point configurations. Consequently, the choice of a distance weighting function is more or less a matter of personal belief, of tradition, or of confidence in the advice of "influential authorities".

This arbitrariness is not, however, the only drawback. The following example will show that distance weighting functions are impaired by a major insufficiency, as they fail to discriminate redundant information.

Consider the configuration shown in Figure 1. The three sample points A, B, and C are equidistant from the estimated point 0. If the variable is isotropic and homogeneous (without trend), any procedure will ascribe the same weight (1/3) to A, B, and C, provided the weights add to one. Now, let us assume that the upper sample point is in fact a cluster of two very close points A and A'. Each of these should get only 1/6, which amounts to assigning 1/3 to the mean of A and A'. Yet, through a distance weighting function,

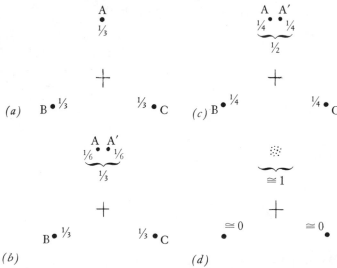

Figure 1   Weights assigned to points used to estimate value at cross (*a*), (*b*): weights correct; (*c*), (*d*): incorrect weights assigned by distance weighting functions without considering spatial arrangement of points.

A and A' get 1/4 each, as do B and C. The cluster AA' is considered to be as informative as the two distinct points B and C. Carrying the argument to extremes, we realize that if A is a cluster of a million points, the points B and C will be almost completely neglected.

More About Least Squares

The conclusion of the preceding paragraph is that it is necessary to take into account not only the situation of sample points with respect to the estimated point, but also interrelationships between sample points themselves. The least-squares procedure achieves this. Still, we claim that it is not thoroughly satisfactory because it disregards the structure of the variable under study.

If the variable is very continuous (topographic elevation in non-mountainous areas, 500 millibar surface height, or piezometric level in an aquifer in the absence of pumping), the fitted surface should be able to honor the experimental points. A weighting scheme is expected to yield results not much different from those of deterministic interpolation procedures such as polynomials. However, there are irregular variables (mineral grades in mines, bathymetric depths, or local temperature in a layer of the atmosphere) and even erratic variables such as porosities and permeabilities in a petroleum reservoir. When the data show such considerable scatter even at a small scale, it makes no sense to constrain the surface to pass through the experimental points. Even if we knew the exact values everywhere, it would probably be impossible to represent them by isolines on a map. Some type of filtering is required. But which filtering method would be best?

It is most important to know precisely and *beforehand* what is to be filtered and what is to be kept. The least-squares technique yields "trends" which are hard to interpret. As Matheron (1971) states "the impression is often created that this famous trend is nothing more than a numerical result brought about by the mode of operation—i.e. perhaps a pure and simple artefact". The conceptual background of trend-surface analysis can be summarized by the following "equation" (Watson, 1969):

$$\text{Value at datum point} =$$
$$\text{value of deterministic function} + \qquad (4)$$
$$\text{random error.}$$

This is not equivalent to:

$$\text{Value at datum point} =$$
$$\text{regional component} + \qquad (5)$$
$$\text{residual}$$

because residuals are not errors. They may account for smaller scale variations of the phenomenon, but they are fully part of it. This fact is admitted by many authors (for example, Harbaugh and Merriam, 1968) who know that if they fit a low-degree polynomial to the regional component, the residuals reflect the main structural trends. As a general rule, correlations between residuals increase as the complexity of the fitted function decreases. Equation (4) cannot hold for any trend model.

Briefly, least squares has the following mathematical background. Each value z_i is regarded as an observed value of a random variable Z_i, the distribution of which depends on non-random parameters which are the coordinates of the point x_i. It is assumed that these random variables Z_i are *uncorrelated*, have a common variance σ^2, and have means given by the linear expression of Equation (2). If these assumptions are correct, least-squares estimators are the best linear unbiased estimators of the regression coefficients, which means that among all unbiased estimators that are linear in the Z_i, least-squares estimators have minimum variance. The important condition here is the non-correlation of the Z_i. *If it is not fulfilled, least-squares estimators are not optimal.* Likewise, the analysis of variance of trend-surface data becomes irrelevant. The mean square deviation

$$\hat{\sigma}^2 = \frac{1}{n}\sum_i [z(x_i) - \hat{m}(x_i)]^2$$

has no significance as to the goodness-of-fit. It is not related to the estimation error $m(x_i) - \hat{m}(x_i)$ nor does it represent the variance of the discrepancy $z(x) - \hat{m}(x)$ at a point x that is not a sample point. Indeed, deviations from the trend are smaller at the x_i than elsewhere, because the estimate $\hat{m}(.)$ has been computed to fit closely to these points (Figure $\hat{2}$).

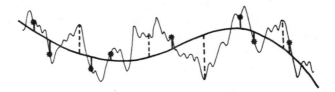

* Sample point

Figure 2   Least-squares fit: errors at sample points are not representative of errors for all points.

Kriging

The term "Kriging" is derived from the name of D. G. Krige, who first introduced the use of moving averages to avoid systematic overestimation of reserves in the field of mining. The conceptual background of Kriging is in essence the same as that of Wiener's optimal filtering. Matheron has generalized the theory to the case of spatial and non-stationary data. The main idea is to consider a spatial variable as a realization of a random function. The appeal to probability theory does not imply any kind of randomness in the phenomenon itself, but is a convenient mathematical formulation that accounts for the complicated behavior of natural spatial data. Furthermore, it provides an easy criterion for the goodness-of-fit, the mean square error. An estimator $\hat{Z}$ of a quantity Z will be called "best" if it minimizes the mean square error $E(\hat{Z} - Z)^2$. It will be the *best unbiased estimator* if:

$$\left| \begin{array}{l} E(\hat{Z} - Z) = 0 \\ E(\hat{Z} - Z)^2 \quad \text{minimum} \end{array} \right. \tag{6}$$

Denoting by $D^2(\hat{Z} - Z)$ the variance of $\hat{Z} - Z$, we know that

$$? \Longrightarrow \quad E(\hat{Z} - Z)^2 = D^2(\hat{Z} - Z) + [E(\hat{Z} - Z)]^2 = 0$$

Thus conditions specified in Equation (6) can be written in the equivalent form,

$$\left| \begin{array}{l} E(\hat{Z} - Z) = 0 \\ D^2(\hat{Z} - Z) \quad \text{minimum.} \end{array} \right. \tag{7}$$

The mathematics of Kriging are an expansion of Equation (7). We may illustrate with one example the derivation of Kriging equations from (7).

The variable under study, z(x), is regarded as a realization of a random function Z(x) on which first- and second-order moments are defined as

$$E[Z(x)] = m(x) \quad \text{mean or "drift" at point x}$$

$$K(x, y) = E[(Z(x) - m(x))(Z(y) - m(y))] \quad \text{covariance function.}$$

It is assumed that m(x) can, at least in appropriate neighborhoods, take the form

$$m(x) = \sum_\ell a_\ell f^\ell(x),$$

where the a_ℓ are unknown but fixed coefficients.

Suppose we want to estimate the true value z(x) by means of an estimator

$$\hat{Z}(x) = \sum_i \lambda^i Z(x_i).$$

The unbiased condition of (7) yields

$$\sum_i \lambda^i m(x_i) - m(x) = 0,$$

thus

$$\sum_\ell a_\ell [\sum_i \lambda^i f^\ell(x_i) - f^\ell(x)] = 0. \tag{8}$$

We want Equation (8) to be true for any values of the unknown a_ℓ. So

$$\sum_i \lambda^i f^\ell(x_i) = f^\ell(x) \qquad (\ell = 0, 1, \ldots, k). \tag{9}$$

The variance $D^2[\hat{Z}(x) - Z(x)]$ is written

$$D^2[\hat{Z}(x) - Z(x)] = \sum_{i,j} \lambda^i \lambda^j K(x_i, x_j) - 2 \sum_i \lambda^i K(x, x_i) + K(x, x). \tag{10}$$

If the λ^i are chosen to minimize Equation (10) subject to conditions specified in (9), we obtain system (11) with the Lagrangian multipliers μ_ℓ:

$$\left|
\begin{aligned}
&\sum_j \lambda^j K(x_i, x_j) - \sum_\ell \mu_\ell f^\ell(x_i) = K(x_i, x) \qquad (i = 1, \ldots, n) \\
&\sum_j \lambda^j f^\ell(x_j) = f^\ell(x) \qquad (\ell = 0, 1, \ldots, k).
\end{aligned}
\right. \tag{11}$$

At its minimum, the variance (Equation (10)) takes the value:

$$D^2[\hat{Z}(x) - Z(x)] = K(x, x) - \sum_i \lambda^i K(x_i, x) + \sum_\ell \mu_\ell f^\ell(x).$$

Similar results will be found when estimating the drift at a point, a block value, or a weighted average.

The linear system (11) has $n + k + 1$ equations for $n + k + 1$ unknowns, which are then weights λ^i and $k + 1$ multipliers μ. It is regular if and only if the functions f^ℓ are linearly independent on the set of the data points:

$$\sum_{\ell=0}^{k} C_\ell f^\ell(x_i) = 0 \quad \forall x_i \Rightarrow C_\ell = 0 \quad \forall \ell.$$

For example, if the drift is a plane, sample points may not be along a single profile, or if the drift is quadratic, sample points may not be on a conic. Now we face the practical question of how to estimate the coefficients of the system, which include $K(x_i, x_j)$, the covariance between sample points, and $K(x_i, x)$, the covariance between sample and estimated points. In cases where several realizations of the random function are available, it may be possible to infer these covariances directly. But in general, we deal with single phenomena with no possible repetition. Then, further assumptions are required.

A first set of assumptions is *wide sense stationarity*:

$$\left|
\begin{aligned}
&E[Z(x)] = m \quad \text{constant} \\
&K(x, y) = K(x - y).
\end{aligned}
\right. \tag{12}$$

These often appear to be too restrictive. No drift is allowed and it is difficult to form an unbiased estimate of the covariance function.

The intrinsic hypotheses are weaker, as only the increments of Z are stationary:

$$\left| \begin{array}{ll} E[Z(x + h) - Z(x)] = ah & (a = \text{constant}) \\ D^2[Z(x + h) - Z(x)] = 2\gamma(h) & (\text{variogram}). \end{array} \right. \tag{13}$$

When a equals zero (no drift), an unbiased estimate of the variogram is:

$$\hat{\gamma}(h) = \frac{1}{2N} \sum_{i=1}^{N} [z(x_i + h) - z(x_i)]^2.$$

When there is a drift, the inference of the variogram is very difficult because of enormous biases. This problem has recently been solved in the scope of a new theory on "intrinsic random functions" (Matheron, 1973). For the moment, let us suppose the variogram is known. It can be substituted for the covariance in the Kriging system (11) to give

$$\left| \begin{array}{ll} \sum_j \lambda^j \gamma(x_i - x_j) + \sum_\ell \mu_\ell f^\ell(x_i) = \gamma(x_i - x) & (i = 1, \ldots, n) \\ \sum_j \lambda^j f^\ell(x_j) = f^\ell(x) & (\ell = 0, 1, \ldots, k) \end{array} \right. \tag{14}$$

$$D^2[\hat{Z}(x) - Z(x)] = \sum_i \lambda^i \gamma(x_i - x) + \sum_\ell \mu_\ell f^\ell(x).$$

This is known as the system of "universal Kriging". Some properties of this system will be demonstrated in the following case study.

A Case Study

Rainfall was measured by 33 rain gauges irregularly located in the basin of Wadi Kadjemeur in eastern Chad (Delhomme and Delfiner, 1973). Among other problems was evaluation of total annual precipitation and contouring precipitation during 13 showers. For the global estimation, the Kriging procedure was compared with other methods in current use, such as Thiessen polygons, surface integration on the map, and arithmetic mean. People readily accepted our global estimates, but some were puzzled by the Kriged maps. To establish a frame of reference we used several methods on the same data, including hand-drawing of contours, trend-surface analysis with first- and second-degree polynomials, and Kriging, once with the actual variogram of the variable and then with an arbitrary non-optimum variogram. The maps are shown on Figures 3 to 6.

Figure 3 shows a hand-drawn map from a report on rainfall and runoff in Chad (Roche, 1968). Figure 4 represents the map contoured after Kriging according to system (14). Our observation is that the Kriged map is smoother than the hand-drawn one. Obviously, the cartographer tried his best

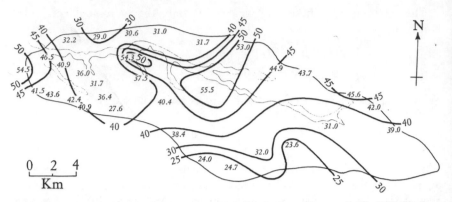

Figure 3   Hand-drawn contour map of rainfall during a shower in Wadi Kadjemeur on August 6, 1966. Measurements in millimeters.

to fit the isolines to the data points. For example, the value 54.3mm in the northwestern part of the basin has been regarded as a local maximum; a 50mm isoline coils around it and the 45mm isoline is forced to make a big detour. In contrast, the Kriging procedure did not pay much attention to this local extreme of 54.3mm, and the closest isoline is labeled 40mm. The same situation occurs for the central values 53mm and 55.5mm. Again in the southern part, the 25mm isoline winds through the basin, whereas it makes a discreet appearance on Figure 4.

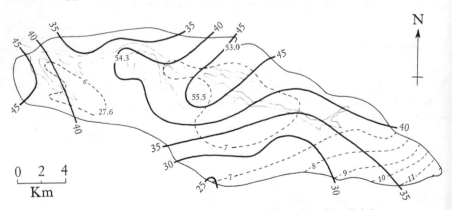

Figure 4   Optimum contour map of rainfall produced by Kriging.

On the whole, the hand-drawn map seems more faithful to the data. Yet, considering it more carefully, we find some strange things. For example, in the southwest the cartographer did not take into account the value 27.6mm which would have altered the shape of the 40mm isoline. Why has the 35mm isoline been skipped in this area? Still, we cannot blame the draftsman, because he had several thousand maps to issue and could not afford to dwell too long on this particular one.

The least-squares interpolations were performed using moving neighborhoods of 12 points each. First-degree polynomials were rejected at once because they obviously failed to reflect the main features of the phenomenon. Second-degree polynomials resulted in the map in Figure 5. As expected, the

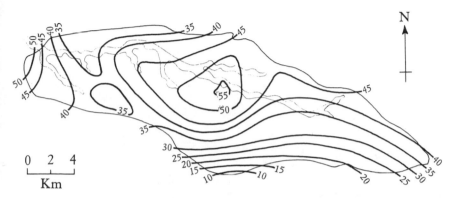

Figure 5 Contoured second-degree polynomial surface fitted by least-squares to rainfall data.

contours do not purport to honor the experimental points. On the whole, major variations are correctly displayed, except for some over- or underestimating due to "edge effects". In the southern part of the basin, estimated values fall to 10mm or less, a drop which is not supported by the data but is merely a consequence of extrapolating the central dome structure.

It seems sensible that the best map is the one which, at each point, has minimum deviation from the actual value. If we take as a mathematical criterion that $E[\hat{Z}(x) - Z(x)]^2$ shall be a minimum at each point x (and not only at sample points), then the Kriged map is by construction the optimum one, at least if linear estimators are used. The estimation variance or its square root, the estimation standard deviation, can also be mapped. The standard deviation has been superimposed as dotted lines on Figure 4. These show where the Kriged map is reliable and where it must be interpreted with caution. The eastern part of the basin, where data are sparse, is less trustworthy than the well-sampled western part; the dotted isolines tell us how much less. For example, we may consider a particular grid point close to the maximum value 55.5mm in the center. Considering both the estimate 48.7mm and the estimation standard deviation of 6.25mm, we see that they are consistent with the value 55.5mm measured at the neighboring sample point.

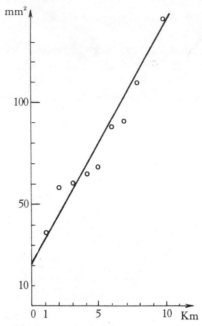

Figure 6 Variogram of rainfall amounts.

The variogram of rainfall amounts (Figure 6) gives an even deeper insight. It is linear with a discontinuity at the origin ("nugget effect"). Such a discontinuity is associated with a large amount of small-scale variability, due either to the phenomenon itself, to observational errors or to both. In the absence of further indications on the behavior of the variable at a scale smaller than the sample spacing, it is impossible to decide between these causes. For rainfall, the nugget effect can probably be explained by local perturbations resulting from instability of the air close to the ground, which make rain fall into the gauge in irregular gusts.

Mathematically, the variable $Z(x)$ can be considered as the sum of two independent *random* terms. These are a continuous term, $Z_0(x)$, and a non-correlated random "noise" $\varepsilon(x)$, with zero mean and variance equal to the amplitude C_0 of the nugget effect, or

$$Z(x) = Z_0(x) + \varepsilon(x).$$

Careful study of system (14) shows two situations:

(1) $x = x_i$ is a sample point. The best estimate of the known $z(x_i)$ is $z(x_i)$ itself and the estimation variance is nil. Kriging is an exact interpolator.

(2) x is not a sample point. The best estimate of $z(x)$ coincides with that of the structured component $z_0(x)$. The totally unpredictable, zero-mean

term $\varepsilon(x)$ cannot have any influence on the estimate itself. Our aim, which is $z(x)$ and not $z_0(x)$, is accounted for by variances which exceed by by the amount C_0 the estimation variances of $z_0(x)$ (Delfiner, 1973a).

Grid points seldom coincide with sample points with an irregular pattern of data. Therefore, in the presence of a nugget effect, Kriged maps represent the features of the structured variable $z_0(x)$. The smooth aspect of the Kriged map (Figure 4) is due to the presence of the nugget effect and not to any arbitrary smoothing. With the same data and another variogram which is continuous at the origin ($\gamma(h) = 15|h|$), Kriging yields a map which scrupulously honors the experimental points even better than the hand-drawn map (Figure 7). A fine map indeed, but an unrealistic one!

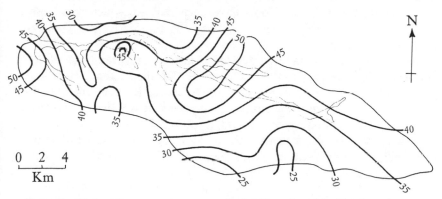

Figure 7   Non-optimum contour map of rainfall produced by Kriging when nugget effect is disregarded.

To understand how disregarding the nugget effect can influence the aspect of the map, especially in the center of the basin, let us consider the grid node closest to the value 55.5mm (Figure 8). The estimation has been made using

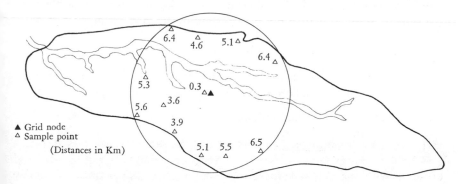

Figure 8   Distances from sample points to a grid node.

12 data points. Figures 9*a*, *b*, and *c* show the weights computed by means of different procedures. The optimum weight for the datum 55.5 is only 62.4 percent, while it would have been 91.6 percent in the absence of noise. This clearly shows the importance of taking the structure into account.

Conditional Simulations

We have just seen that Kriging provides the best linear unbiased estimate built on the data. But an estimation cannot claim to be reality, as it does not completely restore spatial variability. For example, we know that the variogram computed on Kriged values is much more regular than the actual variogram. Now, it is often interesting to visualize the real aspect of the phenomenon. For this, new tools have been devised, which make use of the fact that the variable under study has been considered as a realization of a random function.

The "turning bands" method developed in Fontainebleau (Guibal, 1972; Journel, 1974; Matheron, 1973; Orfeuil, 1972) allows the simulation of other realizations of this same random function. By construction, these have the same structure as the data. But moreover, we would like simulations to retain the measured values at sample points, in order to insure a fair coincidence with what is known of the phenomenon. In other words, among the infinity of possible realizations, we want to select those which honor the experimental points.

Specific properties of Kriging, for example the absence of correlation between estimator and estimation error in the stationary case, provide a theoretical background for the following procedure. On the experimental realization $z(x)$, we write

$$z(x) = \hat{z}(x) + [z(x) - \hat{z}(x)]. \tag{15}$$

Of course the error value $z(x) - \hat{z}(x)$ remains unknown because the true value $z(x)$ is not available. Considering a simulation $s(x)$ it is possible, with the same pattern of sample points, to compute Kriging estimates and write

$$s(x) = \hat{s}(x) + [s(x) - \hat{s}(x)].$$

Now, the error $s(x) - \hat{s}(x)$ can be known exactly. The idea is to substitute in (15) this error measured on $s(x)$ and define the function $c(x)$ as

$$c(x) = \hat{z}(x) + [s(x) - \hat{s}(x)],$$

$c(x)$ is called a *conditional simulation*. It has the same structure as $z(x)$ itself and honors the experimental points. At sample points, Kriging estimates coincide with the actual values; thus $\hat{s}(x_i) = s(x_i)$, $\hat{z}(x_i) = z(x_i)$ and finally $c(x_i) = z(x_i)$.

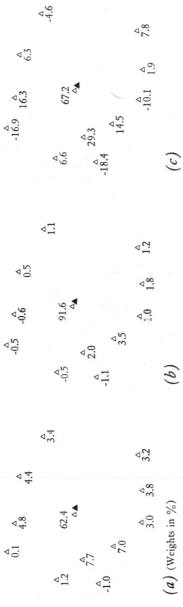

△ 0.1   △ 4.8   △ 4.4

△ 3.4

△ 1.2   62.4 ▲

△ 7.7

△ -1.0   △ 7.0

△ 3.0   △ 3.8   △ 3.2

(a) (Weights in %)

△ -0.5   △ -0.6   △ 0.5

△ 1.1

△ -0.5   91.6 ▲

△ 2.0

△ -1.1   △ 3.5

△ 1.0   △ 1.8   △ 1.2

(b)

-16.9   △ 16.3   △ 6.3   △ -4.6

△ 6.6   67.2 ▲

△ 29.3   △ -18.4   △ 14.5

△ -10.1   △ 1.9   △ 7.8

(c)

Figure 9 Influence of structure on weights assigned points inside circle shown on Figure 8. *(a)* Optimum weights. *(b)* Weights computed with the arbitrary continuous variogram $\gamma(h) = 15|h|$. *(c)* Weights from second-degree polynomial fit by least squares.

Conditional simulations can be considered as variants of the phenomenon. Three of these have been computed on the data of Wadi Kadjemeur. On the maps in Figures 10–12, the 40mm isoline has been emphasized to make

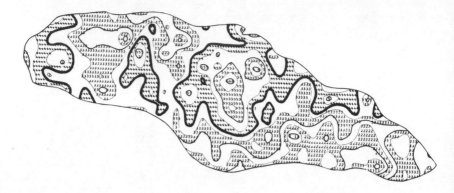

Figure 10   Conditional simulation of rainfall, variation 1.

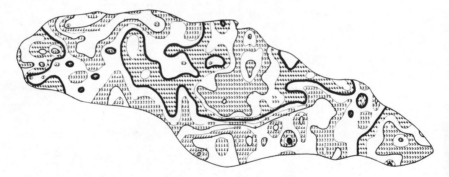

Figure 11   Conditional simulation of rainfall, variation 2.

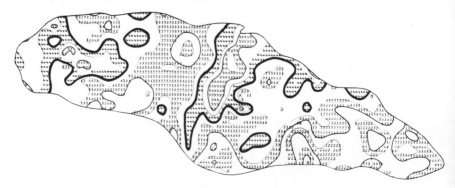

Figure 12   Conditional simulation of rainfall, variation 3.

reading easier. The rather hilly aspect of the map matches quite well what we would anticipate about spatial variability of rainfall during a shower. It can be noted that fluctuations of the variants around their mean, which is the Kriged map, increase with estimation variances associated with Kriging. For example, in the poorly sampled eastern part of the basin, simulated values range from 10mm (Figure 10) to 60mm (Figure 11).

The present case study of Kadjemeur was treated under the intrinsic hypothesis (13) by means of a program called SIMPACK (Delfiner and Delhomme, 1973). This program is also able to deal with more complicated cases, which fall in the scope of a more sophisticated theory outlined next.

Intrinsic Random Functions

Let us return to the problem of inferring covariances or variograms from a unique realization of second-order random function. Difficulty arises with the presence of a non-stationary component, whether interpreted as random or not. The statistical inference of a characteristic requires data that belong to the same parent population; some kind of stationarity is required. Matheron's theory of intrinsic random functions defines precisely which minimum assumptions are actually necessary for applications. This leads to a wider class than second-order random functions, with better properties regarding statistical inference.

We may start from the decomposition

$$Z(x) = m(x) + Y(x),$$

where $Y(x)$ is a random function with zero mean and $m(x)$ a linear combination of functions f^ℓ which will be restricted here to monomials of degree $\leqslant k$.

$$m(x) = \sum_\ell A_\ell f^\ell(x) \qquad \ell = 0, 1, \ldots, k.$$

For more generality, the coefficients A_ℓ are considered as random. In Kriging, we always consider linear estimators of the type

$$\hat{Z}(x) = \sum_i \lambda^i Z(x_i)$$

with λ^i subject to the unbiasedness conditions

$$\sum_i \lambda^i f^\ell(x_i) - f^\ell(x) = 0 \qquad \ell = 0, 1, \ldots, k. \tag{16}$$

As a consequence, in the expression of the estimation error,

$$\hat{Z}(x) - Z(x) = \sum_i \lambda^i Z(x_i) - Z(x)$$

$$= [\sum_i \lambda^i m(x_i) - m(x)] + [\sum_i \lambda^i Y(x_i) - Y(x)],$$

the first term of the right-hand side always cancels and

$$\sum_i \lambda^i Z(x_i) - Z(x) = \sum_i \lambda^i Y(x_i) - Y(x). \tag{17}$$

Hence, if we want to compute and minimize estimation errors, we can work on $Y(x)$ as well as on $Z(x)$.

We may consider the class of all random functions that are equivalent under the action of linear combinations of type (16). These functions $X(x)$ are of the general form

$$X(x) = Y(y) + \sum_\ell B_\ell f^\ell(x),$$

which means that they are all equal to $Y(x)$, up to an arbitrary polynomial of degree $\leqslant k$. In fact, any measure (for example, a set of points x_α and masses λ^α) satisfying

$$\sum_\alpha \lambda^\alpha f^\ell(x_\alpha) = 0 \qquad \ell = 0, 1, \ldots, k, \tag{18}$$

eliminates or filters out polynomials of degree $\leqslant k$, thus yielding:

$$\sum_\alpha \lambda^\alpha X(x_\alpha) = \sum_\alpha \lambda^\alpha Y(x_\alpha)\left(= \sum_\alpha \lambda^\alpha Z(x_\alpha)\right).$$

Notice that quantities such as $\sum_\alpha \lambda^\alpha Z(x_\alpha)$ have the significance of *generalized increments*. For example $\ell = 0$ in Equation (18) shows that the masses λ^α add up to zero.

The minimum assumption required for statistical inference is that these generalized increments are stationary in the wide sense. In other words, all translations of a measure subject to (18) must have the same mean (zero by construction) and the same variance. This is a generalization of the usual intrinsic hypothesis where only differences $Z(x + h) - Z(x)$ (that is, order 0 increments) were concerned. Here, we speak of "intrinsic random functions of order k".

In practice, the most important result of the new theory is that there exists a function K such that the variance of any generalized increment of order k appears in the form

$$D^2\left[\sum_\alpha \lambda^\alpha Z(x_\alpha)\right] = \sum_{\alpha,\beta} \lambda^\alpha \lambda^\beta K(x_\alpha - x_\beta).$$

This function K is the *generalized covariance* of the intrinsic random function Z and is unique up to an even polynomial of degree $\leqslant 2k$. The class of possible models for K is much wider than for ordinary covariances. In particular, generalized covariances can be polynomials of degree $\leqslant 2k + 1$. For example, if $k = 1$ (linear drift), a possible model for K is

$$K(h) = -\alpha_0|h| + \alpha_1|h|^3.$$

With (k = 2) we can use

$$K(h) = -\alpha_0|h| + \alpha_1|h|^3 - \alpha_2|h|^5.$$

Under some conditions on α_0, α_1, α_2, K(h) is conditionally positive definite, which insures that computed variances will be positive. Of course, this is true only for variances of order k increments. The smaller the class of measures, the wider the class of operable covariances.

Notice that Kriging systems remain exactly the same with generalized covariances as they do with ordinary ones. For example, (11) remains unchanged. Polynomial covariances lend themselves to automatic identification. An integrated program named BLUEPACK has been developed (Delfiner, 1973b) which determines the covariance which best fits the data and then computes various Kriging estimates.

Conclusions

The preceding is far from being a complete presentation of the possibilities of Kriging. Broadly speaking, Kriging provides the best linear unbiased estimate for any linear function of the variable z(x), including integrals, derivatives, and Laplacians. For example, these correspond to reserves of ore in place, block-values of ore, weighted averages, strike and dip of geological horizons, velocity of geostrophic winds, and initialization of numerical models. Kriging can also be combined with spline functions. J. M. Monget (1973, personal communication) has utilized spline polynomials in connection with Kriging techniques. The purpose was to obtain, using a ship-board computer, a smooth ocean-current velocity estimate, processed from satellite navigation data. The recent automatization of Kriging techniques should foster numerous new applications.

References

Cressman, G. P., 1959, An operational objective analysis system: *Monthly Weather Review*, v. 87, no. 10, p. 67–374.

Delfiner, P., 1973a, Analyse du géopotentiel et du vent géostrophique par krigeage universel: *Revue de la Météorologie*, No. 25, p. 1–56.

Delfiner, P., 1973b, Présentation du programme BLUEPACK: *Internal Rept.*, Ecole des Mines de Paris, Fontainebleau, 32 p.

Delfiner, P., and J. P. Delhomme, 1973, Présentation du programme SIMPACK: *Internal Rept.*, Ecole des Mines de Paris, Fontainebleau, 26 p.

Delhomme, J. P., and P. Delfiner, 1973, Application du krigeage a l'optimisation d'une campagne pluviométrique en zone aride: *Symposium on the Design of Water Resources Projects with Inadequate Data*, UNESCO-WMO-IAHS, Madrid, Spain, June 1973, p. 191–210.

Guibal, D., 1972, Simulation de schémas intrinsèques: *Internal. Rept.*, Ecole des Mines de Paris, Fontainebleau, 38 p.

Harbaugh, J. W., and D. F. Merriam, 1968, *Computer applications in stratigraphic analysis*: John Wiley and Sons, Inc., New York, 282 p.

Journel, A., 1974, Geostatistics for conditional simulation of ore-bodies: to be published in *Economic Geology*, in press.

Matheron, G., 1969, Le krigeage universel: *Les Cahiers du Centre de Morphologie Mathématique de Fontainebleau*, v. 1, 83 p.

Matheron, G., 1971, The theory of regionalized variables and its applications: *Les Cahiers du Centre de Morphologie Mathématique de Fontainebleau*, v. 5, 211 p.

Matheron, G., 1973, The intrinsic random functions and their applications: *Advances in Applied Probability*, in press.

Orfeuil, J. P., 1972, Simulation du Wiener-Lévy et de ses intégrales: *Internal Rept.*, Ecole des Mines de Paris, Fontainebleau, 29 p.

Roche, M. A., 1968, Ecoulement de surface, alimentation de nappe et transport solide des ouadis Fera, Kadjemeur et Sofoya, Fort-Lamy: ORSTOM, *Rapport définitif 1965-66*, 140 p.

Watson, G. S., 1969, Trend-surface analysis and spatial correlation: Geological Soc. America, *Special Paper 146*, p. 39-46.

Watson, G. S., 1971, Trend-surface analysis: *Jour. Mathematical Geology*, v. 3, no. 3, p. 215-226.

Filtering Process in Surface Generalization and Isopleth Mapping

M. L. Hsu

A geographical distribution consisting of z-values varying in the vertical dimension over the x, y plane is called a statistical surface, each point element being defined by its x, y, and z components. The surface $Z = f(x, y)$ may be determined by a set of spatial data z_{ij} where i and j are within the domain. Geography has been concerned with the analysis and explanation of characteristics of these surfaces. The total surface characteristics may be displayed and studied by means of choroplethic, isarithmic, and other mapping techniques. Furthermore, the complex statistical surface can be decomposed into simpler components and spatial variations examined at different scales and/or times. Both trend and Fourier analysis provide mathematical forms for decomposing surfaces at varying scales or frequencies. The spatial filtering method smooths a surface via a filter or local operator without presupposed knowledge of the analytical form of the surface. Comparisons between the filtering approach and trend and Fourier models are given by Bassett (1972) and Zurflueh (1967). Filtering is related to map generalization, or more broadly, to pattern recognition, spatial predictions, and studies on associations between spatial processes and surface forms. It is also related to the scale problem of spatial data aggregation.

Filtering Process in Isopleth Mapping

An isopleth map is derived from aggregated data based on areal units; the isopleth mapping process pertains to the following major elements (Figure 1). For a given geographical distribution, it is assumed that a continuous and differentiable statistical surface $Z = f(x, y)$ exists; call it the *original surface*. Theoretically, information concerning this surface can be obtained by recording every individual in a small particular area ΔA described by ranges of x and y. In practice, however, data must be enumerated in aggregated fashion upon predetermined areal units. In a data collecting

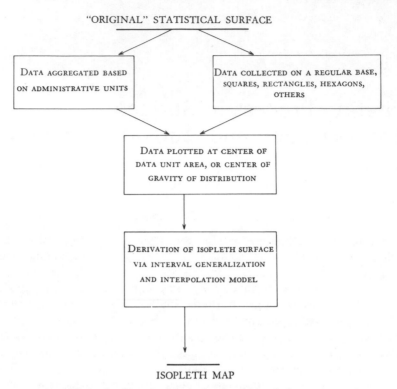

"ORIGINAL" STATISTICAL SURFACE

DATA AGGREGATED BASED ON ADMINISTRATIVE UNITS

DATA COLLECTED ON A REGULAR BASE, SQUARES, RECTANGLES, HEXAGONS, OTHERS

DATA PLOTTED AT CENTER OF DATA UNIT AREA, OR CENTER OF GRAVITY OF DISTRIBUTION

DERIVATION OF ISOPLETH SURFACE VIA INTERVAL GENERALIZATION AND INTERPOLATION MODEL

ISOPLETH MAP

Figure 1   Steps in the production of isopleth maps.

system, administrative subdivisions often constitute the data units; these usually are of varying size, shape, and number of neighboring units. In some instances, the researcher may design his own data base, composed of carefully considered uniform cells. In both cases, however, the data are but sampling statistics (Hsu and Robinson, 1970), since for a given area there can be an infinite number of methods to delineate the data units and to choose the total number of these units, or the sample size. Clearly, each different method of subdivision would result in a different set of areal data. Both the sample size and the method of areal subdivision affect the quality of data and of isopleth maps (Hsu and Robinson, 1970; Morrison, 1971).

In each unit, data may be located at either the center of the area of the data cell or the center of gravity of the distribution within the cell. Based on selected isopleth intervals and a model of interpolation, the isopleth surface is derived from a set of data. Models generally employed fall into one of three types: linear interpolation, point interpolation with a defined local or neighborhood operator, and surface interpolation based on, for example, trend or Fourier equations.

The isopleth mapping process may be simplified further by identifying two types of transformations which link the original surface with the resultant maps (Figure 2). T_2 contains the effects of the generalization obtained from the applications of isopleth intervals and the interpolation model. T_1 is an averaging process.

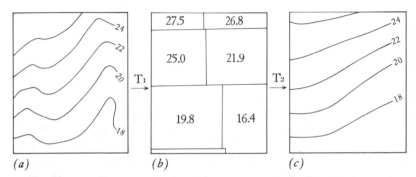

Figure 2   Continuous variable data field (a), yields aggregated areal data (b), which in turn yields isopleth map (c) (illustrations adapted from a larger map by Hsu and Robinson, 1970, p. 38).

When observations from an original statistical surface are aggregated by areal units and recorded as totals or densities of these units, the variation within each unit is "averaged out". This averaging process removes surface features whose wavelengths are smaller than the size of the data unit (Bassett, 1972; Casetti, 1966; Curry, 1966). The size of this unit determines the level of generalization in areal data. The averaging process may be viewed as a form of low-pass filtering (Bassett and Chorley, 1971; Darby and Davies, 1967; Holloway, 1958) or a "regional filter" over the original surface (Zurflueh, 1967). The effect of data aggregation, or T_1, can be measured when we examine the alterations produced by transforming the original surface to a stepwise statistical surface, $Z^* = g(x, y)$, defined by areal data. The Z^* surface can be described by a piecewise continuous function (Protter and Morrey, 1964; Tobler, 1974). In reality, this examination is difficult to perform, since we do not know the original surface. In research, however, an original surface may be defined for experimental purposes. From this surface, areal data and isopleth maps can be developed, and the effect of data aggregation may be observed or approximated.

Research Purposes and Methodological Background

The study of the effect of data aggregation is important to cartography and geographical analysis in a number of ways. First, in mapping, generalization is necessary and desirable, but one important principle is to maintain a constant level of generalization on any one map. The existence of variations in county sizes, for example, suggests the degree of data aggregation by administrative units is far from uniform. In map reading, it is difficult to distinguish to what extent spatial variations shown on a map are "real" and to what extent they have been created by contrasting levels of data generalization. An analysis of T_1 may result in a measure of the acceptance limits of data irregularity. For some very large and/or elongated data units, further data refinement may be required before mapping or other analyses. It should be stressed that the measure of consistency of data aggregation may be based on units in Euclidean or non-Euclidean space. Second, information on the effect of aggregation may be used to select an appropriate level of generalization for mapping. This level must be at or below the sensitive scale of the phenomenon under investigation. Third, from the data surface Z^*, it is possible, in principle, to work back to the original surface, a process of degeneralization (Tobler, 1966, 1969). If this process is adequately defined, it can facilitate modification or sharpening of areal data. It may be possible to provide additional information concerning the unknown original surface, or make "patterns in census data stand out more clearly . . . " (Tobler, 1974).

Studies of the recovery of an original surface or true distribution from observed data are found in many fields, such as astronomy, optics, communications, and picture processing. The methodology employed in these studies, in part, has been based on the convolution of functions,

$$g(x) = \int_{-\infty}^{\infty} h(y)f(x-y)\,dy, \tag{1}$$

where $h(y)$ is the instrumental function, $f(x)$ the original function, and $g(x)$ the observed (Bracewell, 1955; Hildebrand, 1965; Jones, 1955; Petersen and Middleton, 1962). In the spatial context, Equation (1) becomes

$$z^*(x, y) = \int\int_{-\infty}^{\infty} k(u, v)z(x-u, y-v)\,du\,dv, \tag{2}$$

where $z(x, y)$ denotes the true distribution, $z^*(x, y)$ the approximation, and $k(u, v)$ the kernel or distribution of errors (Burr, 1955; Tobler, 1974). In the discrete case this becomes

$$g_{ij}^* = \sum_p \sum_q w_{pq} g_{i+p, j+q} \tag{3}$$

where w is a weighting factor operating over the p, q neighborhood.

More recently, Harmon and Julesz (1973) have sampled and quantized a portrait of Lincoln and produced a "surface" of some 300 small square units similar to a choropleth map. In each unit, grey values have been averaged and shown uniformly. Three different filters were applied to this quantized surface and two of the filtered surfaces show Lincoln's face in a more recognizable form than does the quantized surface. In cartography, it may also be possible to obtain a more "recognizable" view of the original surface by applying the correct filters to the stepwise surface of aggregated data. This implies that certain elements of spatial order and variations that were obscured or distorted by the data-aggregation process could be restored or corrected by appropriate filtering. The resultant filtered distribution would be a better approximation of the original surface.

An Experimental Study on the Effect of Data Aggregation

For this study, two original surfaces were selected. Surface S I, shown in Figure 3, is the surface of a cone described by isarithms which form concentric circles. Surface S II is described by a Fourier series of 49 terms (Hsu and

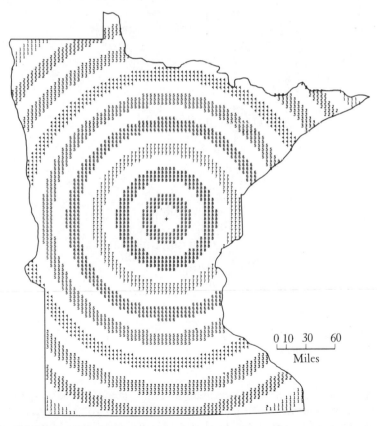

Figure 3   Surface S I. Isarithmic interval is one, and alternate isarithmic "zones" are plotted. For example, zone 1 has "z" values ranging from 2.0 to 2.9, and zone 2 has values ranging from 4.0 to 4.9.

Robinson, 1970; Morrison, 1971, p. 24). On S II there are periodic highs and lows oriented in a north–south direction (Figure 4). Both surfaces are continuous within their domains. The surfaces were digitized and are constructed as "numerical maps" or matrices of 115 by 115 elements. Only the area within the State of Minnesota is shown here.

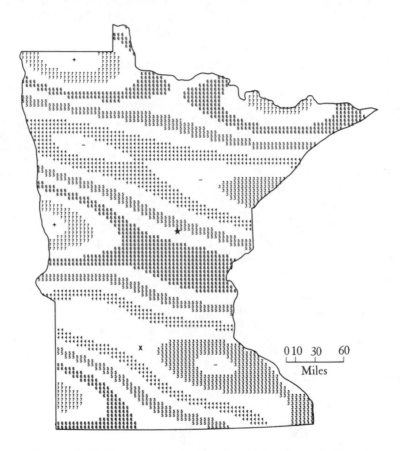

Figure 4 Surface S II. Isarithmic interval is one, and alternate isarithmic "zones" are plotted as in Figure 3. Point x is the central point for S II–B in Figure 11.

Minnesota is used as the experimental base for areal data aggregation. The border of the state was digitized and defined by a 105 by 94 matrix and the state area and irrelevant land outside the state were differentiated. County boundaries within the state were digitized, counties being chosen as the level of data aggregation in this experiment. Digitization was done by superimposing a grid of cells on a state map. Each cell represents approximately 16 square miles.

Filters and the Filtering Process in Data Aggregation

In the usual census-taking procedure, observations within each county are represented by one value or ratio; the parameter of the averaging process is the county size. However, counties vary in size and shape. This means that, in effect, different filter sizes are being applied over various parts of the state. This represents one major difference between the applications of the filtering method in this context and in many other studies. In Holloway's general case, a smoothed or filtered value corresponding to an observation x_t in a time series is

$$\bar{x}_t = \sum_{k=-n}^{m} w_k x_{t+k} \tag{4}$$

Observations are smoothed through x_{t-n} to x_{t+m}, w_k is the weight varying from $-n$ to m, and x_t designates the running mean at time t (Holloway, 1958).

In this study, a two-dimensional filtering process is employed. The filter size (range $-n \leqslant k \leqslant m$) varies from county to county according to their areal extent, but weights (w_k) remain constant within each county. Observations are weighted equally by $1/N$, N being the total observations involved in deriving the mean. This yields a filtered value,

$$\bar{z}_{ij} = \frac{1}{N} \left(\sum_{k=-m}^{m} \sum_{\ell=-n}^{n} z_{i+k, j+\ell} \right) \tag{5}$$

where m and n vary from county to county, and $N = (2m + 1) \cdot (2n + 1)$. The filter is made symmetrical with respect to the central observation of filtering; there is no phase shifting in the series. The sum of coefficients of the filter is equal to unity; thus the mean of each series of county data is not changed.

The 87 counties are considered as filters, and it is necessary to regularize the county shapes. On the basis of the same reference grid, each county was approximated by a rectangle (or square) described by a matrix of an odd number of rows $(2n + 1)$ and columns $(2m + 1)$. This approximation involves a compromise of county shape as well as size, and the effect of shape change is difficult to assess. Since some counties are alike in dimension, only 31 filters are needed to identify all counties.

Filtered Surfaces and Residuals

The original surfaces are described by "numerical maps". Through the application of county filters, each original surface was transformed to a filtered surface of running means (Figures 5 and 6). The filtered surface S I preserves basic spatial characteristics of the original surface, the isopleth zones remaining more or less concentric. However, the highest z-values are reduced on the filtered S I, and the peak area is flattened. S II is more complex, and the averaging generally results in a reduction of z-values in higher areas and an increase in z-values in lower areas.

The difference between the original value and the filtered value gives T_1, the effect of the data aggregation process. This difference is the residual of filtering. To construct the surface of residuals, a high-pass filter may be used in contrast to the low-pass filter used in the averaging process (Holloway, 1958; Zurflueh, 1967). In this study, the residual at a point is

$$R_{ij} = -\frac{1}{N}\left[\left(\sum_{k=-m}^{m}\sum_{\ell=-n}^{n} z_{i+k,j+\ell}\right) - z_{ij}\right] + \frac{N-1}{N}(z_{ij}). \quad (6)$$

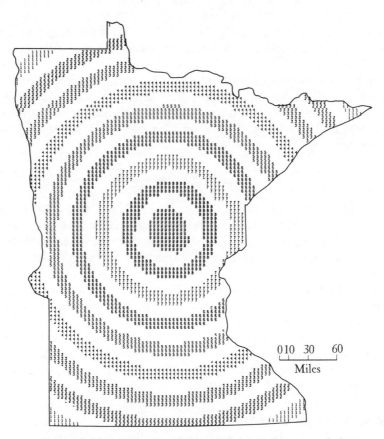

Figure 5   Filtered Surface S I. Isopleth interval is one and alternate isopleth "zones" are plotted as in Figure 3.

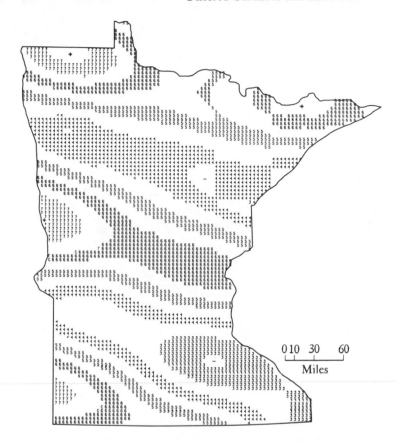

Figure 6 Filtered Surface S II. Isopleth interval is one and alternate isopleth "zones" are plotted as in Figure 3.

Obviously, the sum of the coefficients of the residual filter (matrix) is zero, and values of the residuals form a series with zero mean. The original surfaces were filtered again, this time by county residual filters (Figures 7 and 8). The residual maps, of course, are complementary to their respective filtered maps. In areas of relatively higher original z-values, where the filtered surfaces were being dampened, the residual values are high. For S I, residuals range from -0.05 to 1.16, and for S II, from -1.78 to 2.21. Magnitudes of residuals are reduced because of digitization. On both maps, several residual classes form straight line or angular borders. These reflect locations of county boundaries. Groups of large residuals bounded together by straight lines also represent county boundaries. These illustrate the contrasting levels of data aggregation and the values of residuals among different counties.

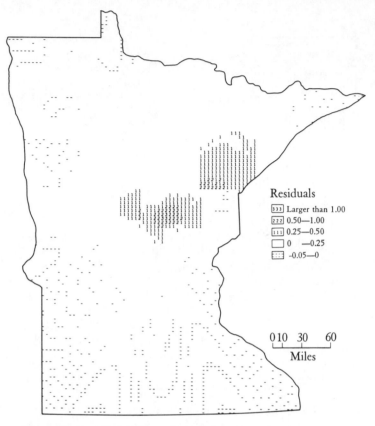

Figure 7 Residual surface obtained by subtracting filtered surface
S I (Figure 5) from original surface S I (Figure 3).

The relative importance of the residuals with respect to the original
surfaces may be evaluated by percentage index

$$I_{ij} = \frac{R_{ij}}{z_{ij}} \times 100. \tag{7}$$

It should be noted that this index measures the aggregation process of a
data collecting system on a *particular* original surface. In other words, the
index varies with the system of data collection as well as with the characteristics of the original surface. This index is also affected by the size of the
grid used for digitizing the map area and the original surface in this experiment. If many experimental surfaces are utilized and a series of residual indices
are computed, these may reveal more precisely their relations with the characteristics of the original surfaces. In general, as spatial gradient increases, so do

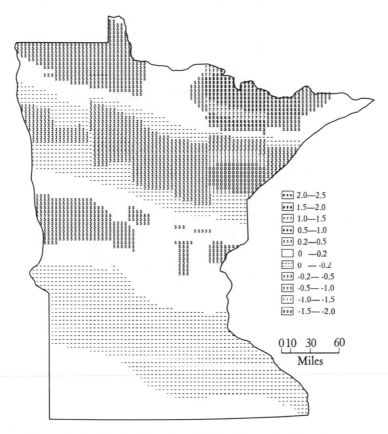

Figure 8 Residual surface obtained by subtracting filtered surface
S II (Figure 6) from original surface S II (Figure 4).

residuals and indices. Since transformation T_1 is an averaging process, it
depresses extremes in z-values. Wherever peaks exist on the original surface,
residuals and indices at these localities will be positive and large. In areas
of troughs or depressions, residuals and indices will be negative and
large.

The filtered value or running mean at the county centroid is an approximation of the areal data as if it had been collected for the county in the usual
census-taking procedure. Indices of residuals at county centroids were
mapped (Figures 9 and 10); these provide an evaluation of the quality of
aggregated data at the county level with reference to the given original
surfaces. For S I, the indices are generally small, ranging within ± 2 percent.
This reflects the fact that surface S I is highly autocorrelated. The range of
indices of S II is larger, from -6.6 to 2.9 percent.

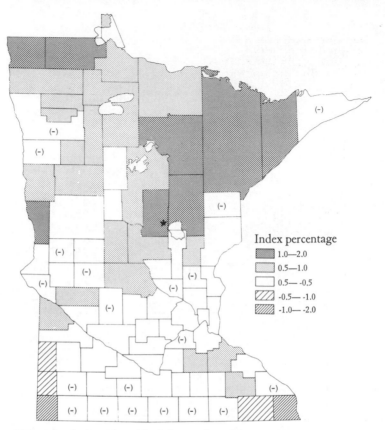

Figure 9 Index of residual for surface S I, as observed at county centroids.

Some tentative conclusions may be drawn from these index maps: (*a*) large or elongated data units tend to generate larger indices, a finding which reinforces an earlier study (Hsu and Robinson, 1970); (*b*) high indices are associated with peaks and troughs, or areas of higher and lower z-values in the distributions; (*c*) in Figure 9, fairly large indices are found in several bordering counties at the northwest, southwest, and southeast corners. These percentages are somewhat exaggerated owing to the low z-values of S I at these localities.

Some attempt was made to separate the effect of the filtering process on values of residuals from the effect of the surface characteristics on these values. On S I, the highest point of the cone surface was chosen, and at this peak a series of 17 filters was centered to derive the running means at this point. The filter sizes ranged from 3 by 3 to 35 by 35. As expected, the filtered value reduces as the filter size increases. The curve S I which describes the relation

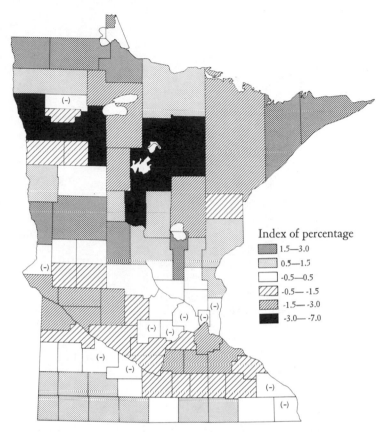

Figure 10 Index of residual for surface S II, as observed at county centroids.

between the filter size and residual index is almost a straight line (Figure 11). The same procedure was repeated on S II twice at different central points. The first point is identical to the peak on S I, and the results are shown by curve S II-A. The second point is located in an area containing lower z-values, shown by curve S II-B. These two curves, differ from S I in slope and, for S II-B, also in direction. In determining residual values and directions (positive or negative), characteristics of the original surface and specific location of the central data point play a decisive role. On a complex surface, these may be more influential than filter size. When a central point is located at the mid-point of a long slope, the residual values are not responsive to increases of filter sizes within the dimension of this slope.

When areal data is utilized for isopleth mapping, some information is lost at the extremities of the surface (Figure 12). Good interpolation models can make adjustments for this type of loss. Likewise, the filtered residual or

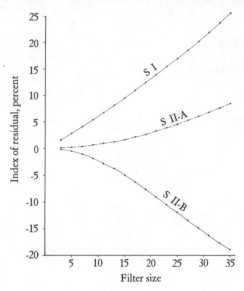

Figure 11 Index of residual (in percent) in relation to filter size.

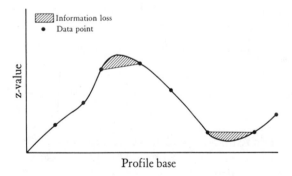

Figure 12 Probable profile of the original surface and information loss in the averaging process.

its index may serve to remedy the information loss, by indicating how the average z-value for a county may be adjusted.

In isopleth mapping, as in other mapping techniques, there are many types of method-produced errors. Spatial filtering can be employed to analyze some of these errors. Since choropleth mapping uses the same type of areal data, inquiries into data aggregation should be applicable to that technique as well. Research along this direction may lead to a better understanding of the original surface.

References

Bassett, K. A., 1972, Numerical methods for map analysis: *Progress in Geography*, v. 4, p. 219–254.

Bassett, K. A., and R. J. Chorley, 1971, An experiment in terrain filtering: *Area*, v. 3, no. 2, p. 78–91.

Bracewell, R. N., 1955, Simple graphical method of correcting for instrumental broadening: *Jour. Optical Soc. America*, v. 45, p. 873–876.

Burr, E. J., 1955, Sharpening of observational data in two dimensions: *Australian Jour. Physics*, v. 8, p. 30–53.

Casetti, E., 1966, Analysis of spatial association by trigonometric polynomials: *The Canadian Geographer*, v. 10, p. 199–204.

Curry, L., 1966, A note on spatial association: *The Professional Geographer*, v. 18, p. 97–99.

Darby, E. K., and E. B. Davies, 1967, The analysis and design of two-dimensional filters for two-dimensional data: *Geophysical Prospecting*, v. 15, no. 3, p. 383–406.

Harmon, L. D., and B. Julesz, 1973, Masking in visual recognition: effects of two-dimensional filtered noise: *Science*, v. 180, no. 4091, p. 1194–1197.

Hildebrand, F. B., 1965, *Methods of applied mathematics*, 2nd ed.: Prentice-Hall, Inc., Englewood Cliffs, New Jersey, 362 p.

Holloway, J. L., Jr., 1958, Smoothing and filtering of time series and space fields: *Advances in Geophysics*, v. 4, p. 351–389.

Hsu, M. L., and A. H. Robinson, 1970, *The fidelity of isopleth maps, an experimental study*: Univ. Minnesota Press, Minneapolis, 92 p.

Jones, R. C., 1955, New method of describing and measuring the granularity of photographic materials: *Jour. Optical Soc. America*, v. 45, p. 799–808.

Morrison, J. L., 1971, Method-produced error in isarithmic mapping: American Congress on Surveying and Mapping, *Tech. Monograph No. CA-5*, 76 p.

Petersen, D. P., and D. Middleton, 1962, Sampling and reconstruction of wave-number-limited functions in N-dimensional Euclidean spaces: *Information and Control*, v. 5, p. 279–323.

Protter, M. H., and C. B. Morrey, 1964, *Modern mathematical analysis*: Addison-Wesley, Reading, Mass., 790 p.

Tobler, W. R., 1966, Numerical map generalization, and notes on the analysis of geographical distributions: Michigan-Inter-Univ. Community of Mathematical Geographers, *Discussion Paper No. 8*, 40 p.

Tobler, W. R., 1967, Of maps and matrices: *Jour. Regional Science*, v. 7, p. 275–280.

Tobler, W. R., 1969, Geographical filters and their inverses: *Geographical Analysis*, v. 1, p. 234–253.

Tobler, W. R., 1974, Linear operators applied to areal data, *in* J. C. Davis and M. J. McCullagh, eds., *Display and analysis of spatial data*: John Wiley & Sons, Ltd., London, p. 14–37.

Zurflueh, E. G., 1967, Applications of two-dimensional linear wavelength filtering: *Geophysics*, v. 32, p. 1015–1035.

Methodology of Computer-Assisted Cartography

P. Yoeli

The use of computers and their accessories such as digitizers, plotters, and CRTs has made it possible to automate certain techniques of map making. Calling these techniques "automated cartography", as has become customary, is somewhat exaggerated, as we are not faced with a new concept of cartography and especially not with fully automated processes. The ultimate aim is to create maps of the well-known type and computers are used to ease, speed up, and perhaps improve "computer-assisted cartography".

"Non-Map" Cartography

Certain conceptual changes are, however, necessary when dealing with maps which are to be used as a base for solution of geometrical problems connected with the Earth's surface. These problems are either purely planimetric, such as the determination of areas, directions, and distances, or three-dimensional such as volume computation, slope analysis, and intervisibility problems. The classical large-scale topographic map seeks to supply the necessary information for all these problems; it is in fact a graphical entity of planimetric and altimetric details, the latter being almost exclusively supplied in the form of contours. Once a topographic map is produced, its manipulation is effected through graphical measurements and their conversion into the numerical answers needed for the problems at hand. Synthesis of terrain details into the form of maps has made classical cartography a purely "map-oriented" discipline, to the extent that it gives the field its name.

The advent of the computer has introduced an additional possibility of purely "cartometrically oriented" cartography. Specific problems may be solved *directly* without recourse to a topographic map, provided the necessary specific data (in principle, part of the data from which classical cartography constructs its maps) are available. This approach might be called "non-map cartography".

Differences Between Conventional and Computer-Assisted Methods

Characteristics and possibilities of the new techniques exert a strong influence on the methods of map making. Formulation of the differences between conventional and computer-assisted map production becomes easier if classifications of maps used in theoretical cartography are introduced. In addition to the classification into "topographic maps" and "thematic maps", the distinction most relevant to computer-assisted methods is the division based on the originality of maps. There are "basic" and "derived" maps. Basic maps are the direct graphic compilation and presentation of original surveys, either topographical or thematic. Derived maps are usually the result of compilation, simplification, and generalization of the contents of basic maps.

As an example of the influence of computer assistance on the method of map production, we may compare the ways of generating a typical basic topographic map in both conventional and computer-assisted form (Figures 1 and 2). The first step is identical for both and comprises the collection and

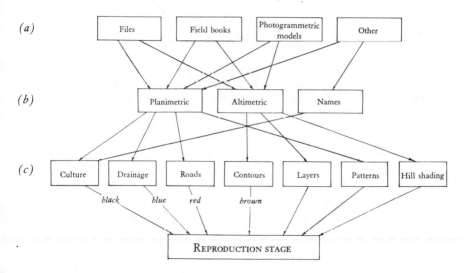

Figure 1 Generation diagram of basic topographic maps by the conventional (manual) approach. (*a*) Data sources. (*b*) Manuscript stage. (*c*) Fair drawing or scribing stage, according to color scheme of map.

preparation of initial sources from which data relevant to the map are taken. For a typical topographic map, this data includes the geodetic base of the map such as coordinates of triangulation points, traverse points, and height points. These usually are taken from surveying department files and from field books or geodetic measurements such as areal triangulation made using

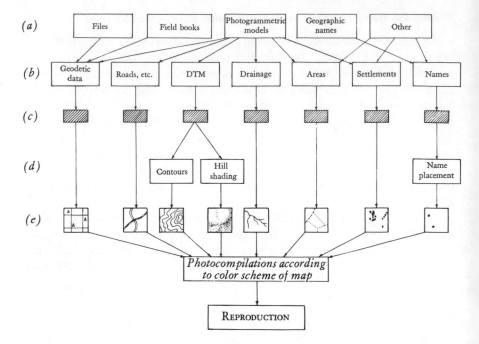

Figure 2 Generation diagram of basic topographic maps by the computer-assisted approach. (*a*) Initial data sources. (*b*) Sources in computer-compatible form (basic data banks). (*c*) Retrieval of relevant data and reduction of data to requirements of scale and format. (*d*) Processing stage. (*e*) Output stage, using plotters and CRTs.

photogrammatric instruments. Topographic contents of the map include planimetric and altimetric details of the ground and are taken, in the case of tacheometric surveys, from field books or field sheets and from photographs in the case of photogrammetric surveys. In addition, this step includes collecting and editing the necessary administrative and informative details such as boundaries, names, and descriptions. This being a basic map, there is in principle no need to collect data from former graphic sources.

From here onward the methods of conventional and computer-assisted cartography part. On the conventional path, preliminary manuscripts are prepared based upon the initial data. These manuscripts are the graphic documentation and compilation of all necessary details comprising the map being produced. Geodetic points, planimetric contents such as roads, drainage, borders, and settlements are plotted, altimetric information is compiled, usually in form of height points and contours, and the list of place names edited. The compilation manuscript can be produced in one sheet incorporating all information or in several sheets, comprising one or more of the groups of the various map items. The manuscript step can be described as the synthesis of material chosen from various sources according to the requirements of the finished map.

Treatment of the manuscript sheet or sheets, the fair drawing or scribing stage, is dictated by the form of reproduction to be used and the number of printing colors chosen. For a multicolored map the items making up the manuscript are separated according to the colors in which they will be printed.

In computer-assisted production (Figure 2) the initial sources must be transformed into computer-compatible form. That is, they must be registered in digital form on a computer-accessible data carrier, such as magnetic tape or disks. These registrations, which may be called "basic cartographic data banks", should preferably be created without reference to a specific map scale and should include an amount of information large enough for the production of a whole range of maps of various scales and types. A good example is the data bank carrying relief information, the "digital terrain model" (DTM). Generated photogrammetrically from a stereoscopic model, the scale of the DTM and the density of the grid should be chosen to serve as the base for computer-executed interpolation of contours on as large a range of map scales as possible, for the computation of hill shadings, and if necessary, for the numerical solution of geometrical problems of the Earth's surface. The same principle applies to all other items such as geographical names, drainage systems, roads, and communications.

Only the next step, retrieval and data reduction, is oriented toward production of a specific map. This is, in a sense, equivalent to the "manuscript stage" of a conventional approach. From the basic data bank only that amount of data needed for the area, scale, and type of map to be produced is retrieved. The necessary degree of generalization dictated by the map scale is achieved at this stage. As an example, from the basic bank of the DTM, the density of the original grid may be reduced so a computer-executed contour interpolation will result in a flow of contours whose degree of generalization is in accordance with requirements of the map scale. This also applies to simplification of drainage systems, and choice of names. This stage presupposes the existence of well-developed computer software.

The following step, the processing stage, must be applied to those items which need further manipulation, including computation of the contour interpolation on the DTM, analytical hill shading (if required), and computation of the placement of names retrieved from the bank according to parameters defined by the map editor. The retrieved, reduced, and processed data are now put out in plotters or CRTs.

So far the process has been completely analytical, with every group of items treated separately. The final synthesis of the various outputs can now begin through photocompilation according to the color scheme chosen for the map.

Digitizing

Assuming the initial sources are in the form of numerical files, name lists, and aerial photographs, fully computer-assisted basic map production has, theoretically, no need for the digitizing of graphic sources other than aerial photographs and field sheets from terrestrial surveys. However, for reasons of convenience and because of the lack of inexpensive photogrammetric digitizing equipment, computer assistance in map production includes digitizing of other graphic sources even for the production of basic topographic maps. Thus we have a third form of map generation, the *hybrid form*, which combines conventional with computer-assisted methods (Figure 3). Parts of the initial sources such as geodetic points and grid are

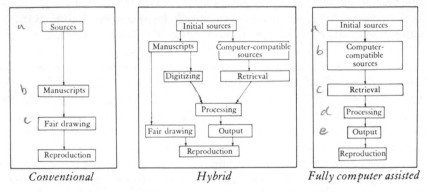

Conventional   *Hybrid*   *Fully computer assisted*

Figure 3 Generation of basic maps by conventional, hydrid, and fully computer-assisted approaches.

directly converted into computer-compatible form and follow the path described earlier. Other items are first compiled into graphic manuscripts from which some are manually turned into fair drawings while others, such as contours and boundaries, are digitized and processed further.

Digitizing is often carried out as an intermediate step between the manuscript and fair drawing stage without further processing of the digitized data, which is then redrawn by a precision plotter that can create a high-quality fair drawing or scribing. In such a mode, electronic equipment replaces professional draftsmen; this is a legitimate form of application, but as far as the automation of the complete process of map production is concerned, a rather limited one.

Derived Maps

The methodological need for digitizing arises for computer-assisted production of derived maps whose initial sources are other maps or graphic materials.

Figure 4 shows the conventional and the computer-assisted methods of generating these maps. The initial stage is identical for both. The sources are usually larger in scale and consequently consist of more detailed maps and other informative, often statistical, material.

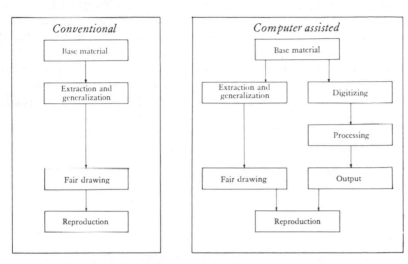

Figure 4 Generation diagram of derived maps by the conventional and computer-assisted approaches.

In the conventional method, relevant data are extracted from the base material and compiled in manuscript form, undergoing the process of generalization and reduction (the adaptation of the amount of information and its graphical form to the scale and character requirements of the new map). The fair drawing and the reproduction stage follow.

With the computer-assisted method the graphic base material or certain of its items are digitized. Generalization is carried out via computer processing with the help of appropriate reduction and generalization software. Taking the relief information as an example, the contours of the topographic base map would be digitized, followed by computer-executed simplification and smoothing of original contours. The degree of computer involvement depends on the type of map concerned, but the system is usually hybrid. Certain items of the derived map are treated in the conventional manner and the manual fair drawings and plotter or CRT outputs combined at the reproduction stage.

Although these examples deal with production of topographic maps, the same deliberations apply in principle to creation of basic and derived thematic maps. The only distinction is that the initial sources and items comprising the map are usually of a different type.

Line-Printer Maps

In the field of thematic cartography, widespread use has been made of computer line printers to print layers of varying density or strings of letters or symbols indicating the flow of contours. Compared with classical cartography these outputs have the great advantage of high-speed production but are graphically inferior to non-computer-assisted creations. Their graphic character is not dictated by optimal cartographic solutions but by the fact that certain computer hardware "is there", Certainly, use of these devices poses an intriguing cartographic challenge. These outputs can best be classified as being part of "computer graphics" in general, which also includes computer-executed drawing of block diagrams and perspective drawings.

Maps by Line Printer

J. T. Coppock

The history of automated cartography has yet to be written, but it seems likely to reveal that many of the earliest attempts to use electromechanical equipment to plot spatial data in their correct relative location arose outside cartography in fields such as physics and biology. In parallel with those developments in automated cartography which have interested cartographers, photogrammetrists, and others concerned with the precise location of data on maps, there have been other advances in computer-assisted methods for making thematic maps which derive little inspiration from conventional cartography. Much of the initiative for such developments has come from users of maps, particularly botanists, economic geographers, meteorologists, and planners. Many of these attempts at practical map making by those more concerned with usable results than with the visual quality of their cartographic output have employed the standard devices attached to electronic data-processing equipment for printing the results of computations, though the maps produced in this way have often been crude and sometimes esthetically unpleasing. Indeed, it seems likely that larger numbers of computer-generated maps of this kind have been produced than of the more conventional products of automated cartography. Admittedly there are now many specialist agencies, notably in military establishments, producing traditional maps (some indistinguishable from their hand-drawn predecessors) on plotters of varying degrees of sophistication. Such machines were comparatively rare until quite recently, whereas every computer installation has some facility, usually a line printer, for recording the results of computations. An additional reason for the large number of maps printed on such devices since the mid-1960s has been the widespread availability of package programs which required little if any technical competence and so could be used by anyone with access to suitable machines. It also seems likely that many of these developments were due to increasing awareness in a wide variety of fields of the potentialities of data processing in general.

What these devices, tabulators, teletypes, and line printers, have in common is that they were designed to print the results of computations rather than to make maps. They are therefore equipped with a set of characters, usually the alphabet in upper case, the digits 0 to 9, punctuation marks, and a range of mathematical and other symbols. Their potentialities for mapping derive from the fact that these characters are, as on most typewriters, printed within a rectangular space of constant size. This grid of possible character locations provides a regular framework for the construction of maps, while the characters themselves provide the symbols required for thematic mapping.

Related Developments

The idea of arranging printed characters in patterns, which is the basis of most map making by line printer, long predates the development of automatic data processing as the Tail of the Mouse in Lewis Carroll's *Alice's Adventures in Wonderland* (1865) shows. What appears to be the earliest attempt in the United Kingdom to use ADP equipment to make maps, those prepared in 1954 for the *Atlas of the British Flora* (Perring and Walters, 1962), relied primarily on the facility for mapping relative location and used only one symbol, a black circle, to map recorded occurrences of the plant species in question. Information on species, the grid references of the 10 km squares of the National Grid in which they had been found, and other data were punched on 40-column cards, a separate card being prepared for each occurrence of each species. The cards were sorted by species on a card-sorter and then, for any given species, by eastings and northings. The cards were then placed in an electromechanical tabulator which had been modified to make the line-feed equal to the spacing of characters on the horizontal axis, so that each character was located within a square. The tabulator was provided with forms pre-printed with outline maps of the British Isles and 100 km squares of the National Grid at a scale such that each character location represented a 10 km square of that grid. As the card deck was read, a black circle was printed in each 10 km square along the first line (reading from north to south) in which an occurrence of that species was recorded. When all such occurrences had been printed (all subsequent cards for a given square being ignored), the paper on the tabulator was advanced one line and the same procedure repeated until all occurrences had been plotted and the map was complete. An average map involving the plotting of about 1000 circles took approximately 15 minutes, compared with a full working day by hand.

This approach arose at a late stage in the planning of the Atlas from the idea "that it might be possible to use the punched cards themselves to produce the maps mechanically" (Perring and Walters, 1962, p. 19). The idea was very simple, for no computation was required and the maps recorded merely the occurrence or non-occurrence of each species. The role of the ADP equipment was simply to record these facts within pre-printed maps, the preparation of which could be justified by the fact that over 2000 maps were required. Yet in essence the basic method is both very similar to that used in mapping by the line printers attached to electronic computers (except that sorting is done within the computer, data are usually manipulated mathematically, and pre-printed map outlines are not generally used), and also anticipates one of the later improvements in line-printer mapping. A similar method was subsequently devised by Bertin and his colleagues (Bertin, 1967), using an electric typewriter on which the line-feed had also been adjusted to give the same increment in both axes. Symbolism was achieved by a series of black circles of decreasing size. It is surprising that Perring's lead does not seem to have been followed and that several years should have elapsed before other methods were attempted.

Another approach, which again anticipates some cartographic developments using the line printer, has been the preparation of figure fields which have been used both as ends in themselves and as aids to the plotting of hand-drawn maps. Examples include the work of Hägerstrand (1955) and Petrini (Hedbom, 1962), and it is probable that further searches would provide examples in other fields. This approach has been continued in the MAP 01 program (Bishop and Gibson, 1966) in which data are printed in squares measuring 0.5 inches by 0.5 inches (i.e., 5 by 3 or 4 characters, depending on the nature of the line printer), and in maps for an agricultural atlas of Scotland (Coppock, 1969). In the latter study, results of computations were printed at the centroid of administrative areas, the decimal point being located as far as possible at the centroid, subject to adjustments to prevent overlapping. Manuscript maps were then compiled from the results by means of transparent overlays or dyeline maps on which administrative boundaries were printed. It seems likely that some of the first recognizable maps to be produced by line printer were of this type, for around 1960 American and British meteorologists were beginning not only to plot figure fields in this way but also to produce isoline maps of meteorological parameters in which the areas between every other pair of contour lines were "shaded" by filling them in with an appropriate digit. Examples of this are provided in the meteorological work by Neilon (1961, U.S. Weather Bureau, personal communication) and Sawyer (1960). Similar maps are available as an option on LINMAP 2 (Gaits, 1969), though digits are printed only at the centroid, any other areas within the map outline being filled in with dots.

Line-Printer Maps

It would be a major research task to attempt to identify the first map to be made by line printer, since many of the necessary records are probably unpublished and it seems likely that parallel developments were in progress in many places and in a wide variety of fields. One of the first major attempts to systematize the production of maps by line printer was undoubtedly that by Howard T. Fisher at Northwestern University which led to the development of the SYMAP program in 1963 and the establishment of the Laboratory for Computer Graphics at Harvard University. Since that date other programs have been developed in a large number of computer centers, though it seems probable that SYMAP is the most widely used. Many of these programs seem to represent parallel attempts to achieve the same ends, sometimes through ignorance of developments elsewhere, but more often because existing programs were unsuitable for machines because of the high level languages used, the incorporation of machine code in the program, or the size of machine required. Thus, the CAMAP program (Hotson, unpublished manuscript) was developed at Edinburgh in full knowledge of the existence of the SYMAP program, because the local KDF 9 computer was too small to run SYMAP and the version then available did not contain an option for choropleth maps. Many such programs have special applications and are of limited value to other users, though they tend to be simple, efficient, and cheap to operate. Others, such as SYMAP, are general purpose and hence large.

While line printers differ in detail and in their suitability for mapping, their general characteristics are fairly similar. The printing area is usually 130 characters wide and the space in which each character is printed is one-tenth of an inch, giving a total width of about 13 inches. Wider printers are available, but they are not generally standard equipment at computer installations. Much wider maps can, however, be produced by printing maps in successive strips, each a maximum of 13 inches wide, which can then be joined together. Most programs perform this operation automatically if a map is requested which is wider than the available printing space. Five strips are probably the maximum convenient number to join together. The resulting maps are not wholly satisfactory because matching strips and joining them neatly is both difficult and time-consuming and the joins are often visible. There are thus many advantages in confining maps to a single width of output paper, provided that the resulting scale is a convenient one. Since maps by line printer are produced on continuous paper, there is no effective limit to their length, though practical considerations suggest an upper limit of eight or nine pages (about 88–99 inches).

The grid within which characters are printed not only provides a means of defining the spatial dimensions of what is to be mapped, but is also one determinant of the grain of the map. Although the characters themselves are of fixed size, the character locations are normally either one-sixth or one-eighth of an inch high and one-tenth of an inch wide, though some printers have facilities for printing at either interval. It follows that a point can be represented only by a single rectangle of these dimensions, a line by a sequence of rectangles (which will be stepped unless the line is either vertical or horizontal in relation to the printer), and an area by a block of characters which can only be approximate unless the true shape is rectilinear and has the same proportions. This discordance between what is to be mapped and its actual representation on the line printer is most acute in respect to lines. There is no doubt that line-printer maps are best suited for the representation of areal data, especially those derived from censuses. A finer grain than that provided by the dimensions of the individual characters can, of course, be achieved by photographic reduction and this has been the normal practice with maps being prepared for publication. For example, in the computer atlas of Birmingham and the Black Country by Rosing and Wood (1971), maps which had been printed in three strips and had a maximum width of 36 inches were reduced five times to 7.2 inches on the printed map. At this final scale, the individual characters of which the shadings were composed are, like those in a screened photograph, barely distinguishable and different categories merely appear as differences in tone.

These shadings are derived from the characters available on the print-chain or drum on the line printer. The individual characters vary greatly in the proportion of space which they occupy, ranging from a dot (.) to the letter (W). For some pusposes, such as regionalization or the mapping of nominal data where it is necessary merely to be able to distinguish one area from its neighbors, there is usually sufficient choice of contrasting symbols available. For working maps, too, the range of available shadings is sufficient for most purposes and useful maps can be obtained using the digits 0 to 9, especially if these are mnemonics of the information being mapped. Also, draftsmen using line-printer maps as compilations for the preparation of hand-drawn maps prefer shadings in which the characters differ greatly in shape and orientation. For maps of ordinal, ratio, or interval data where order is implied, graded shadings will be required. It is possible to select a limited number of characters to represent different shades on the gray scale, for example, . + * O X, but darker tones are difficult to achieve. Characters should preferably be symmetrical and it is desirable to avoid those, such as $, which are likely to have particular significance for map users. Acceptable working maps have been produced in this way, such as maps of agriculture in the European Economic Community prepared in 1972 for internal purposes by the Community's Statistical Office. Maps based on selected characters also have been published in an atlas of the flora of Warwickshire (Cadbury, Hawkes, and Readett, 1971). The range of tones available can be greatly increased by overprinting, or the printing of two or more characters in the same location. Overprinted − and O is darker than O alone, and overprinting O, X, A, and V produces a black rectangle, the darkest tone which can be achieved. By judicious selection of intervals and overprintings it is possible to produce at least ten shades of gray, though six is an appropriate upper limit for most mapping. It should be noted that the penalty attached to overprinting is that it slows the rate of printing, a line with three overprintings being equivalent to four lines of text. It follows that overprinting should not normally be used in the production of working maps. Where users of computer installations are charged according to the number of lines printed, the additional costs of overprinting may even outweigh the advantages of providing greater and more readily perceived contrasts.

Before any maps can be produced the boundaries of the areas to be mapped and any subdivisions within them must be provided in machine-readable form. This can be done by reference either to the grid of character locations or to an external grid, such as geographic coordinates, although this must ultimately be expressed in terms of the character grid when the map is printed. During the early stages of line-printer mapping the former approach was used, map data being coded by reference to the line-printer grid with an origin in the top left-hand corner and coordinates expressed as distances to the right and down from this origin. These references were determined either by measurement or by superimposing a transparent overlay of cells of the appropriate dimensions. Most programs now accept locational references from external grids, such as the Ordnance Survey's National Grid which has its origin to the southwest of Great Britain. The information is converted by the program into a form appropriate for mapping by the printer.

Locations can be defined in one of two ways: by pairs of coordinates as in the SYMAP program, or by detailing the character locations that each area will occupy, as in the CAMAP (Hotson, unpublished manuscript) and CMS (Waugh, 1972) programs. In the former approach, lines and areas are defined by strings of coordinate pairs. Because the line printer cannot locate each vertex more accurately than the nearest character location and because the coordinates occupy a good deal of space in the computer, boundaries are highly simplified. In the SYMAP program, map outlines are limited to 100 vertices, though this number can be increased by breaking the area into a number of "islands", joined by common boundaries. Such an approach characteristically requires a large computer so that the map array can be laid out in core, but any change of scale is possible. In the alternative approach, the map is divided into lines, each of which represents a line of printer output. Each line is coded according to the boundaries which intersect it, the number of spaces between boundaries, and an identifier for each area. The merit of this method is that it can be used with very small computers, since results for each map are computed separately and brought together with the map framework only at the stage of printing. The method also permits more realistic shapes to be achieved by allowing exercise of judgment in allocation of individual cells to particular areas. Even within a large and complex map, as of the 12,000 parishes of Great Britain, only a small part of the map is in core at any one time. The price paid for this approach is less flexibility in changing scale. The ratio of the old to the new scale must be an integer and, with reductions in scale, a factor of 100. A similar approach has been adopted in many programs which map on a regular grid, each cell of which is a data zone. In these circumstances, it is only necessary to provide information on the size of cell, the starting and terminating points of each line, and to arrange the cells in their correct sequence.

Maps based upon grid squares are of increasing importance, especially in planning, as the volume of data collected in this manner grows (Forbes, 1969). However, there is one major problem in using line printers for mapping such data, and that is the fact that characters occupy rectangles rather than squares. Of course, data could be collected by rectangles, but this would be both inconvenient and impractical, because the data serve a variety of purposes. Several other solutions are possible. Values for rectangles could be estimated from those for grid squares; the distortion which results from equating a character location with a grid square could be accepted; map squares could be constructed from groups of rectangles; or the printer could be modified so the dimensions of each character location are the same in both axes. The last appears to be the most satisfactory solution. The first approach requires a further degree of generalization of the data in a way that might bias the results. The second has been adopted by the GRID program (Sinton and Steinitz, 1969), for it can be argued that the distortion is not great where the line-feed is one-eighth of an inch, that the eye can easily compensate for the distortion with practice, and that in problems for which gridded data are appropriate it is not so much their exact location which is important as the cell contents and their topological relationship. These arguments have merit when applied to working maps, but while maps incorporating such distortion have been published (Cadbury, Hawkes, and Readett, 1971), this does not seem a satisfactory solution for maps to be read by non-professionals unfamiliar with the assumptions. The third possibility, the construction of squares which are the least common multiple of the dimensions of the individual character locations (0.5 inches by 0.5 inches, or 5 characters along the horizontal axis and either 3 or 4 on the vertical axis), has been widely used, as in the MAP 01 program. With the SYMAP proximal option, which constructs maps of Thiessen polygons, such squares can be constructed from equally spaced data points identified by single pairs of coordinates with the resulting nearest neighbors forming the squares, though this option is expensive to run. Alternatively, each square can be defined by its vertices, as in the conformal option in SYMAP, or coded as part of the map framework, as in CAMAP and CMS. Unfortunately, though easy to achieve, this solution has two major disadvantages, for the maps are both costly and large, as only 26 cells can be represented on a single width of computer printout.

There are obvious benefits in a solution in which each character location can represent a single square of the grid, as was done with the modified tabulator used for plotting plant species (Perring and Walters, 1962) and the modified typewriter used by Bertin (1967). This has now been achieved at Edinburgh by a relatively simple modification to an IBM 1403 printer at the Regional Computing Centre to give a line feed of 0.1 inch, so that 132 grid squares can now be represented on a single width of computer output. As a byproduct, the quality of other maps produced on this printer has been improved.

Although dot maps of a kind have been produced by line printer, they are not very satisfactory, and most maps are either isoline or choropleth maps. The vast majority of isoline maps represent continuously variable statistical surfaces and imply the existence of data points between which values are computed by an interpolation routine which is part of the program. In printing, the actual isoline may be suppressed and represented only by the boundary between contiguous shadings (Rosing and Wood, 1971). Alternatively, it can be shown as an unshaded line, as approximated by a string of character locations, or as a line which is distinctively printed in a dark shading (Taylor, 1971). Areas between isolines can be left blank or shaded by either distinctive or graded symbols, or every other space between isolines can be left blank. The precise position of each isoline will depend on both the location of data points and the method of interpolation. No difficulty arises when data are samples or collected at points and are (or can be assumed to be) continuously variable, as with most meteorological data. Yet the method is also widely used to display census data by administrative areas. In these circumstances the value attributable to a tract is commonly located at the centroid or approximate centroid of the tract on the questionable assumption that the data are uniformly distributed throughout the tract. Selection of any other location within the tract will clearly alter the positions of isolines. There is also a great variety of interpolation algorithms, each of which makes a number of assumptions. Not one of these can be labeled wholly right or wrong, although the choice of routine will affect the position of the isoline.

The other principal method of mapping by line printer is by some type of choropleth map. Many of the data to be mapped are derived from censuses. These are generally summaries of individual records, aggregated by administrative area in ways which are intended to prevent any disclosure of individual details and hence breaches of confidentiality. Although such data normally relate to specific areas, choropleth maps of a kind can also be produced from point data, as in the proximal option of SYMAP and the approximate choropleth maps of GEOMAP, which are produced by progressively filling the character locations surrounding the data points with the symbol at each point until all locations within the map framework have been filled (Kilchenmann, Steiner, Matt, and Gächter, 1972). Another semi-choroplethic map by line printer is produced by the DOTMAP option in LINMAP. This method is appropriate only for small-scale maps containing a large number of data points. Only one character in each tract is shaded, corresponding to the centroid of the census or other tract, and other locations are filled in with background shading (Gaits, 1969). In towns, where tracts are small, this method generally produces contiguous shaded areas. In the countryside, where tracts are large, the shading of individual symbols is difficult to identify and background shading often dominates such parts of the maps. The most common type of choropleth map, the conformal maps of SYMAP terminology, comprise those in which shaded areas correspond with the administrative areas to which the data refer. Boundaries of such shaded areas may be represented either by the straight boundaries of simplified polygons (or rather their approximation by sequences of characters) or by the character locations identifying each administrative area on the appropriate map framework. As on isoline maps, the boundaries separating different classes of areas may be shown implicitly by a change in symbolism. Boundaries may also be shown explicitly by omitting any shading along an approximate boundary line one character wide or by showing some darker symbol along this same line. If boundaries are explicitly shown, they may be restricted to those separating classes or may include the boundaries of every administrative tract on the map. A major disadvantage of this latter practice is that a large part of the shaded area will be omitted if the administrative areas are small and their boundaries numerous, making the resulting map more difficult to interpret. On balance, it seems best to omit boundaries from the maps themselves and to use a transparent overlay to identify individual areas where this information is required.

Both isoline and choropleth maps (at least those showing ratio or interval data) require decisions about the classes into which the data are to be divided for purposes of mapping. Most programs give users the option of deciding class intervals and have default options which will always provide a standard solution if an alternative is not specified. Standard statistical information, such as mean and standard deviation, and a histogram of values are often provided but this information is not available until the map has been made. Most programs also specify a standard symbolism in default of any instructions to the contrary.

A large proportion of the maps which have been made by means of the SYMAP program consist of isoline maps. In part, this emphasis on isoline maps was a consequence of the fact that earlier versions of the program did not have an option for the production of conformal maps, but the relative cheapness of isoline maps produced by this program has probably also played a part. Such maps have the advantage that they simplify complex data and so facilitate their interpretation. They also avoid the difficulties that arise where boundaries of administrative areas are either unknown or known only with some degree of uncertainty, or where it is not desired to draw attention to the data zones as such. On the other hand, the method exaggerates the importance of isolated anomalous values and is unsuitable where there are marked differences between adjacent areas. In any case, such maps can be drawn much more accurately on digital plotters, for which large numbers of contouring programs exist and where the step size is sufficiently small to give the illusion that lines are, in fact, smooth. By contrast, the line printer, though inappropriate for the representation of lines, is both fast and efficient at shading areas, a task which plotters perform slowly. From this point of view, there is much to be said for using line printers mainly to produce choropleth maps. Such maps also simplify patterns of distribution and appear to be more readily interpreted by those who have little experience in using statistical maps. These maps can, either from boundaries shown on the map or from a transparent overlay, also provide information about specific areas. The method has certain weaknesses, deriving in part from the variable size of administrative areas, but these are as much deficiencies of data as of method. Indeed, in at least some instances maps produced by line printer are more appropriate to the data being mapped than are similar maps drawn by the hand of a skilled draftsman. In British agricultural and forestry statistics, for example, operating units frequently overlap the boundaries of administrative areas so that the data nominally attributed to one area in fact be located in another (Coppock, 1960, 1965). A line-printer map on which boundaries are merely implied at the change from one symbol to another is in many ways a more correct representation of such data than a hand-drawn map on which boundaries are shown precisely by firm black lines.

It is clear that the majority of maps produced on line printers serve two main functions; either as working maps for use by geographers, planners, and others concerned with spatial data, or as maps to display information to others, whether these be policy makers or the general public. The value of line-printer maps to serve the first function is not in doubt and it seems likely, from the experience of a few centers, that the total number of such maps which have been produced by line printers must run into hundreds of thousands. Such maps can provide an initial view of the spatial aspects of a problem, test the consequences of a hypothesis and show where it fits well or badly, suggest possible explanations or factors which have been overlooked, and project existing trends into the future. Provided that the analyst himself can read and interpret the maps, their esthetic quality is of minor importance. Indeed, there are obvious practical advantages in speed and cost if simple maps are produced on which outlines are only approximate, no overprinting is used, and the boundaries of the map are contained within a single width of output paper. There is a danger that the ease with which such maps can be produced in alternative versions, at different scales and with different class intervals, may, in the absence of firm control over the use of computer time, lead to wasteful overproduction. Even in these circumstances, the savings in the time of analysts may more than offset the additional computing costs.

Although the majority of maps made by line printer have probably been of this type, very large numbers of maps intended for a wider readership have also been produced, notably in reports to central and local governments. There is also a growing number of academic publications in which such maps occur, particularly atlases whose production is particularly suited to computer mapping. The first published atlas of line-printer maps appears to have been a mimeographed atlas of Ottawa-Hull (Taylor and Douglas, 1970), though a small number of copies of a privately circulated urban atlas appeared in 1969 (U.S. Bureau of the Census). The first printed atlas of maps produced on the line printer, also of an urban area, appeared in 1971 (Rosing and Wood, 1971). A second edition of an agricultural atlas of England and Wales, in which the hand-drawn maps of the first edition are replaced by line-printer maps, is in press (Coppock) and another agricultural atlas, of which Figure 1 is an example, is in an advanced state of preparation. A computer-generated population atlas of Great Britain is also being prepared. General purpose atlases of Kenya (Taylor, 1971) and Switzerland (Kilchenmann, Steiner, Matt, and Gätcher, 1972) have also appeared, with maps covering a wide range of topics.

The agricultural atlas of Great Britain, currently in preparation, merits special mention because the maps have been produced with the modified printer already discussed. At the scale at which they are run on the line printer, approximately 1 : 2,000,000 a map comprises about 10,000 characters, and each character location represents a 5 km by 5 km cell of the National Grid. The values given to these characters are derived from records for 12,761 civil parishes, the areas of which have been coded at a scale of approximately 1 : 400,000 and are represented by a map framework of about 600,000 characters. Values for each location on the map at the 1 : 2,000,000 scale have been computed by estimating, for those cells which contain parts of more than one parish, the proportions of that cell which can be attributed to each of the constituent parishes and calculating a value from the records of each parish. In computing these values, only a few lines of the map are read into core at any one time. This procedure, though providing only an estimate of the true value (which could be computed only if the data for individual holdings were available and their location known), is probably sufficiently accurate in view of the nature of the original data and the small number of class intervals on most choropleth maps.

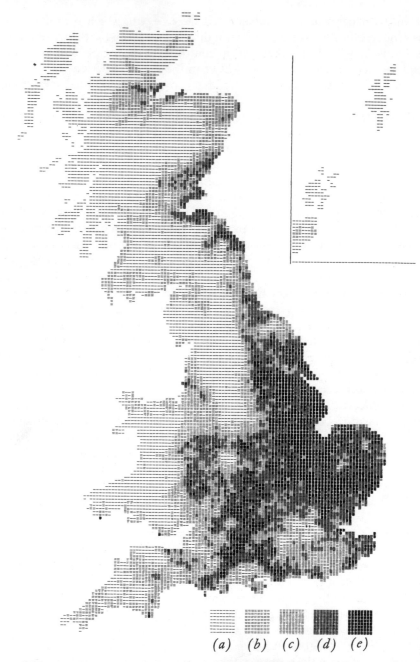

Figure 1   Percentage of all standard man-days on full-time holdings growing wheat in Great Britain in 1970. Source: Ministry of Agriculture, Fisheries and Food, and Department of Agriculture and Fisheries for Scotland.

Possible Improvements to Published Maps

There is little doubt that considerable scope exists for improving the quality of published maps produced on line printers. The first improvements are easily effected, since they are largely procedural. It is relatively easy to improve the method of selecting class intervals, by reading the results of computations onto magnetic tape or disk before any map is prepared, and printing a histogram of the values and other statistical indicators of their distribution, such as mean and standard deviation, as in Figure 2, taken from

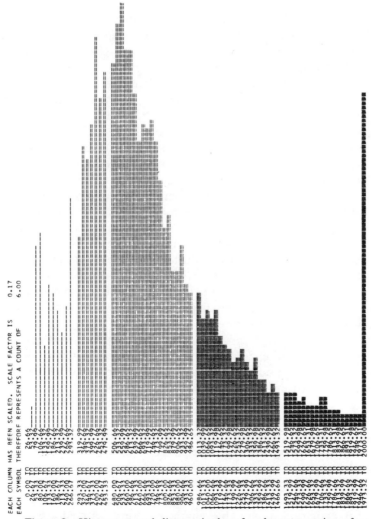

Figure 2   Histogram and diagnostic data for the preparation of a line-printer map of Scotland. Source: Department of Agriculture and Fisheries for Scotland.

data for a map of Scotland. With the help of such information, the map maker can then make a more rational choice of class interval before calling the mapping program and producing the map. Other simple improvements can be achieved by establishing good liaison with the staff of the local computing center. One of the weaknesses of maps produced by line printer is that the wear on printer ribbons is uneven because most numerical results are printed on the left. Printing is therefore not uniform across the printing area and the appearance of maps is often marred by vertical streaks. This difficulty can be avoided if computer operators can be persuaded to insert a new ribbon before batches of maps intended for reproduction are run. Alternatively, double sheets of paper interleaved with carbon paper can be used and the block made from the carbon copy, on which the appearance of characters is no longer dependent on the condition of the ribbon. Such a procedure was followed by Rosing and Wood (1971). A further administrative practice that greatly improves the quality of line-printer maps is the use of a heavy-duty plain paper in place of the much thinner lined paper normally employed.

Interpretation of line-printer maps will also be assisted by the use of overlays, showing road patterns, boundaries, and the like. Such information can be incorporated into mapping packages, being coded in the same way as the map framework, but lines showing roads and other linear features are not satisfactorily represented on line-printer maps. Such information can be more easily and effectively added by superimposing a transparent overlay containing such information at the stage of block making. Good examples of such overlays will be found in the atlas by Rosing and Wood (1971). Similarly, masks can be cut and superimposed during block making to sharpen outlines and give these a more realistic appearance. One kind of overlay superimposed on computer maps which has proved useful at Edinburgh is a map framework of urban areas, woods, rough grazings, and inland water, which can be used to suppress shading in those areas.

Further improvements can be achieved by better symbolism, for the characters on the print-chain or drum have not been selected for their cartographic quality. The modification made to the line feed of the 1403 printer at Edinburgh to provide the grid of square character locations had already made such changes desirable, so an attempt was made to devise a set of characters of more appropriate dimensions better suited to the needs of computer mapping. Preferably these would make overprinting unnecessary. Such aims, while easy to state, were difficult to satisfy. Special character sets can be made, but they are expensive and a much cheaper solution was found by selecting appropriate characters from the large number of special character sets which already exists. In practice, the freedom of choice was somewhat constrained. Suitable characters were selected from an IBM catalog, but these were available only in sets of three, so that it was necessary to accept many characters which were not wanted in order to obtain those which were required. The choice of characters was further restricted by the need to include the standard range of characters so that text and numeric information could be printed. Figure 3 shows some of the special characters available on this print chain. The top line includes those produced by over-printing; the remainder are individual characters. The standard IBM printer has 240 characters arranged in four sets of sixty. Any smaller number of sets will reduce the speed with which the printer operates, so an acceptable compromise was to have two sets of 120 characters. This special print-chain has led, in conjunction with the modification to achieve the square grid, to a considerable improvement in the quality of the maps produced by line printer though at the cost of some reduction in the speed of printing. Even this disadvantage is of only minor importance because the results of computations are written onto magnetic tape and printed offline at appropriate opportunities.

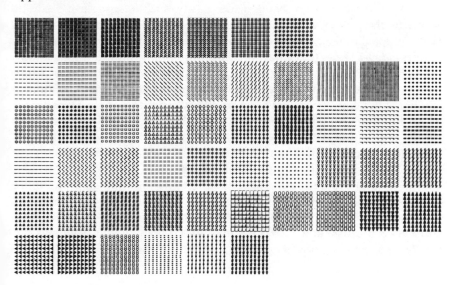

Figure 3 Selected symbols from special print-chain in use with an IBM 1403 line printer at the Regional Computing Centre, Edinburgh.

A further weakness of line-printer maps intended for reproduction is the quality of the lettering produced on the map. Necessary lettering includes information on the map itself (place names and the like), marginal information such as the title of the map, the key to the shadings selected, and the scale. Such lettering has two major weaknesses; it can only be arranged horizontally or vertically (the latter is not very satisfactory because it cannot be read in the normal way) and is restricted to the size of the characters on the print chain which are normally too small, especially after reduction. There are at least four possible solutions to this difficulty. One, used in the SYMAP program, is to construct letters of a size appropriate to the scale at which the final map will be printed by combining characters, coding these in much the same way as census tracts are coded. Coding letters is laborious, and although this procedure has the practical advantage that common information is readily repeated on any maps of the same series and that map and title cannot become separated, the results are not visually satisfactory. Another solution is to add such information by hand before plates or blocks are made, using either lettering pens, adhesive characters, or strips of letters produced on a lettering machine. The last approach is most satisfactory because names can be easily moved and the most appropriate position found by trial and error. Hand lettering is, however, slow in relation to the speed of mapping. A third solution is that any common information to be shown on a range of maps should be drawn on a transparent overlay, which can then be used with the line-printer maps when the blocks are being made. Lastly, such lettering can easily be added by the printer when the map is being printed, a procedure which is being adopted in the printing of the second edition of the *Agricultural Atlas of England and Wales* (Coppock, in press).

One last method of improving the quality of line-printer maps is by the use of color. Colored maps are more readily accepted by those who are unfamiliar with maps, a view that is confirmed by experience in the Department of the Environment with LINMAP and COLMAP. Instead of printing all classes into which the data are divided on a single map, each is printed separately, together with appropriate registration marks, in the darkest tone available. All other information is omitted. Each of these "maps" is then used as a color separation for plate making. The resulting maps are more costly and cannot be produced as quickly as conventional line-printer maps. Their production for a report at Edinburgh, to be reproduced by offset litho, cost between £10.00 and £20.00 per map for computing and plate making, but the cost per copy was very small.

Conclusion

The chief advantages of the line printer as a mapping tool have been its wide availability, the ease with which maps could be produced, and the relatively low cost of such maps. It is difficult to achieve satisfactory comparable costings because of different policies on charging, but at the public service rates charged at the Edinburgh Regional Computing Centre, it has been possible to produce complex maps in batch mode at cost of between £0.50 and £2.00 per map. All these maps would have been more expensive by hand, and some, involving complex calculations on records for more than 12,000 parishes, would never have been attempted. There are, however, not only alternative means of producing maps automatically but also possible substitutes for the line printer itself. Increasing use is being made of visual display units, though their small size, the limited amount of information which can be displayed without excessive flickering, and the practical problems of producing hard copy are obstacles to their wider use. Incremental plotters are increasingly available at computing centers and many more maps will undoubtedly be produced on such equipment. Although it seems unlikely that other forms of printers will displace the line printer in the immediate future, a variety of relatively cheap electrostatic and jet printers are now appearing on the market, often with higher speeds and greater flexibility than the line printer. Computer typesetting, another alternative which produces maps of high quality and offers an immense range of characters and point sizes, is slow and equipment is not widely available, although this method has been used with COLMAP. When CRT display is further advanced, it can be expected to replace the line printer as a mapping device. For the present, most maps produced automatically are probably produced on line printers. While the traditional cartographer may sometimes look aghast at the resulting maps, it should not be forgotten that for many purposes they are sometimes more appropriate than those produced by conventional cartography. In many other instances, while the resolution of such maps is not good, it "is probably as good as is justified by the data" (Sawyer, 1960).

References

Bertin, J., 1967, *Semiologie graphique*: Gauthier-Villars, Mouton, 431 p.

Bishop, K. H., and S. C. Gibson, 1966, *Mapping by 1401 computer using MAP 01*: Subdivision of Transportation, Planning and Programming, New York State Dept. Public Works, Albany, New York, 64 p.

Cadbury, D. A., J. G. Hawkes, and R. C. Readett, 1971, *A computer-mapped flora. A study of the county of Warwick*: Academic Press, London, 768 p.

Casey, F. G., 1954, Punched cards print distribution maps: *Business, the journal of management in industry*, June, p. 67–69.

Coppock, J. T., 1960, The parish as a geographical-statistical unit: *Tidjschrift voor Economische en Sociale Geografie*, v. 51, p. 317–326.

Coppock, J. T., 1965, The cartographic representation of British agricultural statistics: *Geography*, v. 50, p. 101–114.

Coppock, J. T., 1969, An agricultural atlas of Scotland: *Cartographic Jour.*, v. 6, p. 36–46.

Coppock, J. T., in press, *An agricultural atlas of England Wales*, 2nd edition: Faber and Faber Ltd., London, 255 p.

European Economic Community, 1972, Illustration cartographique de données au niveau région: Comité de Statistique Agricole, Office Statistique, Analyse et études, *Doc. F/SB/169*, 101 p.

Forbes, J., 1969, A map analysis of potentially developable land: *Regional Studies*, v. 3, p. 179–195.

Gaits, G. M., 1969, Thematic mapping by computer: *Cartographic Jour.*, v. 6, p. 50–68.

Hägerstrand, T., 1955, Statistiska primäruppgifter flygkartering och "data processing" maskiner: *Meddelanden fran Lunds Universitets Geografiska Institution*, No. 344, p. 233–255.

Hedbom, O., 1962, From manual to automated plotting on thematic maps: *Inter. Yearbook of Cartography*, C. Bertlesmann Verlag, Gütersloth, v. 2, p. 147–150.

Hotson, J. Mc. G., unpublished manuscript, CAMAP: Dept. Geography, Univ. Edinburgh, 4 p.

Kilchenmann, A., D. Steiner, O. F. Matt, and E. Gätcher, 1972, *Computer atlas of Switzerland*: Kummerley & Frey, Bern, 72 p.

Perring, F. H., and S. M. Walters, eds., 1962, *Atlas of the British flora*: Thomas Nelson and Sons, Ltd., London, 432 p.

Rosing, K. E., and P. A. Wood, 1971, Character of a conurbation. *A computer atlas of Birmingham and the Black Country*: Univ. London Press Ltd., London, 126 p.

Sawyer, J. S., 1960, Graphical output from computers and the production of numerically forecast or analyzed synoptic charts: *Meteorological Magazine*, v. 89, p. 187–190.

Sinton, D., and C. Steinitz, 1969, *GRID: a user's reference manual*: Laboratory for Computer Graphics and Spatial Analysis, Graduate School of Design, Harvard Univ., Cambridge, Mass., 19 p.

Taylor, D. R. F., 1971, *A computer atlas of Kenya*: Dept. Geography, Carleton Univ., Ottawa, Canada, 121 p.

Taylor, D. R. F., and D. H. Douglas, 1970, *A computer atlas of Ottawa–Hull*: Dept. Geography, Carleton Univ., Ottawa, Canada, 72 p.

U.S. Bureau of the Census, 1969, Census use study: computer mapping: *Rept. No. 2*, Washington, D.C., 44 p.

Waugh, T. C., 1972, The choropleth mapping system: Edinburgh Regional Computing Centre, Edinburgh, Inter-Univ./Research Centre Series *Rept. No. 7*, 118 p.

Additional reading

Useful bibliographies will be found in D. R. F. Taylor (1971) and in H. Goldstein and J. Wertz with D. Sweet (1969), *Computer mapping; a tool for urban planners*: Battelle Memorial Inst., Urban Studies Center, Cleveland, Ohio, p. 24–30.

Computer Science Aspects of the Mapping Problem

J. A. B. Palmer

This presentation was initially planned as a discussion of many areas in which mapping processes have been automated. However, it became apparent that emphasis should be placed on data structures, especially high level data description. The success in managing data of megabyte dimensions determines whether a large-scale computer graphics system will stand or fall. The requirements of large-scale systems will be examined by looking closely at low levels of data storage and then examining systems of successively increasing complexity.

The methods by which line data are stored are subject to considerations of the eventual use of the data. Generally the intention is to output the data sequence in graphic form as an end product. In this case, the problems are (*a*) to hold the data in minimal storage and (*b*) to present it to the output device in the format needed (that is, to decode it). Preceding this, of course, it is necessary to process the data from the input device to the storage stage. This, however, is the most superficial aspect of the problem.

The interest develops with the need to operate on the data: to store it so that it may be easily manipulated and implicit information may be extracted readily. The sophistication of the method of storage depends on the difficulty of answering the questions posed. Beyond this are the difficulties of access generated by sheer volume of data. Even the most sophisticated technique for some process must be backed up by an overall organization of subtlety and complexity in order to provide a practical degree of access to relevant parts of the data. This is the field of data base management.

Three levels of organization exist in data management: encoding (and conversely, decoding), processing, and organizing. The progression is of increasing complexity and magnitude of concept.

Storage of Line Data

A successful scheme for economical storage of line data must take into account the nature of the data and the resolution required. For example, if all lines in the data set are analytic, then storage of parameters and a routine for generation are likely to be the most efficient. This generally is the case in computer-aided design where, for example, complex surfaces may be represented by Coons patches. However, such methods have not been generally successful in mapping and lines must be represented by strings of coordinate pairs sufficiently close to give the required resolution.

Encoding

Freeman (1961) wrote the premiere article, "On the encoding of arbitrary geometric configurations", twelve years ago. It contains the justification for straight line approximation to an arbitrary curve, which is demonstrated by looking at an arbitrary curve in parametric form, $x = x(t)$, $y = y(t)$, in order to employ single-valued representation. Fourier transforms will give their frequency spectra, from which the sampling interval necessary to achieve a specified precision may be determined. Then, it is possible to consider methods of efficient data representation where the criterion of efficiency is compactness.

From this comes the well known rectangular grid, with lines represented by two types of vectors, diagonals being $1/\sqrt{2}$ and orthogonals 1. The convenience of this form outweighs the difficulties caused by different vector lengths. Representations with vectors of equal length include the four vector orthogonal and six vector triangular representations. These have the advantage of being unchanged under rotational transformation, but have few other advantages. The triangular form requires six vectors, and its binary representation will be unsaturated. With eight vectors, an arbitrary curve may be represented by a string of digits from zero to seven, that is, by three-bit bytes (Figure 1). This yields a relative representation of a curve. In contrast,

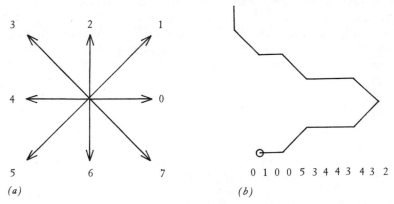

(a)   (b)

Figure 1   Chain encoding (Freeman). Digital representation of eight basic vectors and an example of a continuous line segment stored as a sequence of digits.

an absolute representation of each point to a precision of 0.001 over a given area requires 20 bits per point instead of three. However, there can be instances where absolute representation may be preferable. For example, a point on a line can be located without having to trace back along the line to its origin. Also, if the curves are all straight lines, absolute representation may be more compact.

Investigating further compaction, Freeman suggests that straight lines be represented by generating functions. He demonstrates the ease with which the properties of line length, closure, and area may be extracted. To say that Freeman encoding of lines is the basis of most subsequent graphic work is an overstatement. Nevertheless, the implications of his method of line storage have an effect at many different levels of application.

Freeman did not specify the algorithm now commonly used for performing encoding. That is, given a straight line, construct the sequence of vectors by which it may be approximated most closely. This appealingly simple algorithm was published by Bresenham (1965). The core of the procedure is shown in Figure 2. In the first octant, generate a Freeman chain having the best approximation to a straight line from the origin to (a, b), where a and b are integers. To do this, set a parameter, d, to the value $-a$. Then successively

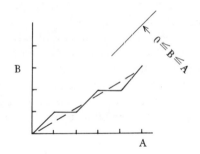

Move from $(0, 0)$ to (A, B)

$$D \leftarrow -A$$

$$D \leftarrow D + \begin{cases} 2(\text{B-A}) & \text{IF } D \geq 0 \\ 2\text{B} & \text{IF } D < 0 \end{cases}$$

$$\begin{cases} \text{DIAG IF } D \geq 0 \\ \text{AXIS IF } D < 0 \end{cases}$$

Move

A TIMES

Figure 2   Bresenham's algorithm for generation of an approximation to a straight line by chain-encoded vectors, shown here for the first octant.

increment d, a times, by a step of size $2b$ if d is negative, or $2(b - a)$ if not. (In this octant, a is greater than or equal to b, so the first step is positive, the second negative.) After each step, increment the chain parallel to OX if d is negative, diagonally if d is positive. After a steps, the point (a, b) will be reached. The scale setting, integer approximation, and octant determination that precede each generation of a segment make the routine appear formidable, but examination of the instructions will reveal that this algorithm is implemented in virtually every computer system for digital plotting.

Boothroyd and Hamilton (1970) pointed out that Bresenham's algorithm can generate slightly different lines in opposite octants and showed how to correct this. Pitteway (1967) developed Bresenham's algorithm so that approximations to conic sections can be produced without much more complexity.

Compaction

Chain-encoded lines are suitable for output on mechanical devices. However, while it is an efficient form of storage for arbitrary curves, it is not efficient for straight line data. With plotting devices of high resolution, larger numbers of increments are needed to generate better approximations to straight lines. The situation develops where the program specifying the output remains unchanged, the same picture looks better, and intermediate storage is increased. Mass storage is an expensive resource to devote to a slow peripheral device such as a plotter, so perhaps it would be more economical to retain absolute coordinates for intermediate storage. Hanlon (personal communication, 1971) has implemented the following compromise (Figure 3) employed in routines written at the Division of Computing Research, CSIRO. All plot files are held as 12 bit bytes, representing relative coordinates.

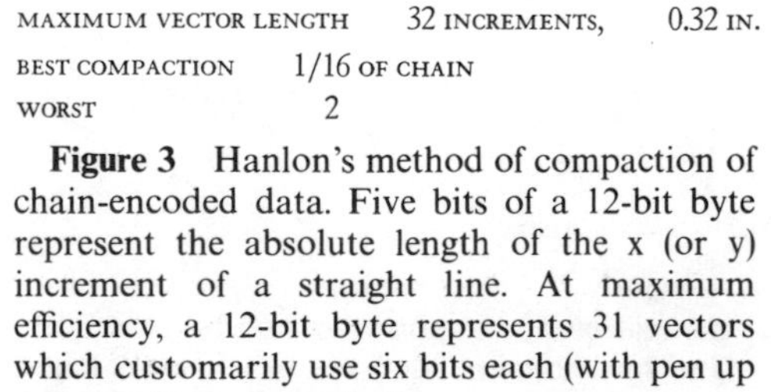

VARIABLE LENGTH RELATIVE

C.S.I.R.O.   12 BIT BYTES,   .01 IN. PLOTTER

$$1\;0\;0\;0\;0\;0\;1\;0\;0\;0\;0\;0$$
$$\uparrow \overbrace{\qquad X \qquad} \uparrow \overbrace{\qquad Y \qquad}$$
$$\text{SIGN X} \qquad \text{SIGN Y}$$

MAXIMUM VECTOR LENGTH   32 INCREMENTS,   0.32 IN.
BEST COMPACTION   1/16 OF CHAIN
WORST   2

Figure 3 Hanlon's method of compaction of chain-encoded data. Five bits of a 12-bit byte represent the absolute length of the x (or y) increment of a straight line. At maximum efficiency, a 12-bit byte represents 31 vectors which customarily use six bits each (with pen up and pen down character).

Each byte can represent a vector of length ± 31, in x and y (-0 is used to indicate "raise pen"). For straight line data, this form of compaction is 16 times as efficient as straight Freeman code. At worst, it is twice as bad. In practice, it averages better than four times as good. The compact representation is generated by the plotting routine, and is decoded by the plotter driver in bytes the size of the plotter hardware buffer.

Among other methods of compacting line data, Pfaltz and Rosenfeld (1967) suggested an interesting form of representation of closed curves that they term "skeleton encoding". A region with an implied boundary is represented by covering it with a matrix of points (Figure 4). Then, a neighborhood of radius r about a point (P, Q) is all points within a Manhattan

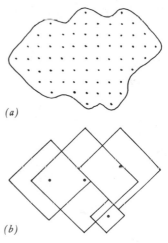

(a)

Figure 4   Skeleton encoding (Pfaltz and Rosenfeld). The area is covered by four squares; hence it can be represented by the coordinates of their centers and the lengths of their diagonals.

(b)

3,(5,5);   4,(8,5);   1,(10,2);   3,(11,6)

distance of (P, Q). This defines a square neighborhood, because the Manhattan distance is the sum of the absolute x and y distances between two points. The region, and implicitly its boundary, is completely described by the centers of the maximal regions and their radii. Skeleton encoding may show to advantage where containment within a region is required. Containment or exclusion can be determined by very simple tests of each center and radius.

Deecker and Penny (1972) have studied the comparative effectiveness of three methods. They give examples of retrieval with criteria of increasing stringency. Vector approximation using variable-length relative vectors is shown to be the ultimate winner.

Map Storage

Having considered basic forms of line data storage, the storage of more than one line, or a complete map, must be examined. Amidon and Akin (1971) consider the problem of compressing a map of lineal data. They start with an initial representation in the form of areal data. This is scanned by a raster. The resulting string is compressed into number pairs that represent value, and the number of times that value occurs. Different methods for compressing the string are tested. They try four directions of scan and expect to find, if the data have any degree of preferred orientation, that the code will provide efficient compression over the areal data (Figure 5). From a number of trials

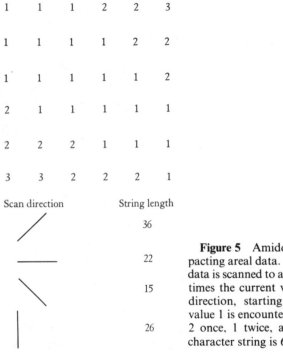

1	1	1	2	2	3
1	1	1	1	2	2
1	1	1	1	1	2
2	1	1	1	1	1
2	2	2	1	1	1
3	3	2	2	2	1

Scan direction   String length

36

22

15

26

Figure 5 Amidon and Akin's method of compacting areal data. For each of four directions the data is scanned to and fro, counting the number of times the current value is repeated. For the first direction, starting at the top left corner, the value 1 is encountered six times successively, then 2 once, 1 twice, and so on. The representative character string is 61 12 21 22 31 12 . . . .

the extent of compression was found to vary from 3 to 95 percent. Variation in the amount of compression is expected because some maps contain more information than others. However, there is no indication how maps stored in this compact form may be used.

Consideration must now be given to problems of retrieval. Magnetic tape is an inefficient medium for the simple storage of maps; microfilm, for example, is more compact, accessible, and cheaper. The important factor is not storage itself, but the automation of interrogation and manipulation. To use maps for selective extraction of data, to seek otherwise unobtainable answers to questions about the map, the data must be not merely stored but structured as well. Unstructured graphic data is useful merely as an intermediary phase to output or from input.

A process for manipulating and examining chain-encoded data directly has been developed by Morse (1968). The basic entity of his data structure is a contour, which is a closed curve. The closure restriction enters into many structures describing line data. Its advantages, which reflect a form of homogeneity, are such that it is worth creating closure artificially. The boundary becomes an essential part of a map, as it is of necessity closed. Contours which are not closed but intersect the edge are said to be closed by inclusion of part of the map boundary. At a higher level, a map has no edge, but in the hidden structure of the data base the separate sheets are as distinct as pages in an atlas.

A contour is represented by a chain of elementary vectors starting from some arbitrary point and continuing around to complete the closure (Figure 6). Redundancy is included to achieve an explicit description. Closure of the contour is indicated by a pointer to the address of the beginning in the row following the end. Similarly, immediately preceding the beginning

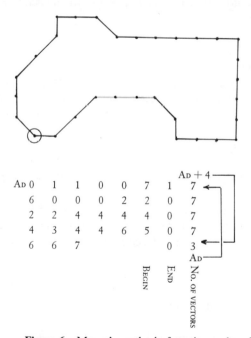

AD	chain vectors					BEGIN	END	NO. OF VECTORS
AD 0	1	1	0	0	7	1		7 ← AD + 4
	6	0	0	0	2	2	0	7
	2	2	4	4	4	4	0	7
	4	3	4	4	6	5	0	7
	6	6	7				0	3 ← AD

Figure 6 Morse's method of storing a closed contour to enable easy recovery. The first seven characters in a word are the chain vectors. The next two indicate beginning and end, and the last is the number of vectors in the word. The word beyond the block points to the start if it is, as in this case, closed, or to another block if that represents a continuation of the contour.

is a pointer to the end. The advantage of these pointers is that a contour may be segmented rather than stored contiguously. This is done where a contour is not actually closed but the closing segment is part óf the boundary. When the map is joined to the next sheet, the pointers are altered to match another artificially closed segment on the adjacent sheet. This sheet in turn may consist of more than one segment. The structure is not, as it stands, sophisticated enough to have more than one contour share the same boundary.

To integrate each contour into a map, hierarchies of tables are used. Each contour is identified by a line in an identification matrix. This matrix contains the address of the start, the absolute coordinates of the starting point, and its identification (that is, what it represents, usually height). These rows are ordered into ascending height; at the head of the hierarchy is a table of "headcells" containing the number of rows with the same identification, and the address of the first row. This is fairly straightforward data structure that enables contour lines to be readily accessed and traversed. It should be noted that there is no attempt at compression, as the scheme is designed to allow rapid access.

Use of Stored Contours

An intriguing problem is the determination of a flight path that avoids terrain greater than a certain elevation. In a non-computer world this might be examined by trying to appropriately position a ruler across a map. Morse (1969) discusses some of the implications of such a task. Basically, the existence of a specified path with respect to regions, or contours, depends on the topology of the regions. There may be many paths that go from one region to another across terrain which does not exceed the maximum allowable elevation, but a graph representation of the regions will enable the paths to be enumerated.

A map and the graph of its contours are shown in Figure 7. A graph is a data form particularly amenable to computer representation as a matrix (Figure 8) and paths through graphs can be determined by well known techniques. From the graphs, all the possible paths from one region to another can be enumerated in terms of their track sequences, where a track sequence is the list of contours that are crossed by the path. In this way, the feasibility of any path can be determined prior to more complex geometrical calculations.

On this map, if the requirement is to find a track sequence that does not include a contour greater than height 1, the only possible path is ABF. Regions bounding the permissible path are C and G. Only when the rapid topological tests have ascertained feasibility are the lengthier geometrical calculations undertaken.

For a flight path it will usually be necessary to find a straight line. Morse uses the term "maze" for the locus of straight lines that intersect certain

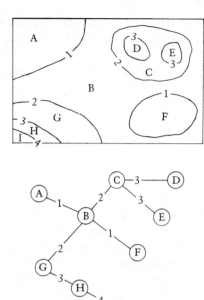

Figure 7 Graph representation of connectivity of regions (Morse). In the graph the regions are nodes, and the separating contours are the connecting arcs.

	A	B	C	D	E	F	G	H	I
A		1							
B	1		2			1	2		
C		2		3	3				
D			3						
E			3						
F		1							
G		2						3	4
H							3		
I							4		

Figure 8 Matrix representation of the graph in Figure 7.

contours and not others. One maze intersects F and avoids C and G. Another avoids C and G and intersects A. The intersections of these areas define a flight path.

In a large map there may be many feasible paths, and a workable search technique is necessary to avoid trying every one sequentially until success is achieved. A strategy suggested by Morse is to always take the alternate path leading to the region having the greatest area. Then, if a dead end is reached along that path, backtrack and try the path leading to the next largest area.

Region Boundaries

A more general method is due to Cook (1967) of the CSIRO Division of Land Use Research in Canberra. His team is engaged in a large-scale investigation of the coastal region of southern New South Wales. Maps of regional boundaries and intersecting lines defining various topographic, economic, and social attributes are being digitized on a D-MAC table.

The D-MAC outputs on paper or magnetic tape the (x, y) coordinates of a point as it is moved over the surface of the table. The string of coordinates requires delimiters for eventual interpretation. These might indicate the beginning of a river, its end, the boundary of a lake, or a reset origin. The operator establishes a menu of delimiters, from which selections can be made by digitizing a specific point. One of the squares on the menu is "move the menu", so the operator can keep it very close to the area being traced.

Cook has developed the following method for holding line data, with its intersecting and overlapping regions, so that types may be extracted. First, certain concepts must be defined. A *boundary* is a line separating two regions and is composed of *edges*, which are straight lines joining points. A *junction* is a vertex with three adjacent boundary vertices. The complexity of relations between entities means that a hierarchical grouping of types is not relevant, so a structure modeled on Ross (1961) was employed.

The structure of the data, although not its full complexity, is shown in Figure 9. Two attributes of the entity "line" are shown. one topological, the other geometric. The first is implied by the pointers to the next line at a junction, always using the same rotational sense. The second is the pair of pointers to end points, which have absolute values of (x, y) coordinates and also the relative (chain-encoded) description of the line joining them as their attributes.

A region has associated with it a junction, which points to a line, whose topological properties enable the next line of the region's boundary to be selected. This well-structured data form enables properties of the entities and their relations to be extracted directly without the need for searching and matching. The system of pointers implies in-core access, so a map of any appreciable size requires a large amount of core. Cook (personal com-

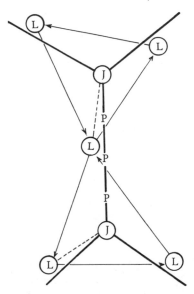

Figure 9 Cook's representation of plane region boundaries. L is a topological attribute of the entity "line", used to determine junction connections, and J is a geometrical attribute defining the position of a junction at the end of a line.

munication, 1972) deals with this by partitioning the map into what he terms "tiles", as the map density increases. Tiles in immediate use are in core; others are on the next level, which may be a drum or disk. A tile contains a limited amount of data. Consequently, the area covered by a tile depends on the density of information in the region which it covers.

The simple binary scheme used allows additions to be made to a map efficiently. When a tile passes a certain data limit, it is split into four. Each new tile is given a new index (Figure 10). This is an elementary tree structure, with terminal nodes easily accessible as the number of branches at intermediate nodes are always the same. The indexing also enables ready retrieval of adjacent tiles. Cook's scheme is large and general. It deals with the difficult problem of looking at lines which cross one another, are not closed, but which are distinguishable by their attributes.

Merrill (1973) developed a different structured form for data, which proves amenable to rapid extraction of features. The only entity used in the scheme is a closed curve, as is the case with the method of Morse. This does not rule out curves which cross the map boundary, nor different curves that intersect. In the first case the curve is closed by the map edge; in the second, a closed

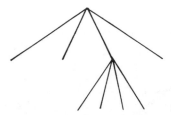

Figure 10 Subdivision of tiles (Cook) and the resultant tree structure.

curve is a complete entity, regardless of its position. Its relation with another closed curve will differ according to whether it intersects, touches, or has no contact with the other curve. In the intersecting case, for instance, the intersections can be extracted, but distinct entities such as junctions do not belong to the structure. The reasons for the type of structure adopted are suggested by an examination of the problem. Questions that might be asked of a map of closed regions are: (*a*) Containment. Is a point inside a region? Is a region inside another? (*b*) Intersection. Do two regions intersect? What is the region of intersection? (*c*) What is the area of a region? (*d*) What is its length? Area and length are straightforward in the most elementary form of storage, as Freeman pointed out. Containment and intersection are less obvious. The traditional method of finding whether a point is within a region is to draw a straight line from the point and count the number of intersections with the boundary. If this number is odd, the point is inside; if even, the point is outside. This is a non-trivial computer operation. Suppose, however, the map were scanned by a television raster. If the single sweep that contained the point were examined, then the analysis would be simple (Figure 11). We will consider an analog to this physical process.

The boundary is first accepted as a set of (x, y) coordinates, in the order that they occur in traversing the boundary. A scan is made with a horizontal line of constant y-value and a check is made on all extrema and inflections to insure that (*a*) extrema have even numbers of points, and (*b*) inflections have odd numbers of points. The original boundary is augmented where necessary during the scan to insure that these conditions are met. Thus, Figure 12 contains 17 points. Starting at the top there are two extrema;

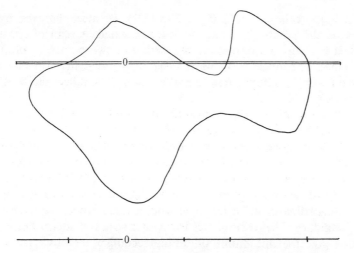

Figure 11 Principle of Merrill's contour storage. One straight line scan through a point and boundary intersections simplifies determination of inclusion/exclusion of the point.

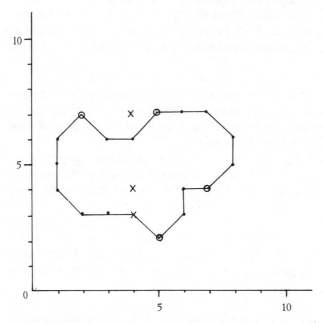

Figure 12 Tightly closed boundary (Merrill). Encircled points have been augmented for consistency of extrema and inflexions. The top line, L6, with y coordinate 7, has six x coordinates, x = 2 and x = 5 being augmented. The xs on the diagram are points used as examples in the text.

one is (2, 7), the other is (5, 7), (6, 7), and (7, 7). To meet the even number requirement, the points (2, 7) and (5, 7) are repeated. A scan of constant y on the next line shows a minimum, but with only two points, so no further point is added. The inflection (7, 4), (6, 4) has (7, 4) duplicated to make it odd. The minimum (5, 2) is duplicated to make it even. The inflection (4, 3), (3, 3), (2, 3) is already odd.

The duplicated points are indicated; this augmented form is called a "tightly closed boundary" by Merrill (1973). Augmentation is necessary for rapid distinction between inflections and extrema. The coordinate pairs are next sorted, first on the y-coordinate, then on the x. Finally, only the extreme values of x and y and y-partitions are stored, where a y-partition is the number of tightly closed boundary points that have the same y-coordinate, followed by their x-coordinates in order of ascending magnitude. These numbers define a boundary. The resemblance to a raster scan is evident. The extreme values that give the minimum containing rectangle are obviously advantageous for giving a quick negative result should that occur during a search.

Examples of the use of this method will be given, referring to Figure 12. Containment is determined by the following rule: A point (A, B) is in or on a boundary if there is a y-partition with y = B, with x contained in an odd–even pair. Thus point (4, 7) on scan line L6 is not contained in any odd–even pair, so it is outside. Point (4, 4) on L3 has its x-coordinate contained in the odd–even pair 1–6, so it is inside, as is point (4, 3) on L2, with 4 in the odd–even pair 4–6.

The extreme simplicity of this operation, which involves no arithmetic other than comparisons and table lookups, demonstrates the power of this data structure. It is evident that the determination of exclusion is the logical NOT of the same operation. The area is simply the sum of odd–even pair differences, with a small correction.

An interesting operation is to find the nearest point on a boundary, to a given point P. This is accomplished by finding the nearest y-partition. Next, find the nearest x in this partition, and compute the Euclidean distance D, from the point P. This narrows the search to all y-partitions not farther than D. Repeat for the next nearest y, and if a smaller D is found, reset D and the limiting y-partition. Continue until the limit is reached. As these examples illustrate, operations proceed by direct search rather than by geometric computation, and schemes for other operations can be similarly devised.

Problems of Data

At the third level of organization it is necessary to store and refer to, or retrieve, very large amounts of data. Problems of data structure may suddenly become much more important than they were at the lowest state.

It is possible that a low level organization of data has been implemented as a prelude to a much larger scheme with the attitude that a change in scale will not alter the total concept. Great ingenuity may be expended on implementing a system for graphic input and storage of maps. Once the input scheme is under way, with its methods of compression and extraction, volume production is planned with the thought that the programming is now finished in detail and extension to a further storage medium such as a disk file is all that is needed. If such a system is to be a success, however, the hardest part is yet to come. Questions that were asked of the trial system may have been answered readily enough, but extension to a medium with greatly increased access time multiplied by the greater lengths of search may produce a geometric deterioration in performance.

What questions are the most time-consuming and how likely are they to be asked? Consider the extraction of a digitized representation of a river system that extends over several sheets of a map. The initial organization should have provided the means for extracting properties of a line with this attribute. If each map out of several hundred has to be retrieved and examined merely to find the total length of a river system, the question will take minutes of computer time to answer.

Terminology in this field has yet to crystallize, but certain terms are now widely used and understood. This discussion is modeled on that by Engels (1972). Consider entities with attributes. An entity has a property and an attribute has value. The entity "town" has the property "name", and attributes such as population, area, rainfall, and altitude, each with a numeric value. Consider how such data could be stored. A data item could consist of town, population, area, rainfall, and altitude. Obviously, the data items could be stored sequentially, which is reasonable if the total size of data is small. A sequential data set is easy to maintain, an item to be added is simply put on the end of the sequence.

To use the file we must examine each entity until a match is found. If some items are used much more than others, they should be moved to the beginning of the file. Such an ordered file may be perfectly adequate for modest applications. On the other hand, suppose all towns in a county are required, with their associated attributes. A further level of organization at once suggests itself; the files should be ordered into sub-files of county. The county would have to be specified for the search, and a table of counties would have to be maintained with pointers to the start of each set of towns within that county. An alternative might be to classify according to first letter of name, although the resulting files might differ markedly in length. The organization would still be the same, with a table of pointers to sequential files.

This principle can be extended, with hierarchies of tables down to a final sequential file. This type of organization is called "indexed sequential". One problem is to make areas in the file large enough for future growth.

That is, to determine how much slack or free space must be carried. Provision must also be made for an overflow area and a mechanism for dealing with overflow.

A third-form, used for fast retrieval of frequently accessed data, is "hash" storage. Here the store address of the data item is derived directly from the property of the data item. The first n characters are called a number and that number is the address. The hashing function has to be designed to give an even distribution over all likely entities. If two entities have the same address, the synonym must be treated by an overflow mechanism just as with an excess in indexed-sequential storage. Storage and retrieval will be slowed by many synonyms, but fewer synonyms will absorb more waste space.

These procedures are all very simple, because only very simple use of the data has been considered. The reason is that all relations discussed so far are one-way. A town, for example, is at a specific altitude. But a further relation is implicit; within a certain altitude range, certain towns occur. With the data organizations described, the only way to answer a question such as "what towns lie within a certain range of altitude?" is by looking at every town. If a few such questions are asked, the system is saturated. This is what data organization really is about. The data should be structured so questions can be answered concerning relations when the relations are expressed in a form containing (*a*) the Boolean operators AND, OR, and NOT, and (*b*) certain functions such as COUNT, AVERAGE, SORT, and SUM.

A technique for organizing data with requisite structure is "file inversion". Figure 13 shows an example of a file to be inverted. The file contains the attribute values of districts. The property of the entity *district* is its name.

ATTRIBUTES OF DISTRICTS,	DISTRICT	REGION	POPULATION	CLASS			
RAINFALL	CLASS	FOREST	PERCENT	MEAN	ALTITUDE		
1901	F	1000	5	45	4000		
2283	W	15000	25	5	1500		
2497	N	1000	15	10	2000		
3301	NW	1000	15	15	2000		
6610	F	0	5	15	4000		

Figure 13   A data file of attributes of districts.

The values of its attributes are given explicitly here. Actual data would, of course, be stored more compactly. For example, there might be 20 logarithmically ascending population classes, so the highest value of that attribute would be 20.

Figure 14 is the inverted file. The population class 1000 has three entries. In this simple example of five districts, any of the apparently variable-length items can be represented by bit strings. A 1 denotes the presence of a specific

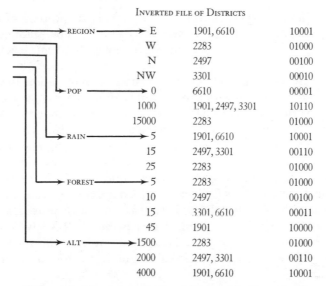

INVERTED FILE OF DISTRICTS

REGION →	E	1901, 6610	10001
	W	2283	01000
	N	2497	00100
	NW	3301	00010
POP →	0	6610	00001
	1000	1901, 2497, 3301	10110
	15000	2283	01000
RAIN →	5	1901, 6610	10001
	15	2497, 3301	00110
	25	2283	01000
FOREST →	5	2283	01000
	10	2497	00100
	15	3301, 6610	00011
	45	1901	10000
ALT →	1500	2283	01000
	2000	2497, 3301	00110
	4000	1901, 6610	10001

Figure 14 The inverted file of Figure 12 (Engels). The right-hand column indicates presence/absence of attributes.

attribute value for a particular entity, and a 0 its absence. We may ask a typical question,

"What districts with population ≥ 1000 have ≥ 10 percent forest?"

The part ≥ 10 percent means in this instance 10 percent OR 15 percent OR 45 percent. As the subsets are ordered, this process is to OR all sets from a certain point. That is,

$$00100 \text{ V } 00011 \text{ V } 10000 := 10111.$$

If we now AND the population string with the ORed strings of forest, the result will emerge from the data with a few simple logical operations (Figure 15). You may check that this is so by a sequential search of the original file.

WHAT DISTRICTS HAVE POP $\geq$ 1000 AND FOREST $\geq$ 10

	1901	2283	2497	3301	6610
POP 1000	1	1	1	1	0
FOREST 10	1	0	1	1	1
LOGICAL AND	1	0	1	1	0
RESULT	1901,	2497,	6610		

Figure 15 Answering a question concerning presence of certain attributes by ANDing two bit strings from the inverted data file of Figure 14.

Inverted files have their difficulties; the worst is the problem of updating. It may be necessary to reinvert them from time to time, since as the files grow, more time is consumed by increasingly frequent reaching into overflows.

A data base is a method of organization of information that enables questions to be answered with a minimum of effort. The actual organization of data on various levels of hardware is extremely complex. A high level language to describe the information relation is needed, from which the data base can be formed. Thus the idea of data independence may be achieved. Languages such as IMS and that of the Codasyl DBTG enable a structured data base to be organized on any installation on which the language is implemented. At the CSIRO Division of Computing Research, a group is implementing the Codasyl Data Base Task Group's proposals for data structure and manipulation. The first user is the CSIRO Division of Land Use Research, for the study of the New South Wales South Coastal region. This effort will demonstrate a practical test of the theories of graphical data organization.

References

Amidon, E. L., and G. S. Akin, 1971, Algorithmic selection of the best method for compressing map data strings: *Communications, Assoc. Computing Machinery*, v. 14, no. 12, p. 769–774.

Boothroyd, J., and P. A. Hamilton, 1970, Exactly reversible plotter paths: *Australian Computer Jour.*, v. 4, p. 20–21.

Bresenham, J. E., 1965, Algorithm for computer control of a digital plotter: *IBM Systems Jour.*, v. 4, no. 1, p. 25–30.

Cook, B. G., 1967, A computer representation of plane region boundaries: *Australian Computer Jour.*, v. 1, p. 44–50.

Deecker, G. F. P., and J. P. Penny, 1972, On interactive map storage and retrieval: *Canadian Jour. Operational Research and Information Processing*, v. 10, p. 62–74.

Engels, R. W., 1972, A tutorial on data base organization: *Annual Review of Automatic Programming*, v. 7, p. 1–64.

Freeman, H., 1961, On the encoding of arbitrary geometric configurations: *Inst. Radio Engineers Trans. Electronic Computers*, v. EC-10, p. 260–268.

Merrill, R. D., 1973, Representation of contours and regions for efficient computer search: *Communications, Assoc. Computing Machinery*, v. 16, no. 2, p. 69–82.

Morse, S. P., 1968, Computer storage of contour map data: *Proc. 23rd Assoc. Computing Machinery Nat. Conference*, v. 23, p. 45–51.

Morse, S. P., 1969, Concepts of use in contour map processing: *Communications, Assoc. Computing Machinery*, v. 12, no. 3, p. 147–152.

Pfaltz, J. L., and A. Rosenfeld, 1967, Computer representation of planar regions by their skeletons: *Communications, Assoc. Computing Machinery*, v. 10, no. 2, p. 119–122.

Pitteway, M. L. V., 1967, Algorithm for drawing ellipses or hyperbolae with a digital plotter: *Computer Jour.*, v. 10, p. 282–289.

Ross, D. T., 1961, A generalised technique for symbol manipulation and numerical calculation: *Communications, Assoc. Computing Machinery*, v. 4, no. 3, p. 147–150.

Relief Representation in Automated Cartography: An Algorithmic Approach

B. F. Sprunt

Relief representation in cartography will be considered in two forms, the planimetric relief map and the obliquely viewed relief diagram. Examples of techniques used to produce these forms manually are presented and discussed in many texts (Imhof, 1963, 1965). Attempts to automate these techniques with example maps and diagrams can be seen in more recent publications (Peucker, 1972; Tomlinson, 1972). This paper is an attempt to identify and formulate in a machine-independent way some of the basic algorithms used repeatedly to solve problems of relief representation in automated cartography.

There has been a tendency for publications to concentrate either on applications through descriptions of large computer-mapping packages or on data structure which is concerned with information coding, storing, and retrieving, with little reference to the links between the two. A gulf appears to exist between computer science and cartographic aspects of relief representation.

If a common data processing language for automated cartography were available, it would be easier to relate different projects in experimental cartography and to relate the whole field to work in other areas of computer graphics. An examination of algorithms in current use may point towards a basic structure for such a language. Relief representation is taken here as a case study.

Published works do not always include details of algorithms, so it is necessary to work mainly in terms of algorithms used by the author. This does not imply that they are necessarily original, optimal, or preferable in any sense; they are merely the most readily available at the time of writing. Most of these algorithms have been implemented as graphics exercises rather than as production programs for automated cartography.

Algorithms for Plotting

It is assumed that the available computer has a drawing device which responds to these two instructions:

MOVE (x, y)   which means move the drawing head from the current position to (x, y) without producing a line.

DRAW (x, y)   which means produce a continuous line from the current position to (x, y).

A map can then be produced by generating plotting lists of coordinate pairs to be processed by the following algorithm defining an operation G(L) where L is a list of lists $L = (l_1, l_2, \ldots, l_n)$.

G(L):

    G1.   Input next list $1 = [(x_1, y_1)(x_2, y_2) \ldots (x_r, y_r)]$

    G2.   MOVE (x_1, y_1)

    G3.   DRAW (x_i, y_i), $i = 2, r$

    G4.   If last list STOP else go to G1

If the list $[(x_1, y_1)(x_1, y_1)]$ is input a dot will be plotted.

    In addition to line work, the drawing device can be made to produce halftone effects by dot clustering. A fixed set of coordinates $C = (x_i, y_i)$, $i = 1, r$ is defined so the following algorithm produces a density level at the area element centered on (x, y) by plotting dots at a subset of C. It operates on a digital picture, $L = (x_i, y_i, k_i)$, $i = 1, n$, $0 \leqslant k \leqslant r$.

H(L):

    H1.   Input list $C = (x_i, y_i)$, $i = 1, r$

    H2.   Input next list element (x, y, k) from L

    H3.   If $k = 0$ go to H6

    H4.   Form the list $1 = \{[(x + x_i, y + y_i)(x + x_i, y + y_i)] \ldots\}$, $i = 1, k$ from list C

    H5.   G(1)

    H6.   If last list STOP else go to H2

Algorithms G and H can provide a wide variety of graphic effects for relief representation on most pen plotters. For CRT plotters, the list C may have $x_i y_i = x_{i+1} y_{i+1}$, $i = 1, r - 1$ to produce repeated exposure on reversal films (Schroeder, 1969).

Before developing programs for relief map and diagram production, a cartographic programmer must be familiar with graphic effects produced by G and H on his own computer equipment. He then can write programs to operate on input data lists to produce plotting lists which he thinks will achieve the required graphic images when plotted.

Input Data Lists

Input data are usually in the form of lists of coordinate triples (x, y, z) which locate points on the surface to be represented. They may be a systematic or random sample of points, or may be a set of lists representing digitized contours. The most convenient form for processing involves grouping of the triples in threes and ordering them to define a partitioning of the surface into triangles. For a random set, an algorithm which groups points into triangles in which the sum of the lengths of the sides is a minimum, and which gives each point approximately the same number of neighbors seems desirable (Bengtsson and Nordbeck, 1964).

Frequently, the data are processed as points over a rectangular grid $(x_{ij}, y_{ij})i = 1, n, \quad j = 1, m$. The following algorithm interpolates a point (x, y, z) at the center of each rectangle of the grid to partition the surface within the rectangular boundary into four triangles.

$T(i, j)$:

T1. Input $i, j, p_{ij}, p_{i,j+1}, p_{i+1,j}, p_{i+1,j+1}$ where $p_{ij} = (x_{ij}y_{ij}z_{ij})$

T2. $x = (x_{ij} + x_{i,j+1})/2; \qquad y = (y_{ij} + y_{i+1,j})/2;$
$z = (z_{ij} + z_{i,j+1} + z_{i+1,j} + z_{i+1,j+1})/4$

T3. Output list $(p, p_{i,j}, p_{i,j+1})(p, p_{i,j+1}, p_{i+1,j+1})(p, p_{i+1,j+1}, p_{ij+1})$
$(p, p_{i,j+1}, p_{ij})$ where $p = (x, y, z)$

T4. STOP

Digitized contours can be processed to produce data points over a rectangular grid by finding their intersections with grid-lines and interpolating with Lagrange and Hermite polynomials (Yoeli, 1967). Intersections with grid lines may be found using INTSEC described below.

Sometimes it is advisable to interpolate further within the basic grid to produce a finer mesh of data points. In this case some curve or surface fitting and interpolating routine may be selected from the many available. A simple algorithm for bridging the gap between two consecutive grid points on a profile is given as an example (Sprunt, 1969):

$F(i, k)$: (interpolates $k - 1$ points between y_i and y_{i+1} as $z_i, i = 3, k + 1$)

F1. Input $i, k, y_{i-1}, y_i, y_{i+1}, y_{i+2}$

F2.   Initialize: $p = 2$, $q = k + 2$, $z_i = 0$, $i = 3$, $k + 1$, $z_2 = y_i$, $z_{k+2} = y_{i+1}$, $z_1 = y_i - (y_{i+1} - y_{i-1})/2k$, $z_{k+3} = y_{i+1} + (y_{i+2} - y_i)/2k$

F3.   If $p + 1 = q - 1$ then $z_{p+1} = z_{q-1} = [3(z_p + z_q) - (z_{p-1} + z_{q+1})]/4$, go to F5 else $z_{p+1} = [3z_p - z_{p-1} + (z_q - z_p)(q - p)]/2$, $z_{q-1} = [3z_q - z_{q+1} - (z_q - z_p)/(q - p)]/2$.

F4.   If $p + 2 = q - 1$ go to F5 else $p = p + 1$, $q = q - 1$, go to F3

F5.   Output z_i, $i = 3$, $k + 1$ and STOP

Repeated applications parallel to the y-axis along grid lines, followed by applications parallel to the x-axis on original and interpolated data points will rapidly fill the interior mesh with points.

Fundamental Processing Operations

Assuming the data have been arranged in the form of a triangular partition of the surface, several commonly recurring operations may be used to process the triangular partition into the required plotting lists. Some of these are well known; for example, sorting a list on a given key or transforming coordinate lists to achieve projection onto a viewing plane for a given viewing point. The two quoted examples will be referred to as SORT and PROJ and will not be detailed here.

Another operation is used in many forms of relief representation and consists of finding the intersection of a list of line, area, or volume elements with a set of parallel equidistant planes. Denoting the operation as INTSEC(S, P) where S is the list of elements and P the set of planes, it may be expressed in its simplest form as an algorithm when S is simply one line segment in space, $S = [(x_1, y_1, z_1)(x_2, y_2, z_2)]$. $P = (a, b, c, h)$ is the set of planes a distance h apart and parallel to $ax + by + cz = 0$, a given plane through the origin.

INTSEC(S, P):

I1.   Input $S = [x_1, y_1, z_1)(x_2, y_2, z_2)]$ and $P = (a, b, c, h)$

I2. $S = [(z'_1, y_1, x_1)(z'_2, y_2, x_2)]$ where $z'_i = \dfrac{(ax_i + by_i + cz_i)}{\sqrt{a^2 + b^2 + c^2}}$,

       $i = 1, 2$

I3.   SORT(S) on z ascending

I4. $z'_i = z'_i/h$, $i = 1, 2$

I5. $j = \lfloor z_1 \rfloor + 1 ; n = \lfloor z_2 \rfloor - \lfloor z_1 \rfloor$

I6. If no more variables in S go to I8 else go to I7

I7. For next variable, w' in S form a new list $(w + s*dw) = W$, where $w = \lfloor w_1/dw \rfloor * dw$; $dw = (w_2 - w_1)/(z_2' - z_1')$; $s = 1, n$; go to I6.

I8. Output j, n, lists W and STOP

Note that $\lfloor k \rfloor$ indicates the greatest integer less than k. The algorithm may be implemented to take advantage of special cases:

(1) If the points in S lie in a line perpendicular to P, then the output will be simply j and n, indicating the range of intercepts on an integer scale.
(2) If the points lie in a plane perpendicular to P and parallel to the x-axis, then the output indicates the range together with a coordinate associated with each point of the range.
(3) In other cases there will be two coordinates associated with each point on the scale.

It is assumed that INTSEC will operate on lists of lists of S. For example, a list may define a polygonal boundary whose interior is to be shaded with parallel lines. One execution of INTSEC on the list will define the end points of the required shading lines.

Applications

Contour Maps

The plotting of isarithms by computer is well documented. The "contour map" as a form of relief representation is so familiar it has conditioned to some extent our perception of relief from maps. The basic idea of contour mapping is to plot the traces formed where a set of equidistant parallel planes intersect a surface. Several efficient algorithms exist to create these traces (Cottafava and Le Moli, 1969) and they may be easily adapted to produce other cartographic representations such as those produced by Tanaka's orthographical relief method (Peucker, 1972; Sprunt, 1972a).

If the data are presented as a list of lists A, output from algorithm T, three forms of maps may be created.

(1) "Horizontal" contour maps M, viewed on a horizontal picture plane from vertically above, are given by $M = PROJ[INTSEC(A, P_1)]$ where P_1 defines a horizontal set (Figure 1).
(2) "Oblique" contour maps M, viewed on a horizontal picture plane from vertically above, are given by $M = PROJ[INTSEC(A, P_2)]$ where P_2 defines an oblique set (Figure 2).

Figure 1   Horizontal contours, viewed on a horizontal picture plane from above.

Figure 2   Oblique contours, viewed on a horizontal picture plane from above.

(3) "Perspective" contour maps M, have an arbitrary viewing point and picture plane and are of two types:

$$M_h = PROJ[INTSEC(A, P_1)], \text{ with } P_1 \text{ a horizontal set,}$$

$$M_v = PROJ[INTSEC(A, P_3)], \text{ with } P_3 \text{ a vertical set.}$$

The latter projected profile method is the one in most common use. Strictly, the list A should have added to it the polygonal boundaries of the four sides of the surface and its base.

Hidden Lines

The problem of hidden lines in perspective contour maps is a particular case of the general hidden-line problem. For the purposes of this paper, a projected point (x, y, z) on a contour at level $z = z_r$ is visible if it is outside the union of the interiors of all projected contours at levels $z = z_s$ for $z_s > z_r$.

Let R_j be the projected interior of the jth contour. Assume the contours are sorted in ascending order by distance from the viewer so R_1 is the projection of the highest contour section in type M_h and the front contour in type M_v. We can then form $V_i = \bigcup_{j=1}^{j=i} (R_j)$, the required union or "cumulative mask". The piece of a projected contour interior which is hidden is $Q_i = V_{i-1} \cap R_i$. The visibility of (x, y, z) reduces to testing if the projection of a point is in a specified region.

Problems of union and intersection of two closed regions and point-in-region problems have recently been solved in a paper by Merrill (1973) using y-partitions of tightly closed boundaries. His idea may be extended to the regions enclosed by a projected contour and may be implemented in terms of the algorithm INTSEC. If $R = (R_i)$, $i = 1, n$ is the list of required regions,

$$R = \text{SORT}[\text{INTSEC}(\text{PROJ}\{\text{SORT}[\text{INTSEC}(A, P_1)]\}, P_2)]$$

Here, P_1 is a set of horizontal contour planes, and A, the partitioned surface as defined for perspective maps. The projection is arbitrary, P_2 being a set of planes perpendicular to the viewing plane and parallel to the x-axis in the viewing plane. The first sort orders on the basis of contour height, the second sort orders on y-values on the viewing plane.

It is also possible to define $V = (V_i)$, $i = 1, n$ as an operation CUMASK(R) using the algorithm described by Merrill (1973) for the union of two regions. Surface line information, presented as plotting lists B, may be processed in a manner similar to points on contours and visibility checked against a cumulative mask in V. When a run of one or more hidden points is found in a list in B, the points are deleted, the current list is closed, and a new list opened for subsequent points.

An alternative approach is to map hidden areas Q' on the digital model in a single forward scan of the input data list (Douglas, 1971) and to project and plot only $B \cap \bar{Q}'$.

NERC/Experimental Cartography Unit FORTRAN IV program BDPMK2 for drawing block diagrams (Sprunt, 1972a) uses x-partitions of vertical profile projections to solve the hidden-line problem, in common with many similar programs which have been in use since the early 1960s. Figure 3a shows typical output from BDPMK2, with horizontal contours

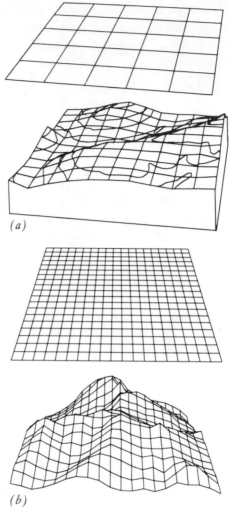

Figure 3   Block diagrams (a) with contours as additional surface information, (b) in typical "fishnet" form.

plotted as surface information. Figure 3b shows as a block diagram the surface used for all other figures in this paper.

Enhancement of the Relief Effect

Some experimental work on relief representation by computer has sought to enhance the relief effect conveyed by a contour map or diagram by the application of shading or the use of particular sets of surface lines.

Analytical hill shading has been successfully automated by calculating the light intensity $I = \cos(e)$, over a partitioned surface (Yoeli, 1967). The cosine of the angle e between the normal to a facet of the surface and the direction of illumination is calculated as follows:

For a surface (z_{ij}), $i = 1, n$, $j = 1, m$ and an illumination source with direction cosines S_x, S_y, S_z $Y(i, j)$:

Y1. Input $i, j, (z_{i,j}, z_{i,j+1}, z_{i+1,j+1}, z_{i+1,j}) = (H_A, H_B, H_C, H_D)$

Y2. $a_x = \text{const.}, a_y = 0, a_z = [(H_B - H_A) + (H_C - H_D)]/2,$

$\quad b_x = 0, b_y = \text{const.}, b_z = [(H_D - H_A) + (H_C - H_B)]/2$

Y3. $\cos(e) = \dfrac{S_x(a_y b_z - a_z b_y) + S_y(a_z b_x - a_x b_z) + S_z(a_x b_y - a_y b_x)}{\sqrt{(a_y b_z - a_z b_y)^2 + (a_z b_x - a_x b_z)^2 + (a_x b_y - a_y b_x)^2}}$

Y4. density $D = \log[1/\cos(e)]$

Y5. $H(D)$

Y6. If last facet STOP else go to Y1.

Yoeli used character overprinting in a line printer implementation of H, but the algorithm has been more recently implemented on a CRT display (Peucker, 1972).

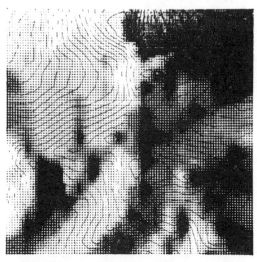

Figure 4 Relief shading with shadows, produced by overprinting.

Figure 5   Relief shading with alternative form of shadow production.

A similar form of rendering, which is not strictly hill shading, has been tried for relief enhancement in which shadows are incorporated (Sprunt, 1969) (Figure 4). In another scheme employed in the same project, cosine values from 0 to $(+\cos)_{max}$ correspond to densities 12 to 0, and cosine values from 0 to $(-\cos)_{max}$ correspond to densities 25 to 12 (Figure 5).

Another possible scheme using algorithm H for output is to process the surface list A through INTSEC as for the oblique contour method and use the number of contour crossings per facet as input to algorithm H. Tanaka (1932) indicated that the contour density was a reasonably good approximation to shadow density in this instance. Figure 6 shows a half-tone interpretation of this approach.

Relief contour methods (Tanaka, 1950) simulate the illumination and shadow effect of contours on an illuminated surface. Thickening of contours away from the light source has been automated by Peucker (1972). Figure 7 shows an example of this technique produced by the writer; Figure 8 shows the alternative form. Both methods use the sign of cos(e) in algorithm Y or its equivalent to determine orientation of facets.

Hachures may be produced in crude form (Figure 9) by the procedure, $M = \text{PROJ}[\text{INTSEC}(A, P_i)]$ where P_i is varied for each triangle in A. P_i is chosen as a vertical set of planes with the direction of P being perpendicular to the direction of horizontal contour segments for the current triangle. The value of h is given by $h_i = d \cot \theta_i$ where d remains constant for all triangles and θ_i is the inclination of the current triangle to the horizontal.

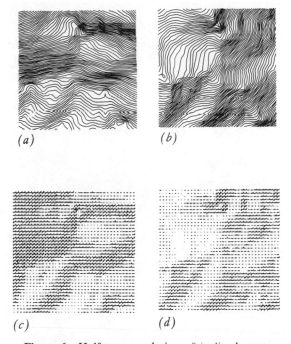

(a)   *(b)*

(c)   *(d)*

Figure 6 Half-tone rendering of inclined contour method.

Figure 7 Relief contours produced by thickening contours away from the light source.

Figure 8   Relief contours produced as light lines toward light source and dark lines away from light source.

Little work has been published on selection of an optimal set of lines for defining a surface. An artist achieves this selection instinctively and economy of line is a feature of the best manual relief representations. Certain optimal sets can be located automatically. Douglas (1971) enhances the appearance of perspective views by delineating boundaries between visible and hidden parts of a surface. A similar attempt was made by Sprunt (1969) on half-tone perspective views (Figure 10).

Course and ridge lines can be located and plotted using an algorithm which has been described for defining streams in simulation studies (Sprunt, 1972b). The surface is partitioned and the immediate neighbors for each point are located. For each point examined in turn, an immediate successor is defined as the neighboring point which is lower than the chosen point and which joins it with the steepest slope. This defines a partial ordering so that points on the surface can be subjected to a topological sort (Knuth, 1968).

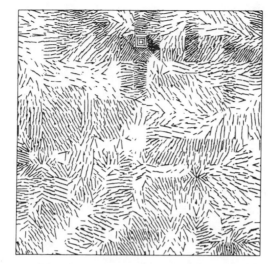

Figure 9 Hachures produced by automated procedure.

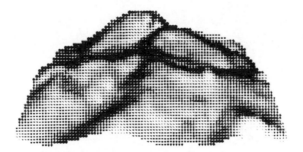

Figure 10 Half-tone perspective view with boundaries of hidden areas emphasized.

All points with more than a specified number of predecessors are linked to form the courses. By negating all z-values in A, and reapplying the algorithm, ridges can be defined.

Conclusions

There appear to be a few basic algorithms which, if incorporated in a suitable programming language, would allow relief maps to be generated by simple commands. It is suggested that this approach would produce greater flexibility and opportunity for creative use by cartographers than is currently available through general purpose packages. Further studies in this direction might bring to light a set of primitives which could form the basis for a special purpose computer language for automated cartography or a symbolic language for theoretical cartography.

Note on Illustrations

With the exception of Figure 3a which is a two kilometer square sampled over an 11 by 11 grid, all illustrations show an area approximately 1.2 kilometers square which was sampled over a 20 by 20 grid. The former has an elevation range of approximately 60 meters and the latter approximately 300 meters. For Figures 4, 5, and 10, algorithm F was used to interpolate to a 96 by 96 grid. Figures 1, 4, 5, and 10 were plotted on a SC4020 plotter; others were plotted on a drum-type incremental pen plotter driven by an ICL 4130 computer.

References

Bengtsson, B., and S. Nordbeck, 1964, Construction of isarithms and isarithmic maps by computer: *BIT*, v. 4, p. 87–105.

Cottafava, G., and G. Le Moli, 1969, Automatic contour map: *Communications, Assoc. Computing Machinery*, v. 12, no. 7, p. 386–391.

Douglas, D., 1971, VIEWBLOK: A computer program for constructing perspective view block diagrams: *Revue de Geographie de Montreal*, v. 26, p. 102–104.

Imhof, E., ed., 1963, *International yearbook of cartography*: George Philip and Son, London, 231 p.

Imhof, E., 1965, *Kartographische Geländedarstellung*: Walter de Gruyter & Co., Berlin, 425 p.

Knuth, D. E., 1968, *The art of computer programming*: Vol. 1, Fundamental algorithms: Addison-Wesley Publishing Co., Reading, Mass., 262 p.

Merrill, R. D., 1973, Representation of contours and regions for efficient computer search: *Communications, Assoc. Computing Machinery*, v. 16, no. 2, p. 69–82.

Peucker, T. K., 1972, Computer cartography: Assoc. American Geographers, Commission on College Geography, *Resource Paper No. 17*, 75 p.

Schroeder, M. R., 1969, Images from computers and microfilm plotters: *Communications, Assoc. Computing Machinery*, v. 12, no. 2, p. 95–101.

Sprunt, B. F., 1969, Computer-generated half tone images from digital terrain models: *MSc Dissertation*, Dept. Mathematics, Univ. Southampton, 80 p.

Sprunt, B. F., 1972a, Contours in perspective: Paper presented at Inst. British Geographers Annual Conference, Aberdeen, Scotland, 18 p.

Sprunt, B. F., 1972b, Digital simulation of drainage basin development, *in* R. J. Chorley, ed., *Spatial analysis in geomorphology*: Methuen & Co., London, p. 371–389.

Tanaka, K., 1932, The orthographical relief method of representing hill features on a topographical map: *Geographical Jour.*, v. 79, p. 213–219.

Tanaka, K., 1950, The relief contour method of representing hill features on a topographical map: *Geographical Review*, v. 40, p. 444–456.

Tomlinson, R. F., 1972, Geographical data handling: *Inter. Geographical Union Commission on Geographical Data Sensing and Processing*, Ottawa, 1350 p.

Yoeli, 1967, The mechanization of analytical hill shading: *Cartographic Jour.*, v. 4, no. 2, p. 82–88.

The Computer Version of Three Relief Representations

T. K. Peucker, M. Tichenor, and W. D. Rase

The cartographic representation of surfaces is of growing concern to many disciplines of the Earth and social sciences. Hand in hand with this goes the demand for methods which provide easier and quicker comprehension of the surface being displayed. One of the reasons for this expanding interest is the increasing number of instances where a rapid understanding of the surface features is required, even if this must be achieved at the expense of the precision of the surface representation. A road or street map, for example, gains little by the inclusion of contour lines as a driver can spend only a brief time searching through a set of isarithms.

The problem therefore is to present three-dimensional data with an immediate impression of depth and relative distance. This can be accomplished through different types of binocular and monocular vision. Binocular vision, although in many ways closest to the perception of an actual surface model, is inadequate for most applications since it requires special equipment and a setup which is too inflexible for many needs.

Three-dimensional impressions can be produced by several types of monocular vision: movement, one and two point perspective, differences in size, shades and shading, structure in the representation, hidden parts elimination. Automated graphic animation is not yet in a state which makes its use feasible as "three-dimensional maps". The components of perspective, differences in sizes, and visibility which are used in the production of block diagrams have the disadvantage that they may hide parts of the surface and produce varying impressions depending on the view angle.

Hill shading, on the other hand, offers many advantages and few disadvantages for the cartographic representation of surfaces. Maps of shaded relief are planimetrically correct; they are vertical views and therefore can be overlaid with any other information such as transportation networks, settlements, and so forth. They have the disadvantage of imposing a varying graytone on the map which makes other features stand out differently

187

depending on the intensity of the shading. However, there are solutions to this too.

Almost 100 years ago it was suggested by Wiechel (1878) that a method of hill shading could be based on a strict mathematical foundation by calculating the shading density on discrete points of the surface. Let ε be the angle between the normal vector to the tangential plane at a surface point and the beam of light. If the light intensity is I, then the illumination I_ε at a surface point is equal to the product of I times the cosine of ε.

$$I_\varepsilon = I \cos \varepsilon.$$

If a surface is white and perfectly matte, it reflects the same amount of light it receives. The ratio between light intensity and reflected light, $I : I_\varepsilon$, is the opacity. The shading intensity of a surface point or the shading density is the logarithm of the opacity,

$$D = \log \frac{1}{\cos \varepsilon}.$$

Wiechel suggested computing the shading density at discrete points, interpolating to produce a map of "isophots" (lines of constant shading), and consequently darkening the interval areas. Since at that time, the computation of even a very small number of densities was prohibitive, Wiechel suggested simplifications which all but negated the advantages of the method and reduced it to the traditional manual method.

Several attempts have been made to approach Wiechel's ideal formula by methods which maintained its precision but at the same time made the production of maps feasible. The most successful researcher is Kichiro Tanaka, who has developed three methods of analytical hill shading. Several computer-based approaches have also been produced, the ones by Yoeli being the most successful so far. Our attempts concentrated on a numerical and hardware improvement of Yoeli's approach and the computer implementation of two methods published by Tanaka. It will become clear that it is usually not satisfactory to duplicate a manual method by computer, but it is necessary to implement the basic idea.

Relief Contour Method

An increasing area of the Earth's surface is already recorded in machine-readable form as surface isarithms. Isarithms are the features most easily and accurately digitized with automatic coordinatographs, or digitizers. This is because it is only necessary to trace along a line and record locations at increments of movement through length of time. The relief contour method may therefore be useful for debugging purposes and creation of fast relief representations of digitized isarithms. For a better understanding of the procedure, and the necessary alterations for its usage with the computer, a short outline of Tanaka's (1950) method is in order.

The basis of this method is that an obliquely illuminated unit of surface reflects light according to its position with respect to the light source. This enables a numerical value of brightness to be defined for any point on the surface. If t is the thickness of the white or black contour lines, then:

$$t = t_0 \cos \theta$$

where θ is the angle between the direction of the light source and the direction of slope on the surface, and t_0 is the maximum thickness of the contour line. If the angle is less than 90°, the contour line is white, but if the angle is larger than 90° then the contour line is black. If we call d_0 the vertical difference between a pair of isarithms near a point, and γ the slope gradient between two isarithms in a small area, then the horizontal distance between two isarithms in this area becomes:

$$t_0 = d_0 \cot \gamma.$$

At this point, Tanaka introduces k, known as the "line factor", which gives a measure between the maximum thickness t_0 and the vertical distance between two isarithms d_0:

$$t_0 = k \, d_0.$$

The problem is thus reduced to finding the best value for k. Taking ρ as the relative brightness of the untreated surface or white contour line, ρ_0 as the neutral background or gray surface, and ρ' as the dark contour line, then

$$k = \rho_0/(\rho - \rho_0) \quad \text{and} \quad k' = \rho_0/(\rho_0 - \rho')$$

where k and k' are line factors for the light and dark contour lines, respectively. Tanaka suggests values between 1. and 2. for k, the first for very rough terrain, the second for very shallow terrain.

Tanaka employs a rather simple drawing method. A drafting pen is filed down so its thickness is equal to t_0, the maximum thickness of the contour line. This pen is then used with a fixed orientation equal to the direction of the light so that it thins out when θ approaches 90°.

The Computer Approach

Again, if d_0 is the vertical distance between two isarithms and t_0 is the maximum width of the black or white contour line, then:

$$t_0 = \cot \alpha \, d_0$$

where α is the elevation of the sun. If $\cot \alpha = k$, the line factor in Tanaka's work is the cotangent of the sun's elevation. It is important to choose k so that no shadows overlap. As an operational approach, the following method is suggested: Construct a profile of length T. Along this line, add up the elevation traversed (positive and negative), giving the total relief along the cross-section, D. If the isarithms were equally spaced along the profile, D/T would be the average gradient. In other words, each isarithm would cast a shadow exactly onto the next lower line. Thus a factor must be introduced which represents the proportion of t_0 which should be covered by the contour line. Here, this proportional factor is chosen arbitrarily. In order to obtain acceptable results over all of the map, the profile should be constructed in an area of very rough terrain which has a high density of isarithms. Thus,

$$t_0 = (Tp/D) \, d_0$$

where p is the proportionality factor.

Procedure. The program described makes the assumption that the light source is in the northwest and that each contour line is digitized sequentially with an indication whether the slope is ascending on the right or left of the line.

In the program, one segment of a contour line bounded by two neighboring points P_1 and P_2 is processed at a time. As each point on the contour line casts a shadow of equal length t_0, the thickness of the contour therefore depends on the direction of the segment. It must be decided, however, whether the line is to be drawn in white or black. For this, increments in the x-direction ($d_x = x_1 - x_2$) and in the y-direction ($d_y = y_1 - y_2$ are summed

$$d = d_x + d_y$$

		if this expression is	
		positive	negative
if the slope	right	white	black
ascends to the	left	black	white

In the case of a black contour, a point P_{s1} is constructed with the coordinates

$$X_{s1} = X_1 + \sqrt{t_0}$$
$$Y_{s1} = Y_1 - \sqrt{t_0}$$

In the case of a white contour, the signs are reversed. P_{s1} is a point along the outer rim of the shaded contour.

In this version of the program, no white contour is drawn although this could be introduced easily and would not take more time than that required for the additional drawing with a multi-pen plotter. Since blackening with the pen plotter consumes a large amount of plotting time, several options have been left open:

(1) t_0 is chosen relatively large,

$$\frac{D}{T} > t_0 > \frac{D}{2T}$$

and the boundary line for the contour is drawn with a dotted line. In this case, the shadow must be blackened by hand.

(2) t_0 is chosen relatively small,

$$\frac{D}{2T} > t_0$$

and the darkened line serves as a visual approximation of the shading. (3) a relatively thick pen is issued for drawing the isarithm and the procedure is rerun n times where

$$n = \text{integer } \frac{t_0}{p} + 1$$

and p is the pen width. In this case

$$\left. \begin{array}{l} X_{s1} = X_1 + i\dfrac{t_0}{p} \\[2ex] Y_{s1} = Y_1 - i\dfrac{t_0}{p} \end{array} \right\} \quad \text{for } i = 1, 2, \dots, n.$$

The procedure is programmed as a subroutine which processes one contour line at a time. This makes it very flexible and versatile. It has been used with digitized contour-line data and in connection with a general contouring program. Figure 1 shows an example from Banff National Park, Alberta. Scale is approximately 1:100,000.

Orthographical Relief Method

The orthographical relief method was considered by its two groups of authors to be a very fast and exact procedure, especially in comparison with vertical profiles. Its great advantage, however, was that it "permits construction of a perspective-like view of the terrain that is planimetrically correct" (Robinson and Thrower, 1957). Topographic features could be included without transformation, an orthographical relief map could be overlaid onto a topographic map of the same scale, and there would be no hidden areas, provided the surface had no overhanging parts.

The basic idea of this method is relatively simple. A surface can be intersected by a series of inclined planes, yielding the same number of isarithms (horizontal contours) as there are intersections of the planes with the surface.

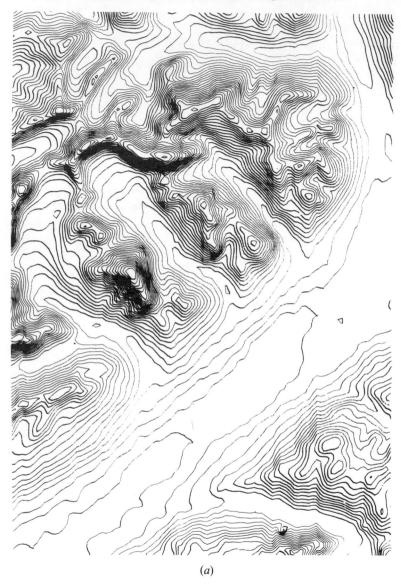

(a)

This produces a series of inclined planes with the same number of "inclined contours" (Tanaka, 1932) or "traces of parallel inclined planes" (Robinson and Thrower, 1969). The skill in application of the method lies in the selection of the density of traces, the dip of the planes, and the orientation of the azimuth.

The procedure is relatively fast and easy to perform, even by inexperienced draftsmen. Let the inclined plane have the angle θ, and let h be the distance

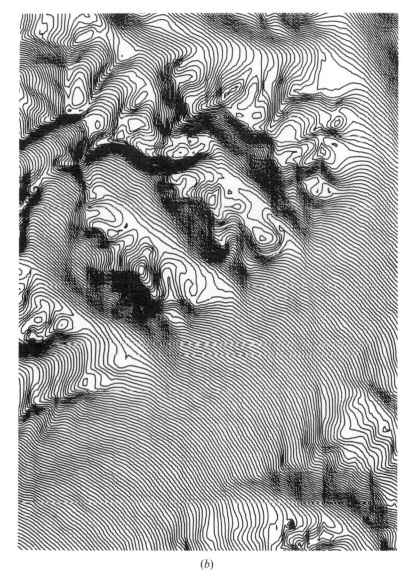

(*b*)

Figure 1 (*a*) Contour map of part of Banff National Park, Alberta. (*b*) Same area shaded by the relief contour method.

between each pair of horizontal contour planes. The intersection of the two types of plane will be a straight line with the orientation of the azimuth. Considering a set of horizontal planes, one inclined plane will produce a set of parallel lines with the spacing D, where

$$D = h \cot \theta.$$

Intersections of the isarithms with the straight lines give control points for the traces of inclined planes. If the inclined planes are arranged in parallel and at equal spacings of D, a series of traces can be drawn. Tanaka (1930) chose θ as 45°, assuming that sunlight would also fall at an angle of 45°. He used a closed succession of inclined planes and drew dense contours to give the impression of relief by means of light and shading. Robinson and Thrower (1957), on the other hand, used inclined planes with $\theta = 30°$. They also used fewer isarithms per height-unit, spacing the planes more widely. Their purpose was less to give the impressions of relief but rather "to define forms as they might be seen from an oblique view".

A strong critique of this method recently appeared, stating that "owing to the average viewer's preconditioning to vertical profiles, inclined contour maps are easily misinterpreted, and even the experienced map reader is not psychologically prepared to interpret surface form accurately from oblique sections" (Oberlander, 1968, p. 802). Robinson and Thrower (1957) had already eliminated this perceptual error by after-treating the inclined contours according to the illumination of the subarea. Lines were dashed in areas of a high light-intensity and intermediate lines were added in dark areas, assuming a light source in the northwest or west. It should be mentioned that this represents a logical contradiction to Tanaka's original method since it is based on two simultaneous light sources, one from the south and the other from the northwest or west. A more logical correction of the possible misinterpretation of inclined contours was already mentioned in a commentary to Tanaka's original article which suggested turning the map 135° clockwise.

It would be difficult to program the manual method without changes. Although intersection of contour lines with lines of constant y-dimension does not pose any conceptual problem, the tracing of inclined contours becomes a major task in the vicinity of ridge lines and river lines. There are two possible solutions of the "turning-point problem". Mathematical functions could be applied and the contour drawn accordingly. The results, however, could differ greatly from reality and would therefore not be acceptable. The second approach would be to code the ridge and course lines and intersect them with the inclined planes. This, however, would make the program inefficient as it would use different methods for the turning points and the rest of the inclined contours. It was therefore decided to use surfaces defined by a regular grid of z-values and intersect this grid with a series of inclined planes. From the general equation for a plane,

$$ax + by + cz + d = 0,$$

the third dimension can be obtained

$$z = \frac{ax + by + d}{-c}.$$

If the plane goes through the origin, then

$$z = \frac{ax + by}{-c}.$$

Let the parameters a, b, and c be the components of the unit vector $N\{a, b, c\}$. If α is the azimuth of the inclined plane, or the angle between the inclined plane and the horizontal, and β the projection of the unit vector onto the horizontal plane, then

$$R = \sin \alpha$$

$$a = -R \sin \alpha$$

$$b = -R \cos \alpha$$

$$C = \cos \beta.$$

Because the calculation of intersections of a surface with horizontal planes is computationally simpler than calculation of intersections with inclined planes, it was decided to subtract the unit plane from the surface and then compute contours. The "normalized" surface is then

$$z_{1ij} = x_i \sin \alpha \sin \beta + y_j \cos \alpha \sin \beta - z_{0ij} \cos \beta,$$

where z_{0ij} is the original surface. The implemented procedure allows for variable azimuth and angle of inclination.

Analytical Hill Shading

Another method of planimetrically correct relief representation is the "analytical hill shading" method developed by Yoeli (1965, 1966, 1967). The method is again based on a regular grid of z-values and on Wiechel's (1878) principal of surface illumination. In one grid cell the inclination of the surface can be represented by the cell's vectors in the x- and y-directions. Denoting the four corners of a cell 1, 2, 3, 4 and starting at the southeast corner, the z-components are given by

$$Z_x = \frac{(Z_2 - Z_1) + (Z_3 - Z_4)}{Z}$$

$$Z_y = \frac{(Z_4 - Z_1) + (Z_3 - Z_2)}{Z}.$$

If the sides of the grid cell are of unit length, the two vectors X and Y can be defined as

$$X: \quad X_x = 1, \quad Y_x = 0, \quad Z_x = \frac{(Z_2 - Z_1) + (Z_3 - Z_4)}{Z}$$

$$Y: \quad X_y = 0, \quad Y_y = 1, \quad Z_y = \frac{(Z_4 - Z_1) + (Z_3 - Z_2)}{Z}$$

Given the light vector S with its components X_s, Y_s, Z_s, the light intensity can be computed:

$$I = \cos e = \frac{X_s(Y_xZ_y - Z_xY_x) + Y_s(Z_xX_y - X_xZ_y) + Z_s(X_xY_y - Y_xX_y)}{(Y_xZ_y - Z_xY_y)^2 + (Z_xX_y - X_xZ_y)^2 + (X_xY_y - Y_xX_y)^2}$$

As can be seen in his article, Yoeli (1966) produced some results using a line printer. Since the resolution of a regular line printer is 10 by 8 elements per inch, the map was reduced drastically (by at least a factor of 10) to reveal an acceptable impression of shading. The applicability of the method therefore clearly depends on better instrumentation. One solution could be a half-tone film plotter driven by a computer-generated tape. In Figure 2 an example of

Figure 2   Banff National Park area represented by analytical hill shading, done on a half-tone film plotter.

this approach is shown. For grids of 40 by 50 to 150 by 150 points, the gray-shading was computed and then interpolated linearly to a grid ten times as large in both dimensions.

The examples seem to indicate that the methods are feasible for automation of relief shading. However, several problems are still awaiting a solution. Since Wiechel's equation gives the relief shading with only one light source, tests must be performed to create more general shadings. The greatest problem, however, is the size of the matrices which must be handled; these may contain several million points. Linear approximations of the Wiechel equation and a switching solution for the method of inclined contours are presently being investigated.

References

Oberlander, T. M., 1968, A critical appraisal of the inclined contour technique of surface representation: *Annals Assoc. American Geographers*, v. 58, p. 802–813.

Robinson, A. H., and N. J. W. Thrower, 1957, A new method for terrain representation: *Geographical Review*, v. 47, p. 507–520.

Robinson, A. H., and N. J. W. Thrower, 1969, On surface representation using traces of parallel inclined planes: *Annals Assoc. American Geographers*, v. 59, p. 600–603.

Tanaka, K., 1930, A new method of topographical hill delineation: *Memoirs, College of Engineering, Kyushu Imperial Univ.*, v. 5, no. 3, p. 121–143.

Tanaka, K., 1932, The orthographical relief method of representing hill features on a topographical map: *Geographical Jour.*, v. 79, p. 213–219.

Tanaka, K., 1950, The relief contour method of representing topography on maps: *Geographical Review*, v. 40, p. 444–456.

Wiechel, H., 1878, Theorie und Darstellung der Beleuchtung von nicht gesetzmaessig gebildeten Flaechen mit Ruecksicht auf die Bergzeichnung: *Civilingenieur*, v. 24, p. 335–364.

Yoeli, P., 1965, Analytical hill shading: *Surveying and Mapping*, v. 25, no. 4, p. 573–579.

Yoeli, P., 1966, Analytical hill shading and density: *Surveying and Mapping*, v. 26, no. 2, p. 253–260.

Yoeli, P., 1967, The mechanization of analytical hill shading: *The Cartographic Jour.*, v. 4, p. 82–88.

Hidden-Line Removal from Three-Dimensional Maps and Diagrams

B. F. Sprunt

The main purpose of this paper is to examine algorithms for solving the so-called hidden-line problem in three-dimensional maps and diagrams. An attempt is made to place it in a more general context by a brief consideration of some related spatial problems. Applications of hidden-line algorithms are not limited to problems of displaying surfaces. They may also be used to derive quantitative measures of surface properties, since they enable a particular form of accessibility to be defined, that of visual accessibility or intervisibility. The hidden-line problem is simply a particular, three-dimensional constrained case of what in general form is the problem of accessibility within a network.

The Hidden-Line Problem

If one object is held in front of another and viewed as a two-dimensional scene, the boundaries between the two objects can be seen at a glance and, if required, the boundaries can be outlined. The boundaries, if drawn on the objects themselves, will enclose hidden parts of their surfaces. Repetition of this task with the eyes closed is much more difficult, although this is effectively the task facing the programmer using a "blind" computer. There may be several feasible solutions, so approximations to those solutions are sought which are optimal with respect to programming and processing costs.

In its simplest form the problem of hidden points and lines may be considered with reference to the profile of a section. Figure 1 illustrates two situations: (*a*) where the viewpoint is within the range of the profile, and (*b*) where it is outside the range. Hidden parts may be mapped directly onto the profile itself, or onto a base line or any other arbitrary line. These two situations are indicated in Figure 1 by thickened lines.

Throughout this paper, unless otherwise stated, it is assumed that the surfaces viewed are opaque and that if a point A is visible from point B, then

198

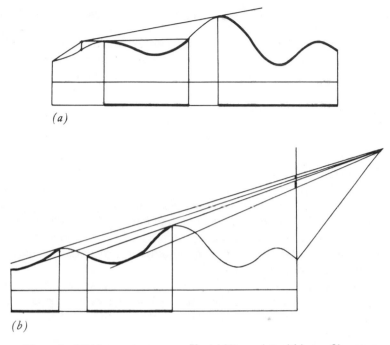

(a)

(b)

Figure 1   Hidden parts on a profile. (a) Viewpoint within profile range. (b) Viewpoint outside profile range—hidden areas indicated by heavy lines.

B is visible from A. In other words the relation is symmetric, giving a concept of intervisibility. A point A is defined as being visible from B with respect to a given profile, if the straight line joining A and B does not intersect the profile. From the definition of convexity for point sets, it follows that any two points on a concave depression of the profile are intervisible.

In order to describe the problem more formally, a profile may be represented by n points with ordinates z_i, $i = 1, \ldots, n$ and a visibility function defined by $v_{ij} = 1$ if point j is visible from i, $v_{ij} = 0$ otherwise. An n by n intervisibility matrix $\mathbf{V}$ can then be constructed for the profile and analyzed in the same way as a binary connectivity matrix associated with a graph. It may be noted that the probability p_i that a point selected at random on the profile is visible from the ith point is given by

$$p_i = \frac{1}{n} \sum_{j=1}^{n} (v_{ij})$$

and a general measure of intervisibility over the profile is

$$I = \frac{1}{n^2} \sum_{i=1}^{n} \sum_{j=1}^{n} (v_{ij}).$$

In addition, the function defined by p_i, $i = 1, \ldots, n$ may be mapped and related to the original function z_i.

The ideas illustrated by Figure 1 can be easily extended to mapping hidden areas on a surface, or their projections onto a base or arbitrary viewing plane. When visibility is mapped with respect to a single viewpoint it is best computed as a bit plane and then plotted with respect to a relief map (Peucker, 1972, p. 44). For a more general consideration of intervisibility on a surface z_{ij} defined by n by n points, an (n^2 by n^2) binary intervisibility matrix can be constructed and the surface p_{ij} mapped.

Applications of "visual accessibility" are found in two-dimensional and three-dimensional mapping by automated methods. Problems arise due to projection of a three-dimensional model onto a two-dimensional viewing plane. Other spatial problems involve illumination from a point source creating shadow areas (Appel, 1968) and calculation of potential insolation over a terrain surface. The former is identical to perspective projection problems while the latter requires only isometric projection to determine shadow areas (Sprunt, 1970).

Problems associated with intervisibility in the landscape include movement of personnel in war games and the siting of building within the landscape. However, only the cartographic problems will be considered here.

Two-Dimensional Cases

All hidden-line problems imply a three-dimensional model of some kind but it is convenient to consider the operations of windowing and symbol placement in automated cartography as two-dimensional cases (Figure 2). When only part of a map is to be drawn from a larger digitized base map, only those point and line elements falling within a given rectangle are plotted. Other elements of the digitized map are considered to be hidden. The problem is solved by an algorithm which tests if a given point or line segment (two points) lies within a rectangle. Alternatively, the algorithm may be used to suppress elements within the rectangle for subsequent name placement.

In thematic mapping, symbols may overlap at a given point, as in Figure 2b–d. The solution to this problem will depend on the nature of the mapping technique. A picture-processing approach enables the problem to be solved at a sequence of points in a raster while line-plotting techniques demand that regions must be examined for line suppression. Peucker (1972, p. 51) discusses these problems and indicates that for point display, a system of priorities is used to decide the symbol to be plotted. All other cases reduce to locating regions which overlap and establishing some kind of pre-sorting on probability of overlap to save searching time. Interactive choice may also be a very convenient and efficient method of deciding which lines to suppress.

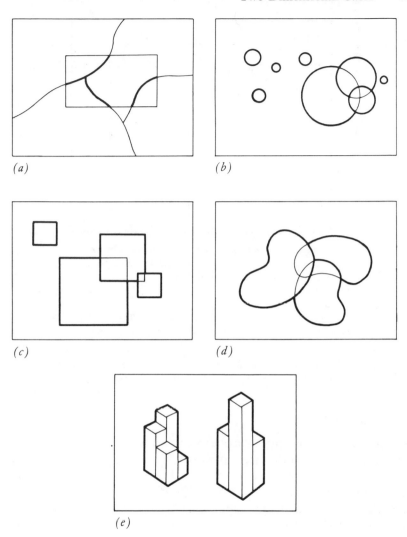

Figure 2 Intersecting regions on a map. (*a*) Windowing, in which only part of a map is drawn from a larger digitized base map. (*b*)–(*e*) Examples of symbol placement, in which hidden lines must be eliminated from overlapping symbols or areas on a map.

In some instances the symbol itself is a three-dimensional form with its own inherent hidden-line problem, but this again reduces to a problem of intersecting regions (Figure 2*e*).

The problem of intersecting regions is solved most simply if the boundaries of the regions are first encoded to enable a regular partitioning of the region to be made. Figure 3 illustrates one form of encoding using intersections on a

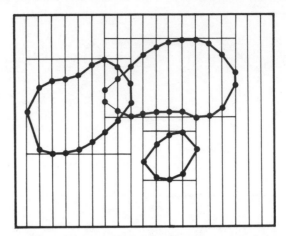

Figure 3 Detecting intersecting regions by partitioning, where boundaries are encoded using intersections on a vertical set of lines.

vertical set of lines, while the method of Freeman chain encoding (Freeman, 1961) is the best for general use. Merrill (1973) solves the problem of intersecting regions by first determining if the bounding rectangles of the region intersect and then testing for intersections on the ordered partitions of the region. All hidden-line problems can be solved by this method.

Three-Dimensional Cases

Jenks and Brown (1966, p. 857) define three-dimensional maps as "perspective representations of obliquely viewed statistical or topographic surfaces". They suggest that maps of this type could be used to illustrate submarine environments, airport facilities, development of hurricanes, intersecting statistical surfaces, or movement of fog, smog, and other air pollutants. They also point out that "three-dimensional maps are conceptualized views of what the distributive surface might look like", and describe a manual method of construction which is still commonly used. One must note, however, that selecting an oblique view almost invariably implies that there will be hidden areas and consequent loss of information. This applies to statistical surfaces as well as topographic surfaces. It is interesting to note that by requiring a map or diagram to exclude "hidden information" which we do not really want to lose, we introduce what is probably the most difficult part of programming for automatic solution. The problem can be avoided by displaying all lines, including the hidden or "back lines", but this generally leads to confusion. The user is unable to mentally reconstruct the desired image unless a device such as an anaglyph presentation or stereoscopic pair is used.

In generating an image by computer we are displaying the form of a model that we have constructed in some way. Optimal solutions to the hidden-line problem are different for different models. By imposing constraints on the kind of model we use and the kind of view we take, we may drastically reduce the amount of computation involved in the solution. For example, if we limit the model of the surface to one single-valued continuous function, solutions are much simpler than if we allow multiple, closed or interpenetrating surfaces. If we only wish to display isometric projections rather than perspective projections of the surface, the solution is again simplified. Similarly, one-point perspective with hidden-line removal is simpler than two-point perspective which is in turn simpler than three-point perspective. The optimal algorithm for hidden-line removal in automated cartography is therefore tied to the requirements of the map user as well as to the efficiency of its execution on the computer. Frequently, acceptable results can be obtained from very simple, restricted-view programs requiring minimal programming effort. It is also unnecessary to insist that the computer does the complete job. If hidden lines can be removed most efficiently by "painting out" at the production stage, then that is the optimal algorithm for the job.

Hidden-Line Algorithms

It is possible to summarize briefly the procedures used to produce displays of conceptualized models of three-dimensional objects.

(1)   An object or scene is defined by points, lines, surfaces, or combinations of these three elements.

(2)   All points and lines on the object are projected onto a plane by a mathematical transformation.

(3)   An image of the object or scene is formed by displaying or drawing the results of the transformation.

Hidden-line algorithms may be incorporated at step (2) or (3).

The problem of hidden-line removal has received considerable attention in computer-aided design (CAD). Forrest (1968) noted three basic techniques among the many attempts to solve the problem efficiently.

(1)   Comparison of every point, vertex, edge, line, face, or surface with every other component of the objects in the viewing region. Sophisticated analysis can reduce the number of comparisons to be made.

(2)   Scanning the objects by a ray or raster, or by a cutting plane. Intersections of the objects with the ray or plane are counted and only the intersections nearest the view plane are displayed.

(3)   The Warnock approach involves concentrating only on those areas which the visibility changes, much as the eye concentrates on regions of complexity and ambiguity in a drawing. This is achieved by repeatedly dividing the picture into quadrants.

An object may be specified as a patchwork of mathematical functions or by sets of points or curves lying on its surface. As a particular example, objects may be defined as a connected sequence of polygonal faces. This appears to be most satisfactory in CAD, yielding efficient hidden-line algorithms.

Output images may be line drawings produced as a sequence of plotted vectors or half-tone images produced by raster display techniques. The most efficient forms of hidden-line algorithms appear to be adaptable to both forms of display.

Since Forrest's survey, Jones (1969) has suggested a new approach which is suitable for scenes in which the viewer may see into or through objects. Objects are described by a set of discrete cells which are bounded partly by faces of the original objects and partly by artificially introduced transparent faces. Cell faces may be opaque or may have a number of transparent openings. Each cell is required to be a convex polygon and to be shared by two adjacent cells. The structure may be represented by a linear graph and for a chosen viewpoint a directed subgraph defines the avenues of sight. The graph structure may be searched recursively to explore all possible avenues through windows.

Galimberti and Montanari (1969) have published an algorithm for eliminating hidden lines in the representation of a perspective view of concave and convex plane-faced objects on the picture plane. Ricci (1971) has extended this approach to include the case where lines are included in addition to those defining edges of faces.

Display of Statistical or Topographic Surfaces

Hidden-line techniques most commonly used for displaying a topographic surface are restricted forms of type 2 in which only the nearest element of a surface along a viewing ray is displayed. They take advantage of the fact that a topographic surface may be considered as a single-valued function of two variables and may be defined by an array of altitudes over a rectangular grid. Although this technique seems to be most suitable for presenting terrain and continuous statistical surfaces, it has seldom been mentioned in computer science, literature, presumably because of its restrictions (Brauer, 1968; Williamson, 1972).

Alternative algorithms have been devised for drawing mathematical functions of two variables with hidden-line removal (Kubert, Szabo, and Giulieri, 1968) in which each point in a grid is checked against all other points on a vertical cutting plane through the grid and the viewpoint. Rohlf (1969) implemented this algorithm to produce excellent visual results for polynomial trend surfaces in geological applications, but the algorithm is very inefficient and not recommended.

By defining the surface as a sequence of stacked profiles, the type 2 algorithm can be implemented in one forward scan of the surface, thus reducing considerably the number of comparisons to be made. Resulting profile diagrams are well known through the SYMVU package, a Tobler-Rens derivative dating to the mid-1960s. Wray (1970) also implemented the profile method of producing isometric drawings of terrain and Sprunt (1970) used the algorithm for carrying forward a "visibility profile" when displaying perspective views in line and half-tone plots. Essentially, the carrying forward of a "visibility profile" defines hidden areas or "shadow areas" on the terrain surface which can then be mapped (Douglas, 1971; Sprunt, 1972).

Two other forms of three-dimensional diagrams have received attention, the display of geographical data in histogram form for regularly and irregularly shaped spatial units (Figure 4). In the former, data values are given over a two-dimensional grid of cells and vertical, square, or rectangular prisms are erected with heights proportional to some function of data values. This

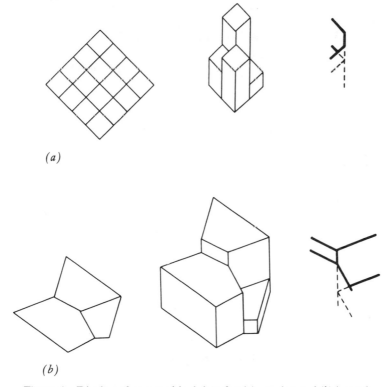

(a)

(b)

Figure 4   Display of geographical data for (a) regular and (b) irregular spatial units. Hidden lines at a vertex are shown with broken lines.

type of diagram has been produced by Tobler (1969, p. 247) using a sequential profile scanning method; an isometric version has been presented by Brooks and Pinzke (1971). In the latter case the data values are associated with irregular polygons on which the prisms are erected.

For simple projection, a forward scan algorithm will determine visibility in the case of columns on a regular grid of cells. For the irregular case, Tobler (1973) has used a type 1 algorithm in which the outer normal of each of the prism faces is compared with the viewing ray to determine if a face can be seen. A similar procedure is used for the tops of the prisms. Exposed faces are then compared with hidden faces for coincidence. Hidden faces and overlapping edges are deleted immediately. Every remaining edge is then compared with every remaining face and top. Edges completely behind any single face are deleted. Every remaining edge is compared with every other edge. If they intersect on the picture plane, each point of intersection is recorded. A point halfway between intersections is tested for visibility against every face and top, using inverse projective equations to find its positions in space, testing to see if it is behind the face, and inside the picture plane polygon representing the face. If this midpoint is visible, the segment between these intersections is drawn.

The procedure for determining hidden parts can be improved by ordering the faces on their nearness to the viewing plane and examining for overlap only those faces which lie within the distance range of a given face (Figure 5).

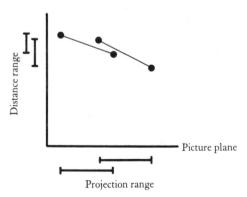

Figure 5   Testing vertical faces for overlap; only those faces within the distance range of a given face are examined.

This amounts to a forward search through a list of pointers within the given range.

An alternative approach is to draw these diagrams sequentially, based on the faces incident to a given vertex of the base net of areal units as shown in

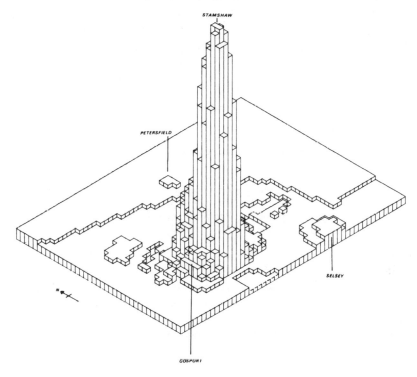

Figure 6 Preference surface mapped in histogram form and plotted by computer, with names added manually. (Data supplied by M. Bateman, Portsmouth Polytechnic.)

the extreme right diagrams of Figures 4a and 4b. Figure 6 shows an example in which the surface was rapidly plotted by computer using this approach; the names were added manually.

In conclusion, it should be noted that there may be limitations on the size of data sets which can be efficiently plotted by the techniques described, because all data must be available for searching unless a sequential method can be used. Hidden areas on a terrain surface can be mapped sequentially using a "tiling" approach. Figure 7 shows a basic tile defined by four data points within which 12 further points have been interpolated. The 4 by 4 points in the lower left corner are used to define points unique to this tile, and their visibility map is defined by 16 bits for convenient storage. It is necessary to carry forward visibility profiles for two sides of each tile to determine visibility and to pass forward the updated visibility profiles for the adjacent tiles to the north and to the east. Very large surfaces can be processed in this way to yield a compact binary visibility map against which surface information may be efficiently processed.

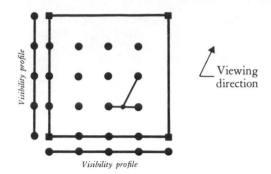

Figure 7   Basic tile for sequential mapping of hidden areas. ■ data point, ● interpolated point, • point on profile where visibility is checked.

For stepped surfaces, there is a limitation on the number of faces that can be included. Digitized boundaries of irregular units yielding high-order polygons are not worth plotting by the techniques described, without first simplification to low-order polygons.

There is no "best" general purpose method. The user must examine the cartographic problem at hand and select from the wide variety of algorithms available to him to obtain the optimal solution for himself and the map user.

References

Appel, A., 1968, Some techniques for shading machine renderings of solids: *American Federation of Information Processing Soc.*, v. 32, p. 37–45.

Brauer, C., 1968, A computer program to plot an isometric projection of a solution space surface: Computer Science Dept., Univ. Utah, *Internal Rept. TR-4-9*, 11 p.

Brooks, W. D., and K. G. Pinzke, 1971, A computer program for three-dimensional presentation of geographic data: *Canadian Cartographer*, v. 8, no. 2, p. 110–125.

Douglas, D., 1971, VIEWBLOK: A computer program for constructing perspective view block diagrams: *Revue de Geographie de Montreal*, v. 26, p. 102–104.

Forrest, A. R., 1968, A survey of techniques for removing hidden lines: Cambridge Mathematical Laboratory, Cambridge Univ., *CAD Group Document No. 19*, 10 p.

Freeman, H., 1961, Techniques for digital computer analysis of chain encoded arbitrary plane curves: *Proc. National Electronics Conference*, v. 17, p. 421–432.

Galimberti, R., and U. Montanari, 1969, An algorithm for hidden line elimination: *Communications, Assoc. Computing Machinery*, v. 12, no. 4, p. 206–211.

Jenks, G. F., and D. A. Brown, 1966, Three-dimensional map construction: *Science*, v. 154, no. 3750, p. 857–864.

Jones, C. B., 1969, A new approach to the "hidden line" problem: Centre for Computing and Automation, Imperial College, London, *Rept. CG 69/5*, 19 p.

Kubert, B., J. Szabo, and S. Giulieri, 1968, Perspective representation of functions of two variables: *Jour. Assoc. Computing Machinery*, v. 15, no. 2, p. 193–204.

Merrill, R. D., 1973, Representation of contours and regions for efficient computer search: *Communications, Assoc. Computing Machinery*, v. 16, no. 2, p. 69–82.

Peucker, T. K., 1972, Computer Cartography: Commission on College Geography, Assoc. American Geographers, *Resource Paper No. 17*, 75 p.

Ricci, A., 1971, An algorithm for the removal of hidden lines in three-dimensional scenes: *The Computer Jour.*, v. 14, no. 4, p. 375–377.

Rohlf, F. J., 1969, GRAFPAC, graphic output subroutines for the GE635 computer: *Kansas Geological Survey Computer Contribution 36*, 50 p.

Sprunt, B. F., 1969, Computer-generated halftone images from digital terrain models: *MSc Dissertation*, Dept. Mathematics, Univ. Southampton, 80 p.

Sprunt, B. F., 1970, Geographics: a computer's eye-view of terrain: Inst. British Geographers, *Area*, no. 4, p. 54–59.

Sprunt, B. F., 1972, Contours in perspective: Paper presented at Inst. British Geographers Annual Conference, Aberdeen, Scotland, 18 p.

Tobler, W. R., 1969, Geographical filters and their inverses: *Geographical Analysis*, v. 1, p. 234–253.

Tobler, W. R., 1973, A computer program to draw perspective views of geographical data: Dept. Geography, Univ. Michigan, Ann Arbor, 7 p.

Williamson, H., 1972, Hidden line plotting program (J6). Algorithm 420: *Communications, Assoc. Computing Machinery*, v. 15, no. 2, p. 100–103.

Wray, W. B., 1970, FORTRAN IV CDC 6400 computer program for constructing isometric diagrams: *Kansas Geological Survey Computer Contribution 44*, 58 p.

Representation of Geographic Surfaces within a Computer

J. L. Pfaltz

By a surface we simply mean a function f of one or more variables. In geography, these functions usually are those whose independent variables denote geographic position; that is, functions f (x, y) of two variables where (x, y) denotes a point within a geographic coordinate system. A topographic surface in which altitude is a function of position is the standard prototype. Functions of a single variable are seldom called "surfaces" (because their graphic representation is simply a line drawn over the coordinate axis), but we will use them to illustrate simple concepts that will be extended to two-dimensional surfaces. Surfaces of higher dimension (functions of n variables) are important in social and economic theory, but are not easy to visualize or represent graphically. These will be ignored in this paper, except to point out results which can be generalized to higher dimensions.

Surfaces, like functions of a single variable, can be basically represented in one of three ways. In mathematics, the most common method of definition is by a functional expression such as

$$f(x, y) = x^3 + 3x^2y - 5y + y^3$$

which permits the simple calculation of its value given any combination x, y.

Surfaces also may be defined in "tabular" form where the value of f is given for a selection of representative arguments. To find an arbitrary value of f, a "table lookup" must be performed to determine the value of the nearest known point and use it to approximate the desired value. Generally we refine the approximation by means of an interpolation scheme involving values of neighboring known points. To simplify table lookup and interpolation procedures, the surface is often represented over a regular discrete grid. Thus a two-dimensional array (or matrix) of values becomes the archetype of this method of representation.

The third basic technique involves quantizing the range of values of f, rather than quantizing the domain of the function into a discrete grid. f is thus a "step function" and corresponding to each of the quantization intervals $(f_0, f_1]$, $(f_1, f_2]$, ..., $(f_{n-1}, f_n]$ is an associated region R_i such that for all $(x, y) \in R_i f_{i-1} \leq f(x, y) < f_i$. Delineation of these regions yields, in graphic form, the familiar contour map. This technique has been employed in computing (Boehm, 1967; Pfaltz and Rosenfeld, 1967), but representing boundaries of regions (contours) involves many of the problems of representing the original surface and requires an algorithm to determine region membership of any specified point. The technique does not appreciably simplify the problem of storing surfaces, and a contour map does not lend itself to computer processing.

Of the three methods of representing surfaces, the first is clearly superior. Unfortunately, for most surfaces encountered in real life there is no *compact* expression to represent the surface. Consequently geographers represent most surfaces in a computer by a large mass of numbers denoting the functional value f for various points (x, y). These large collections of values provide two problems in computer applications. The first problem is that of sheer storage; the second, and possibly most important, is one of access.

The computer is customarily regarded as a magnificent device for processing large amounts of data. This is only true in a sense. Consider a typical FORTRAN program. It seldom contains more than 50 declared variables. Even though the value assigned to a single variable may be changing constantly, as in an iterative loop, there are still fewer than 50 named items of data that can be referenced at any one time. Even if some of the declared variables are arrays (50 by 50 is a large array in most FORTRAN programs), we are still operating with a relatively small number of distinct items of data.

Scientific programming, as exemplified by FORTRAN, is perhaps exceptional. Business data processing programs operate on files containing hundreds of thousands of distinct records. Closer inspection shows that most such programs operate on sequential files. The program itself can reference only a few data items at any given time: its internally named variables, the record that has been currently read, and possibly the next record that "will be read".

Even with "random access" hardware it is still extremely difficult to reference and use an arbitrary item of information in a large file. The generally mediocre accomplishments of management information systems (MIS) attest to this. An item of information must have associated with it a unique identifier which serves to locate the desired data. (In theory, information can be accessed in terms of its current value, as in "the set of all elements with value 5.7". In practice the cost of such "content-addressable" or "associative" memory is prohibitive except for certain specialized high-density applications.) In machine language, the storage address serves as the unique identifier. In a higher level language a symbolic variable name is used as the referencing identifier. Associated with each symbolic identifier is a procedure to locate the item in storage.

Thousands of distinct, unique identifiers simply cannot be managed in a program. One of the beauties of array notation is that this is unnecessary. A single array name identifies the entire file; suffixes (subscripts) to this name identify individual elements by a standard accessing convention. But even if a surface is represented as an array and array notation is used, points of the surface identified by other than the geographic position, such as the "highest peak", cannot be accessed without an exhaustive sequential search. The problem of access is far more important and difficult than problems of representation and storage. It is primarily a conceptual problem which is completely machine-independent.

Surface Modeling by Locally Valid Analytic Surfaces

When possible, the representation of surfaces by a compact mathematical expression, preferably a polynomial (or power series), is clearly the best. Wierstrass's well-known approximation theorem states that any continuous surface can be approximated with arbitrarily small error by a polynomial of sufficiently high degree. Such polynomials can be derived by standard least-squares surface-fitting programs. But for surfaces of any significant irregularity, to obtain anything more than a crude approximation, the degree of the approximating polynomial must be inordinately high. The number of coefficients, m, that must be calculated and stored increases as $(m + 1)^2$. One simple way to keep the degree m of the approximating expression down to a manageable size is to limit the domain of validity of the expression. Over a small enough region of the surface even a linear polynomial (plane) can be a very accurate representation. However, outside their domains of validity, such approximations characteristically differ greatly from the actual surface.

A possible solution is to subdivide the domain of the surface into many small regions over which the surface cannot be too iregular and create a collection of approximating expressions that accurately represent the surface. The problem is that two adjacent representing expressions seldom yield a surface that is continuous along their common boundary. The resulting surface is almost certainly not "smooth" across the boundary in the sense that its first, and possibly higher order, partial derivatives are continuous (Figure 1). Methods exist for forcing continuity with various degrees of smoothness across these "surface patches". Representation by "surface splines" is one such technique, but requires solution of a fairly complex system of partial differential equations to insure that desirable global properties are preserved.

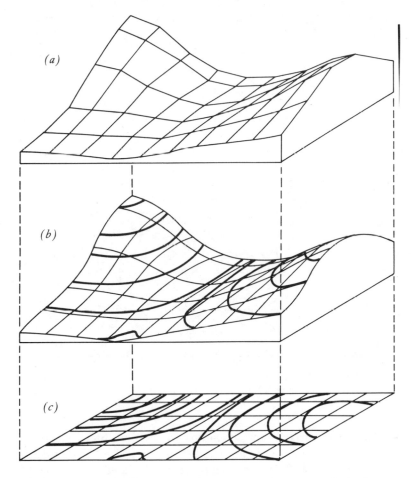

Figure 1 Approximations to a two-dimensional surface. (*a*) By first-degree polynomial (planar). (*b*) Original surface. (*c*) By contour map. (Reproduced by permission of Journal of Geophysical Research.)

A different approach involving multiplication of preliminary, but overlapping, approximations by appropriate weighting functions has been developed by Dr. John Junkins and Mr. James Jancaitis of the University of Virginia. It efficiently yields surfaces of cartographic quality and is being tested by the U.S. Army Topographic Command for routine map production. Figure 2 shows a surface digitized by the Army's UNAMACE digitizer, and the resulting contour map generated by their software. Using 1600 observations, Junkins first made 324 preliminary linear approximations using a standard least-squares routine. Weighted averages of these were combined to

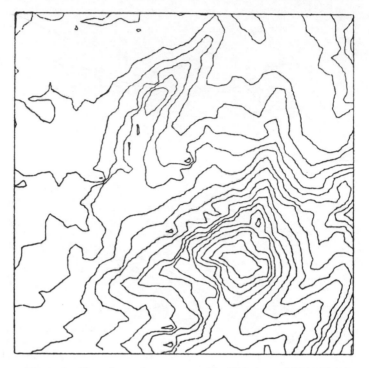

Figure 2 Plot of raw data generated by U.S. Army UNAMACE digitizer. 1600 (40 by 40) measured data points.

produce 289 final surface representations which were fourth-degree polynomials in two variables. Figure 3 is a contour plot of the final surface representation. In all, 7225 coefficients were calculated and stored. Total execution time, including contour plottings, was 24 seconds on a CDC 6400.

Before examining Junkins' procedure in detail, the mathematics underlying the technique should be considered. For initial simplicity, let us consider a one-dimensional case, a simple function $f(x)$ such as Figure 4 represented piecewise by approximating functions, each valid over an interval of length k. We first establish preliminary approximations, g_i, which are valid over intervals of length 2k. (In Figure 4 each of these g_i are second-degree polynomials, but any analytic function may be used.) Now suppose $g_i(x)$ approximate $f(x)$ over $[x_{i-1}, x_{i+1}]$ and $g_{i+1}(x)$ approximates $f(x)$ over $[x_i, x_{i+2}]$. We wish to combine $g_i(x)$ and $g_{i+1}(x)$ to obtain a final approximation $f_i(x)$ over $[x_i, x_{i+1}]$ with the property that

(a) $f_i(x_i) = g_i(x_i)$
(b) $f_{i+1}(x_{i+1}) = g_{i+1}(x_{i+1})$.

Figure 3 Contour plot of functional surface model generated from data of Figure 2, using 289 locally valid surface patches.

Thus we wish to determine appropriate weighting functions $w_i(x)$ and $w_{i+1}(x)$, and let $\hat{f}_i(x) = w_i(x) \cdot g_i(x) + w_{i+1}(x) \cdot g_{i+1}(x)$. From conditions (a) and (b), we want

$$w_i(x_i) = 1 \qquad w_{i+1}(x_i) = 0$$
$$w_i(x_{i+1}) = 0 \qquad w_{i+1}(x_{i+1}) = 1.$$

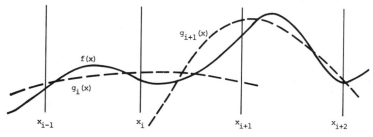

Figure 4 One-dimensional surface, $f(x)$, with overlapping preliminary approximations, $g_i(x)$ and $g_{i+1}(x)$.

The simplest such weighting functions are the linear functions:

$$w_i(x) = \frac{-1}{x_{i+1} - x_i}(x - x_{i+1})$$

$$w_{i+1}(x) = \frac{1}{x_{i+1} - x_i}(x - x_i).$$

These are illustrated in Figure 5, together with $\hat{f}_i(x)$.

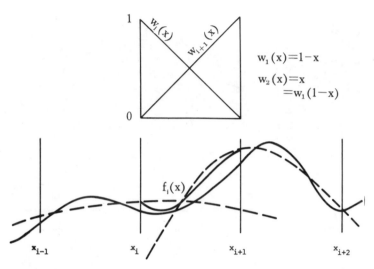

$$w_1(x) = 1 - x$$

$$w_2(x) = x$$
$$= w_1(1-x)$$

Figure 5   Linear weighting functions, $w_i(x)$ and $w_{i+1}(x)$ and (below) resultant locally valid surface function $f_i(x) = w_i g_i + w_{i+1} g_{i+1}$.

Although each of the patches $\hat{f}_i$, $\hat{f}_{i+1}$ will fit together in a continuous fashion, their first derivatives need not be continuous (that is, there may be an "angle" at x_{i+1}). This effect can be eliminated by using third-degree weighting functions having the additional properties

(a') $w_i'(x_i) = w_i'(x_{i+1}) = 0$
(b') $w_{i+1}'(x_i) = w_{i+1}'(x_{i+1}) = 0$

as illustrated in Figure 6. To see that these boundary conditions are sufficient, we may differentiate

$$\hat{f} = w_i \cdot g_i + w_{i+1} \cdot g_{i+1}$$

to obtain

$$\hat{f}' = w_i' \cdot g_i + w_i \cdot g_i' + w_{i+1}' \cdot g_{i+1} + w_{i+1} \cdot g_{i+1}'.$$

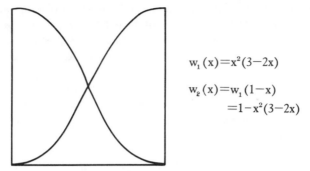

$$w_1(x) = x^2(3-2x)$$

$$w_2(x) = w_1(1-x)$$
$$= 1 - x^2(3-2x)$$

Figure 6 Third-degree weighting functions (one-dimensional case) that guarantee continuity of both $f(x)$ and $f'(x)$.

Simple substitution shows that

$$\hat{f}_i(x_i) = g_i(x_i) \qquad\qquad \hat{f}'_i(x_i) = g'_i(x_i)$$

$$\hat{f}_i(x_{i+1}) = g_{i+1}(x_{i+1}) \qquad \hat{f}'_i(x_{i+1}) = g'_{i+1}(x_{i+1})$$

insuring continuity of both the function and its derivative. The solution of this boundary value problem yields the third-degree polynomials,

$$w_1(x) = x^2(3 - 2x)$$

$$w_2(x) = 1 - x^2(3 - 2x) \qquad\qquad (1)$$

$$= w_1(1 - x)$$

Returning to the original example given in Figure 5, we have made second-degree initial approximations and used first-degree linear weighting functions. Consequently, after multiplication the resulting approximating patches are third-degree polynomials of the form:

$$\hat{f}_i(x) = \sum_{i=0}^{3} c_i x^i.$$

Storage requirements for the representation will be four real numbers (the coefficients, c_i) for each interval in the domain of the representation.

We may qualitatively consider some of the storage tradeoffs that are available. The length of the interval $[x_i, x_{i+1}]$ may be increased so there will be fewer intervals and fewer coefficient sets to be stored. Alternatively cruder initial approximations g_i could be used, perhaps first-degree linear functions. Then $\hat{f}$ will consist of second-degree patches and only three coefficients would be stored per interval. However, more intervals would probably be necessary to maintain a constant error tolerance. Readily the factor 1.333

is the breakeven point. Conversely, the total number of intervals could be reduced by refining the initial approximating functions g_i, perhaps by using third-degree polynomials. Now, however, five real coefficients must be stored per interval patch. These ideas of optimal storage are all extensible to the two-dimensional case.

Precisely the same approach can be used with two-dimensional surfaces $f(x, y)$; except four, instead of two, overlapping preliminary surfaces are needed, as shown in Figure 7, As before, the final local surface is obtained as the sum,

$$\hat{f}(x, y) = \sum_{i=0}^{4} w_i(x, y) \cdot g_i(x, y)$$

where the $g_i(x, y)$ are any preliminary local surfaces. The only problem is determination of appropriate weight functions $w_i(x, y)$. Clearly we want the local surface $\hat{f}_i$ which is valid over the region $[1, 2, 3, 4]$ (Figure 7) to join continuously with all four neighbors. Consider, for instance, the join along the line $1 \rightarrow 2$ with the local surface immediately above. Continuity will be maintained if the only contributions to the value $\hat{f}(x, y)$ (and partial derivatives of $\hat{f}$) for points (x, y) on the boundary $1 \rightarrow 2$ come entirely from the preliminary surfaces $g_1(x, y)$ and $g_2(x, y)$ centered at the points 1 and 2, respectively. That is, there is zero contribution from the preliminary surfaces $g_3(x, y)$ and $g_4(x, y)$.

These conditions, together with the natural requirement that $\Sigma_{i=1}^{4} w_i(x, y) = 1.0$ for all points (x, y) in the region, establish a classical boundary value problem which Junkins, Miller, and Jancaitis (1973) have solved. In general there are many solutions, but the polynomial solutions of minimal degree are unique. They are

$$w_1(x, y) = x^2 y^2 (9 - 6x - 6y + 4xy)$$

$$w_2(x, y) = w_1(1 - x, y)$$

$$w_3(x, y) = w_1(1 - x, 1 - y)$$

$$w_4(x, y) = w_1(x, 1 - y)$$

(2)

Comparison with Equation (1) shows that

$$w_1(x, y) = [x^2(3 - 2x)] \cdot [y^2(3 - 2y)]$$

$$= w_1(x) \cdot w_2(y)$$

Jancaitis and Junkins (1973) have since shown that generalization to n-dimensional surfaces by simply multiplying lower order weight functions is valid. This provides a very elegant feature of this method of surface modeling. Once weighting functions sufficient to guarantee continuity of the kth order

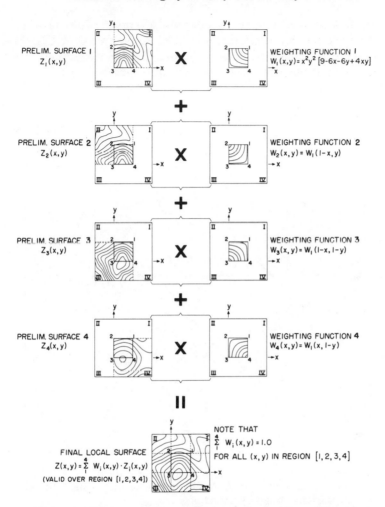

Figure 7 Schema of process to determine locally valid analytic two-dimensional surface patch. Note that preliminary approximations are denoted Z_i instead of g_i as in text. (Reproduced by permission of Journal of Geophysical Research.)

derivatives have been determined for the one-dimensional case they can be extended to the n-dimensional case without solving a large system of partial differential equations.

We now consider the practical application of the analytic surface model. Junkins, Miller, and Jancaitis developed the technique primarily as a cartographic technique, not as a method of computer representation and storage of surfaces. To estimate its utility in the preparation of maps, compare the plot of the analytic surface determined from 1600 raw measurements (Figure 3) with Figure 8 which was plotted by the U.S. Army from 6400 UNAMACE measurements that had first been smoothed. Figure 8 is perhaps the best indication of what the original surface "really" looks like.

Figure 8   Contour plot drawn from 6400 smoothed UNAMACE measurements made by U.S. Army. (Reproduced by permission of Journal of Geophysical Research.)

All the surface models shown in this paper have been generated using first-degree (planar) preliminary local approximations to the surface (determined by least-squares fit) and third-degree weighting functions given in Equation 2, resulting in fourth-degree surface patches of the form

$$f(x, y) = \sum_{i=0}^{4} \sum_{j=0}^{4} c_{ij} x^i y^j$$

involving 25 coefficients, c_{ij}. Figure 9 illustrates a series of surface models in which only the size of the region (interval) of validity has been altered. Let n denote the length of a side of a region of validity, so that each region of

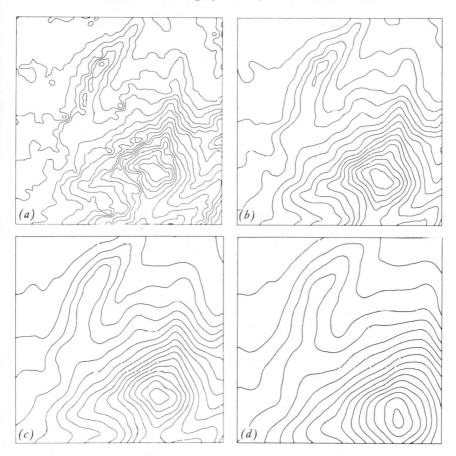

Figure 9   Four analytic surface models using different intervals of validity. (a) $n = 1$, (b) $n = 2$, (c) $n = 3$, (d) $n = 4$. (Reproduced by permission of Journal of Geophysical Research.)

validity encompasses $(n + 1)^2$ grid points. Each of the preliminary surfaces must be valid over a region of size $2n$. In Figure 9a $n = 1$; the preliminary surfaces, g_i, are planes obtained from a least-squares fit to nine measured data points, yielding 1369 locally valid surface functions. (Although in this case the underlying grid of the final surface model corresponds to the grid by which the measurements were made, this is not necessary. Since the preliminary local surfaces are planes, only three measured points are necessary to determine them, and they may be placed anywhere within the region.) In Figure 9b (identical to Figure 3), $n = 2$; so preliminary planes were determined from 25 data points, yielding 289 locally valid functions. In Figures 9c and d, $n = 3$ and 4; thus sets of 49 and 81 data points determined the preliminary functions, yielding 121 and 49 locally valid functions, respectively.

The weighted average of four preliminary surfaces naturally tends to "smooth" the surface, and it is evident from the series of plots in Figure 9 that the size of the regions of validity has a major effect on the degree of smoothing. A reasonably objective measure of smoothing (Junkins, Miller, and Jancaitis, 1973) is the ratio of the standard deviation of the function surface values with respect to the measured values, over the known standard deviation of the measuring process itself. This smoothing ratio is close to 1.0 in Figure 9b, matching our intuitive perception that this is the most faithful representation. Figure 9a is clearly "under-smoothed", while Figures 9c and d are "oversmoothed", having ratios significantly greater than 1.0. However, oversmoothing may be useful in suppressing the micro-structure of the surface to obtain dominant trend surfaces.

How effective are locally analytic surfaces as a method for the computer storage of surfaces? Since these local surface functions are fourth-degree polynomials, each requires 25 real coefficients for representation. Conse-quently, to represent the 289 surface functions of Figure 9b, 7255 real co-efficients must be stored. This seems unattractive when compared to the original 1600 raw measurements. If these storage requirements are compared to 6400 (which may be a more appropriate reflection of the degree of accuracy of the surface model) the ratio is more nearly one, but still unfavorable.

Against this, however, it must be remembered that the analytic surface model representation is in a more readily usable form. To obtain the value of any point on the surface, it is necessary only to evaluate a polynomial. If the surface is represented by the 1600 (or 6400) raw data points an inter-polation procedure must be executed to obtain values of non-grid points. More importantly the slope or gradient of the surface at any point can be accurately calculated by simply differentiating the polynomial representa-tion. It is the familiar tradeoff of storage efficiency versus computational efficiency.

We can consider two possible ways of compressing the storage required by functional surface models. First of all, this system was designed to produce plots of cartographic quality, hence the surface patches were constrained so that their first partial derivatives were continuous (to avoid minor angles in the contour lines). For many applications it may be sufficient to have the surface values themselves be continuous. In this case we could use as weight-ing functions first-degree polynomials of the form

$$w_1(x, y) = w_1(x) \cdot w_1(y)$$

$$= (1 - x) \cdot (1 - y) = 1 - x - y + xy.$$

Consequently the final surface patches would be only second-degree poly-nomials represented by nine real coefficients. Only 2601 words of storage would be necessary to represent the 289 locally valid patches of Figure 3, with little expected loss of accuracy.

An alternative approach might be to store only the preliminary surface, not the final weighted surface patch itself. Using this procedure the surface of Figure 3 can be represented using only 972 words of memory. But a price would be paid in execution. To retrieve a single point would require eight memory accesses, one to each of the four overlapping preliminary surfaces, one to each of the four weighting functions, followed by a simple calculation.

While it may be debated whether Junkins' analytic surface models offer significant economies in the representation of two-dimensional topographic surfaces, it is one of the few that generalize to n-dimensional surfaces, which are likely to be of increasing importance in geographical applications.

Bit Plane Representation of Surfaces

Suppose we decide to represent a surface over a regular (x, y) grid so the mathematical model is simply an m by n array whose elements correspond to a single observed value on the surface. Virtually all programming languages handle doubly subscripted arrays under the convention that value of each element of the array is represented by a single machine word; the entire file (identified by the array name) is stored in a standard columnwise (or row-wise) fashion. To obtain the functional value f(x, y) of any point on the surface, it is only necessary to convert the geographic coordinates x and y to integer subscripts i and j, access the array, and return the value of the "nearest" element (or possibly perform a simple interpolation based on value of neighboring elements).

Since it is so easy to reference and work with points on the surface, array representation seems to be a natural choice. There is a catch, however. Even a moderate-sized surface, say 100 by 100, requires 10,000 words of high-cost core storage. Larger surfaces, or several surfaces of this size, quickly devour main memory. Even on virtual storage machines one begins to pay dearly for the overhead of page swapping.

There are two immediate possible solutions. The surface can be stored as a file on peripheral storage with each row (or column) of the array as a separate logical record. Processing routines can be written that require less than 10 rows in core at any one time (Johnston and Pfaltz, 1967). Such software is not difficult to write and generally is superior to paging by the operating system since memory swapping can usually be minimized.

Alternatively, two or more element values can be packed in a single machine word. With only 10 bits any integer in the range [0, 1023] can be represented. If we are willing to represent surface values with no more than 10 bit accuracy, we can pack from 3 to 6 (depending on the computer) array elements in a single machine word with a corresponding three- to six-fold saving in storage. Quantization of a nominally real-valued surface to an integer-valued surface with 10 bit accuracy is perhaps less drastic than it appears. On a detailed contour map with 20-foot contour intervals (which is a quantization of the surface values) this corresponds to a range from sea level to 20,000 feet. Even if the surface file is in peripheral storage, the saving from quantization is worthwhile. The catch is that every information access requires either a packing or unpacking operation. Furthermore, the packing scheme is not readily adaptable to the requirements of the surface. A surface that requires only five-bit accuracy still wastes storage. A surface that requires 11-bit accuracy necessitates an entirely new packing scheme.

Either of these two methods of storing large arrays of values requires an investment in software, either to access values, or to pack and unpack values. Given such an investment, radically different storage techniques can be considered; bit-plane encoding is an example.

We will assume that all surface values are integer. (Bit plane encoding of real-valued surfaces is possible, but the resulting real arithmetic is orders of magnitude slower.) Let k denote the number of bits in a machine word, and let z_{ij} denote $f(i, j)$ or the ijth element of the surface array.

First consider a binary surface, where all elements have value 0 or 1. Since the value of each element (point of the surface) is a single bit we may pack k elements into a single machine word. An m by n binary array requires (m by n)/k words of storage; this is clearly the most effective possible compression. The (m by n)/k words used to represent the binary surface we will call a "bit plane", or simply a "plane".

But what about surfaces that are not binary? Suppose surface values lie in the range [0, 63] requiring six bits for their representation. Precisely the same "packing" scheme is used, but only the low-order bits of all z_{ij} values are stored in a single plane, the bits of next higher significance in a different plane, and so on, until six separate planes are used to store each of the six bits necessary for the representation. An illustration may make this concept clearer. Suppose for concreteness that z_{ij} has value 45, that is

$$z_{ij} = 45_{10} = 101101_2$$

The low order bit, 1, is stored in the ijth position of plane 1; 0 is stored in the ijth position of plane 2 and so on as illustrated in Figure 10. Conceptually the value, z, of any point on the surface is read "vertically" through a "stack" of bit planes.

Bit-plane encoding has several advantages and disadvantages. Only one packing procedure is necessary, since representation of surfaces whose values lie in a larger (or smaller) range requires only the addition (or deletion) of more planes from the stack. Consequently, storage requirements can be optimally adjusted to the nature of the surface. In image processing applications, bit-plane encoding permits efficient handling of several large arrays (100 by 100 are typical, 500 by 500 are not unusual) in a single program. Furthermore, on most computers basic operations at the bit level are executed in the CPU registers in parallel. Consequently, k points of the surface can be processed simultaneously.

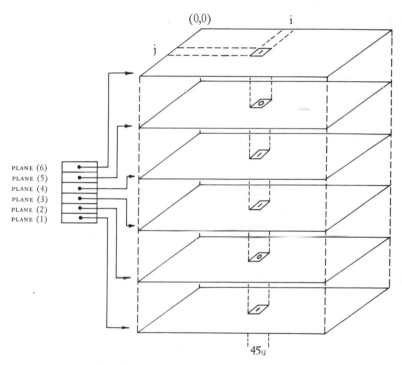

Figure 10 Representation of a z-value in a stack of planes. (Reproduced by permission of Journal of Geophysical Research.)

On the other hand, access to any single point, z_{ij}, of the surface is incredibly inefficient. To retrieve a single six-bit value, six separate accesses must be made to each of the planes containing the representation, then the individual bits assembled in a single word. As a consequence, standard procedures which operate on a surface in a sequential fashion, one point at a time, simply cannot be employed. The method of surface representation effectively demands algorithms which operate on all points of a surface simultaneously, or in parallel.

Since parallel processing of geographical surfaces is relatively uncommon this paper will conclude with a few examples of parallel surface processing. All programs were written in PAX, a FORTRAN-based parallel picture processing language developed at the University of Maryland (Butt, 1968; Johnston, 1972). All routines reference only entire surfaces (stacks of planes); in none are individual points on the surface referenced or processed.

Figure 11 illustrates the 40 by 40 surface generated from the same set of raw UNAMACE data employed in Figure 2. In this case the data were first quantized to six significant bits (64 distinct values). For graphic clarity, however, in this and succeeding figures only the five high-order bits are represented in the printout.

```
43223321        111      21      1112233455
3222221         22111 12311       112233456
321111          2211  123321     1112223467
21111111111   1111111134311        11223453
211121    1   1121212345211        1122268
22111111111  111223345422111       1123556
2211111  111111234556653212111111111123356
211122111111123457775422222222211 112244
1111211111112234548975321122222331 111235
211121111212345788632223333223442 111235
22222222222344698A75322333334542112244
2211122222234556A7543334443345431 11222
2221122222344799875333444444456432  1211
222223222334569977434565555556653211112
22332322335467997444456666655564321112
2322223333456998644566877666678543221123
3334333334569976555688877789Aa653322245
3333333435456987655539998889BCA76433454
433343333456A7976668889A999AUEA9754567
44444344432289877787AAABAABDEFDA866668ABR
4444444468888878899AUCHDCEG4EBA877BADB
444445555699A8988899ACCDEFFGJJFDBABABACA
54455555A899889989BBRCEGGHIJLJGFFCCCCCB8
5555655548A89999AABDEEGEFIMMOKIGGEECC976
55566655578A9AAHBDEFFFIMMMMPMJHGEUCBAA8
555566656789BACCCBEFIINOPRRUMJIHGEACDDA
5555677777A8ABCCDLFGKLNQRKTQPGLKIGFUDEUB
56666787779AADDEFFHMOGSUTURGPMKJHFDEFED
5666777677A9ACDEGGFLKQRUVVVSSOLJHFEFGGG
5667777889AAAFEFHJKMMNOORUVVUTOMKHFFGHHG
66666778699BCNFEHJJKKLMNPRTUUSSOMJIGHHIJG
677677889ACEFGHHHHHHIKKMQRTSQPMKIGHIJJIG
7779788898CDEFGGFGGHIKKJPGQPOMLJIIJJKKIF
67778889AABDJEEDEEFGIJLMNPPOMLJIJJLLKJGE
88A888989ABBRCDDEEEGHIKLOONMLKKKKLMLJHEC
9988999AAAAARBDDEFFGGKMONNMLLLMMMMLKFEA
A9AA89AAAAABCCOEDDCHGJMNOOMMMNOONNMJHFCA
9AA9999AABBCCCEFHJIJKKMOOONNOOOPOMLKFECB
9898AAAAARCCDEFGIHGLMNOPPOOOQQUONMJHGCB9
9RAAAAAABBACDDEFHJKMNPPQGQPPGQQPMKJFECA9
```

Figure 11   Quantized 40 by 40 surface employed in Figure 2.

Surprisingly this surface is "too small" for a system designed to process large arrays. It was expanded four-fold to produce the slightly smoothed 80 by 80 surface illustrated in Figure 12. All subsequent procedures operated on this surface. Figure 13 illustrates a contour map drawn on a plotter for comparison with Figure 3. A second program was written to find "ridges" of the surface. Figure 14 shows the resulting binary surface (ones denote ridge points), while Figure 15 shows these ridge points overlaid on the original surface. (The contours of Figure 13 have been entered by hand.) The results are clearly not of cartographic quality, but they are satisfactory for many purposes and were cheap to produce.

```
3332211122221111          111111          111          111111111122333334443
343322222332211           111111          11211         11111122233334444454
333222222222111           11111111        11122111      11111222333334456564
23222111111111            11211111111111122331111        11111222333334456565
232211111111111           11211111  1111223332111        111111222222333321
222111111111              1111111111  1112233332111       11111122222233345676
121111111111111111111111  11111111111111113344332111       11112222333345676
11111111111111111111111   11111111111111112334431111       11111122223335676
1111111111111    11       11111111111122234444321111        11111122223355676
11111111111111    111     11111111122212233444321111        1111112223356676
1211111111111111111111    111111122223334444433221111111    111112233445565
1211111111111111111111    11111122233333444444432211111f1   11111123344565
1221111111111     1111111111111122233344445655544322111111111111111111223334455
121111111111111111111111111111122334455566544322111111111111111111223334454
22111111111111111111111111111122334456666766543222211221111111221111  11122223444
121111111111111111111111111122334445677776544322111222222222221111    11111122343
1111111111111111111111111112223334444467877654332111112222222222233211  11111122344
1111111111111111111111111112223334455567888764433221112222222222333321  11111122344
11111111111111111111111111223344456789A987664332222233333333222233333211  1111122344
111111111111111111112233445678988A87654322223533333332233443211 1111112233444
121222222222211111122233333445689AAA976543322223333333333333444432111111111233443
122222222222222222222223334445689A98765433222333333333344443211111111111233443
222111111112222222222233445449999777554433333333344443211 1112233322
22211111111222222222223334556799998765433333333334444444333344553321 11112222221
122221111112222222222233446678998765433333334444444444444455543321 11121111
122222111122222222222233445676899987765433334444444444444555443211  11111111
12222222228222222223334444556789987766443335445555544554565443211111111111111
12222222223322222223333445567698987654433444556555555554566654332111111111111121
2223333223333222225333456678998764544444445665555555566444332211111111111122
22233333223333222223335456677899876944444455566666665555556443222111111111122
22341222222223333333334456689878664444455667777766666666677765443222111112233
233333232222333333333345668987765444445567777776666667777654332221111112233
2333333333333333333334456689887655555555567877777778899865443332211123444
333333333333333333333456689877665555555588877777778998AA99665443352222234444
33333333333333333334455668987766555555778888877789ABBAA976655443344444443
333333333333333333456789788766655555778889987788998B88BA9776644333444555554
333333333333333334556778877666666667788999998889ABCCA76875444555556776
3333334433333333334566777888776666666778888999999999ACC0CBA9877654456678997
34333344443334444332236778888877666677777789999AAA999AABCDDDDCBA98766556677899AA8
34444444433444433334456788888777777778888899AABBABBBCCDDFFGFDCAA9977777776ABBA8
34444444444333444445567888887777777788889999AABBABBCCCCDEFGGGEDBAA9877777789ABCCA8
34444444444444455667898888888887788AA999AABBBCCCDDEEEFFGHHGFDCBAA99999999AABBA7
34444444444444445556788998888888888899999AABBCCCDDEEFFFGIIIHFEDCCBAAAAAAAAAABB97
44444444554445556778888888888888999AAAAABCCDEFFFGGGGHIJJIIGFEEDDBBBBBBBBBBBA86
444444445556778888888888888899AABBBCCDEFFFGGHIIJKKJIGFFFFECCCC8BBCBAA976
44444445555544444557788888889999999AAABCCCDDEEEEFGHJKKLMLJIHGFFFFDDDCCBBA998765
444444555555554445577889999999AAABBCCDDDDEEEFGHIKLLLMMKJIHGFFEDDDCCBBA986765
4444455556655555557788999999AAABBCDDDEEEEFFHIJKKLLLNNLKJIHGFFFDDCC8AA99998
4445555566663555556777889AAAAAAABBBBDDDDEFFFFHIKLLLMMMNNLKJIHGGFEDDCCBAAAAAA97
4455555566666666666777789AAAABBBBCBBCDEFGHIIJLMNNOOPPPPONMMLJIHHGGFFEDCCCCCDCCA8
4555555566666666666777767777789AAABCCCDDDEFGIJKLMNOPPQQQRRPPOOONLJJIHGGFEDDCDDDDCB9
4555555566666677766778899AAACCCCDDEEEEFGJLLMQOPQRRRRSRQPOOONLKJJIHGFEDDDDDDDDLA
4556666666666777777777899AAACCDDDEEFEFGIJLMNOPQRSSSSSSRQPPOOMLJJIHGFEEJDDDEEEDDA
4556666666777777777778999AABBCDDDEFFFFFIJJKNOPQRSSTTTTTSSRQQPNMKJIHGFFEDDDEFFFFFC
4556666666777777777788999ACCDDDEEFFGGFGJJJKMOPPQRSSTTTTTSRRQNMLKJIIGFFEEDEEFFFFFC
4556666666677777778A8899999ACDDDEEFGHIIIKKKKMMMNNOOPRSSTTTTTSSRQNMLKJIGFEEEEFFGGGGFC
45566666666777777788899AAAABDDDDEFGHHIJJKKKLLMMNPQSSTTTTTSSRQNMLKJIGGFEEFFFGGGGFC
456666666677777788999AAABBCCDEDEFGHHIIIJJJJJKKLLMMNOPPRSSSSSRRRQNMLKJIHGFFFFGGHHHHGC
4666666666777777778999ABCCCDDEEEFGGHHIIIIJJKKLLMNPQRRSSSSSRRQQPNMLKIIHGFFFGGGGHIMGC
5666666666777777899AABBCCDDEFFFFGGGGGGHHHHIIJJJKLMOPQQRRRQPOONLLJJIHGGFGGHHHII1HFC
5666666667777778889999AABBCCDDEEFFFGGGGGGGGGGIIJJJKLOPPQQQQPOONMLKJIHGGGGGHHIII1HGEB
56677777777788889999AABBCCDDDEEFFFFFFFFFGGHIIJJJJJMOPPPPOONMMLKJIIHHGGHHIIJJJJIIHGFB
56777777777888899999AAABCCDDDDDDDDDEEEFFGGHIIJKKLMMNOONNMLLLKJJIIHHIIIJJJJJJJIHGFDA
56777777778888899999AAABBCCDDDDCDDDDEEFFGGHIJKLMMNNNNMMMLLLJJIIIIIIIJJJKKKKJJIHFFDA
67777777788888888999AAAAABBCCCCCDDDDDEFFGGHIIJKLMMMMMLLKKJJJJJJJJJJKKKKJJIHGEDCA
687777777788888888999AAAABBCCCCDDDDDEFFFGGHIJKLMMMMNMMLKKJJJJJJJJKKKLKKJJIIGFEDC9
788877788888999999999999AAAABBCCCCDDDEEEFFFFFGIJKLMMMMMLLLKKKKJJKKLLLLLLKJJIGFDCB8
79887777888899999999AAAABBCCCCCDDDDDEEFFGGHIJLKLLMMMMLLLLKKKKKKKKLLLLLLLLJJIHFEDCA8
799307777888899999999AAAABBBCCDDDCDCDFFFGGIJLLMMMMMLLLLKLLMMMMMMMMLLLKJIHGFECBA7
7998887778899999999AAAAAABBBCCDDDDDDDDFGGGHIKLMMMNMMLLLLLMMMMMMMMLLLKJIGFFDCBA8
79988888888899999999AAAABBCCCDDDEFFGGGGIIIIJKLMMNMMLLLLMMMMMNNNMMLLKJIIGFODCBA8
798888888999999999AAAAABBCCCCDEEFGGHHHHIJJJJJLMNNNNMMMMMNNNNNNNNMMLLKJJIFEDCCBA8
788888888999999999AAAAABBCCCDDEEFFGGGGFGJKKKKLLMMMMNOOOONNNMMLMKJIHGFECCCBA97
78888888999999999AAAAABBCDDDDEFFFGGGGGHJKLLLMMMMNOOONNNNNOOPPOONNMLKJIIGFFECBAA97
7989799AAAAAAAAAAAAAABCCCCCDDEFGGHHIIJKLLMMNNOOO0O0O0NNNNNOOPPOONNMLKJJIHFEDDCBAA97
5767778888888888888888899AAAAABBCDDEFFGGHHIIIJJJJJJJJJJJJJKKKJJIHGFFEDCBBAA98775
```

Figure 12 Corresponding expanded 80 by 80 surface smoothed by one iteration of local averaging.

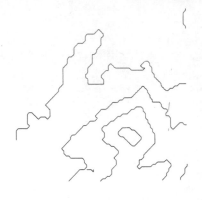

Figure 13 Contour plot of figure field shown in Figure 12.

Figure 14 (*below*) Ridges on the surface of figure field shown in Figure 12.

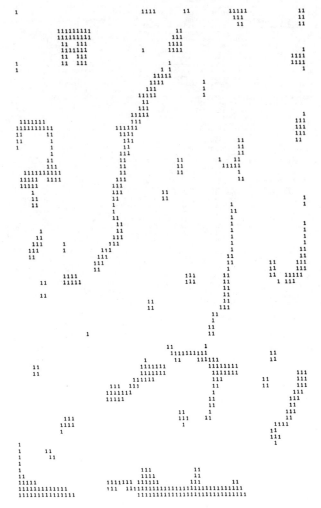

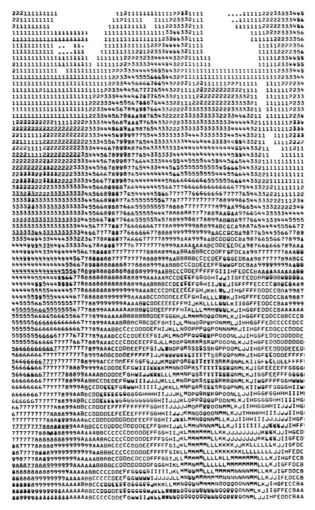

Figure 15 Ridges from Figure 14 superimposed on the original surface.

Acknowledgment

This work was supported in part by NSF grant GJ-31626 and ONR grant 00014-73-C-0109.

References

Boehm, B. W., 1967, Tabular representation of multivariate functions with applications to topographic modeling: *Rand Corp. Tech. Memo RM-4636-PR*, 80 p. Available from NTIS as AD 649330.

Butt, E., 1968, The PAX picture processing system: Univ. Maryland Computer Science Center, *Tech. Rept. 67*, 65 p.

Jancaitis, J. R., and J. L. Junkins, 1973, Modeling n-dimensional surfaces using a weighted function approach: presented 54th Annual Meeting of American Geophysical Union, Geodesy section, Washington, D.C.

Johnston, E. G., 1972, The PAX user's manual: *Air Force Cambridge Research Lab. Scientific Rept. No. 7*, AFCRL-72-0304, 300 p.

Johnston, J., and J. Pfaltz, 1967, A collection of picture processing routines: Univ. Maryland Computer Science Center, *Tech. Rept. 43*, 87 p.

Junkins, J. L., G. W. Miller, and J. R. Jancaitis, 1973, A weighting function approach to modeling of irregular surfaces: *Jour. Geophysical Research*, v. 78, no. 11, p. 1794–1803.

Pfaltz, J. L., and A. Rosenfeld, 1967, Computer representation of planar regions by their skeletons: *Communications, Assoc. Computing Machinery*, v. 10, no. 2, p. 119–125.

Programs of the Harvard University Laboratory for Computer Graphics and Spatial Analysis

A. H. Schmidt and W. A. Zafft

Recent decades, indeed recent years, have seen considerable advances in the process by which graphic displays of data are created. Many of these advances can be traced, directly or indirectly, to the development of automated or computerized methods of producing maps. As production methods have changed, the capability for displaying data has found diverse uses and gained new importance. Indeed, even the name of the end product invokes this evolution: "map" versus "graphic display of data". The word "map" is more limited in context and implies more of a geographer's bias than does the term "graphic display".

Producing a map by the traditional hand method can be a formidable task. Great care and much labor are needed to create even a moderately complex map. Given these constraints, it is not surprising that before automated methods for producing maps were developed, a map was a precious item, similar to a book before the invention of the printing press. Maps tended to be general in content, so they could be used by as many people as possible. Production of specialized maps for small audiences was infeasible in all but a few instances.

The development of computerized mapping methods relaxed many of the constraints imposed on traditional map production. It is becoming clear that the advantages of computerized mapping do not primarily relate to the physical production of maps, as computer-drawn maps are often less precise than hand-drawn ones, and in many instances more expensive. Rather, computers allow greater flexibility in the manipulation of data and graphic symbolism. Obviously, the capability of automatic data handling allows a user to produce individualized maps showing specialized data. A more subtle advantage concerns the manipulation of symbolism. It is based on the fact that patterns in the data are often enhanced or suppressed by the nature of the symbolism used in creating a map. Computers allow a user to experiment with his data and with map characteristics to find the symbolism, map contents, and scale which best communicate information about the data. They provide this capability by enabling the user to quickly and easily specify production of a map.

As is common with innovations, computerized map production has changed from difference-in-degree to difference-in-kind. Thus, experiments in computer mapping are most valuable and successful, not when they merely attempt to duplicate previous methods, but when they seek to develop new capabilities. These new capabilities include the creation of different types of maps such as three-dimensional plots and the use of maps for new purposes, often involving data analysis rather than just data display. The resulting integration of man and machine can be a paradigm for other fields, since it weds the computer's ability to manipulate data and symbols and to create patterns with man's ability to seek out, recognize, and interpret these patterns. This, in turn, places greater responsibility on the user. He must develop greater sophistication in specifying and analyzing graphic displays of data so that he can make full use of the capabilities being developed while recognizing and avoiding the bias inherent in any display of data.

One way of working toward this goal is to allow the user maximum opportunity to make his own maps. He can learn by doing, if he is given the proper set of tools and aids. Computerized mapping can provide the tools to enable both the novice and the sophisticated user to create maps and, what is more important, to help the novice become a sophisticated user.

The Laboratory for Computer Graphics and Spatial Analysis was established in 1965 with a grant from the Ford Foundation to the Harvard University Graduate School of Design. Since its inception, the Laboratory has conducted research in general spatial systems theory. This work has involved investigations in spatial patterns occurring in architecture, city and regional planning, and other design professions. Other research has been organized in theoretical geography, particularly in the theory of surfaces as related to spatial structure and spatial processes for geographic phenomena, the macrogeography of social and economic phenomena, and central place theory.

Much of the effort of the Laboratory has been in the development and dissemination of programs which can be used by both the novice and the sophisticated map maker. Initial work at the Laboratory centered on the SYMAP program. Substantial modification and improvement has been made in this program, as well as in the other programs that have been developed. Recent investigations have been directed to applications involving specialized output devices, such as pen plotters and cathode ray tube (CRT) plotters. New programs are also being developed to aid in the manipulation of large files of geographic data, describing the outline (in x–y coordinates) of various geographic areas. Comprehensive data banks are being assembled which describe such features as the outlines of the countries of the world, outlines of the states and counties in the United States, and information on various U.S. metropolitan areas. Users will be able to combine these geographic files with their own specialized data to greatly simplify the production of thematic maps. The Laboratory is also developing techniques for computerized animation for the presentation of spatially variable time-series data.

Computer Programs

Much of the following discussion emphasizes the SYMAP program, for a number of reasons. SYMAP is the most widely known and distributed mapping program (approximately 300 copies of SYMAP have been distributed by the Laboratory), and in many ways it is the precursor of other programs. Not only was it developed first, but other programs, including those developed elsewhere, often draw from the design or the capabilities of SYMAP. For example, some programs are merely specialized versions of SYMAP, designed for particular output devices or for use with a particular kind of data. Other programs make use of SYMAP's input conventions, organizing the input in a series of packages, each describing a particular type of feature of the map. The provision of a series of mapping options, with default actions when the option is not used, has been widely imitated. And finally, some programs use SYMAP as a preprocessor. The most common examples of this are programs that require regularly spaced geographic data as input. In these and other ways, SYMAP has demonstrated and encouraged advances in graphic display techniques.

SYMAP

Work on the SYMAP program was started in 1963 by Howard Fisher at Northwestern Technological Institute. Further development followed establishment of the Laboratory for Computer Graphics at Harvard University in 1965. Substantial modifications in SYMAP were made by Russel and Shepard, whose work has been extended by Reine.

SYMAP is designed to produce graphic displays of spatially distributed data with as few constraints as possible. SYMAP produces output on a standard line printer; specialized output devices are not needed. It is designed to require little prior experience with computers or with mapping. Great flexibility has been included in the program, so that both the novice and sophisticated user can use SYMAP to the best of their respective abilities. SYMAP includes over 35 options for controlling the characteristics of the output map, all of which have defaults. SYMAP can produce contour, conformant, or proximal maps. Several maps can be produced for a single input deck, as SYMAP can internally save information for re-use in successive maps.

Contour (isopleth) maps are used to describe a continuously varying data function from observations made at discrete locations. SYMAP interpolates from known data point values to construct a continuous surface. Interpolated points on the surface are assigned to an interval. A unique printer character is used to represent each interval and the computed surface is displayed using the appropriate symbol at each print location.

Conformant (choropleth) maps are used to depict values given to pre-defined data zones, where a zone may be a point, a line, or an area. A unique symbol is assigned to each value interval, as with contour maps, and the symbolic representation of the data is displayed.

Proximal maps construct zones around each data point using a nearest-neighbor criterion. Each constructed zone is assigned the value of the enclosed data point and a symbol is printed throughout the zone. Proximal maps do not interpolate between known data values, although they do compute distances between data points.

The SYMAP interpolation algorithm for contour mapping can compute a continuously differentiable, regularly spaced data surface from a series of irregularly spaced input values. The interpolation algorithm can be controlled by the user through the use of relative or absolute limits on interpolation, by altering the number of data points used to compute unknown values, or by the inclusion of barriers to interpolation. The algorithm uses a weighted average of known data values, based on an inverse distance model, with correction for other characteristics of the data surface such as special configurations of the data points. The resulting computed surface passes through each of the known data points.

Input to SYMAP is given in a series of "packages", each of which describe one type of feature of the area to be studied. These specify the outline of the map area, the location and value of data points, and the location and content of map "cosmetics" such as legends, titles, or special features such as rivers, highways, and railroads. Standard formats have been provided, or the user can specify his own input format, and can manipulate or transform the data before transferring information to SYMAP. Another package is used to define the characteristics of each output map: its size, scale, contents, number and range of data intervals, and symbolism used for each interval. Special symbols can be used to identify the location of data points, the contour or zonal boundaries, and background. SYMAP can also store the values of the computed data surface for input to other programs. The mapping options enable the user to tailor the output to his requirements, while allowing him the opportunity to produce an adequate map with as little effort as possible.

SYMAP is widely used in both academic and non-academic applications in the fields of geology, geography, archaeology, city and regional planning, architecture, economics, medicine, biology, and physics. About 50 percent of

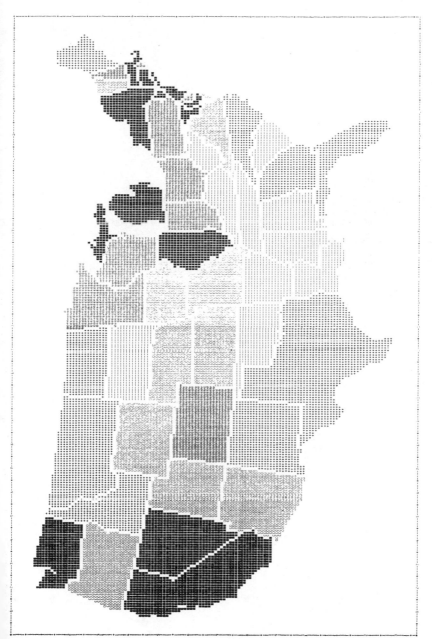

Figure 1 SYMAP conformant map showing 1970 median family income for the U.S. by state.

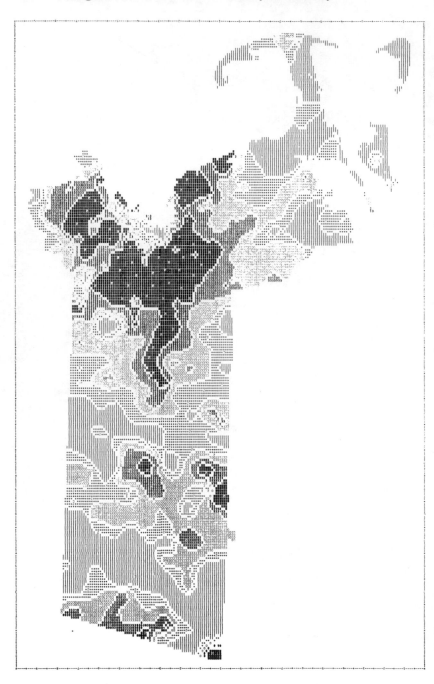

Figure 2 SYMAP contour showing 1970 median family income for Massachusetts by town. Contour lines computed on the basis of town centroids.

the SYMAP installations are at universities, and 25 percent each at governmental and private institutions. SYMAP manuals have been translated into several languages, including German, Spanish, and Japanese. Part of this acceptance is the result of the flexibility and generality of SYMAP, as it imposes few preconceived notions on what the user wants to do.

SYMAP is written in FORTRAN IV Level G. It can be run in 150K bytes of core memory on an IBM 360/40 computer, and has been modified to run on Burroughs, CDC, DEC, GE, Honeywell, ICL, RCA, Siemens, UNIVAC, XDS, as well as other IBM computers. The cost for a SYMAP plot similar to those shown in Figures 1–3 is approximately $4.

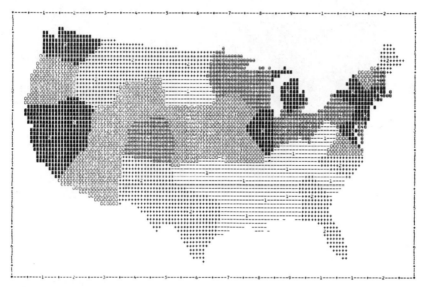

Figure 3 SYMAP proximal map of 1970 median family income for the U.S. by state. Proximal zones computed on the basis of state centroids.

CALFORM

The CALFORM program was initially written by Robert Cartwright in 1969, under the sponsorship of the University of Missouri. Since then, the program has been extensively revised and modified. CALFORM produces conformant (choropleth) maps on a pen or CRT plotter, and hence produces maps with greater precision and quality than is possible on a line printer. The resulting maps contain shading symbols which represent values attributed to each data zone. CALFORM can also produce simple outline maps containing no data value information.

CALFORM contains many options similar to those in SYMAP. Input to CALFORM is organized in a similar way as a series of input "packages"

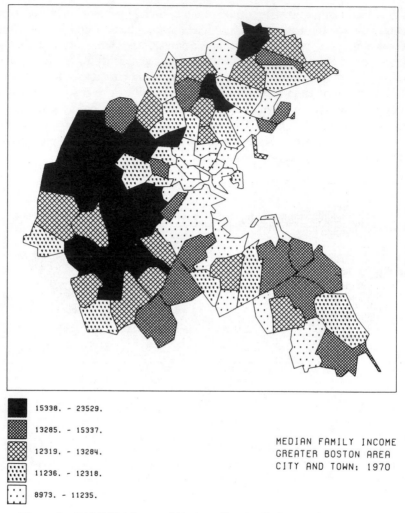

15338. - 23529.

13285. - 15337.

12319. - 13284.

11236. - 12318.

8973. - 11235.

MEDIAN FAMILY INCOME
GREATER BOSTON AREA
CITY AND TOWN: 1970

Figure 4   CALFORM map of 1970 median family income for the Boston
SMSA by towns.

describing particular components of the map production process. These
specify the location and shape of the data zones, the legends and title, and the
values associated with each zone. The map size and type, the number and
range of data levels, and the shading symbols associated with each level may
also be defined by the user. CALFORM, like SYMAP, contains defaults
for many options to aid the novice.

Data zones are defined in the CALFORM program by listing a unique
number assigned to each node. The list of node numbers for a zone is then
combined with a list giving the x–y coordinates of each node, to specify the

size and location of the zone. This procedure is more efficient than that used by SYMAP, since the x–y location of each node is specified only once. One particular advantage of this scheme is that it interfaces with work being done at the Harvard Laboratory on geographic base files. Many of the data banks being assembled will be accepted by CALFORM without modification, which will greatly facilitate the creation of thematic maps.

CALFORM is frequently used to produce conformant maps for photographic reproduction, often after preliminary analysis has been done using SYMAP. CALFORM is written in FORTRAN IV Level G. It requires 150K bytes of core memory on an IBM 360/40 computer and has been modified to run on CDC and XDS, as well as other IBM computers. The program has also been modified to run in 100K bytes of core memory. CalComp plotter software must also be provided. If the program is to use a CRT plotter, additional minor modifications are needed. Costs for use of CALFORM are related to the size of the output plot; a plot similar to that shown in Figure 4 costs approximately $1, plus plotting time (1–3 hours at approximately $8/hour). Figure 4 shows a CALFORM plot made on a CalComp plotter. Income data by city and town for the Greater Boston Standard Metropolitan Statistical Area is shown. This plot may be compared to Figures 5 and 6, which show similar data plotted by SYMVU.

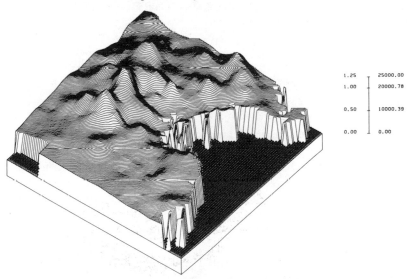

```
                                          1.25      25000.00
                                          1.00      20000.78

                                          0.50      10000.39

                                          0.00       0.00
```

MEDIAN FAMILY INCOME: GREATER BOSTON AREA BY CITY AND TOWN - 1970
AZIMUTH = 51   ALTITUDE = 45
*WIDTH = 5.00   *HEIGHT = 1.77
* BEFORE FORESHORTENING

Figure 5 SYMVU map of 1970 median family income for the Boston SMSA by towns. View from the southeast. Data values initially computed by SYMAP program using contour mapping option.

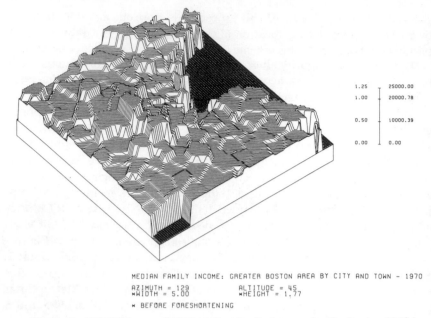

MEDIAN FAMILY INCOME: GREATER BOSTON AREA BY CITY AND TOWN - 1970
AZIMUTH = .129   ALTITUDE = 45
*WIDTH = 5.00   *HEIGHT = 1.77
* BEFORE FORESHORTENING

Figure 6   SYMVU map of 1970 median family income for the Boston SMSA
by towns. View from the southwest. Data values initially computed by SYMAP
program using conformant mapping option.

SYMVU

Initial work on the SYMVU program was done by Waldo Tobler at the
University of Michigan in 1965. The basic program was written by Frank
Rens and others at the Harvard Laboratory. Muxworthy at the University
of Edinburgh has also contributed to its development.

SYMVU generates a three-dimensional perspective view of a surface, using
a pen or CRT plotter. SYMVU can display contour (isopleth), conformant
(choropleth), and proximal maps of greater precision and quality than
SYMAP can produce, although it has greater constraints on the input data.
SYMVU automatically omits those parts of a surface that are hidden from
view. Once a surface is defined, a user can produce successive views, each
having different characteristics.

SYMVU requires a matrix of regularly spaced data values as input and
cannot interpolate between irregularly spaced data, as SYMAP does. Thus,
SYMAP is often used to preprocess data for input to SYMVU. A gridded
surface computed by SYMAP can be temporarily stored for use with
SYMVU, or if the data are in matrix form initially, they may be used directly.

One advantage of SYMVU is that data do not need to be classified into
intervals since SYMVU can display continuous data. This allows the user to

display more of the detail of his data structure than can be displayed with a two-dimensional view. SYMVU can produce plots with as few as three control cards, plus the data values. However, almost 30 options are provided to alter plot production, including plot size, orientation, tilt, symbolism, and vertical scaling.

SYMVU can be used whenever SYMAP is used, if greater precision or quality is needed and if the restrictions on input data are met. Plots produced by SYMVU have enjoyed great acceptance, with many users claiming a dramatic improvement in readability over more traditional plots. Computer requirements for SYMVU are similar to those of CALFORM, except 220K bytes of core memory are required on an IBM 360/40 computer. A plot from SYMVU similar to those shown in Figures 5 and 6 costs approximately $4.

These figures show two views of income data for the cities and towns in the Greater Boston Standard Metropolitan Statistical Area. Note both the change in orientation and the shift from a contour to a conformant map structure.

GRID

The GRID program was developed by David Sinton and Carl Steinitz in 1968, and is a simplified, special purpose version of SYMAP. It is designed to efficiently display large quantities of information collected at regular grid intervals. Output is produced on a standard line printer.

GRID accepts a matrix of data values as input and assigns each value to a grid cell, based on the sequence in which the values are read and on the user-specified dimensions of the data matrix. Each data value is assigned to a specific value range; each range is assigned a unique graphic symbol. Output from GRID consists of the symbolic representation of the data values. GRID can also produce a "dot map" of the data.

The user can specify the characteristics of the data and the intervals used. He must specify the symbols used in printing the map, as there is no default option, and can include legends and text for the map. Although GRID is designed for rectangular areas, provision has been made for describing irregularly shaped outlines. There is no maximum size for the input matrix, since each line of input is immediately converted into a line of output. However, input value may be manipulated by other routines which then pass on modified values to GRID prior to creation of the output map. The size of the output map is a function of the size of the data matrix and the size of the output cells.

GRID is used whenever gridded data sources are available, as in aerial surveys of natural resource data. It has also been used to perform sieve mapping and to do composite variable or index mapping. Program specifications are similar to those of SYMAP, except only 100K bytes of core are required on an IBM 360/40 computer. Typical cost for a GRID map with

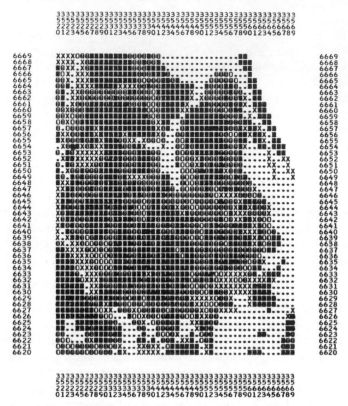

Figure 7   GRID map of foundation characteristics, showing six classes mapped on a 49 by 49 grid.

10,000 cells (100 by 100 matrix) is approximately $2–3. Figure 7 shows results of a study on foundations and ground subsurface characteristics, as produced by GRID.

Selected Publications on SYMAP and Related Programs

The following publications are available from the Laboratory for Computer Graphics and Spatial Analysis, Graduate School of Design, Harvard University, Cambridge, Mass., U.S.A.

Dudnik, E. E., 1971, SYMAP user's reference manual for synagraphic computer mapping: Univ. Illinois Dept. Architecture *Rept. No. 71-1*, 114 p. Describes the installation and use of SYMAP.

Harvard University Laboratory for Computer Graphics and Spatial Analysis, 1971, *GRID manual version 3*, 38 p. Describes installation and use of GRID.

Harvard University Laboratory for Computer Graphics and Spatial Analysis, 1971, *SYMVU user's–operator's reference manual*, 60 p. Describes installation and use of SYMVU.

Harvard University Laboratory for Computer Graphics and Spatial Analysis, 1972, *CALFORM manual*, 81 p. Describes installation and use of CALFORM.

Harvard University Laboratory for Computer Graphics and Spatial Analysis, 1973, *LAB-LOG, Catalog*, 30 p. Summary of materials available from Harvard University Laboratory for Computer Graphics and Spatial Analysis.

Harvard University Laboratory for Computer Graphics and Spatial Analysis, 1973, *Selected projects*, 400 p. Describes projects involving computer mapping and use of programs.

Shepard, D. S., 1968, A two-dimensional interpolation function for computer mapping of irregularly spaced data: Harvard Univ. Papers in Theoretical Geography, *Geography and the Properties of Surfaces Series Paper No. 15*, 20 p. Discusses the SYMAP interpolation algorithm for estimating values from irregularly spaced data points.

The SURFACE II Graphics System

R. J. Sampson

Geologists, especially those engaged in exploration for natural resources, have a great need for automated methods of creating maps. Much of the raw data of exploration is now stored in computer data banks. This information includes analyses of rock samples, measurements of geophysical properties, and data from wells and boreholes. Commonly, an exploration geologist must utilize hundreds or thousands of observations, each consisting of many variables, in the development and evaluation of a prospect. All of these variables must be considered in the form of maps, so spatial relationships become apparent.

The search for resources could be accelerated if the step from data bank to geologic exploration map were automated. Many geologic parameters such as subsurface structural configuration, variations in geomagnetic or gravity fields, and changes in mineralogic composition can be expressed as contour maps. Contour maps are especially useful in the exploration for oil and gas, where they are used to depict the form of subsurface strata. These maps delineate features which hopefully form traps for hydrocarbons. The maps are drawn from data collected from wells previously drilled in the area or from measurements of seismic reflections from buried horizons.

The potential value and utility of automatic contouring programs has occurred to many people, and dozens, perhaps hundreds, of computer programs have been written for this purpose. They range from simple, inefficient routines in the public domain to highly sophisticated, proprietary graphics systems priced at many tens of thousands of dollars. The algorithms vary greatly in their approach to the contouring problem, and also vary greatly in the degree of success which they achieve in a given mapping situation (Walden, 1972). Unfortunately, the performance of an automatic contouring method cannot be predicted from the magnitude of the price tag or the complexity of coding within the program.

Development of an optimal contouring program is hindered by the almost total lack of theoretical guidelines. Statistical theory of spatial variability is sketchy and of little use in practical situations such as those which arise in geologic exploration. Empirical guidance is also in short supply because of the highly proprietary nature of most commercial systems and the natural reluctance of their authors to submit their programs for comparative analysis.

The Kansas Geological Survey, in common with most other geological organizations, has long recognized the potential worth of a powerful computer contouring system for use in the Earth sciences. However, unlike most other groups, the Survey not only possesses a massive computer data bank of geologic information, but also has a directive to perform basic as well as applied research. This provides an incentive not only to use an automatic contouring system, but also to investigate the fundamental nature of spatial variability and the contouring problem itself. The cost of developing a sophisticated contouring package might be prohibitive if it were not for our mandate to conduct basic research; this allows us to write off our development costs against the fundamental knowledge gained about the way certain geologic variables change through space.

Over the past four years the Kansas Geological Survey has been developing a computer graphics system called "SURFACE II". The system is primarily designed to create subsurface structural contour maps of data contained within our well-data file. However, it also has features designed to allow us to investigate problems in spatial variability. Because conflicting opinions exist as to the "best" method of contouring irregularly spaced data, SURFACE II is written in an extremely flexible manner so the behavior of contouring algorithms themselves can be investigated. Our contouring system is not a finished package. Indeed, it will probably never be "finished", as it is designed to grow and to be modified as the objectives of our research change.

Because of the dual purpose which SURFACE II serves, we have established certain goals which have been used to guide development of the system. Although these goals could be articulated in different ways, basically we are concerned that (a) the system be easy to use by anyone, whether computer scientist or field geologist, (b) the system be easily transportable so it can be moved from one computer system to another, and, finally, (c) the system have a modular structure which can be easily modified to allow for experimentation. This discussion will concentrate on programming decisions taken to achieve these goals.

Structure of SURFACE II

SURFACE II is a large computer software system for manipulation and display of spatially distributed data. The system, in general, will display the form of any variable characterized by values "located" in coordinates defined by two other variables. The only inherent restrictions are that the coordinate variables must be orthogonal and the mapped variable must be single valued.

To insure that the system could be easily used by a novice with no training in programming, it was necessary to develop a simple control language which uses English-like words to identify each operation. These words form a series of instructions or *commands* which are understood by SURFACE II. The *name* is the first four characters of each command, but a longer, complete word can be used to help identify the command to the user. Following the command name is a list of parameters associated with its operation. These parameters are written in a free format, each being separated by a comma. Not all parameters must be given, as most have an assumed value which is used if an explicit value is not supplied.

Use of a free format was chosen for two teasons. Firstly, it makes writing the documentation for the system easier. It is only necessary to describe the purpose of a command and the order of the associated parameters; elaborate coding instuctions are not needed. Secondly, it is easier for a user to set up an input deck in free format, especially when using a remote terminal for job input. A direct consequence is reduction in the number of failed runs resulting from erroneous instructions.

Commands in SURFACE II can be divided into two categories. These include *active* commands which cause an operation to be performed and therefore must be given each time the operation is to be executed. *Secondary* commands affect the operation of active commands. If a secondary command is not given, assumed values for the parameters of that command will be used automatically. Also, once a secondary command has been used, its parameters stay in effect until replaced by another occurrence of that command.

Another important feature of the command language is that the order of occurrence of most commands is not mandatory. Commands are read in and saved until a PERFORM command is encountered. Then the active commands are executed according to a predetermined sequence. Secondary commands are automatically associated with their proper active command. Each time an active command is executed, a printed report is generated which describes all parameters and options used during its execution.

The various active commands are executed in the following order:

>INPUT
>DATA MANIPULATION
>OUTPUT
>GRAPHIC OUTPUT.

This series of operations is repeated until there are no more commands to execute or until a STOP command is encountered. If the predetermined sequence of execution is not the one desired by a user, the active commands can be separated by PERFORM commands. PERFORM overrides the automatic sequence and causes commands to be executed in the order in which they appear. This gives an advanced user great flexibility in the operation of the program.

Another important feature which simplifies use of the program is that not all user errors are fatal. A typical user error would be specification of an invalid value for a parameter. The program will automatically generate an error message given complete details of why the command is incorrect and what course of action has been taken. The assumed value for the parameter is then used in place of the erroneous value and execution continues. This "fail-safe" feature is important because on the first attempt to produce a map from an unfamiliar data set, the best choice of parameters to properly represent the data may not be obvious. For example, the most effective grid size, contour interval, or map size may have to be deduced by trial-and-error. If the user can obtain *any* results from his initial attempt, then the computer run may not have been a total waste, even if there are errors in the parameters. Any new data set generally has a few bad values which must be located and corrected. Gross data errors often can be spotted at once in a map because they appear as a tight group of closed contour levels, with the central value being much different from surrounding values. Even a map made with erroneous parameters may be useful in spotting these bad data points.

To achieve the second goal of transportability, it was important that the contouring system be as machine-independent as possible. The Kansas Geological Survey uses the University of Kansas computer and has little control over acquisition of new hardware or changes in the current hardware configuration and operating system. As the Survey has a small programming staff, it is important that changes in the university computation center do not necessitate massive changes in our program library. In addition, the Survey provides services to the geological profession and it is desirable that the SURFACE II graphics system be transportable to other facilities with minimal effort. Therefore most of the system is written in a selected subset of the current version of FORTRAN IV. Restrictions placed on the FORTRAN language include:

(1) No mixed-mode arithmetic is used

(2) No random I/O is performed

(3) Format generator is not used

(4) Type statements such as REAL*8 and INTEGER*2 are not used

(5) Only subscripts of the form C, V, V $\pm$ C, K*V $\pm$ C are used

(6) Characters are handled only in A1 or A4 format

(7) All references to file numbers in I/O statements are variable.

SURFACE II now runs on the Honeywell 635 computer using the FORTRAN Y compiler and on the IBM 360/370 computer using OS with the FORTRAN G or H compiler.

Machine-dependent routines comprise less than 10 percent of the total number of routines and tend to be very simple. Some of these are optional and could easily be replaced with dummy routines. Typical examples of machine-dependent features include routines to pack and unpack characters and extract and insert bits in a word. The time of day and certain other data must be obtained from the operating system for labeling and the timing of processing. It is also necessary to obtain elapsed processor time from the operating system and to obtain information about specific I/O files. The table of machine-dependent constants used by the system must be initialized by a FORTRAN routine specific to the computer used. Of course, a routine also must be custom-tailored to interface the particular plotters used in a specific computation center.

The current SURFACE II system has approximately 19,000 FORTRAN and assembler language statements in more than 100 routines, although about 25 percent of the FORTRAN statements are comment cards. The final system is expected to have 25,000 to 30,000 statements in more than 150 routines. The system is large and still growing, but does not demand all of the memory of a large computer system for its operation. This is achieved by using overlays and having only a small fraction of the system in core at one time. Overlays are used at four levels. Level 1 consists of the mainline program and subroutines callable by more than one level or callable by the lowest level. This includes 19 routines which reside in core during job execution. Level 2 consists of "submainline" routines, one for each of the principal parts of the system. These consist mostly of calls to Level 3 routines and logic control statements. The routines control the order in which the active commands are executed. Level 2 contains eight routines and eight segments.

Level 3 includes the routines that do most of the work and where most of the coding exists. Each active command is broken into one or more modules that appear in this group of routines. Fifty-one routines and 44 segments are implemented at this level. Level 4 consists of utility subroutines callable by Level 3 routines. These comprise 28 routines and 11 segments.

The programming goal is to minimize the amount of memory used by overlaying as much of the system as possible. An attempt is also made to minimize the size of the largest routine in core at each level. With this technique, it is not necessary to be concerned about minimizing the number of routines or restricting the ultimate size of the system.

It is difficult to define a "typical" memory requirement, because it is difficult to describe a "typical" contouring problem. Using the Honeywell 635 computer, it is possible to run a data set consisting of 500 irregularly spaced control points and to construct a grid matrix containing 70 columns and rows using only 25K words of memory (Honeywell 635 words contain 36 bits). The program and I/O buffers require 17K words leaving 8K of the 25K words for storage of data. Since the user specifies at run time the amount of memory available, all memory in excess of the amount required for the program is assigned to COMMON, to be used to store data. SURFACE II does not utilize fixed sizes of arrays, so all of COMMON could be used to store data points, leaving no room to store the grid matrix, or vice versa. In practice, of course, some combination of sample data and grid matrix is stored in this part of memory. If the user does not provide SURFACE II with enough memory to execute the specified commands, execution terminates with a message telling how much additional memory will be required. Since memory cost is one of the most expensive charges associated with running a job, the user must be careful to specify the optimum amount of memory.

On an IBM 360/67 using OS/MFT, memory requirements are very different. In this computer, memory size is fixed by the size of the partition used. No charge is made for the amount of memory, so all memory available in the partition can be used for the program. This is done by determining the size of the program and all I/O buffers, and then adjusting the dimensions of the COMMON array to make up the difference. For example, with a partition size of 260K bytes, the COMMON array could be as large as 160K bytes. Because the program and I/O buffers will require approximately 100K bytes of the 260K partition, it would be possible to process large data sets including as many as 5000 to 6000 sample points and creating grid matrices having up to 200 columns and rows.

Contour Maps

Isoline drawings, or contour maps, constitute the largest category of output created by users of SURFACE II. Examples of user applications include structural contour and isopach maps made for petroleum exploration, topographic and population-density maps for use by geographers, and exotic maps such as trend-residual and filtered maps created for a variety of research purposes.

Before a map can be drawn, the surface must be represented in the computer as a rectangular grid of points. Contouring consists of calculating the locations of specified isolines through this grid. The perimeter of the grid is searched until the range in value between two successive points includes the value of a contour line. The location of the line at the perimeter is found by interpolation. Once this starting point has been located, the contour line is followed through the grid matrix to its end. When all contour lines that intersect the edge of the map have been located, the interior of the grid is searched for closed contour lines. At this time, the interiors of closed contours are examined to determine if they represent depressions or highs.

In tracing contour lines through the grid matrix, the situation may arise where two corners of a grid cell are higher and two are lower than the value of the contour line entering the cell. Three possible paths exist for contour lines through such a cell, as shown in Figure 1. In SURFACE II, contour

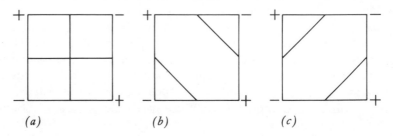

(a)   (b)   (c)

Figure 1 Possible paths of contour lines through a cell having two corners higher and two corners lower than the value of contour line entering cell. (a) Unacceptable solution using crossing contour lines. (b) Solution if average of corners is higher than contour line. (c) Solution if average of corners is lower than contour line.

lines are not allowed to cross, eliminating the solution shown in Figure 1a. A choice is made between the two remaining alternatives on the following basis. First, the value at the center of the grid cell is estimated by finding the average of the values at the corners of the cell. If the value at the center is greater than the contour level being traced, the solution shown in Figure 1b is used; if the center is lower than the contour level, the solution in Figure 1c is used.

Once all contour lines have been calculated, the order in which they will be plotted is determined. This is done by a sorting procedure that insures that travel of the plotter carriage with the pen off the paper is as small as possible.

Finally, the contour lines are prepared for drawing on the map. At this stage the lines can be smoothed to reduce their angularity, which is a function of the coarseness of the grid matrix. The smoothing procedure used is a weighted average of two circular arcs (IBM, 1969). As an example, to smooth line segment FG in Figure 2, circular arcs are calculated which pass through EFG and FGH. Then, n equally spaced intermediate points are calculated on each circular arc. The location of an intermediate point on the contour line is the weighted average of corresponding intermediate points on the circular arcs. The weight for arc EFG is 1 at F and decreases linearly to 0 at G. The weight for arc FGH is 0 at F and increases linearly to 1 at G.

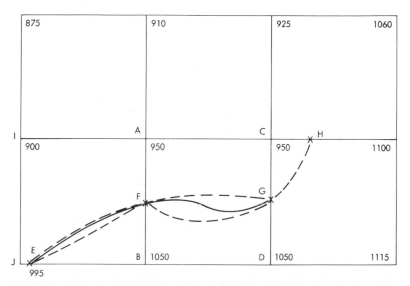

Figure 2   Contour line smoothing performed by averaging overlapping circular arcs (dashed lines) to obtain continuous contour line (solid line). (Courtesy of International Business Machines Corporation.)

Annotation is added to the contour lines at this stage. This includes labeling, the drawing of heavy or bold lines, and hachuring of contour lines around closed depressions. Bold lines are made by the simple expedient of drawing back along the contour line after offsetting a small amount parallel to the original line.

Selecting the places where annotation is to be inserted into a contour line is an interesting challenge, because it has a disproportionate influence on user acceptance of the finished map. In SURFACE II, labels are placed at least one inch or a distance equal to the length of a label (whichever is greater) in from the map edge. Labels are then spaced at specified distances along the contour line. However, labels can be placed only where the contour line is "straight enough" to accept them. This is determined by the check shown in Figure 3. The perpendicular distance between line AF and points on the contour line replaced by the label (points B, C, D, and E) must be less than half the height of a character used in the label.

Line annotation is only one of many features under user control in SURFACE II. Although these parameters have no effect on the accuracy of the graphic representation, they strongly influence esthetic acceptability of the finished product. The use of most of these features is optional under the "fail-safe" system, so the user may elaborate upon the appearance of the final output to any desired degree. An outline of the available parameters is

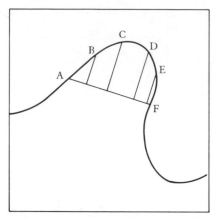

Figure 3   Determination of degree of curvature on contour line for placement of labels.

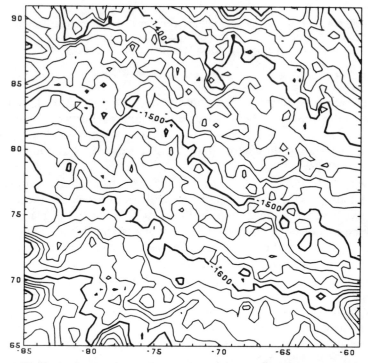

Figure 4   Contour map of subsurface structural configuration on the top of the Lansing Group (Pennsylvanian) in Stafford Co., Kansas. Elevations in feet below sea level. Geographic coordinates given in miles from an arbitrary origin. Approximately 1200 wells were used for control.

Table 1.   Options under user control that affect appearance of finished contour map

---

A.   Adjustment of map size or scale
B.   Annotation of map border
     Character location
     Origin of scale
     Frequency of annotation
     Size of characters
     Character format
C.   Posting of data points on map
     Type of symbol
     Label size
     Label format
D.   Adjustment of contour interval
     Origin of contour scale
     Contour spacing
     Unequally spaced contour levels specified by table
E.   Contour line annotation
     Size, frequency, and format of labels
     Specification of heavy lines
     Specification of hachured lines
F.   Smoothing of contour lines
G.   Plotting of outlines on map

---

given in Table 1. Figure 4 shows a subsurface structural contour map of the top of the Lansing Group (Pennsylvanian) in Stafford County, Kansas. The map was made using many of the options of SURFACE II.

Transect Plots

In addition to isoline maps, transect or block diagrams may be produced from grid matrices. A transect diagram is a perspective or isometric projection of a surface, and for many persons is easier to visualize than a contour map. However, a transect plot cannot easily be used for quantitative analysis, so its applications are primarily pictorial. Figure 5 shows a block diagram representation of topography in the Lawrence, Kansas, area. Figure 6 is an illustration of a potential energy surface formed by H_2 reacting with an H atom (J. Remark, personal communication, 1973).

In the construction of these diagrams, hidden lines are automatically removed and some plotter optimization is done to reduce drawing time. The pen tracks down one line in the x-direction and returns back along the next parallel line. All lines are drawn in the x-direction, then all lines in the y-direction. The hidden line algorithm used is an extensive modification of the procedure developed by Kubert, Szabo, and Giulieri (1968) and by Rohlf

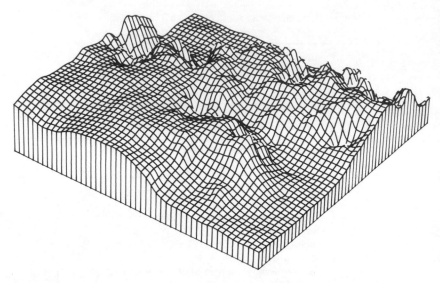

Figure 5 Perspective block diagram or "fishnet" plot of topography near Lawrence, Kansas. Data taken from northern half of Wakarusa 7½ minute Quadrangle.

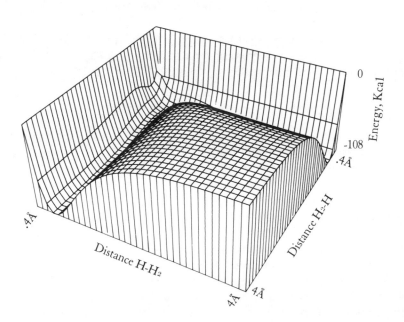

Figure 6 Block diagram showing potential energy surface formed by hydrogen molecule (H_2) reacting with hydrogen atom.

(1969). The user can adjust all scale parameters, including viewing angle and viewing distance, which control the perspective effect on the block.

Line Printer Maps

It might seem strange that a plotter system should contain options to produce line printer maps, but there are practical reasons for having this capability. Maps can be made on a line printer at a much faster rate than on a line plotter, because turn-around time is shorter for the line printer, which runs continuously, than for peripheral or off-line plotters, which require special handling. The cost of printing a map usually is much lower than the cost to plot a map of the same physical dimensions, although resolution in the printer map will also be lower. However, line printer maps can be used to check the choice of contour interval and variables of scale and grid size before a final map is plotted. These maps also provide an inexpensive method of checking data sets for drastic errors (keypunch or coding mistakes), as these may appear as obvious "post holes" or peaks on the contoured surface.

SURFACE II will construct line printer maps of any desired size, so the problem of resolution can be solved by making a very large map for subsequent reduction. Unfortunately, the extra steps negate the cost savings which is the principal attraction of line printer maps. The limited character set available on a printer is a constraint on the number of contour intervals that can be shown, and the restricted number of density steps that can be created by overprinting limits the range of shading that can be produced. Some of these inherent constraints are apparent in Figure 7, which is a line printer map of the same data used to create Figure 4.

Data Manipulation

A variety of commands are included in SURFACE II for manipulation of data, particularly for interpolation from irregularly spaced data points to the nodes of a regular grid. This must be done if contour maps or transect diagrams are to be drawn of irregularly spaced data, and also if certain transformations are to be made. For example, derivative and filtered maps can be made only if the data are in gridded form. General surface-to-surface operations, such a subtracting two surfaces to find their difference (isopach map construction) is possible only if the surfaces are defined at the nodes of a regular grid.

The method used for interpolation to a grid is a two-part, weighted average of nearest neighboring data points around each grid node. In an initial pass, the slope of the surface is estimated at every data point. A search procedure finds the nearest n neighbors to the data point being considered and fits a weighted trend surface to these points. Weights inversely

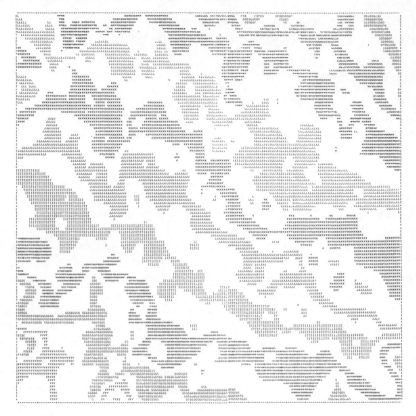

Figure 7 Line printer contour map of surface shown in Figure 4.

proportional to the distance from data point being evaluated are assigned to the other points. The constant of the fitted regression equation is adjusted so the plane passes through the data point (Figure 8). If the search procedure has not found at least five points or if the simultaneous equations of the fitted plane do not have a solution, the coefficients of the regional trend are used as the local trend. The coefficients of the trend are saved for each data point.

The second part of the algorithm estimates the value of the surface at the grid nodes. A search procedure finds n' nearest neighboring data points around the node to be estimated. The x, y coordinates of the grid node are substituted into each of the local trend-surface equations associated with these data points, in effect projecting these local surfaces to the location of the node (Figure 9). A weighted average of these estimates is then calculated, weighting each slope by the inverse of the squared distance between the grid node and the data point associated with the slope. If a data point lies at or

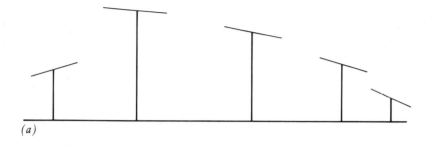

(a)

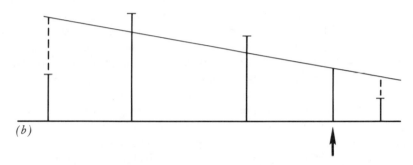

(b)

Figure 8 (a) Interpolation from irregularly spaced data points to a grid requires calculation of local dip at every data point. (b) Local dip at a data point (shown by arrow) is found by fitting least-squares surface to surrounding points, subject to constraint that plane passes through the data point.

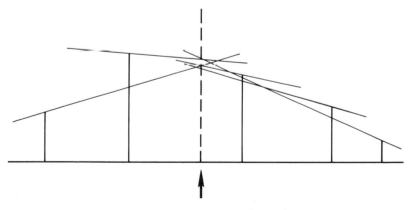

Figure 9 Local dips at control points are projected to grid node (arrow). Value assigned to node is weighted average of these projections.

very near to a grid intersection, the value of the data point is used directly as the value of the grid node. This two-step interpolation method was devised by Osborn (1967) and has been widely used in other contouring programs (Jones, 1971; Walters, 1969). A similar interpolation procedure, also using two steps, was originally described by Batcha and Reese (1964) and is contained in several commercial systems (IBM, 1965; Walters, 1969).

One critical difference between the various contouring programs that interpolate to a regular grid is the way in which "nearest neighbors" are defined and found. Because some search techniques may be superior to others in certain situations (primarily reflecting the nature of the data point distribution), SURFACE II provides a variety of search patterns that may be selected by the user. The simplest method finds the n nearest neighboring data points, in a Euclidean distance sense, regardless of their angular distribution around the point being estimated. This method is fast and satisfactory if control points are distributed in a comparatively uniform pattern but provides poor estimates if the data are distributed at close intervals along widely spaced traverses. A quadrant search, which imposes the additional constraint that a minimum number of points must be taken from each of the four quadrants around the estimated point, is superior for highly irregular data distributions. A further elaboration is the octant search, which obtains specified numbers of nearest points (usually one or two) from each octant around the point being estimated. The procedures require finding and testing more neighbors than a simple search, but the testing procedure is a logic operation and does not greatly increase search time. An entirely different type of search procedure finds all points within a radius r of the point being estimated. This approach requires a modified interpolation algorithm, because the number of points used in the estimating equation varies from area to area across the map. At the present time, the first two search procedures are available in SURFACE II, and the second two procedures are being implemented.

A different approach to interpolation is use of universal Kriging, developed by Matheron and his associates (Blais and Carlier, 1967; Matheron, 1963, 1971) and described in another context by Thompson (1956) and Switzer, Mohr, and Heitman (1964). Kriging provides an optimal estimate of the surface at every point; that is, the interpolated surface will have minimum error. This is achieved by taking into account prior knowledge about the spatial autocorrelation between sample data points. The method requires a "structural analysis" to determine the form of the two-dimensional autocorrelation function of the surface before contouring can begin. The universal Kriging algorithm used in SURFACE II was developed by Olea (1972, 1974) in a joint research project of the Kansas Geological Survey and Empresa Nacional del Chile. Although universal Kriging is more expensive than conventional interpolation procedures, it also provides a map of the expected error contained in the estimated surface (Figures 10 and 11).

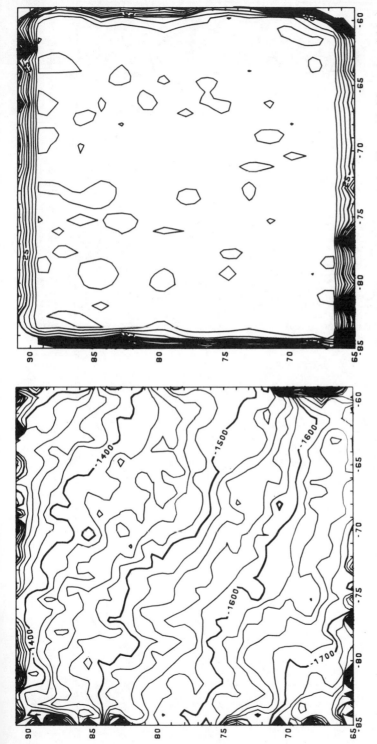

Figure 10 Contour map of area shown in Figure 4, constructed by universal Kriging, using quadratic drift and 7 mile neighborhood.

Figure 11 Expected error map for Figure 10. Mapped variable is number of feet within one standard deviation of estimated surface. Lowest contour lines (closed contours in center of map) are ± 5 feet; contour interval is ± 5 feet.

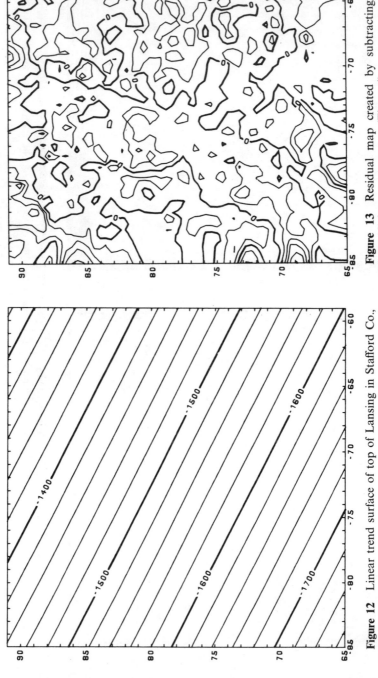

Figure 12 Linear trend surface of top of Lansing in Stafford Co., Kansas.

Figure 13 Residual map created by subtracting trend surface (Figure 12) from contour map (Figure 4).

Trend-surface analysis is the name applied to a widely used method of surface estimation which employs a global-fit procedure. In contrast to local-fit procedures discussed above, all data points are considered simultaneously in this method, which attempts to approximate the form of the surface by a function of the two geographic coordinates. In essence, trend-surface analysis is a two-dimensional extension of least-squares curve fitting. An extensive discussion of the method is given in this volume by Whitten. SURFACE II will calculate polynomial trend surfaces of irregularly spaced data and generate contour maps of the trends and residuals. Figures 12 and 13 show a linear trend surface and residual map of the Stafford Co., Kansas, subsurface data.

An entirely different method of creating a regular grid of information from irregularly spaced control points is the calculation of distance functions. The grid matrix from which these maps are made is a function solely of the spatial distribution of data and not of the data values. Examples include maps showing the distance from every point on the surface to the nearest data point, or the average distance to the nearest specified numbers of data points. Figure 14 shows the distance of every point in Stafford Co., Kansas,

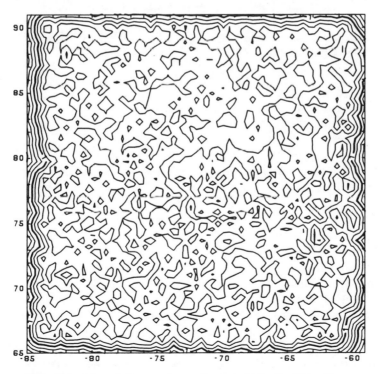

Figure 14   Map of distance from all points in Stafford Co., Kansas, to nearest control well. Contour interval is one-fourth mile.

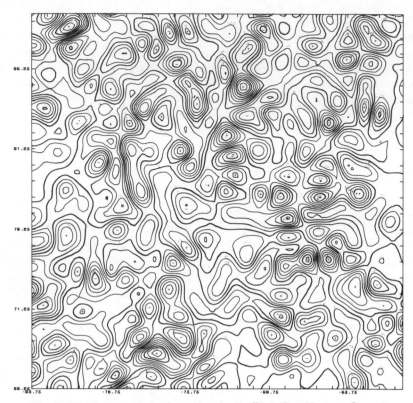

Figure 15 Structural configuration in Stafford Co., Kansas, filtered to enhance structures having a spatial wavelength of two miles.

from the nearest control well, and can provide valuable information about control point densities and about the reliability of contour maps made from this data.

Once a regular grid has been created, the matrix can be transformed in a variety of useful ways. A map can be "filtered" by convolving the grid matrix with a smaller filter matrix, as described by Robinson in another article in this volume. SURFACE II provides for input of a filter matrix and calculation of a filtered map. Figure 15 shows the top of the Lansing formation in Stafford Co., Kansas, filtered to enhance structures having a spatial wavelength of two miles.

Derivatives of surfaces also can be calculated, producing maps showing rate of change of slope in a specified direction. Figure 16 is a map of the derivative of the Lansing structural surface taken in the direction of the regional dip, which is approximately to the southwest. Structural slopes having a component in the same direction as the regional trend produce

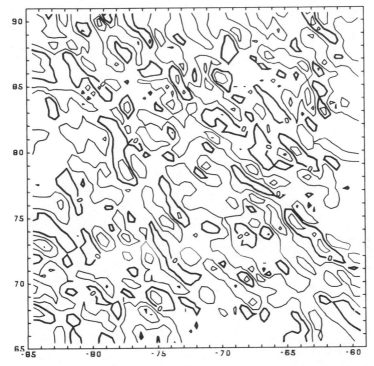

Figure 16 Derivative of structural configuration in Stafford Co., Kansas, taken along regional trend as given by linear trend surface (Figure 12).

positive derivatives, crests and troughs of structures have zero derivatives, and areas having slope components opposite the regional trend have negative derivatives. The up-dip flanks of closed anticlinal structures appear on derivative maps as regions of negative slope, providing a useful clue to potential hydrocarbon traps. Also, it is possible to identify the "spill-over point," defining the maximum closure volume, on a derivative map with more assurance than on a structural contour map.

Plotter and line printer graphics are only part of the output from SURFACE II. The program also generates statistics and graphs describing the quality of the surface approximation which has been made. These analyses allow the performance of the system to be checked, and provide the user with a powerful tool for investigating interaction between the contouring algorithm and the data set being mapped. Figure 17 shows one form of graphic analysis, a plot of original data values versus the value assigned to the fitted surface at the control points. For a completed contour map which contained no error, the plot would be a straight line. If the

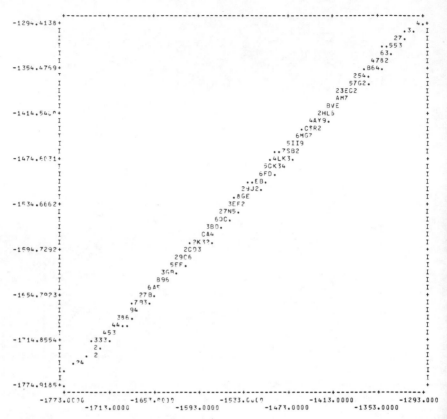

Figure 17 Plot of original subsurface elevations in feet (ordinate) versus estimated elevations in feet back-calculated from grid matrix (abscissa). Numbers and letters on plot represent successively greater numbers of points.

interpolation algorithm is creating a biased estimate of the surface configuration, the plotted line will be distorted. The spread of points about the line is an indication of the amount of small-scale fluctuation in the mapped variable. The interpolation algorithm may tend to smooth a highly erratic set of data points, resulting in a large scatter of points on this diagram. Figure 18 shows essentially the same information in another form, as a plot of error versus values of control points. If there is a systematic tendency for interpolation errors to be associated with specific values of the surface, this tendency will be apparent on this diagram.

SURFACE II can be used to create contour maps and other graphic output of a quality comparable to those produced by advanced commercial software packages. The routine drawing of maps and diagrams will probably constitute the greatest use for the system, but hopefully research capabilities

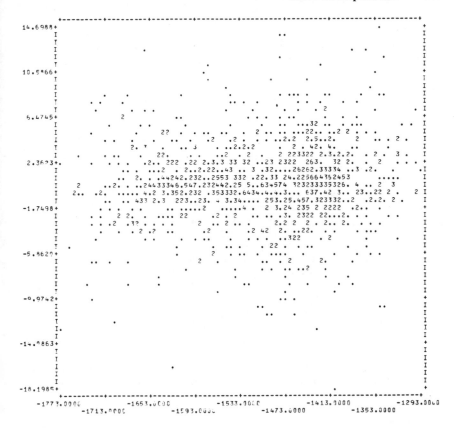

Figure 18 Plot of original surface elevations in feet (abscissa) versus error in feet (original value − estimated value back-calculated from grid matrix) at each control point.

have been designed into SURFACE II that give it greater potential. A variety of alternative contouring algorithms are already implemented, as are a number of different nearest-neighbor search routines. Other algorithms will be added, enabling the system to emulate the performance of almost any other contouring system. By holding portions of the system constant and varying other portions and parameters, it should be possible to eventually deduce an optimum system configuration for the display of any specified type of surface. It also should be possible to evaluate the performance of most implemented or proposed contouring systems independent of such influences as machine size or speed. We hope that SURFACE II will be a valuable tool for the investigation of what has been an obscure area of computer application.

References

Batcha, J. P., and J. R. Reese, 1964, Surface determination and automatic contouring for mineral exploration, extraction, and processing: *Colorado School Mines Quarterly*, v. 59, p. 1–4.

Blais, R. A., and P. A. Carlier, 1967, Applications of geostatistics in ore evaluation: *Ore Reserve Estimation and Grade Control*, v. 9, p. 41–68.

IBM, 1965, *Numerical surface techniques and contour map plotting*: IBM Data Processing Application, White Plains, New York, 36 p.

IBM, 1969, *1130 numerical surface techniques and contour map plotting (1130-CX-11X) programmer's manual*: IBM, White Plains, New York, 78 p.

Jones, R. L., 1971, A generalized digital contouring program: NASA Langley Research Center, Hampton, Virginia, *NASA TN D-6022*, 78 p.

Kubert, B., J. Szabo, and S. Giulieri, 1968, The perspective representation of functions of two variables: *Jour., Assoc. Computing Machinery*, v. 15, no. 2, p. 193–204.

Matheron, G., 1963, Principles of geostatistics: *Economic Geology*, v. 58, p. 1246–1266.

Matheron, G., 1971, The theory of regionalized variables and its applications: *Les Cahiers du Centre de Morphologie Mathématique de Fontainebleau*, v. 5, 211 p.

Olea, R. A., 1972, Application of regionalized variable theory to automatic contouring: *American Petroleum Inst. Special Rept.*, Project 131, 191 p.

Olea, R. A., 1974, Optimal contour mapping using universal Kriging: *Jour. Geophysical Research*, in press.

Osborn, R. T., 1967, An automated procedure for producing contour charts: U.S. Naval Oceanographic Office, *IM No. 67-4*, 54 p. Available from NTIS as AD807617.

Rohlf, F. J., 1969, GRAFPAC, graphic output subroutines for the 635 computer: *Kansas Geological Survey Computer Contribution 36*, 50 p.

Switzer, P., M. Mohr, and R. E. Heitman, 1964, Statistical analyses of ocean terrain and contour plotting procedures: Dept. Navy, Bureau of Ships, NObsr-81564, SS-050, *Rept. No. 1440464*, 85 p. Available from NTIS as AD601538.

Thompson, P., 1956, Optimum smoothing of two-dimensional fields: *Tellus*, v. 8, p. 384–393.

Walden, A. R., 1972, Quantitative comparison of automatic contouring algorithms: Kansas Oil Exploration Decision System, *Tech. Rept. Module Surface*, Kansas Geological Survey, Lawrence, Kansas, 115 p.

Walters, R. F., 1969, Contouring by machine: a user's guide: *Bull. American Assoc. Petroleum Geologists*, v. 35, no. 11, p. 2324–2340.

Design and Use of the New Linmap-Colmap System[*]

G. M. Gaits

Experience with the Old Linmap System

During the period 1968–73 over 900 maps, many in color, were produced by the Old Linmap System. Users and operators as well as the designer of the system collected considerable experience in this period, which led to the redesign of the Old System.

In operation many design faults in the Old System were uncovered. It was found that the method adopted for digitizing zone boundaries (for choropleth = ZONEMAPS) and their treatment by the system produced incorrect display where boundaries were (or should have been) common. Also, when mapping many subjects over the same area at the same scale in separate runs, it was necessary to repeat the time-consuming process of setting up the graphic image of the area inside the computer. Obviously, if serial production of maps were planned, this process should not be repeated more than necessary. Furthermore, many usable byproducts of map processing were not saved during a run; these could have facilitated further processing either on subsequent runs of LINMAP or by other systems. Inconsistencies were discovered in statistical processing, which on occasion led to obscure if not incorrect results. Other minor aspects of system design also needed rectification.

Many users felt that their needs were not suitably catered for by the Old System. They wanted a cheaper method for producing high quality monochrome output. They wanted to be able to specify free-form arithmetic expressions to be used in computing. They wanted a method for displaying potential values (number of people within a certain distance). They wanted more statistical listings and the capability of using logic operators in deciding whether a record was of interest. They wanted many other capabilities, some of which even the New System cannot supply. The Old System therefore served a very useful purpose, apart from producing a large number of

[*] Crown Copyright

267

maps, by bringing user needs to the fore. Any of these factors taken independently might not have called for a comprehensive redesign of the Old System. Taken together they provided an overpowering case to do so. This was accomplished in 15 months by one of the most experienced British software houses on the basis of an extensive specification of the features and facilities the New Linmap–Colmap System should have.

Structural Design of the New System

Figure 1 illustrates the conceptual framework of the New System, designed from the outset as a spatial data processing package to operate on locationally referenced (geocoded) data files. The first box indicates that the system was designed to accept any data file, be it a national register of hospital or educational installations or censuses of population, employment, or production. In short, the system was conceived to operate on any data file which

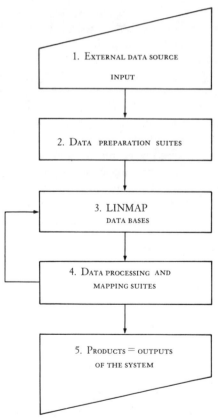

Figure 1 Conceptual framework of New System LINMAP.

contained records of place-related data. The second box of Figure 1 represents data preparation suites through which external files must pass before they become suitable for processing by the Linmap system. Once the external file has passed through the preparation stage it becomes part of an off-line magnetic tape library which constitutes the Linmap Data Base (box 3). The data processing and mapping suites (box 4) then call up the required files from the data base on request and undertake the desired processing. Figure 1 indicates a loop back from box 4 to 3 which represents the capability of the system to pre-process data for later production and thereby to expand its own data base. Box 5 indicates the products or output of the New System.

Figure 2 shows the three data preparation suites. The Point Data Preparation Suite was designed as a general utility processor to match records of

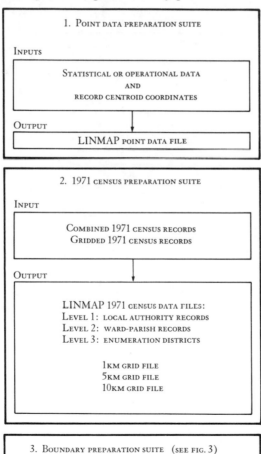

Figure 2 Data preparation suites used in New System LINMAP.

external data files lacking National Grid Coordinates with a corresponding file containing the required coordinates. The 1971 Census Preparation Suite was designed to prepare data from this source for processing by the New System. As this census already incorporates location references for each record, the suite performs only a simple conversion of the source file into Linmap format and separates out the various levels of records. The Boundary Preparation Suite is illustrated by Figure 3. The New System may operate on either the segment file or on the boundary file of closed-up polygons. The suite also permits reconstitution of boundaries or boundary sets using updated segment files. A segment may have up to 500 vertices and a boundary over 4000 vertices. Both segments and boundaries may be smoothed by the

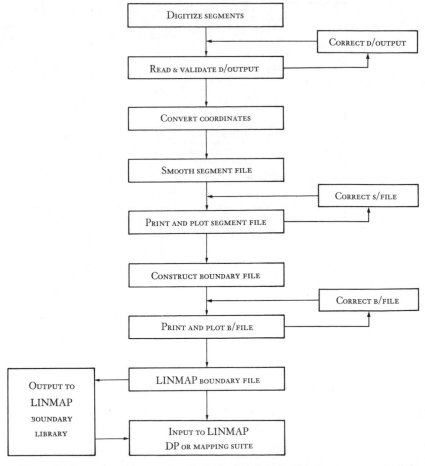

Figure 3   Boundary Preparation Suite for LINMAP. This is one segment of the data preparation suites shown in Figure 2.

suite to keep the number of vertices within these limits. There is no limit on the number of segments or boundaries the output file may contain.

The Data Processing and Mapping Suite is the heart of the New Linmap System. Figure 4 shows only a very general picture of the layout of this suite. The process begins with a user map order. The request is checked by the Linmap Service-Unit where queries are clarified and the request translated onto Linmap coding forms. These forms look very much like a small program calling functional macros and identifying their parameters. These are punched onto cards and submitted to the computer. The first main program CONTROL is in fact a compiler and process controller. It checks syntax in

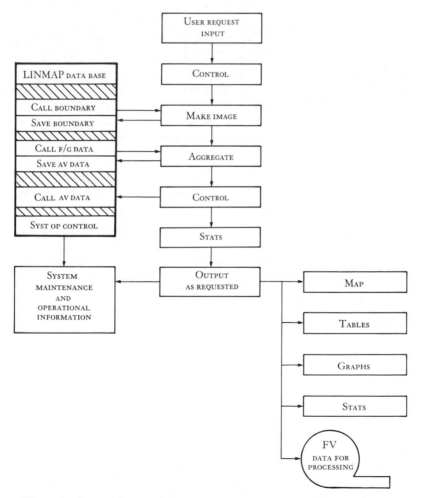

Figure 4 General layout of the Data Processing and Mapping Suite in the New System LINMAP.

the macros and their associated parameters, calls on-line system files and off-line data files, sets up the processing sequence, and oversees its execution.

If the request calls for a map whose boundary has not yet been mapped, the main program MAKEIMAGE is called. This creates a binary image of the (blank) map at the scale and in the style requested. This binary image may be "saved" and re-used when the same area, at the same scale and in the same style, is used for mapping other subjects.

Once the system has determined the area of interest it scans the relevant data file and extracts those records which fall within the area. Two main programs, AGGREGATE and COMPUTE, carry out this task. The role of the first is to sort relevant data points into their positions on the map and to carry out all logical inclusion/exclusion tests on records. The second performs all necessary computation specified in the user request. Output at this stage may be a preprocessed data file which is written into the Linmap Data Library for future processing, or an internal file for mapping and producing the various products the user requested. CONTROL, AGGRE-GATE, and COMPUTE call in various modules for statistical processing, formatting, and sorting which are needed to prepare output. At the end of the run the system automatically updates all file directories and internal files and produces system monitor output.

Products of the New System

The user may obtain any or all of the following forms of output: maps, sets of standard statistical measures, sets of graphs or histograms, sets of tables or listings, data files for further processing. Some of these are always output by the system. Others, including maps, are optional and produced only when specifically requested.

Map Output

Maps may be produced in one of three forms: on the line printer, on the linotron in monochrome (Figures 5 and 6), or in color. Line-printer maps (LINMAPS) are by far the cheapest, but also the least pleasing form of output. They are quickest to produce and suitable for research work or pre-processing of data, rather than for inclusion in reports or for wide circulation.

Linotron maps (COLMAPS) may be produced in two forms. The MONO-CHROME version, using specially designed gray scales, is suitable for illustrating reports and for wider circulation. The difficulties of achieving a recognizable gray scale, however, make these maps less readable than the COLOR version. They are, on the other hand, cheaper to produce and print than are colored maps.

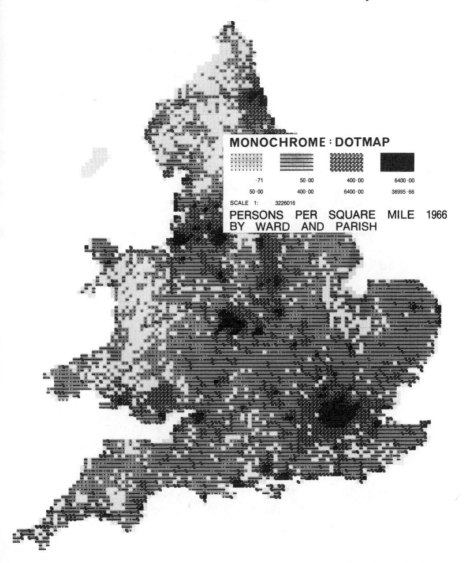

Figure 5 Monochrome dotmap of population density by ward and parish, from 1966 census data.

The system permits users to make up their own shading by specifying the character overprint, up to four layers, for Linmaps. A user has three sets of shades to choose from for monochrome output and more will be added in the future. For colored maps, the user may specify his scheme of color overprinting, using up to 10 layers, or may separate each shade for a different color or tint.

Figure 6 Monochrome gridmap of workers per acre of cropland, displayed on the basis of the British National Grid System.

Map Styles

Dotmaps are made by printing a shade (using the line printer or linotron) at the position on the map where the location of one or more data centroids fall. Computed data values are sorted into as many as 10 class intervals, each allocated a distinctive shade (Figure 5). *Gridmaps* display data on the basis of the British National Grid System. The user may specify any size of grid. The shading system is similar to that of dotmaps except the relevant shade covers the whole grid square (Figure 6). *Zonemaps* are the customary choropleth style of data presentation.

Potmap (potential map) is a new style of output. It may be based on a dotmap when the user specifies that the potential should be calculated for every nth character on every nth line. It may be based on a gridmap when a grid size is stipulated and the potential calculated at the center of the grid square. In the first case, intermediate character positions are left unshaded; in the second, the map has the appearance of a gridmap. When specifying potential maps the user may specify a "radius of a circle of influence" in meters. This is applied to each potential location to identify those centroids which may contribute to that location. The circles may overlap so the same centroid may contribute to more than one location. The user also may specify a "distance function" to weight each centroid according to their distance from the locations they contribute to, thereby modifying the value of their contribution. As an alternative, the New System permits the user to specify the location of up to 60 positions for which potential values can be calculated. Each location may have a different circle of interest and while the distance function must be the same, each location may have a "weighting factor" specified by the user.

Statistical Output

The New Linmap System may process data on the basis of aggregation areas, on the basis of the source records, or on both. The user, therefore, can examine statistics of the subject at both aggregate and discrete levels.

The Linmap system provides two standard methods of delimiting class boundaries. The Quantile Method groups previously ordered data into classes so that each class contains the same number of observations. In the Percentile Method, the class interval is standard and depends on the range of the data. A third method of delimiting class boundaries allows the user to specify the values of class intervals. All three methods are limited to no more than 10 classes.

In many cases the user does not wish to consider values less than or more than some specific value. The Linmap system permits the user to specify lower and upper "thresholds"; all values falling outside the specified range are ignored by the system. In practice, this is equivalent to specifying the lower bound of class 1 and the upper bound of the highest class.

The Linmap system always calculates the following statistical measures on data values after sorting into 100 equal interval classes:

Mean
Median
Mode
Range
Variance
Standard deviation
Coefficient of variation

and for each display category:

Minimum class value
Maximum class value
Class mean
Number of values in class
Sum of values in class
Percentage of total values.

Four different graphs or histograms can be produced by Linmap if required. These can be produced for each "map" either at aggregation area level, at record level, or at both levels. The graphs include: frequency distribution, logarithmic (base 10) frequency distribution, cumulative frequency distribution, percentage frequency distribution. These graphs are plotted on the basis of 100 equal interval classes between the minimum and maximum values processed, or within thresholds if these are specified.

Some Facilities in the New System

The New System can process two data files simultaneously. These may be files of the same statistical series but collected at different times, or two files from different sources but both collected at about the same time. The system, however, requires one-to-one parity between the two files. One major application of this facility is the study and mapping of changes between the 1966 and 1971 population censuses.

As data may be hidden somewhere on hundreds of magnetic tapes, Linmap has capabilities for *conditional processing*. The user may specify logical conditions to delimit his interest to his specific problem. All logical and relational operators are available. Reference can be made to any part of the record and relationships between parts of the record expressed in a mathematical formula. This facility should prove to be an extremely powerful tool for testing spatial hypotheses and relationships.

Data may be transformed using the Free Formulae Computation facility. Up to 10 variables may be created on the basis of 50 data values in the records. The relationship between these variables can be expressed in a mathematical equation whose product is the final value to be mapped. Any of the following operators may be used to construct the equation:

+	plus
−	minus
*	multiplied by
/	divided by
**	raised to the power
LN	log to base e
LG	log to base 10
C	constants

The equation may be nested with brackets but cannot exceed 140 characters.

In the Old System, boundaries of a set of consecutive zones had to be submitted as a file to indicate a zonemap. The New System automatically finds those zones which fall partly or wholly in the area to be mapped. The blank images of such zonemaps can be saved for repeated processing.

The New System permits specification of the line density (number of lines per inch) and character density (number of characters per inch) required. On Colmaps, line and character density are always the same, as the output character is always square. On Linmaps, line densities may take values of 6, 8, or 10; character densities are usually 10.

Colmap text output through the linotron may include capitals, lower case, bold, or italics anywhere in the text. Print size may be varied between lines. Users can therefore design the main title, subtitle, and footnote annotations on maps.

The New System permits data files to have from 1 to 4000 items recorded in the data fields. However, within each file the record length is fixed. When new fields are added, the header information is updated. There is no limit to the number of records in a file or to the number of reels a file may occupy.

Systems Information

The New Linmap System was developed on the ICL 1905F computer at the Central Computer Agency of the British Government. The system has now been installed at the Department of the Environment's ICL 1906A at the Hastings Computer Centre. Software was written in ICL Plan to run under the George 3 operating system. The New Linmap system is wholly machine and OS bound. This is the result of a policy decision in the Department of the Environment to devise the most efficient system for in-house use.

The system may occupy 32K of 24 bit words in the central processor although many constituent programs require much less space. In addition, Linmap uses four 9-track and one 7-track tape drives and one disk pack, in addition to George 3 requirements. A card reader, line printer, and MOP terminal are also needed. Production work is done in batch mode. The mapping and boundary preparation suites consist of 28 programs, 8 subroutines, and over 100 modules. The total number of executable core instructions is 54,645 ICL 1900 plan statements. The full listing of the source programs contains 67,215 lines, including non-executable comments.

Mapping Population Census Data

Gaits (1969) described the method adopted in coordinate referencing the 18,000 records in the Ward-Parish tables of the 1966 census. The work, while tedious, was not particularly difficult or cumbersome. It was completed within 12 months and required about two man-years of effort for coding the base maps, digitizing, and building the Linmap file. The file contained 381 data items supplied by the census office for each Ward-Parish record, to which acreage values were added, making the final records 382 items long. The file was organized into a National File containing England, Wales, and Scotland on two magnetic tape reels. Ten regional files, one for each economic planning region (EPR) of England and separate ones for Wales and Scotland were also created in order to reduce read time when areas the size of EPRs or smaller were required for mapping. For national or inter-regional mapping, the National File was used.

The 1971 census opened up an entirely new vista for spatial analysis and mapping. The authorities, partly due to the success of the Linmap system decided that locational referencing should form part of the census. The Department of the Environment and the Office of Population Surveys and Census conducted a series of field trials during 1968 and 1969 to establish the feasibility, cost and preferred method of location referencing in the 1971 census.

The release of census information on a collection area basis is now well advanced. Records are processed and released by county and lower level records are nested within higher level records. For each area unit record, there are four physical records which together contain about 1600 enumerated facts.

During processing a "centroid" coordinate is computed for each Enumeration District, Ward/Parish, and Local Authority and written into their record header. It is not necessary to digitize these centroids as was the case in the 1966 census. They are immediately available for Linmapping or, in fact, for any spatial analysis and processing.

Preparations for Mapping the 1971 Census

The Department of the Environment has ordered a complete copy of both area and grid records on magnetic tape as well as on microfilm. For processing reasons, however, the data were requested not by geographical counties but by Economic Planning Regions. The 1971 Census Preparation Suite will be used to separate out the various record levels and to combine the four census records into one physical record for each area. The first EPR was delivered in 1973 and its preparation started immediately. Mapping commenced in late 1973. In late 1974, grid data should start to arrive. These will be held on National Files (GB) only, as the New System permits reading to begin with any reel of a multi-reel file.

Parallel with assimilation of the 1971 census data, the Linmap Boundary Library is being prepared for mapping. Three files of this Library are of considerable interest. These are:

(1)   1971 Local Authority Boundaries (1.4K)
(2)   1974 Local Authority Boundaries (0.5K)
(3)   1971 Ward/Parish Boundaries (18.0K)

Files (1) and (2) will be used for the production of zonemaps from both 1966 to 1971 censuses. These maps should illustrate the inter-censal change of population characteristics for historical and for operational purposes. File (3) will be used for subregional and structure planning purposes and for town and city display.

Possible Lines of Map Production

Current estimates put Department of the Environment demand at 5000 census "maps" during the 1973–78 period. Demands emanating from other departments of the government have not yet been assessed. Total production output of the New System may well be in excess of 10,000 "maps". However, a third of the production is expected to output only statistical products. Even so, the number of maps staggers the imagination and calls for planning of production lines or map series. It is necessary that maps produced for wider use have common parameters to permit their correlation. Such parameters should specify the area, scale, type and style of mapping. Consideration of the combinations of standard areas, map types, and map styles suggests between 99 and 165 possible production lines. The most important production line, however, is to provide any map of any area to any customer; that is, to produce maps on demand. It is impossible to estimate precisely what customers may want. However, it is hoped that the New System will be able to supply it.

The National Atlas

The New Linmap System is ideally suited for the production of statistical atlases. Not only does it create high quality graphic output from the mono-chrome and color options but it also has considerable data processing capability. Added to these features the existence of the Linmap Data Base will provide an unrivalled opportunity to publish an Atlas (or a series) economically. An "Atlas of Population and Housing Characteristics of Great Britain" is visualized in seven thematic volumes:

(1) General Characteristics of Population
(2) Employment Characteristics
(3) Ethnic Characteristics
(4) Housing Characteristics
(5) Migration Characteristics
(6) Travel to Work Characteristics
(7) Mixed Characteristics.

Each volume would display up to 40 subjects at approximately 1:2.5 million scale showing 1971 and 1974 Local Authorities on the basis of 1971 census data and where possible the inter-censal change (1966–1971) for 1974 Authorities. Each volume would contain up to 100 maps together with selected histograms.

Such an Atlas, if produced, would constitute a source of information of inestimable value on the population characteristics of Great Britain entering into the last quarter of the 20th century. It would be a task worth doing, and worth doing well.

Acknowledgments

The New Linmap System is the product of team work. Nick Attwater smoothed the path of the work along the official channels; his programmers coded the new PDP and 71 Census DP Suites; Gill Hackman advised on customer requirements; and Ray Tucker designed the new linotron gray scale. However, most of the credit should go to the fifteen-man coding and four-man design teams of Computer Analysts and Programmers Ltd. under the supervision of Jim Pearce.

This paper is published with the knowledge of the Department of the Environment but does not necessarily represent the policies or views of that Department or of any other UK Government Department, Agency, or Office which may be mentioned in the paper.

References

Gaits, G. M., 1969, Thematic mapping by computer: *Jour. British Cartographic Soc.*, v. 6, p. 50–68.

Office of Population, Censuses and Surveys, 1970, Geocoding in the 1971 census: Office of Population Census and Surveys, *Information Paper No. 1*, 11 p.

Office of Population, Censuses and Surveys, 1972, Statistics for grid squares: Office of Population Census and Surveys, *Information Paper No. 5*, 6 p.

Office of Population, Censuses and Surveys, 1973, A guide to 1971 census statistics: Office of Population Census and Surveys, *Information Paper No. 6*, in press.

The Practical Use of Trend-Surface Analyses in the Geological Sciences

E. H. T. Whitten

The statistical method for analyzing mapped data most commonly encountered in the geological literature is possibly trend-surface analysis; this is reflected by many American and British books (Chorley, 1972; Davis, 1973; Koch and Link, 1971; Krumbein and Graybill, 1965) and by reviews in the Soviet Union (Romanova, 1968) and Czechoslovakia (Peska, Klomínský, and Sattran, 1970). Although comprising a powerful set of tools, the techniques are beset by a plethora of practical and mathematical problems and pitfalls that are not widely appreciated. In the space available, it is difficult to explain fully all of these difficulties. The basic mathematical models are simple and well documented in the literature; no attempt is made to review this aspect, although some of the key references are cited. Users of trend-surface analysis need to guard against employing one of the many "canned" computer programs that are now available without thoroughly understanding what the method accomplishes and how. Even more important is the unequivocal definition of the objectives of the analysis in terms of the actual samples used, the sampled population, and the target population that is of real interest (Whitten, 1961). Although the mathematical problems must not be overlooked (Watson, 1972), a review of the large Earth sciences literature in which trend surfaces have been used suggests that the latter topic requires infinitely more attention.

In attempting to condense such a complex subject, it is likely that individual statements may be oversimplified or non-rigorous. Therefore, what follows must be considered a mere outline, rather than a complete formal presentation.

The Trend-Surface Models

Trend-surface analysis comprises a series of techniques for filtering data; in most instances a measured variable z (elevation, quartz content, etc.) is

282

assumed to be a dependent variable with respect to the geographic, spatial, independent variables x and y. The initial objective of the analysis is to use a series of filtering processes to identify the function z = f(x, y) that isolates and represents (1) the essential features of the regional variation pattern of z and (2) the local and the error components ("noise") included in actual observations of z. It is an objective, quantitative, descriptive technique. Unfortunately, the geological objectives are commonly ill-defined, but they usually include use of the mathematical function to prepare a contoured map of z that purports to estimate interpolated, noise-free values of z at *all* x, y points in the map area. Sometimes, even extrapolation beyond the geographic limits of the observed data points is attempted. Such extrapolations necessarily involve critical assumptions about unmeasured samples in the target population. The objectives also commonly involve an additional step—use of the trend map to draw economic or genetic conclusions about the dependent variable or the objects on which that variable was measured. Before using trend-surface analysis for any set of data, it is imperative that the objectives be rigorously defined and that the constraints involved be carefully enunciated. The ready availability of computer programs has led to widespread use of trend-surface methods and, frequently, to ignoring the full geological meaning of the data used.

If the observed data (z) are completely error free, a function z = f(x, y) could be chosen so that the computed value of the dependent variable ($\hat{z}$) always equals the observed value (z = $\hat{z}$) at each datum point; the bicubic-spline surface is such a function designed to achieve this objective (deBoor 1962; Koelling and Whitten, 1973; Whitten, 1969; Whitten and Koelling, 1973). Functions which cause z = $\hat{z}$ at all observed data points do not yield trend surfaces. In the Earth sciences, observational data almost invariably incorporate both (1) experimental or observational errors and (2) localized variability that appears to be irrelevant to the total or regional pattern. The latter commonly has considerable geological importance. The concept is that the filtering process removes these two components from the observed data in order to expose the regional pattern. In practice, a simple function with linear or nonlinear coefficients is chosen. The best coefficients are then estimated for the particular data; for this purpose, the standard method of least squares is commonly used. The more common linear models used are:

(a) Orthogonal algebraic polynomial for gridded data (a regression analysis in which the coefficients of the polynomial are uncorrelated is called orthogonal) (deLury, 1950; Grant, 1957; Oldham and Sutherland, 1955).

(b) Nonorthogonal algebraic polynomial for irregularly spaced data with the form:

$$z = a_0 + a_1x + a_2y + a_3x^2 + a_4xy + a_5y^2 + a_6x^3 + \ldots + \varepsilon$$

where the coefficients are not independent and ε is a random error term (Grant, 1957; Krumbein, 1959).

(c)   Nonorthogonal algebraic polynomial for irregularly spaced three-dimensional data, i.e., $z = f(x, y, w)$, where w is the third spatial dimension (Peikert, 1963).

(d)   Orthogonal algebraic polynomial for irregularity spaced data (Whitten, 1970).

(e)   Double Fourier series (trigonometric polynomial) for gridded data (Harbaugh and Preston, 1965; James, 1966a).

(f)   Double Fourier series (trigonometric polynomial) for irregularly spaced data (James, 1966b) with the form:

$$z = \sum_{i=0}^{KC} \sum_{j=0}^{LC} cc_{ij} \cos\left(\frac{2\pi iy}{M}\right) \cos\left(\frac{2\pi jx}{N}\right) + \sum_{i=0}^{KC} \sum_{j=1}^{LS} cs_{ij} \cos$$

$$\left(\frac{2\pi iy}{M}\right) \sin\left(\frac{2\pi jx}{N}\right) + \sum_{i=0}^{KS} \sum_{j=0}^{LC} sc_{ij} \sin\left(\frac{2\pi iy}{M}\right) \cos\left(\frac{2\pi jx}{N}\right) +$$

$$\sum_{i=1}^{KS} \sum_{j=1}^{LS} ss_{ij} \sin\left(\frac{2\pi iy}{M}\right) \sin\left(\frac{2\pi jx}{N}\right)$$

where

M = fundamental wavelength in y-direction,
N = fundamental wavelength in x-direction,
KC = maximum cosine harmonic in y-direction,
LC = maximum cosine harmonic in x-direction,
KS = minimum sine harmonic in y-direction,
LS = minimum sine harmonic in x-direction, and

$$\begin{matrix} cc_{ij} \\ cs_{ij} \\ sc_{ij} \\ ss_{ij} \end{matrix} = \text{coefficients of the series.}$$

By far the most widely represented in the literature is (b), although (f) has become popular more recently; commonly a first-degree polynomial (type b) is combined with the Fourier series model (f) (see Whitten, 1968a, 1969, p. 230). The more recently developed orthogonal-polynomial model for irregularly spaced data (d) has many advantages over the other polynomial models. These advantages will undoubtedly lead to significantly expanded use of this model in the future. Numerous variants of these models have been introduced. For example, some authors have included additional terms such as trigonometric or exponential terms in an attempt to achieve a closer fit to the actual data. This approach is referred to later but, on the whole, such variants have little to commend them as trend-surface models.

The versatility of Fourier series for approximating continuously variable distributions and the probable inherent harmonic nature of many geological and geophysical phenomena would suggest that for many purposes, double Fourier series trend surfaces might be superior to polynomial surfaces. Though widely used, it cannot be anticipated that polynomial or Fourier series have genetic significance for the spatial variability of most Earth science variables. In all of these models the coefficients have little or no physical significance. From an understanding of the physico-chemical and mechanical principles that have genetic significance in controlling the original distribution of the dependent variable, a differential equation could be erected and used as a nonlinear approximating equation. The coefficients, if correctly chosen, could have physical significance. For such reasons, future emphasis will undoubtedly be placed on models with nonlinear coefficients. James (1968, 1970) demonstrated the technique of building and using nonlinear equations for trend-surface analysis. This method found ready application to geochemical problems, but, to date, few have designed nonlinear equations for the traditional domain of trend-surface analysis of mapped variables.

The algebraic and computational steps for methods (b) through (f) are well documented in the literature. A selection of the computer programs that have been published is listed with the references. Difficult problems with the inversion of ill-conditioned matrices are encountered in many programs for (b); some superior programs provide methods for solving the simultaneous equations without matrix inversion (Whitten, Krumbein, Waye, and Beckman, 1965). Computational problems of this type do not arise with the simple arithmetic steps involved in the orthogonal polynomial for irregularly spaced data. Because there is no computer program for this particularly useful method in the public domain, a FORTRAN IV listing is to be published (Whitten, in press).

Space does not allow dealing with moving-average methods (Krige, 1966), Kriging (Matheron, 1970; Watson, 1972), or spatial filtering (Robinson, Charlesworth, and Ellis, 1969; Whitten and Koelling, 1973), which are all types of trend-surface analyses in the widest sense of the term. Each has its own advantages, disadvantages, and special features. The sampling and practical problems that arise in attempting to make effective use of these significant and powerful techniques are similar to those involved in poly-nomial and Fourier series trend-surface analyses.

Despite the computational and mathematical difficulties, the main problems in the practical use of trend-surface analyses are conceptual; for example, fundamental questions involve how "good" a particular trend surface is and the degree of similarity of two different surfaces.

"Goodness" of Fit

Estimating how "good" a particular trend surface is depends upon answering the question: "How good for what purpose?" This question is commonly unanswered or the answer is left ill-defined. Superficial answers are provided by the two commonest measures. The first of these is a statistic expressing the proportion of the total corrected sum of squares of the mapped data, calculated by

$$ SS = \frac{\sum\limits_{i=1}^{n} \hat{z}_i^2 - \left(\sum\limits_{i=1}^{n} \hat{z}_i\right)^2 \Big/ n}{\sum\limits_{i=1}^{n} z_i^2 - \left(\sum\limits_{i=1}^{n} z_i\right)^2 \Big/ n} \times 100\%. $$

For over a decade, this value has commonly been referred to by geologists as the sum of squares reduction, or the reduction of the sum of squares, of a map although other names have been used (e.g., the term "percentage of goodness-of-fit of the trend surface" was used by Davis, 1973, p. 329). In essence, this is a measure of the sum of the squares of the deviations (distances) between each original datum point and the computed surface; for standardization, this sum is expressed as a percentage of the sum of the squares of the deviations (distances) between each original datum point and the mean value of the dependent variable. It is worth noting that for the one-dimensional case $z = f(x)$, the SS for the first-degree equation $z = a_0 + a_1 x$ is $100.r^2 \%$, where r is the customary linear correlation coefficient.

In general SS provides a measure of the goodness-of-fit to the observed data points, but it does not necessarily provide a significant measure of the goodness of the surface as a prediction for the test of the target population. However, it is the latter, rather than the former, objective that geologists most commonly have in mind. The SS can vary from 100 percent when the surface passes through every observed datum point, to a very low value when the observed values are so scattered that they lie well away from the computed surface. Thus, the departure $(z - \hat{z})$ of the observed points from the computed surface affects the SS, as do:

(a) the number (n) of datum points; increasing n tends to decrease the SS.
(b) the degree of the polynomial or the order of the Fourier series; as the number of the terms in the fitted equation increases, the goodness-of-fit increases.

These three factors affecting SS can be evaluated conveniently by the second commonly employed technique which involves analysis of variance and the simple F-test (Dawson and Whitten, 1962). These tests permit formal confidence levels to be associated with a particular trend surface as a mode of representing the actual samples used (although this is not commonly a significant objective in itself). An example of an analysis of variance table from Dawson and Whitten (1962, Table 2) is:

Source of variation	Sum of squares	Degrees of freedom	Mean square	F	Confidence level
Due to linear component (first degree)	7180.333	2	3590.166	37.68	≫99.95
Deviations from linear (n − 1)	15623.404	164 ⎯ 166	95.264		
Due to linear + quadratic (second degree)	8416.195				
Due to linear (first degree)	7180.333				
Due to quadratic alone	1232.865	3	410.955	4.598	>99.5
Deviations from quadratic	14390.539	161	89.382		
Deviations from linear	15623.404				
Due to linear + quadratic + cubic (third degree)	8884.296				
Due to linear + quadratic (second degree)	8416.195				
Due to cubic alone	468.101	4	117.025	1.320	≃ 75
Deviations from cubic	13922.438	157	88.677		
Deviations from quadratic	14390.539				

Increasing the SS is easily achieved by increasing the degree of the polynomial (or order of the Fourier series) used, but the following questions are raised in the process:

(1) Consideration of the degrees of freedom makes it obvious that there must be more data points than coefficients in the particular equation used. Three times as many data points as coefficients is a safe guide to the minimum number of data points to use.

(2) For polynomial trend surfaces, it has been found that with equations of degree greater than 3 or 4, "wild" extremae appear in the computed surfaces in regions that have low density of data points. Low-degree surfaces rarely develop such spurious features, except at the map boundaries.

(3) With increasing degree (or order), increments of SS are commonly uneven but are dependent on the particular data set. Uneven increments raise numerous additional problems which are discussed below.

(4) When a low-degree polynomial is fitted to data, discrete areas of positive and negative residuals (differences between computed and observed values of the dependent variable) tend to occur. Many authors have suggested increasing the degree (or order) until autocorrelation of residuals is reduced to an acceptable, prescribed, low level (Agterberg,

1964). In many cases, polynomial or Fourier series have been augmented by additional terms (usually exponential or trigonometric) in an attempt to increase the SS. The mathematical steps involved are sound, but the procedure is questionable from the point of view of objective.

Points (3) and (4) need more background for full appreciation. deLury (1950) and Grant (1957) gave reasonably precise mathematical definitions of the "trend". The observed value of the dependent variable comprises the true value plus a small error component (observational error, clerical error, etc.). Trend-surface analysis attempts to separate the trend from the residuals, where the latter include the error components. For orthogonal polynomials and gridded data, Grant computed the z^2-array which, in effect, sets out the proportion of the total variability accounted for by each of the orthogonal polynomial coefficients. A representative z^2-array follows (Whitten, 1970, Table 3):

	x →									
	5446836.19	268589.35	32296.98	43730.51	76315.49	93634.56	66217.65	43070.91	.	.
y ↓ 2681685.96	158828.81	126275.04	85841.02	7263.71	89535.27	105326.31	14903.70	.	.	
244723.17	11965.90	7473.51	65358.63	5768.75	7219.34	668.60	.	.		
59267.87	3305.34	33699.11	601.36	5661.60	732.58	.	.			
14922.91	46940.85	19159.90	52.16	9917.46	.	.				
820.43	1154.62	71.49	17.80	.	.					
1037.45	724.58	1579.61	.	.	.					
39.84	1482.94	.	.							
664.66	.	.								
.	.	.								
.	.	.								

Proceeding from the first-degree terms (two nearest top left corner of array) to those for successively higher degrees (which are found in the diagonal rows successively farther towards the bottom right corner of the array), there tends to be a sudden significant drop (dashed line in the example) in the contribution to the total variability of the individual coefficients. Those contiguous high values in the z^2-array define the trend, i.e., those polynomial coefficients to be used in the orthogonal polynomial equation to define the trend. Spasmodic large terms may occur over the rest of the z^2-array below the dashed line and be associated with considerable SS, but they are part of the residual according to Grant's and deLury's definition. Because nonorthogonal polynomials for irregularly spaced data do not readily permit calculation of the contribution of each coefficient, this original and very desirable definition of trend has not been widely used. In fact, most available computer programs only permit calculation of nonorthogonal coefficients of the complete first degree, the complete first and second degrees, the complete first, second, and third degrees, and so forth. With nonorthogonal polynomials all coefficients change as the degree is changed, because the coefficients are not independent. The more recently developed orthogonal polynomial model for irregularly spaced data permits the z^2-array to be scanned, and those terms in the true trend to be identified and used alone for the mapping equation (Whitten, 1970, Fig. 1b). This is one of the features which makes this model superior to the standard, nonorthogonal model. To date, however, very few maps of irregularly spaced data have been published in which the true trend has been identified and mapped.

In most cases where high-degree polynomial surfaces have been published, a satisfactory SS for that surface, or a high confidence level based on analysis of variance, has been taken as justification for their use. Commonly, SS increments erratically; for example:

Surface A	B	C	D	E	F	G	H
Degrees 1	1 & 2	1, 2 & 3	1 thru 4	1 thru 5	1 thru 6	1 thru 7	1 thru 8
SS 3	27	47	48	49	51	71	95

Judging by numerous published accounts, the large SS of 95 percent for the complete eighth-degree polynomial (H) in this example would commonly be used to justify placing reliance on the eighth-degree map. The confidence level based on an F-test and analysis of variance for the complete eighth-degree surface is likely to be very high. However, the confidence level for the added sum of squares associated with the increment from degree N to degree $(N + 1)$ should be tested (Chayes, 1970); the first time a step from degree N to degree $(N + 1)$ is encountered that does not add a significant increase in SS (when tested in relation to the degrees of freedom associated with the added coefficients), computation should stop. Maps of degree higher than N should not be used as trend surfaces. In the above example, the increments from C to D, D to E, and E to F are all likely to lack significance. If this proves to be the case, C would be the highest degree polynomial surface that should be used. The large increases in SS between F and G and between G and H, although significant in themselves, would be relegated to the residual component. This is not the common practice in published literature but it parallels, as nearly as possible within the limitations of the nonorthogonal method, deLury's and Grant's original definitions, and is to be recommended when the orthogonal model is not available. However, there is at least one type of situation in which going to a higher degree is justified when a lower increment is insignificant. If, for example, the dependent variable defines a symmetrical "basin", the first-degree surface could have a SS approaching zero and the second degree might account for, say, 95 percent of the total variability and fairly be considered to represent the trend (Baird, Baird, and Morton, 1971).

Clearly, adding miscellaneous nonpolynomial terms to an algebraic polynomial function in order to increase the SS is predicated on the assumption that the surface most nearly passing through all of the data points is best. Such a philosophy seems to be a departure from the whole trend concept. The approach is appropriate where the data are known to be error free and the local minor features are equally important as, and not to be differentiated from, the broad regional effects. However, if this is the objective, a more efficient route is to use a spline function explicitly designed to pass through every datum point (Whitten and Koelling, 1973).

Another approach to assessing the desirability of a computed surface is to consider confidence bands about the trend surface. Unfortunately, currently available methods have very limited value. Krumbein (1963) showed that, for first-degree polynomial trend surfaces, the confidence bands are narrowest near the center of the map area and diverge radially outwards. Although Agterberg (1964) attempted to extend the method to high-degree polynomial surfaces, Krumbein and Graybill (1965) refrained from such an extension because it has yet to be shown how to accommodate the severe problems associated with the cross-product terms of the independent variables.

Yet another approach is to divide the total data set into two separate, but geographically interpenetrating, subsets (Agterberg, 1964; Koch and Link, 1971, p. 67). The contoured trend surfaces computed for each subset can be compared. Similar maps would lend credibility to the correctness of each, although there are real problems associated with objective comparison of two contoured maps. Alternatively, the trend surface for subset A can be used to calculate values ($\hat{z}_A$) at the sites of samples in subset B. Then, the value of $|\hat{z}_A - z_B|$ for each datum point from subset B yields a measure of the ability to predict raw values of subset B, and thus of the predictive value of the trend surface prepared for subset A data. The significance of such tests depends critically upon the levels of variance of the dependent variable and it would be inappropriate to draw conclusions about the tests without prior careful evaluation of the total variance pattern (although the latter type of information is rarely available).

The orientation of the reference geographic axes has no effect on polynomial trend-surface results. That is, identical maps and SS are produced, no matter what orientation the reference axes have. However, double Fourier series trend surfaces are "axes dependent". If different, orthogonal, geographic axes are used, the SS barely changes but the shape of the computed map surface may change markedly. The so-called "boundary effects" are much more extreme for polynomial surfaces, especially those of higher degree, than for Fourier surfaces. Near the geographical boundary of the data array, lack of restraint imposed by actual data allows the polynomial function to assume unrealistic values of the dependent variable. With the Fourier trend surface, built-in restraints of the trigonometric functions make such effects less obvious. To escape the problem, only that part of a trend surface well within the geographic limits of the data should be utilized.

All standard trend-surface techniques assume that the dependent variable is a continuous variable; that is, there are no discontinuities such as faults within the area. Where the data density is high, an unsuspected discontinuity such as a fault may be reflected by a belt of strong positive residuals parallel to a strong negative belt (Whitten and Beckman, 1969, p. 1056). James (1968, 1970) developed a nonlinear model suitable for fitting a "faulted polynomial surface" to subsurface stratigraphic data and gave numerous illustrations of its use.

For the double Fourier model (f), selection of the fundamental wavelengths parallel to the reference axes is critical. Unless the dominant wavelengths inherent in the data are known from prior knowledge, current methods require empirical iteration to select reasonable wavelengths. The set of smallest Fourier coefficients results when the most appropriate fundamental wavelengths have been identified and used. Krumbein (1966) compared several characteristics of polynomial and Fourier models in map analysis.

The spatial distribution of the data is critical in all trend-surface analyses, although the effects of poorly distributed data are less obvious with Fourier series trend surfaces. The least-squares criterion used in trend surfaces results in the computed surface being more constrained in areas where data are clustered. Where data points are sparse or absent, occasional points far removed from the computed surface have a relatively small adverse effect on SS and thus have little effect in constraining the shape of the computed surface. A completely uniform distribution of data points throughout the area is optimal. Certain geophysical surveys yield observations at the nodes of a regular grid but, in almost all other branches of the Earth sciences, data tend to be unevenly distributed or clustered due to such restraints as the locations of outcrops or conditions of accessibility. All current methods of "orthogonalizing" originally irregularly spaced data (that is, interpolating values at the nodes of an orthogonal grid) involve strong subjective biases that commonly outweigh any supposed benefits stemming from use of gridded data (Whitten and Koelling, 1973). Eliminating geographic clusters by using average values of all data points falling within specified unit areas is not satisfactory. The variance of average values is less than that of the raw data, so that average values based on strongly clustered data result in areas of low variance, while areas of sparse data retain the original larger variances. Standard polynomial models assume that the variance of the dependent variable is constant over the map area. Although complex models appropriate for use when the variance changes spatially have been devised, they have not been widely used. This is, in part, because positive information about the variance is rarely available and is difficult to obtain.

Data for the Dependent Variable

Perhaps the most critical issues in using trend-surface analyses concern the raw data rather than the mathematical models themselves. Trend surfaces have been used for almost any available set of spatially distributed data. In a majority of these instances, enthusiasm for the method has apparently distracted attention from the nature of the data, the underlying geological problem, and definition of the objective. Some of the issues to be considered are:

(a) the geographic or spatial distribution of the "samples" or observation points,

(b) the levels of variance of the dependent variable,

(c) the continuous or discontinuous nature of the dependent variable,

(d) the relationship of the samples (or observation points) to the sampled population and, more particularly, to the target population that is of basic interest, and

(e) the distribution statistics of the dependent variable. This topic is not discussed here, but care is needed in assessing trend surfaces computed for data that are strongly skewed. Use of a transformation to normalize the dependent variable has sometimes been advocated, but such procedures lead to additional problems that are beyond the scope of this presentation.

Consider two specific types of study involving the variability of granitic rocks: (1) the Lacorne–La Motte–Preissac granitic complex, Quebec, Canada (Dawson and Whitten, 1962), and (2) the Caledonian and Variscan granites of the British Isles and western Europe (Hall, 1969, 1972), the igneous rocks of eastern Siberia (Vistelius, Ivanov, and Romanova, 1972), or the phosphorous content of the granitic rocks of North America (Vistelius and Hurst, 1964). For one lithic unit such as the Lacorne Granite, the ideal sample array for computing a trend surface is likely to involve observations at the nodes of a grid across the entire unit, and extending beyond the geographic limits of the area for which the surface is required. Almost all real data sets provide an uneven spatial coverage; some areas are devoid of data, others have relatively clustered data. Even data from economic geology tend to be of this type (for example, dense data along drives and raises and sparse data in between). Trend surfaces yield poorer fits in data-deficient areas. It is well known that variables measured for a statistically adequate set of samples permit quantitative statements to be made about the sampled population that the samples represent. However, unless the sampled and target populations happen to coincide, which is unusual, statistical inferences cannot be drawn about the target population; it is only possible to make subject-matter inferences about the target population (Whitten, 1961).

Extending trend-surface contours across unsampled parts of a batholith lends an erroneous impression of precision to the implicit and explicit predictions. Of course, manually drawn contours make analogous predictions about the unobserved target population, but they are obviously subjective in nature (Whitten, 1972*a*). In weighing the relative merits of *a* computed map representing a data set as opposed to *the* correct map, the geologist must decide how uneven a data distribution he can tolerate. It is impossible to evaluate a given trend surface unless the spatial locations of the data points are clearly indicated. Even then, evaluation requires assumptions about the several levels of local variability. The problem of obtaining an even distribution of data points is still more difficult when a three-dimensional array is involved (Peikert, 1965; Whitten and Boyer, 1964).

Spatial levels of variance of the variables are critical. For example, when a set of chemical or modal analyses is available for one hundred 1 kg samples from a batholith, it would be common to treat each analysis as an accurate representation of the geographic domain that extends half way to the next sample. Minor analytical and clerical errors are recognized. However, if a new set of samples were to be collected with each new specimen 10cm, 1m or 10m from each sample of the first set, would there be a significant change in the analytical values? In most cases, the answer would be "yes", although Whitten (1968*b*, 1972*b*) showed that the density of replicate Aulanko Granodiorite samples yielded almost identical trend-surface maps. Similarly, if 10g, 100g, or 50kg samples had been taken, instead of 1kg specimens, would the results differ? Clearly, in general, the answer is "yes". If, as is commonly the case, the new data would be significantly different, is it realistic and reasonable to use trend-surface analyses (or any other statistical technique) to predict the regional pattern and the local residuals on the basis of the original data set? In attempting to separate the regional trend or effect, the locally significant geological anomalies, and random error, one must be convinced that each datum employed is a realistic and statistically significant representative of the geographic domain from which it was obtained. Besides assuming that a polynomial or Fourier function can portray realistically the geometry of the regional data surface, far more assumptions must be made about the data than are commonly justified or commonly realized. Unfortunately, levels of variance for each variable are in general different so that sampling appropriate for a trend surface of, for example, the specific gravity of 5kg samples is likely to be significantly different from the sampling needed for mapping the yttrium content of biotites or the amount of gold in channel samples of the same lithic unit.

A regional study of variation in the Caledonian and Variscan granites of northwestern Europe, the orogenic igneous rocks of eastern Asia, or the phosphorous content of North American granites raises other interesting problems. Standard trend-surface models assume that each dependent variable is continuous across the entire geographic area. Suppose that one to ten analyses were available for each discrete granite mass. The actual analyses at their respective geographical locations, or the arithmetic means calculated for each granite mass, could be used. Apart from the very real problem of how representative the original analyses are for their respective granite masses, the next questions are whether the populations of dependent variables are continuous, and what are the objectives of fitting trend surfaces to such data. Contours *between* the discrete granite masses imply predictions about the *intervening* areas, where neither data nor members of the target population exist. In the examples cited, it is difficult to define any conceptual meaning for the gradients across the contours in those areas in which igneous rocks do not occur; the bases and constraints of this particular problem have not been fully explored. If there is reason to assume that the observed variables are continuous functions of x and y, the isolines could estimate that continuous variation. In this event, if an unsampled igneous massif occurs its composition would be predicted by the isolines, although interpolation and extrapolation present even more problems than usual. Trend-surface analysis is a very powerful tool, but in situations of this type it is appropriate to determine whether it is more useful than discriminant analysis of Q-mode factor analysis for attaining the objectives of the research. In several instances, the apparently easy method of trend-surface analysis has been used when more direct, and less equivocal, answers could have been obtained using other well known statistical tests.

Conclusion

This discussion is a mere outline of a fascinating subject. Making maps is fundamental to the Earth sciences. In attempting to make quantitative and objective maps, trend-surface techniques can be very valuable. Unfortunately, the mathematical and computer techniques and capabilities are currently ahead of the geological understanding of the data, and the questions and objectives being assayed. As already mentioned, care must be exercised in avoiding the acceptance of *a* computer-produced map rather than *the* statistically significant portrayal of the target population of interest.

Acknowledgment

This work was supported by a grant from the U.S. Army Research Office—Durham (Grant number DA-ARO-D-31-124-72-G54).

References

Agterberg, F. P., 1964, Methods of trend surface analysis: *Colorado School Mines Quarterly*, v. 59, p. 111–130.

Baird, A. K., K. W. Baird, and D. M. Morton, 1971, On deciding whether trend surfaces of progressively higher order are meaningful: discussion: *Bull. Geological Soc. America*, v. 82, p. 1219–1234.

*Canright, R. B., Jr., and P. Swigert, 1968, PLOT3D—a package of FORTRAN subprograms to draw three-dimensional surfaces: Lewis Research Center, Cleveland, Ohio, *NASA Tech. Memo. X-1598*, 32 p. Available from NTIS as N68-28240.

Chayes, F., 1970, On deciding whether trend surfaces of progressively higher order are meaningful: *Bull. Geological Soc. America*, v. 81, p. 1273–1278.

Chorley, R. J., ed., 1972, *Spatial analysis in geomorphology*: Methuen & Co. Ltd., London, 393 p.

*Cole, A. J., 1969, An iterative approach to the fitting of trend surfaces: *Kansas Geological Survey Computer Contribution 37*, 27 p.

Davis, J. C., 1973, *Statistics and data analysis in geology*: John Wiley & Sons, Inc., New York, 550 p.

Dawson, K. R., and E. H. T. Whitten, 1962, The quantitative mineralogical composition and variation of the Lacorne, La Motte, and Preissac granitic complex, Quebec, Canada: *Jour. Petrology*, v. 3, p. 1–37.

deBoor, C., 1962, Bicubic spline interpolation: *Jour. Mathematics and Physics*, v. 41, p. 212–218.

deLury, D. B., 1950, *Values and integrals of the orthogonal polynomials up to* n = 26: Univ. Toronto Press, Toronto, Ontario, 33 p.

*Esler, J. E., P. F. Smith, and J. C. Davis, 1968, KWIKR8, a FORTRAN IV program for multiple regression and geologic trend analysis: *Kansas Geological Survey Computer Contribution 28*, 31 p.

*Ewen-Smith, B. M., 1971, Algorithm for the production of contoured maps from linearized data: *Nature*, London, v. 234, p. 33–34.

*Good, D. I., 1964, FORTRAN II trend-surface program for the IBM 1620: *Kansas Geological Survey Spec. Dist. Publ. 14*, 54 p.

Grant, F., 1957, A problem in the analysis of geophysical data: *Geophysics*, v. 22, p. 309–344.

Hall, A., 1969, Regional variation in the composition of British Caledonian granites: *Jour. Geology*, v. 77, p. 466–481.

Hall, A., 1972, Regional geochemical variation in the Caledonian and Variscan granites of western Europe: *Inter. Geological Congress XXIV Canada*, Sect. 2, p. 171–180.

*Harbaugh, J. W., 1963, BALGOL program for trend-surface mapping using an IBM 7090 computer: *Kansas Geological Survey Spec. Dist. Publ. 3*, 17 p.

Harbaugh, J. W., and F. W. Preston, 1965, Fourier series analysis in geology: *Univ. Arizona, College of Mines*, v. 1, p. R1–R46.

*Harbaugh, J. W., and M. J. Sackin, 1968, FORTRAN IV program for harmonic trend analysis using double Fourier series and regularly gridded data for the GE-625 computer: *Kansas Geological Survey Computer Contribution 29*, 30 p.

*Howarth, R. J., 1971, FORTRAN IV program for grey-level mapping of spatial data: *Jour. Inter. Assoc. Mathematical Geology*, v. 3, p. 95–121.

*James, W. R., 1966a, The Fourier series model in map analysis: Office Naval Research, Geography Branch, *Tech. Rept. No. 1*, ONR Task No. 388–078, Contract Nonr 1228(36), 37 p. Available from NTIS as AD631716.

*James, W. R., 1966b, FORTRAN IV program using double Fourier series for surface fitting of irregularly spaced data: *Kansas Geological Survey Computer Contribution 5*, 19 p.

*James, W. R., 1968, Least-squares surface fitting with discontinuous functions: Office Naval Research, Geography Branch, *Tech. Rept. No. 8*, ONR Task No. 389–150, Contract Nonr 1228(36), 51 p. Available from NTIS as AD647867.

*James, W. R., 1970, Regression models for faulted structural surfaces: *Bull. American Assoc. Petroleum Geologists*, v. 54, p. 638–646.

Koch, G. S., Jr., and R. F. Link, 1971, *Statistical analysis of geological data*, Vol. 2: John Wiley & Sons, Inc., New York, 438 p.

Koelling, M. E. V., and E. H. T. Whitten, 1973, FORTRAN IV program for spline-surface interpolation and contour map production: Geocom Program, in press.

Krige, D. G., 1966, Two-dimensional weighted moving average trend surfaces for ore valuation: Jour. South African Inst. Mining Metallurgy (*Proc. Symposium Mathematical Statistics Computer Applications Ore Valuation*), p. 13–79.

Krumbein, W. C., 1959, Trend-surface analysis of contour-type maps with irregular control-point spacing: *Jour. Geophysical Research*, v. 64, p. 823–834.

Krumbein, W. C., 1963, Confidence intervals on low-order polynomial trend surfaces: *Jour. Geophysical Research*, v. 68, p. 5869–5878.

Krumbein, W. C., 1966, A comparison of polynomial and Fourier models in map analysis: Office Naval Research, Geography Branch, *Tech. Rept. No. 2*, ONR Task No. 388-078, Contract Nonr 1228(36), 45 p. Available from NTIS as AD635476.

Krumbein, W. C., and F. A. Graybill, 1965, *An introduction to statistical models in geology*: McGraw-Hill Book Co., New York, 475 p.

*Lee, P. J., 1969, FORTRAN IV programs for canonical correlation and canonical trend-surface analysis: *Kansas Geological Survey Computer Contribution 32*, 46 p.

Matheron, G., 1970, Random functions and their application in geology, in D. F. Merriam, ed., *Geostatistics*: Plenum Press, New York, p. 79–87.

*Miesch, A. T., and J. J. Connor, 1968, Stepwise regression and nonpolynomial models in trend analysis: *Kansas Geological Survey Computer Contribution 27*, 40 p.

*McIntyre, D. B., 1963, Program for computation of trend surfaces and residuals of degree 1 through 8: Dept. Geology, Pomona College, *Tech. Rept. 4*, 24 p.

*McIntyre, D. B., D. D. Pollard, and R. Smith, 1968, Computer programs for automatic contouring: *Kansas Geological Survey Computer Contribution 23*, 76 p.

Oldham, C. H. G., and D. B. Sutherland, 1955, Orthogonal polynomials: their use in estimating the regional effect: *Geophysics*, v. 20, p. 295–306.

*O'Leary, M., R. H. Lippert, and O. T. Spitz, 1966, FORTRAN IV and MAP program for computation and plotting of trend surfaces for degrees 1 through 6: *Kansas Geological Survey Computer Contribution 3*, 48 p.

*Peikert, E. W., 1963, IBM 709 program for least-squares analysis of three-dimensional geological and geophysical observations: Office Naval Research, Geography Branch, *Tech. Rept. No. 4*, ONR Task No. 389–135, Contract Nonr 1228(26), 72 p. Available from NTIS as AD420274.

Peikert, E. W., 1965, Model for three-dimensional mineralogical variation in granitic plutons based on the Glen Alpine Stock, Sierra Nevada, California: *Bull. Geological Soc. America*, v. 76, p. 331–348.

Peska, V., J. Klomínský, and V. Sattran, 1970, Použití trendové analýzy v geologických vědách: *Časopis pro mineralogii a geologii*, v. 15, p. 145–161.

*Preston, F. W., and J. W. Harbaugh, 1965, BALGOL program and geologic application for single and double Fourier series using IBM 7090/7094 computers: *Kansas Geological Survey Spec. Dist. Publ. 24*, 72 p.

Robinson, J. E., H. A. K. Charlesworth, and M. J. Ellis, 1969, Structural analysis using spatial filtering in Interior Plains of south-central Alberta: *Bull. American Assoc. Petroleum Geologists*, v. 53, p. 2341–2367.

Romanova, M. A., 1968, Trend-analiz dannykh geologicheskikh nablyudenii (osnovnaya literatura) (Trend analysis of geologic data (basic literature)), in M. A. Romanova and O. V. Sarmanov, eds., *Voprosy matematicheskoi geologii*: Nauka Press for the V. A. Steklov Mathematical Institute of the Academy of Sciences of the U.S.S.R., Leningrad, p. 284–288.

*Sampson, R. J., and J. C. Davis, 1966, FORTRAN II trend-surface program with unrestricted input for the IBM 1620 computer: *Kansas Geological Survey Spec. Dist. Publ. 26*, 12 p.

*Turner, A. K., 1968, FORTRAN IV programs to develop contour maps of three-dimensional data: *Joint Highway Research Project No. C-36-72A*, File No. 1-6-1, Purdue Univ., 86 p. Available from NTIS as PB179245.

Vistelius, A. B., and V. J. Hurst, 1964, Phosphorous in granitic rocks of North America: *Bull. Geological Soc. America*, v. 75, p. 1055–1092.

Vistelius, A. B., D. N. Ivanov, and M. A. Romanova, 1972, *Atlas trendov soderzhanii glavnykh porodoobrazuyushchikh okislov v magmaticheskikh porodakh severo-vostoka Azii* (Atlas of the trends of the major oxides in the magmatic rocks of north-east Asia): Laboratory of Mathematical Geology, Leningrad, pages not numbered.

Watson, G. S., 1972, Trend surface analysis and spatial correlation: *Geological Soc. America Spec. Paper 146*, p. 39–46.

Whitten, E. H. T., 1961, Quantitative areal modal analysis of granitic complexes: *Bull. Geological Soc. America*, v. 72, p. 1331–1360.

*Whitten, E. H. T., 1963, A surface-fitting program suitable for testing geological models which involve areally distributed data: Office Naval Research, Geography Branch, *Tech. Rept. No. 2*, ONR Task No. 389-135, Contract Nonr 1228(26), 56 p. Available from NTIS as AD406919.

*Whitten, E. H. T., 1968a, FORTRAN IV CDC 6400 computer program to analyze subsurface fold geometry: *Kansas Geological Survey Computer Contribution 25*, 46 p.

*Whitten, E. H. T., 1968b, O dispersii nekotorykh priznakov granitnykh porod (Variance of some selected attributes in granitic rocks), *in* M. A. Romanova and O. V. Sarmanov, eds., *Voprosy matematicheskoi geologii*: Nauka Press for the V. A. Steklov Mathematical Institute of the Academy of Sciences of the U.S.S.R., Leningrad, p. 240–252.

Whitten, E. H. T., 1969, Trends in computer applications in structural geology, *in* D. F. Merriam, ed., *Computer applications in the Earth sciences*: Plenum Press, New York, p. 223–249.

Whitten E. H. T., 1970, Orthogonal polynomial trend surfaces for irregularly spaced data: *Jour. Inter. Assoc. Mathematical Geology*, v. 2, p. 141–152.

Whitten, E. H. T., 1972a, Enigmas in assessing the composition of a rock unit: a case history based on the Malsburg Granite, SW Germany: *Geological Soc. Finland Bull.*, v. 44, p. 47–82.

Whitten, E. H. T., 1972b, Conceptual models for three-dimensional variability of rock units: *Inter. Geological Congress XXII India 1964 Report*, Pt. 16, p. 25–38.

Whitten, E. H. T., 1974, Orthogonal-polynomial contoured trend-surface maps for irregularly spaced data: *Computer Applications*, in press.

Whitten, E. H. T., and W. A. Beckman, Jr., 1969, Fold geometry within part of Michigan Basin, Michigan: *Bull. American Assoc. Petroleum Geologists*, v. 53, p. 1043–1057.

Whitten, E. H. T., and R. E. Boyer, 1964, Process-response models based on heavy-mineral content of the San Isabel Granite, Colorado: *Bull. Geological Soc. America*, v. 75, p. 841–862.

Whitten, E. H. T., and M. E. V. Koelling, 1973, Spline-surface interpolation, spatial filtering, and trend surfaces for geological mapped variables: *Jour. Inter. Assoc. Mathematical Geologists*, v. 5, no. 2, p. 111–126.

Whitten, E. H. T., W. C. Krumbein, I. Waye, and W. A. Beckman, Jr., 1965, A surface-fitting program for areally distributed data from the Earth sciences and remote sensing: *National Aeronautics Space Administration Contractors Rept. CR-318*, 146 p.

* These articles contain trend-surface analysis computer programs; not many of these publications are specifically cited in the text. NTIS signifies National Technical Information Service, U.S. Department of Commerce, Springfield, Virginia 22151. These reports can be purchased for $3.00 per copy by citing the code number.

Computer Applications in Land-Use Mapping and the Minnesota Land Management Information System

M. L. Hsu, K. Kozar, G. W. Orning, and P. G. Streed

The concept of rational use of land resources is not new, but the general public's awareness of the limited nature of our land resources and the urgent need for optimal utilization of them are phenomena of this decade. In order to manage land resources effectively and plan for the future, it is essential that we comprehend the land utilization of the past and present. To achieve this, we need a vast amount of information on land resources and related socio-economic variables. When dealing with a large area, such as a major region or country, automation becomes necessary for carrying out the tasks of information collection, analysis, and updating. Accordingly, the State of Minnesota has established an automated land information system to facilitate the work of resource management and planning.

The Minnesota Land Management Information System (MLMIS) is being developed under the auspices of the Minnesota State Planning Agency and the University of Minnesota Center for Urban and Regional Affairs. The system is primarily a result of four studies which began in 1966: (*a*) a study on lakeshore development of the Brainerd area in Crow Wing County (Orning, 1967); (*b*) the subsequent Minnesota Lake Shore Development Study (Borchert and others, 1970*a* and 1970*b*); (*c*) a report on state land holdings by the Minnesota State Planning Agency (1968); and (*d*) the state land-use mapping project (MLMIS, 1971). During these studies, it became apparent that a statewide data system was essential. Therefore, MLMIS aims at providing extensive information to officials, planners, and researchers in decision-making and policy formulation concerning Minnesota land and water. The study works toward establishing a statewide data base for land-related information, such as land use, land ownership, land value, land characteristics, and government land-use controls.

298

The Basic Data Unit

Basic Data Unit — parcel

The choice of a basic data collection unit is crucial to an information system. In Minnesota, it was decided that the basic unit for statewide coverage should be the 40-acre parcel, the smallest consistent unit in the U.S. land survey system. The first-order reference axes for the system are the 32 pairs of locally defined principal meridians and base lines (parallels). The second-order references are tiers of townships and ranges (Figures 1 and 2). A township, which is defined by a pair of township and range lines, is a 36-mile square. Within a township, there are 36 sections (one-mile squares), and in each section, 16 forty-acre parcels.

There are nearly 1.4 million of these 40-acre parcels or data cells in Minnesota. Most blocks of land, whether in public or private ownership, have as their edges the boundary lines of 40-acre parcels. The parcel divisions are reflected in agricultural areas as field lines, in forested areas as timber cutting boundaries, and in cities as major streets. In fact, in cities, major commercial developments often occur on section corners of the U.S. land survey. These lines and cells describe the manner in which the landscape of Minnesota has been divided and shaped. The 40-acre parcel is important in other ways, because it is the base for many governmental records at the county, regional, state, and federal levels. The cell structure also lends itself to computer mapping.

The MLMIS is designed for planning studies at the state, regional, and county levels, and is not intended to be a municipal or urban information system. Special care, however, is being taken to assure that data collected below the level of 40-acre units can be aggregated and incorporated into MLMIS. Generally, these data are maintained for municipal or county subdivisions. One such example is an urban study employing 10-acre data cells (Robinette, 1971).

The Geocoding System

The locational content of data in Minnesota consists of the following hierarchies: the state, county, township, section, and parcel. The geocoding system in MLMIS contains identification codes for all these elements. In addition, it encodes the minor civil divisions (MCD) which are administrative subdivisions comprised of townships, incorporated places, and other areas. The MCD and the county identification are adopted from the U.S. Bureau of the Census. Centroids of the MCD are recorded in latitude and longitude, correct to the nearest 10 seconds. The ability to locate a 40-acre parcel by a point reference to spherical coordinates has yet to be perfected, but in the future, one point of each parcel may be identified in latitude and longitude. At present, each 40-acre parcel is uniquely defined by a serial number of 14

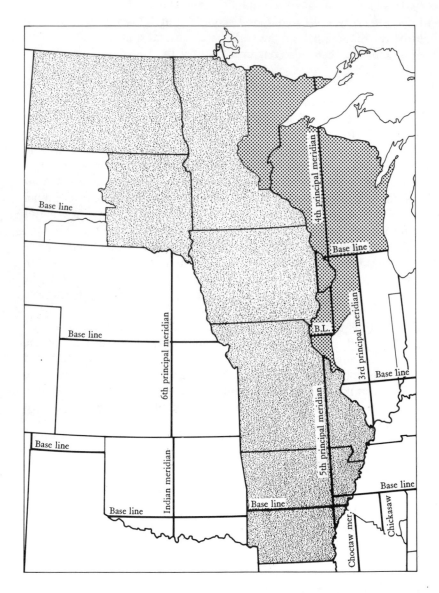

Figure 1   The U.S. land survey system. The State of Minnesota is governed by the fourth and fifth principal meridians and their base lines.

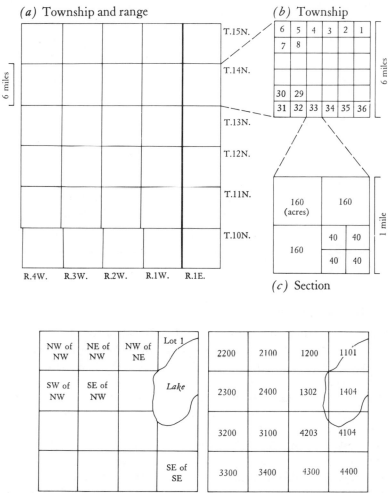

Figure 2 Scheme for describing land divided according to the township and range convention. (a) Arrangement of townships. (b) Division of a township into sections. (c) Subdivision of a section into quarters and quarter-quarters. (d) System of legal description. (e) Numerical code used by MLMIS for description of a section.

characters, and parcel data may be displayed on township maps (Figure 2 and Table 1).

In the U.S. land survey system, some townships are not precisely 36 square miles. In these irregularly shaped townships, some sections contain more than 16 parcels per section and these "extra" parcels are identified by a

Table 1.   Characters of parcel identification

Type of location	Number of characters	Example
County	2	31
Township	3	055
Range*	3	262
Section	2	36
Quarter-Quarter Section (40-acre parcel)	2	31
Government Lot†	2	09

* The last character in the range serial is a directional code.

† All parcels which are not exactly 40 acres were originally surveyed in size by the government and called government lots. Ownership is not implied.

special code. Approximately 10 percent of the townships need some adjustments.

Major Information Sources

There are four major data sources for MLMIS: (a) various levels of government, including county, state, and federal; (b) the U.S. Bureau of the Census; (c) the University of Minnesota excluding MLMIS; and (d) the MLMIS itself. Census data may be used directly by the MLMIS, since the system has adopted the census areal codes. In contrast, data and records provided by other governmental agencies may be used only after some reorganization of data elements.

At present, the main body of data in the MLMIS is the complete coverage (1.4 million cells) of state land-use types and water orientation. In the United States, other data systems comparable to the MLMIS are described by Swanson (1969) and Denenberg, Corbin, and Alsberg (1972). However, neither has so large a number of data cells. Information on water orientation was obtained from aerial photographs and from county highway maps. Seven types of orientations denote wherever a 40-acre parcel adjoins a lake, stream, or ditch. Information on land use was interpreted from aerial photographs into a nine-category classification established so the interpreters could determine the land-use types with minimum consultation of other data sources (Orning and Maki, 1972, Appendix C). The nine categories are: forested, water, marsh, cultivated, pasture and open, urban residential, urban non-residential or mixed residential, extractive, and transportation. The dominant land use was identified for each 40-acre parcel by a three-man team, two interpreters and one map recorder. Double interpretation facilitated accuracy. The basic unit of interpretation was a township within which section lines were followed. Each regular section was divided into 16 forty-acre parcels based on field lines and timber cut edges, as well as a transparent reference grid. It was assumed that these parcels cover all surface area, including water bodies. Cases which were difficult to determine from photographs were resolved by field checking.

MLMIS Data Structure

The data are presently maintained on 12 machine-readable magnetic tapes—each tape containing one development region as defined by the State of Minnesota except for Development Region 3 which is on two tapes. A development region contains one to eleven contiguous counties.

Each unique record of a parcel has the following four components: a 14-character identification key, minor civil division (MCD) number, longitude and latitude of the MCD centroid, and seven types of data. These data types are land use, water orientation, federal land ownership, relative ownership (full or partial of the parcel, federal ownership only), geomorphic region, state land class, and soils. The last three types are completed for only a small number of counties.

The Procedures of Data Input

The procedure of data input to MLMIS employed before 1973 was traditional, containing the following steps. For each 40-acre parcel, land information was coded on maps (scale 1:24,000), locational and land information was recorded on mark sense cards, the card was read, checked, and finally transferred onto tapes.

Now, a new method of data input has been developed, called the CRT data entry system. A CRT (cathode ray tube) is connected to a CDC 6600 computer via a CDC 3200 (Figure 3). At this experimental stage, only one county, Itasca, is programmed into the CRT data entry system. This system consists of a locational directory and data files. Data on 40-acre parcels may be called onto the CRT (Figure 4) for an area one-half of a township at a time; this limitation is fixed by the screen which allows only 50 characters horizontally and 20 vertically. Each parcel is designated by a two-digit code, spatially forming a small square resembling the "map image" of a parcel on a township map. Subroutines are available for displaying either the data as stored on the computer tapes or as a map with coded symbols for one-half of a township. Entering new data, correcting, and updating information can be performed easily, and the results of these operations are viewed immediately on the screen. Hard copies of the final records are produced by line printer.

The CRT input procedure is most effective with graphic source materials such as maps and photographs, but it is not limited to such usage. If source

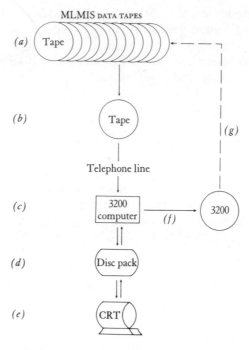

Figure 3 Outline of CRT data entry system. At the 6600 computer, data are read off tape files (*a*) and transferred to special file (*b*) which is sent by telephone to 3200 computer (*c*). Data are then written on disk pack (*d*) for random access. User can request display of townships on CRT (*e*) and can enter and correct data. These are sent back to disk pack. When user is finished, updated file is returned (*f*) to 3200. To be developed is a link (*g*) to return data to 6600 magnetic tape files.

materials are comparable in scale to the screen imagery, they may be used directly for data input. Results of data entry may be checked immediately by viewing the spatial patterns on the original materials and that on the screen. If only one class of data exists within a township, such as forested land, the data entry may be completed by a single request call on CRT. If the township has a predominant class, this may be entered first for the entire township. Then other classes may be input in areas where the data fall under these classes. Currently, the CRT data entry system is being implemented, and for Itasca County, a dozen new types of data such as county zoning and school districts are entered for each 40-acre parcel.

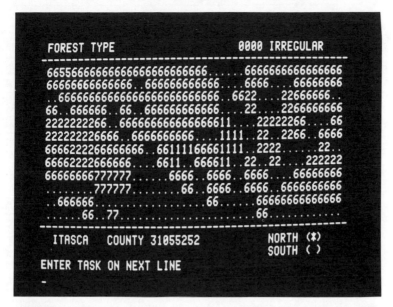

Figure 4 CRT display of forest types in northern one-half of a township, Itasca County. Numeral 1 denotes white pine, red pine and jack pine, 2 spruce-fir, 6 aspen-birch, and 7 unproductive.

Procedure of Data Retrieval

At present MLMIS does not have a user-oriented program for retrieval of data from the system. Data are stored on tapes by state development regions and by counties. In order to obtain data on 40-acre parcels of several townships in different counties, for example, a special program would have to be written to search for the requested counties, the townships, and so forth. A simple request for data would cost approximately $8.20 at the Minnesota computer system, not including the time for program writing and submission. However, the situation will be improved in the near future with the installation of a data retrieval package, System 2000.

Display and Analysis of Land Information

Computer mapping is the primary mode of data display for MLMIS. Line printer, CalComp plotter, and CRT have been utilized for cartographic work. A MINNMAP program produces maps based on data from 40-acre parcels (Figure 5). The most substantial application of MLMIS to date is the statewide multicolored land use map at 1 : 500,000. A line printer produces a gray-tone township map in each of the primary colors (red, yellow, and blue). The township maps can then be pasted into blocks of six townships, and these

Figure 5 Line-printer map showing land-use zoning in a township in Itasca County.

blocks aligned and photographically reduced (Figure 6). A plate is made for each of the colors required for printing the resultant map. This map, which contains 1.4 million data cells, would have been difficult to produce by conventional cartographic procedures, even though the reproduction method just described was also tedious. Presently, other mapping methods are being developed.

With the CalComp plotter a large area such as a county, region, or even the entire state can be mapped in a single computer submission. This eliminates the need for combining printer outputs of small areas (Figures 7 and 8). On a state or county map, each plotted symbol represents one 40-acre cell. Different numerals, symbols, and/or colors are employed to differentiate classes.

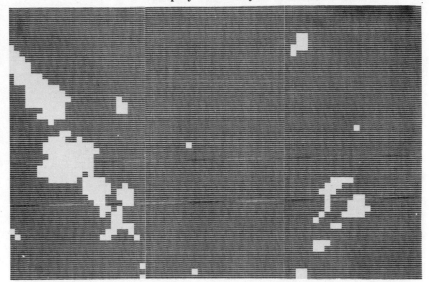

Figure 6   A block of six township maps produced on line printer. Later this and other blocks were pasted together to make the negative for yellow printing plate.

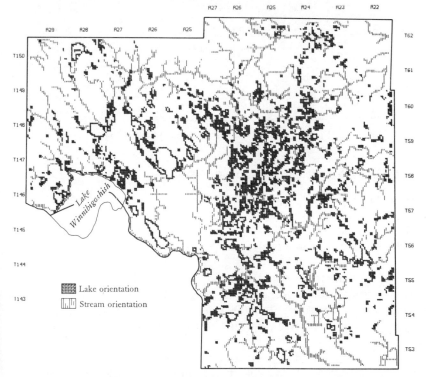

Figure 7   Plotter map showing water orientation, Itasca County.

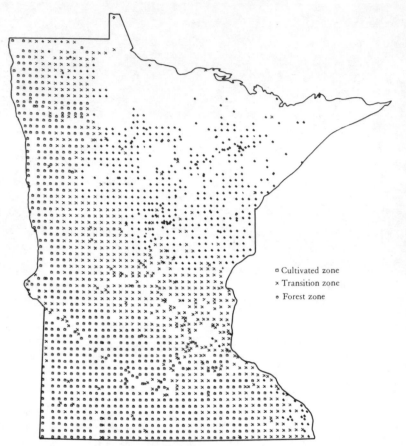

Figure 8　Plotter map of land-use patterns, based on MCD data.

Data Updating and Potential Information Source

Since land utilization changes through time, information sources and methods for data updating are of utmost importance to a data system such as MLMIS. One potential information source which is being investigated is satellite imagery, via a grant to the State Planning Agency from NASA (Brown and others, 1973). The Earth Resources Technology Satellite (ERTS-1) provides imagery in the form of 70mm positive transparencies and color-combined slides which can be projected for interpretation at scales ranging from 1:30,000 to 1:250,000. Nine-inch bulk transparencies are being analyzed by density level slicing with an Interpretation System VP-8 image analyzer.

Thus far, research has shown good results from satellite images with regard to urban and extractive land uses. In urban places with populations of 7000 and more, areas of different urban functions can be detected, making possible a refinement of the two-class urban land-use type now employed. In mining areas, area measurement and extractive feature classification can be carried out with sufficient accuracy. Preliminary studies on density of artificial surfaces in the Twin Cities indicate that with some ground truth it will be possible to collect data on impermeability by one-mile cells, and to map the degree of impermeability in the urban area. Moreover, a model for urban run-off may be developed based on the data on impermeability and storm sewer networks (Brown and others, 1973).

MLMIS is an ongoing study; thus far most efforts have been placed in areas of data collection, improvements of input and output procedures, and mapping programs. Some progress, however, has been made in data analysis, model formulation, and prediction. Much of the value of MLMIS has been in research which meets current needs in land management and planning. More recent studies include an investigation of land for development in northern Minnesota (Rusch, Borchert, and Orning, 1972), a recreational resource study on lakes in the St. Paul area (Wietecki and Orning, 1973), a study of legal controls in relation to land use (Gilbert, 1973), and development of the Rapid Analysis Fiscal Tool or RAFT (MLMIS and CURA, 1972). RAFT is a group of computer programs to create and manipulate a data base to be used in the analysis of current laws and proposed alternative policics on state taxation.

The creation of the MLMIS has been made possible by the promotion of long-term cooperation and coordination among reseachers, planners, and public officials. It has been as much a political exercise as it has been an information system study. The ultimate goal of the MLMIS, of course, is not simply one of data accumulation, but to provide pertinent information and to improve the quality of public and private decisions affecting the environment.

References

Borchert, J. R., G. W. Orning, J. Stinchfield, and L. Maki, 1970a, *Minnesota's lakeshore, resources, development, policy needs*: Dept. Geography and the Center for Urban and Regional Affairs, Univ. Minnesota, Minneapolis, 47 p.

Borchert, J. R., G. W. Orning, J. Stinchfield, D. Pederson, and L. Maki, 1970b, *Minnesota's lakeshore, statistical summary*: Dept. Geography and the Center for Urban and Regional Affairs, Univ. Minnesota, Minneapolis, 72 p.

Brown, D., M. Meyer, J. Ulliman, R. Eller, J. Gamble, S. Prestin, and D. Trippler, 1973, ERTS-1 application to Minnesota land use mapping: Minnesota Land Management Information System, Univ. Minnesota, Minneapolis, *Rept. No. 3*, 8 p.

Denenberg, S. A., C. C. Corbin, and P. A. Alsberg, 1972, *NARIS, A natural resource information system*: Center for Advanced Computation, Univ. Illinois, Urbana, 15 p.

Gilbert, W., 1973, Minnesota land use laws: a classification of statutory powers: Minnesota Land Management Information System, Univ. Minnesota, Minneapolis, *Rept. No. 5*, 215 p.

MLMIS, 1971, *State of Minnesota land use map, 1969*: Center for Urban and Regional Affairs and Minnesota State Planning Agency.

MLMIS, and Center for Urban and Regional Affairs, 1972, Rapid analysis fiscal tool, *Annual Report for 1971–72*: Univ. Minnesota, Minneapolis, 44 p.

Minnesota State Planning Agency, 1968, *A state land inventory*: Minnesota State Planning Agency, St. Paul, 15 p.

Orning, G. W., 1967, The process of lakeshore development in Crow Wing County: *Unpublished M.A. thesis*, Dept. Geography, Univ. Minnesota, Minneapolis, 51 p.

Orning, G. W., and L. Maki, 1972, Land management information in northwest Minnesota—the beginning of a statewise system: Minnesota Land Management Information System, Univ. Minnesota, Minneapolis, *Rept. No. 1*, 75 p.

Robinette, A., 1971, *Land use prototype study, Empire Township, Dakota County, Minnesota*: School of Landscape Architecture, Univ. Minnesota, Minneapolis, 97 p.

Rusch, P. G., J. R. Borchert, and G. W. Orning, 1972, Land for development adjoining northern Minnesota's national recreational corridor: Minnesota Land Management Information System, Univ. Minnesota, Minneapolis, *Rept. No. 2*, 48 p.

Swanson, R. A., 1969, *The land use and natural resources inventory of New York State*: Office of Planning Coordination, New York State, Albany, 20 p.

Wieteki, K., G. W. Orning, 1973, Lakes in Ramsey County, recreational resource, use, policy implications: Minnesota Land Management Information System, Univ. Minnesota, Minneapolis, *Rept. No. 4*, 107 p.

Information requests should be directed to Mr. G. W. Orning, director of MLMIS or Dr. K. Kozar, Systems Director.

The Evaluation and Prediction of Visual Clustering in Maps Symbolized with Proportional Circles

G. F. Jenks

Maps are communicative devices designed to display spatial information in two-dimensional format. To some map makers and map users these displays are considered to be areal data banks or storehouses of a myriad of separate and isolated individual facts. Other map makers and map users turn to the map as a communicative device because the two-dimensional format allows them to display, and see, the new information which derives from the juxtaposition of sets of symbols. The following paragraphs are directed toward this latter type of map information transfer and little or no attention is paid to the search and retrieval of specific facts from single symbols.

In carrying out our daily activities we all make visual comparisons between different kinds of animate and inanimate objects. How many times, for instance, have you heard a new grandmother say of her first grandson, "He has his father's nose". One often hears a similar statement such as, she is the "spitting image" of her mother. Similarly, automobiles are visually compared, as are pieces of furniture, articles of clothing, houses, trees, and even whole cities or broad geographical regions. We accept these comparisons as normal pursuits although we often disagree with, or fail to perceive, the resemblances that others see.

In the pursuit of scientific knowledge we find many who practice some form of visual comparison. Botanical taxonomists visually compare leaves, twigs, and other parts of plants in their classification of vegetation, as do zoologists with animals, ornithologists with birds, and entomologists with insects. Geologists visually compare rocks; geomorphologists, landforms; anthropologists, human features; and geographers compare landscapes and maps. In contrast to our daily relationships, when a scientist makes visual comparisons we expect that a formalized procedure has been followed. For example, there may be a series of specific features that are observed and collated. This may be done using a set of standard objects, as in the case of museum samples, or by graphic and verbal cues incorporated into field books or texts. At any rate, the expectation is that scientific visual comparisons will be more consistent than those made by untrained individuals.

While authors often ask readers to visually compare one map with another there is no assurance that such comparisons are valid. Since visual comparison of objects is a complex psychophysical process (Arnheim, 1971, p. 60–63; Zusne, 1970, p. 221–243), several relevant questions about map reading come to mind. What attributes of map symbolization and design assist readers in perceiving spatial patterns? Do readers see individual symbols or clusters of symbols when making map comparisons? What psychological processes are utilized in visual map comparison, as for example, attitude, experience, motivation, and memory? What attributes of a map, such as its complexity, color, texture, pattern, and size, aid readers in the comparison task? Do map readers as a group see similar patterns on a map or is the regionalizing process highly individualistic? This latter question is particularly important since authors have assumed that patterns are perceived in identical form, texture, size, and complexity by everyone.

In this study an inquiry is made into several aspects of the visual comparison of maps symbolized with proportional circles. Specifically, five questions are set forth and tested: (1) Can map readers consistently evaluate sets of proportional circles in terms of how they are clustered? (2) Do map readers see regions on proportional circle maps and do these regions appear similar to all readers? (3) When comparing pairs of maps symbolized with proportional circles are readers consistently able to evaluate pattern similarity? (4) Are the common mathematical and statistical measures of pattern adequate gauges of visual map comparisons? (5) Is it possible to predict the visual levels of similarity between maps if readers do not perform according to numerical measures?

Clustering of Proportional Circles

Gestalt psychologists have studied how people visually integrate a number of separate graphic elements into a composite form. Kohler (1947) discusses the problem of the visual properties of shape and how our familiarity with a certain feature and its graphic articulation aids us in seeing that feature in a complex visual field. This is the basis of much work in automated processing of remotely sensed images, where attempts are made to sort out selected landscape features from surrounding visual noise.

In other psychological studies, certain Gestalt qualities or principles of visual organization have been formulated by Wertheimer and further elaborated by Arnheim (1971, p. 66–72). Several of these apply to map reading, including proximity, similarity of shape, similarity of color, similarity of size, good continuation, and good closure. These principles of visual grouping can be demonstrated in simple diagrams such as those shown in Figure 1. Proximity as a grouping theory is clear in the comparison of diagrams *a* and *e*. Groupings of similar colored elements as in *a* or *d* are easier to perceive than those of different colors as in *c*. Similarity of shape and its effect upon grouping is illustrated by comparisons of *a* and *d* with *f*. Note that it is also easier to see the grouping of similar sized objects as in *a* than those of varying sizes in *d*. The good continuity in *g* is easier to see than that in *h*, although the latter has a degree of good continuity. Although Dent (1970) has given us a beginning in relating these Gestalt principles of visual perception to map design, few of them have been tested in a visually complex environment such as that found in the normal thematic map.

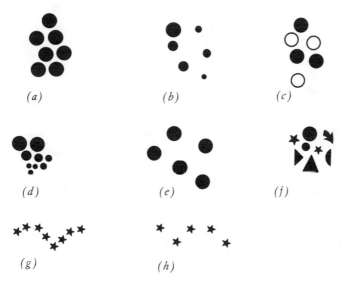

Figure 1 Clusters of symbols illustrating some of the principles of the psychologist Wertheimer. Note it is easier to see a cluster when all symbols are the same size, shape, and color, and when they are grouped closely together. (Differences in color are represented by open and solid symbols.)

There is another aspect of the map design problem which needs elaboration. In much of the work done in remote sensing the task has been to eliminate visual static by reducing the obscuring elements in an attempt to recognize known Earth phenomena. The cartographer places individual symbols on the map where these features occur on the Earth. He hopes that he can design his map so that he limits visual static and he expects his reader to see an agglomeration of symbols by some process of visual integration. Clearly these visual groups of symbols are not known shapes which the map reader can anticipate and seek through an organized search procedure.

Instead, the map reader perceives irregular forms, regions, or patterns, because his eye and brain combine to create them without prior knowledge of their existence.

With this background in mind two experiments were devised to test these grouping concepts using typical circle symbols. In the first experiment 20 groups of controlled dyads or triads of circles were constructed. The circles in the triads were composed of sets which were either tangent or were spaced at distances equal to one-half of the diameter of the smaller circle. The total amount of black in each triad was equal to that of all other triads. The circles in the dyads were also presented in tangentially and radially spaced sets but the amount of blackness was varied considerably. The 20 sets of circles are shown in Figure 2.

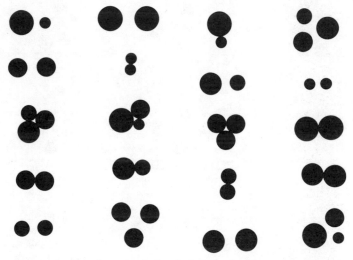

Figure 2 Dyads and triads of circles created to give different visual impressions of clustering. They were first presented to the respondents in this form to adapt them to the task of rating the degree of clustering. Later each set was seen individually and clustering was rated on a five-point scale.

The unordered sets of circles (Figure 2) were presented to the respondents to adapt them to the task to be performed. After adaptation each respondent then looked at one set of circles at a time and rated the degree of clustering on the five-point scale:

        5   Very clustered
        4   Somewhat more clustered than unclustered
        3   Equally clustered and unclustered
        2   Somewhat more unclustered than clustered
        1   Very unclustered.

One hundred respondents performed the clustering task: the composite ratings of these decisions made it possible to array the circle sets in order of visual ranking (Figure 3). It should be noted that these rankings proceed

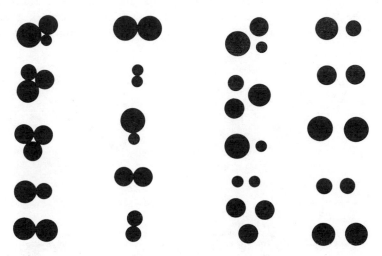

Figure 3 Sets of circles from Figure 2, re-ordered in terms of degree of visual clustering. Most will agree with this ordering which places tightest clusters in the upper left and the loosest clusters in the lower right.

down each column from the top left to the bottom right. The top three sets of circles in the left-hand column were rated as very highly clustered with a median rating of 5 and means varying from 4.7 to 4.5. The next seven sets of circles, the tangent pairs, were given median ratings of 4 and the means ranged from 4.1 to 3.8. Two sets of circles, each a triad with varying sizes of circles, were given median ratings of 3 but the means were below that value, 2.8 and 2.6. All other circle sets were given median ratings of 2 with means varying from 2.2 to 1.8. Interestingly enough, respondents used the rating "very unclustered" quite parsimoniously, since five sets of circles had modal values of 1 but no set had a median or mean value approaching 1.

Results of this experiment indicate that potential map readers do, in fact, see sets of circles in clusters and that they are reasonably consistent in their visual rankings. The standard deviations obtained were never higher than 1.2 and the majority were below the 1.0 level. A further degree of consistency is found in the rankings as shown in Figure 3. Note that there is a logical ordering of the circle sets and that in only one case is this ranking disturbed. In that case, the widely spaced dyad with small circles is one rank above those dyads with larger and radially spaced circles.

Regions on Proportional Circle Maps

In the second clustering experiment six maps of the value of a crop in South Carolina were presented to 100 respondents. The mapped distributions (Figure 4) were selected to give a broad range of patterns. Since these maps were to be utilized in a later experiment, the total amount of black (the area of all circles) was controlled so that it is approximately equal for all maps.

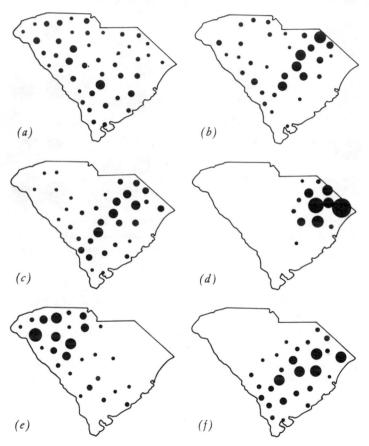

Figure 4 Six maps created with proportional circles which have been controlled to display the same area of black on each map. Maps were selected to display a wide range of patterns and differing degrees of clustering.

Respondents were directed to draw lines around regions or "areas of sameness" on each of the six maps. Lines shown superposed upon the maps in Figure 5 represent the summation of this task. Each isoline represents the decision of 10 percent of the sample with the 30 percent, 60 percent, and

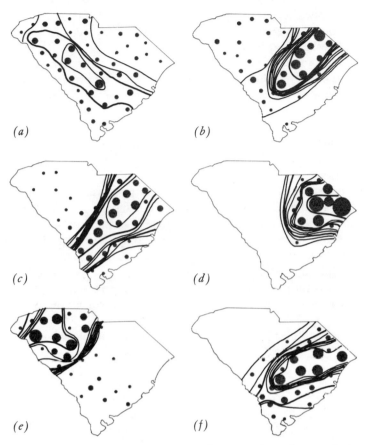

Figure 5 Isolines on these maps indicate number of respondents who agreed upon limits of visual regions. Closely spaced isolines indicate general agreement on regional boundaries while loosely spaced isolines show that respondents were either unable to see groupings clearly or they did not agree on where boundaries were located.

90 percent levels being emphasized by a heavy line. On Figure 5, maps *b*, *d*, and *e*, there are nine isolines, the innermost outlining an area which 90 percent of the respondents agreed to be clustered. Grouping of lines into dark bands on a map indicates that there was a high degree of agreement or consensus on the limits of a visual region. A loose arrangement, and a lesser number of isolines, indicates that respondents were in disagreement or unable to define regions. The pattern of lines on Figure 5*a* indicates this latter reaction. Although the level of regionalization on Figure 5*c* and *f* is less certain than on Figure 5*b*, *d*, and *e*, it is only slightly so, because the central regions are defined by either 70 percent or 80 percent isolines. While the

author is satisfied that this group of 100 readers did in fact see regions in the six proportional circle maps, he is well aware of the need for more than a graphic or verbal description of this visual process.

The area of, and the distance between, circles on a proportional circle map seems to be closely related to the visual regionalizing process. If this is true, it can be hypothesized that a potential surface for any given map in Figure 4 should be highly correlated with the visual isolines drawn on the same map in Figure 5. To test this hypothesis the centers of each of the 46 counties of South Carolina were used as sample points and a potential surface for each distribution was calculated. Because the circles on the maps were also centered at these county centers it was possible to correlate visual responses with the potential surface. Thus, a clustering response of 98 percent of the respondents for the large circle on Figure 5d could be paired with the potential of 2.46 at that point. This concept of modeling has commonly been used in demographic and economic studies in geography (Berry and Marble, 1968, p. 130–148; Cole and King, 1968, p. 503–511; Knos, 1962) and its application here is simply an extension of these "gravity" or "potential" concepts. Correlations resulting from a comparison of the percentage of respondents grouping circles into clusters and the potential values are presented in Table 1.

Table 1. Correlation between Symbol Potential and clustering (see Figure 5)

Map	r
a	0.6154
b	0.8111
c	0.8114
d	0.9169
e	0.8394
f	0.8450

From a psychophysical point of view one can argue that the potential model is not an appropriate measure since the reader of a map may not be able to see details over the total area of the map in a single fixation. Under this assumption it follows that lines drawn to delineate regions could only have been constructed in segments, and that these segments of boundaries probably were drawn between areas with significantly different degrees of blackness. To test this hypothesis, a circle was floated across each map, so that its center was located at each of the county centers. Thus, it was possible to obtain a measure of the total blackness in the immediate environment of each county by summing the areas of all circle symbols whose centers fell within the floating circle. The radius of the circle used was one-ninth of the width of the experimental maps. This size seems to conform to the area which can be seen with a high degree of clarity during fixation (Graham, 1965, p. 47–50; Pirene, 1967, p. 28–29). The correlation between the number of groupings of circles and the blackness of the fixated environment of the circles is presented in Table 2.

Table 2.   Correlation between Responses and Blackness of Visual Environment (see Figure 5)

Map	r
a	0·6887
b	0·8564
c	0·8895
d	0·908
e	0·8818
f	0·8946

The two sets of correlations in Tables 1 and 2 give added proof that map readers do see regions on proportional circle maps and that they see these regions with a high degree of consistency. Without further testing, the psychophysical processes involved in these regionalizations cannot be deduced, but the high correlation coefficients indicate that distance between circles, area of circles, and the immediate environment around a given circle all play a part in verbal clustering. In any case, the findings indicate that a third experiment involving map comparisons could be fruitfully undertaken.

Visual Comparisons of Proportional Circle Maps

Authors and teachers have assumed that the similarities they see between patterns on maps are seen in the same manner by other map users. There is little proof of the accuracy of this assumption in the cartographic literature and three studies seem to indicate it is an erroneous concept (Jenks, 1973; McCarty and Salisbury, 1961; Wood, 1973). However, visual map comparisons cannot be discarded as a useful communicative technique because the task set for the map reader in these three studies was highly variable and the methodology used for measuring success was not uniform. Starting with the premise that the visual map comparison task is a psychophysical process, it may not follow normal statistical or mathematical laws of order as tested by McCarty and Salisbury (1961). Expanding upon this premise leads to the question of whether a group of map readers is capable of performing a comparison task with consistency both between pairs of maps and logically in terms of the sequencing of map pairs. These concepts led to the development of an additional visual map reading experiment using the six crop maps of South Carolina. (For a lengthier discussion of these concepts, refer to Corcoran, 1971, p. 54–58.)

In this third experiment respondents were given copies of the crop maps (Figure 4) and asked to make comparisons between all possible pairs of maps. The comparisons were rated on a five-point scale between the following extremes: "5—the maps look very much alike" and "1—the maps look very different". The results of this experiment are presented in Figure 6 in the form of a series of histograms placed between each map pair. The map pairs are in rank order based upon the mean response of 100 evaluations. The pair with the most similar rating (b–c) is presented first and the pair with the least similar rating (a–d) is presented last.

The rating scale utilized to arrange pairs of maps in Figure 6 is open to interpretations which need further explanation. The mean, median, mode, and a rank for each comparison are given in Table 3. These measures of

Table 3.   Mean, Median, Mode, and Rank for 15 Visual Map Comparisons (see Figure 6)

Map Pair	Mean	Median	Mode	Rank
a–b	2.61	3	3	12
a–c	2.47	2	2	11
a–d	1.08	1	1	1
a–e	2.06	2	2	8
a–f	1.75	2	1	4
b–c	4.31	4	5	15
b–d	1.88	2	1	6
b–e	2.20	2	1	9
b–f	2.88	3	2	13
c–d	1.67	1	1	3
c–e	2.04	2	1	7
c–f	3.66	4	4	14
d–e	1.44	1	1	2
d–f	2.39	2	2	10
e–f	1.83	1	1	5

central tendency are derived from linear interval scaling and there is no proof that the visual task performed by the respondents follows such a scale (Corcoran, 1971). As a result, a ranking was thought to be more appropriate for ordering the map pairs so further analyses could be made (Helmstadter, 1964, p. 20–21). The mean value was selected as the ranking score because

Figure 6   Fifteen possible pairs of six crop maps of South Carolina shown in visual order from least different to most different. Histograms show responses on a five-point scale in which 5 represents "look alike" and 1 represents "look different".

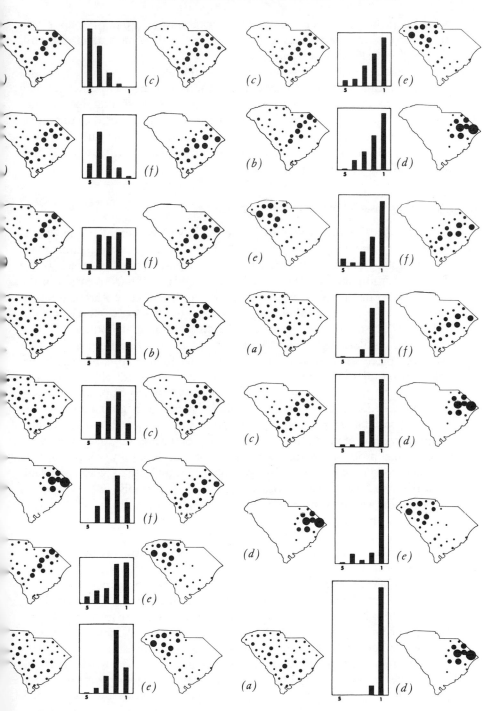

there is a problem of ties in other scales. Furthermore, 11 pairs of maps retain the same rank under all measures and no map pair is more than one rank different regardless of the scale used.

The ranking of map pairs along the visual scale seems to be logical and cartographically rational. Maps that seem to be visually very different were consistently rated so by the respondents as were those that had similar patterns. Between these extremes is a lesser, but not unexpected or unacceptable, degree of consistency. Numerous psychological studies attempting to determine distinguishable differences in form seem to corroborate these findings (Graham, 1965, p. 553f).

Predicting Visual Map Comparison Rankings

The map is a visual communicative device having certain attributes which set it aside from many other design problems. The map designer must place his symbology in locations prescribed by their position on the surface of the Earth. Additionally, he is more or less obliged to follow convention in the geometric forms he uses to symbolize his final product. Within these constraints, however, he can alter size, color, and contrast so the map he creates is his own personal interpretation of the distribution under study.

Ideally, the designer would like to predict the information transfer that will take place when readers see his map. In visual map comparison this information might be how well or how poorly readers will be able to relate the map patterns. If a measure of visual similarity between maps was available he could test his products prior to publication and redesign them if they did not meet specified standards. A partial goal of this reasearch was to attempt to find a method of predicting visual rankings of the maps used in experiment three. This problem is somewhat like that explored by Clarke (1959), Flannery (1956), Williams (1956), Wright (1966), and others who have dealt with the visual similarity or dissimilarity of map symbols. In this instance, however, the visual comparison problem involves the pattern or clustering of symbols on a map rather than the accuracy with which the value represented by an individual symbol can be determined.

Geographers have long been interested in map comparisons and a number of numerical methods of measuring pattern characteristics have been developed, as have certain techniques for the comparison of patterns on two or more maps. These techniques are well summarized in Cole and King (1968, p. 163–338) and in a number of other texts on statistical geography. Several promising procedures for pattern analysis and comparison were selected, including product–moment correlation of circles on one map with those of another, three potential models, and several local visual environmental area measures including six with floating circles which were described previously. A contiguity measure and a centroid measure were also examined.

In each of these procedures, values were calculated for the 46 counties on each map and a product–moment correlation calculated for all possible map pairs. The 15 correlation coefficients for a given comparison were then ranked and a Spearman rank correlation calculated between the ranking and the visual ranking. None of these measures was considered to be a reliable predictor of the visual comparisons since the highest correlation obtained was 0.65.

The lack of success in attempts to duplicate visual rankings of maps became a concern and resulted in a detailed pair-by-pair study of the visual differences between maps and the correlation coefficients that were obtained. One aspect of the inability to predict visual rankings is graphically illustrated in Figure 7. The product–moment correlation between maps *b* and *f* resulted

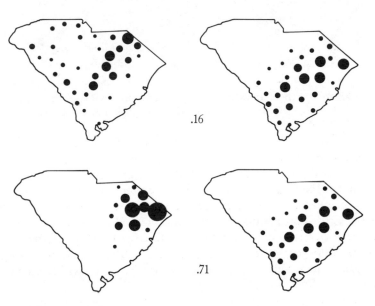

Figure 7   Correlation coefficients between each map pair represent numerical relationship between patterns on the maps. These values would be reversed in the visual rankings as shown in Figure 6.

in a coefficient of 0.16 and between maps *d* and *f* of 0.71. The visual rankings for these maps was reversed and the upper pair of maps in Figure 7 were considered to be much more alike than the bottom pair by the 100 respondents. There are two probable causes for these differences between product–moment and visual correlation. In the top pair (Figure 7*b* and *f*) there are a number of small circles on one map which are paired with empty areas on the other. In addition, the larger circles, while somewhat similar in pattern, are offset from one map to another. Both of these conditions contribute to a low product–moment correlation even though the visual response indicates a degree of pattern similarity. In the case of the bottom pair of maps (Figure 7d and f) the large circles on one are coincident in location with many of those on the other. The large empty areas are also located in similar positions giving added impetus to a relatively high product–moment coefficient. On the other hand, the maps have very different numbers of circles and this difference may have a strong influence on the low visual correlation.

Translation in position of patterns on maps causes them to appear different, but apparently these locational differences are less important in visual than in numerical comparisons. This concept is illustrated in Figure 8

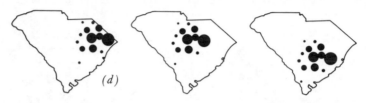

Figure 8   These maps have a high degree of visual similarity but a very low correlation coefficient would be obtained if they were compared numerically.

where the circles shown on map d have been moved both horizontally and angularly. Clearly these maps are visually similar because the circle patterns are identical. Numerical analysis of these patterns using product–moment correlation, potentials, or similar measures yields very low similarity indices, however. Cross-correlation provides one method of evaluation and if the proper lags were utilized correlation coefficients of 1.0 could be obtained. This procedure was discarded because the author could not imagine a circumstance in which readers of these maps would consider them to be identical.

Analysis of the type just discussed led to the development of a map sampling technique which would take into consideration numbers of circles, size of circles, and the translated positions of circles. This technique utilizes a network of columns and rows similar to those shown in Figure 9. Black dots represent centers of each of the 46 counties of South Carolina and all maps were constructed with circles centered on these points.

Using these columns, rows, and dots it became possible to compare two maps in the following manner. First, the number of circles in a given column on one map was subtracted from the number of circles in the same column on the other map. The absolute differences in number of circles for all rows and columns were then tabulated and these 15 sums, one for each possible map pair, were ranked and correlated with the visual rankings. The Spearman

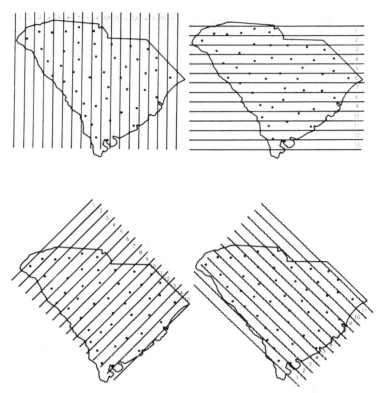

Figure 9 Columns and rows used to evaluate differences between patterns on proportional circle maps. Dots represent centers of counties in South Carolina. Differences in number of circles or area of circles were assigned to the column or row in which the county center appears.

correlation coefficient was 0.93 for vertical columns and horizontal rows, 0.89 for angular columns and rows, and 0.91 when both sets of columns and rows were used. These coefficients are significantly higher than the highest ($\rho = 0.65$) obtained by previous methods.

Difference in pattern blackness of the maps was measured by obtaining the sum of the area of black circles in a given column or row and subtracting this from the blackness in the same column or row on the second map. These absolute sums were then ranked and correlated. In this case Spearman correlation coefficients were 0.83, 0.79, and 0.81 for the vertical, angular, and combined networks. While these coefficients are lower than those obtained for differences in numbers of circles, they are reasonably high comparative measures.

In the final manipulation of these data, the sum of differences in numbers of circles on a map was multiplied by the sum of differences in blackness for the same map. Rank correlation between these products and the visual rankings yielded a coefficient of 0.90.

High correlation coefficients resulting from the sampling network of columns and rows makes it possible to rank maps on a numerical scale which is essentially the same as that obtained by visual evaluation. However, it cannot be assumed that this brief study solves the problem of visual map comparison. More research with an expanded sample of mapped patterns is needed. An analysis of the most efficient scale for the network of columns and rows is also needed, as is some method of standardizing the procedure so that maps of different areas can be compared.

In conclusion, it has been determined that readers of proportional circle maps do see regions and that they see these regions with a high degree of consistency. Further, readers can effectively make visual comparisons between two or more proportional circle maps and these comparisons can be simulated by numerical analysis. With this knowledge in hand cartographers can use this type of map knowing that regional or pattern information is being transferred from the map to the reader.

References

Arnheim, R., 1971, *Art and visual perception*: Univ. California Press, Berkeley, 443 p.

Arnheim, R., 1972, *Visual thinking*: Univ. California Press, Berkeley, 344 p.

Berry, B. J. L., and D. F. Marble, eds., 1968, *Spatial analysis*: Prentice-Hall Inc., Englewood Cliffs, New Jersey, 490 p.

Clarke, J. I., 1959, Statistical map-reading: *Geography*, v. 44, p. 96–104.

Cole, J. P., and C. A. M. King, 1968, *Quantitative geography*: John Wiley and Sons, Inc., New York, 692 p.

Corcoran, D. W. J., 1971, *Pattern recognition*: Penguin Books, Baltimore, 216 p.

Dent, B. D., 1970, Perceptual organization and thematic map communication: *Place Perception Research Rept. No. 5*, Cartographic Lab., Clark Univ., Worcester, 368 p.

Flannery, J., 1956, The graduated circle: A description, analysis and evaluation of a quantitative map symbol: *Ph.D. Dissertation*, Geography Dept., Univ. Wisconsin, Madison, 196 p.

Graham, C. H., 1965, *Vision and visual perception*: John Wiley and Sons, Inc., New York, 637 p.

Helmstadter, G. C., 1964, *Principles of psychological measurement*: Appleton-Century-Crofts, New York, 248 p.

Jenks, G. F., 1973, Visual integration in thematic mapping: Fact or fiction?: *1973 Yearbook of Cartography*, Kartographisches Institut Bertelsmann, Gutersloh, p. 27–35.

Knos, D. S., 1962, *Distribution of land values in Topeka, Kansas*: Center for Research in Business, Univ. Kansas, Lawrence, 33 p.

Kohler, W., 1947, *Gestalt psychology*: New American Library, New York, 222 p.

McCarty, H., and N. Salisbury, 1961, Visual comparisons of isopleth maps as a means of determining correlations between spatially distributed phenomenon: *Research Rept. No. 3*, Geography Dept., Univ. Iowa, Iowa City, 81 p.

Pirene, M. H., 1967, *Vision and the eye*: Chapman and Hall, London, 187 p.

Williams, R. L., 1956, Statistical symbols for maps: Their design and relative values: *Office of Naval Research Rept. No. 609(03)*, Yale Univ., New Haven, 115 p.

Wood, D., 1973, I don't want to, but I will: *Ph.D. Dissertation*, Geography Dept., Clark Univ., Worcester, Mass., in preparation.

Wright, R., 1966, Selection of line weights for solid, qualitative line symbols in series on maps: *Ph.D. Dissertation*, Univ. Kansas, Lawrence, 130 p.

Zusne, L., 1970, *Visual perception of form*: Academic Press, New York, 547 p.

The Relevance of Cartography

D. P. Bickmore

It may well be that the title that I have chosen for my paper is simply the defense mechanism of an aging cartographer. I suspect that there are some "spatial data processors" who regard cartographers as dinosaurs left stranded by the computer technology of today. Obviously I have some sympathy with this point of view, but I have also observed some of the dilemmas in which computer graphics, geographical information systems, and the like have been enmeshed over the last few years.

One of the several definitions of the word "map" that appears in the Oxford Dictionary dates from a source of 1586, where it was used to describe "a circumstantial account of a state of things" ("circumstantial" is defined as "full of circumstances, details or minutiae"): not a bad objective 400 years later! Maps, of course, have been made from the earliest days as an obvious and inescapable human reflex to the question, "where is it?". But there is perhaps some slight significance that the term "cartography" first appears in English literature as recently as 1859, when exact surveying was becoming one of the technologies necessary both to geographical exploration and to civil engineering and administration. I am in no way competent to take you on an historical tour of the developments of cartography over the last century, but there are two particular aspects of this development to which I do want to draw your attention in passing: the industrialization of cartography and the definition of topography.

First, the industrialization of cartography. Whatever may be the reasons, there is no doubt that many billions of dollars are now spent annually on this subject. It is, of course, difficult (and, I believe, irrelevant) to say where surveying finishes and cartography starts, but my guess is that in Britain alone cartography commands a £10 million-a-year budget, and the world figure is probably greater by at least two orders of magnitude. The maps of a country are quite a good index of its status in the international technology league. Not only is cartography big business, it is also something of a monopoly, very largely carried out by government, and, indeed, by a small magic circle of highly specialized, and sometimes military, acolytes.

Another aspect of the industrialization of cartography is seen in the build-up of teams of surveyors ranging the countryside to produce a steady flow of draft maps or revisions for centralized drawing offices and for fast running printing machines. To some degree the pace is set by the printing machines on the old syndrome that the more powerful the machine, the faster the production, and hence, the cheaper the product. The machine insists on being fed by the production line, which in consequence has to be kept slimmed down to a standardized product. This is a situation discouraging to experiment or change, but presumably all over the world the general public thinks it knows what a map is, and rests all too content. The arguments in the last five years for introducing computing into cartography have been most successful when they have sought only to introduce a box of electronics into the existing flow line, without altering either the data collection process or the design, i.e. "more of the same thing, more quickly, and no messing about!". In the standard industrial process the cartographer has tended to become a mini-functionary, discouraged both from new design interests that stimulated his eighteenth century predecessors and from new topics and philosophies that excite contemporary geographers. At the same time he is concerned, perhaps overly so, with the "circumstances, details and minutiae" of his product; its conformity to precise specifications, its exact printing register, and all the unshowy and repetitive discipline that his particular industrial process demands. Is this discipline, part-way between the geographer, the scribe, and the engineer, a relevant asset in the jungle of "spatial data processing"?

If engineers, many of them military ones, have drilled the process of cartography into an industrial discipline, there has also been a tendency to freeze the content. Topography has become invariant, an *idée fixe* over the world during the last 100 years. It provides a delineation of "the state of things" in qualitative terms. Let us look briefly at the elements of topography at virtually any scale:

(1) Framework of reference (graticule or grid)
(2) Land and water surfaces; relief and drainage
(3) Vegetation and land use
(4) Communications
(5) Human settlement, boundaries, place names
(6) Economic activity
(7) Landmarks.

And all this in one map, for anywhere in the world! My purpose in this article is a double one, both to draw attention to the many unquantitative aspects of topographic mapping and to emphasize the interrelation of these different elements of the continuum of landscape that the topographic map tries to assemble as a single picture. Indeed, the cartographer's ambition is to sandwich separable elements together so as to preserve visual interrelation, but in so doing there is the danger that the content of nearly everything he handles is over-simplified. Thus rivers on topographic or atlas maps do not record flows; nor do roads or railways; the relief is only the outer shape of the geological bone structure. The symbol for mine or factory says nothing quantitative about its production; the built-up area defines neither the population nor its characteristics.

During the last 50 years there have been many who were not content with the general purpose map. Specialty mapping or "thematic cartography" has grown in interest, but still remains a 10 percent part of the field. Why is this, especially at a time when more and more different quantitative aspects of a region are significant for planning? Partly because the production system demands a standard, straightforward product; partly because data for special maps are often not available (either because it simply has not been collected, or because it has been collected by "other" organizations for non-mapping purposes and often has been boiled down into statistical tables sometimes to preserve "confidentiality"); or more often because mapping has been seen as a slow, expensive, and unquantified exercise irrelevant to decision making. These are important areas where computer techniques should help.

One of the main fields in which specialty mapping has grown is that of national atlases, and I will use illustrations from the Atlas of Britain (Bickmore and Shaw, 1963) to underline the range of problems that are involved. As one of the editors, at least I can claim to know the inner horrors of these maps as well as anyone, and a mild celebration of the tenth anniversary of publication seems in order. I refer to the Atlas of Britain also because it was, in 1959, out of the birth pangs of this elephant that the notion grew that in computer cartography might lie an "easier" way of handling this morass of data. Oxford has a reputation as a home of lost causes! Since the object of these illustrations is to show something about the "relevance of cartography", there are several matters which should be borne in mind.

The first of these concerns data and the problems that are inherent in assembling data from a wide range of different sources into a "bank" or "compilation" from which graphic displays such as maps and statistical tables can be made. One built-in bedevilment of this compilation process is the inevitable tendency of data to change, either as a result of additional knowledge and further surveys, or because of the time over which something is measured (e.g., production in a factory or population in a parish). Another bedeviling factor is the relative positional reliability of different types of data (superficial versus solid geology, for example) to be shown on the same map. Yet another is that different data sets are all too frequently based on different boundaries within the same region, e.g. census and soil boundaries. These data problems unfortunately are not dispelled by one wave of the computer.

Wherever the compilation or data bank dares to be ambitiously "circumstantial" these problems arise.

The second matter concerns graphics. All the information presented on a map is to be read by eye from paper. The resolving power of the eye enables it to differentiate to 1/10mm where provoked to do so. Clearly, therefore, conciseness is of the essence and high resolution graphics are a common denominator of cartography. There are tricks, too, of colors, lines, and point symbols that suggest that there is some subtlety within the cartographic language. Here the capabilities of the high resolution plotter in a computer system offer interesting potential to extend the language as opposed only to mimicking it.

Thirdly, there are always limitations imposed by time, cost, and resources available. High resolution mapping of "spatial data" is expensive and there are no rewards for a product that fails to emerge from the pipeline. (In the particular case of the Atlas of Britain it was decided that all the maps would be published together in one volume and not singly as available.) For those in the future who attempt to build composite data banks, I commend the disciplines of atlas production. I have often identified myself with the bowed shoulders of the figure of mythological Atlas staggering off the cartouches of eighteenth century maps. Let no one underestimate the management qualities necessary in cartography, and, I believe, in any effective application of spatial data processing by computer.

Now let us turn to some "spatial data," albeit processed largely by hand and 10 years ago. The object of the Atlas of Britain was to present an inventory of resources: that at least is a current need. The maps I have selected primarily pose questions about whether this data could be processed today as economically, as truthfully, and as readably by computer methods.

I should briefly introduce the Atlas by explaining that it is the result of approximately 50 man-years of work and was published by the Clarendon Press of Oxford University in 1963 at £25 per copy. It has 200 pages of maps, each 15 inches by 20 inches. The majority of these are at 1:2M scale (32 miles to 1 inch) and cover the whole of Great Britain and Northern Ireland. There are also sections of regional maps at 1:1M and 1:500,000 scales. Subject matter ranges from geology, vegetation, climatology, forestry, agriculture, mining, industry, communications, to a series of sociological subjects.

Figure 1, from page 3 of the Atlas of Britain, is a map of physical features at 1:2M scale. I wish to draw attention here to the use of a toned layer (in dark green on the original) for land below 25 feet in altitude, and another one (in yellow on the original) picking out areas between high and low tide. Data for representing this information on very small-scale maps are not easy to come by. In the case of the 25-foot contour, compilations had to be made from maps at 1:25,000 and reduced by a factor of nearly 100. Had this relief information about Britain been available on magnetic tape, the task

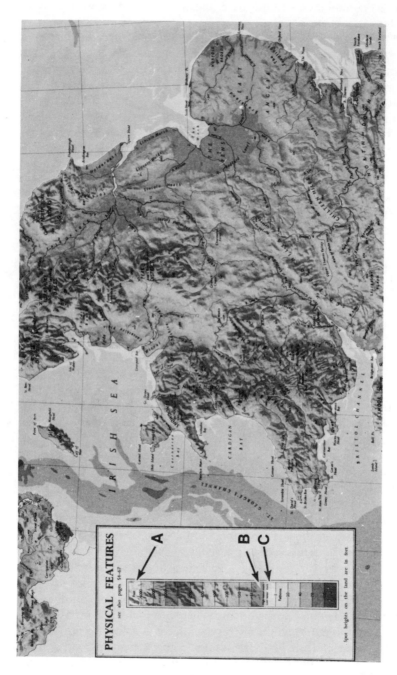

Figure 1 Physical features map with toned layers indicating elevation. Note tones representing extremely small areas of high ground (A), areas of ground lower than 25 feet (B), and intertidal areas (C). From page 3 of the Atlas of Britain. (Reproduced by permission of the Clarendon Press, Oxford.)

of extracting it for these very small scales would have been extremely simple and the possibility of computing metric contours or slope maps (through our automatic contouring program) would have been feasible. On the other hand, the cost of putting this information onto tape may simply not be worthwhile.

I would also draw attention to the toned layer that represents land over 4000 feet. Logic dictates an increasing scale of altitude/color, but these small top peaks are minute islands even on the ground and are difficult to show by color in any sense equivalent to their rather dramatic height. I suggest that this problem of "losing" critical small areas is common in the graphics, though not in the statistics of spatial data processing, an argument in favor of a computer system which can provide both.

Much of the stepped effect of layers has deliberately been smoothed off by the use of hill shading. Note that both the layers and the hill shading are derived from contours, but that no contour lines are shown. Computer techniques can select and produce layers quickly and cheaply, but automatic hill shading at this resolution, while feasible, seems likely to be very extravagant in computer time. There are, however, other techniques of relief display by computer that seem worth exploring, such as the anaglyph and perspective diagram.

Figure 2 is taken from page 13 of the Atlas and presents the Permian and Triassic geology of Britain. It is one of a series on which geological systems are mapped separately. I want to direct attention to the fineness of detail which is feasible where there is selection of what is shown. Cartography has far too often smoothed and generalized its patterns for no adequate reason. This map also has attempted to handle the three-dimensional nature of this particular topic by the diagrams of borehole information (in appropriate color coding) that are presented around the map. Geological mapping seems to remain a colorful but two-dimensional business and so far not strongly influenced by the three-dimensional analyses of subterranean surfaces that are attempted by the more exotic computer programs devised for oil exploration. There is scope here for bringing the two together with the aid of computer graphics.

The next map (Figure 3) is taken from plate 24 and deals with the temperature and salinity of sea water. This information is derived from the marine equivalent of boreholes, which are illustrated on the top of the figure. Of course, the layers which have been derived from this very limited amount of data may have somewhat humble reliability; I think there is some danger that their unreliability may be lost in the rather exciting colors by which they are displayed in the original plate. This is a case where human interpolation seems likely to be preferable to machine contouring.

Figure 4 is a map of the averages of annual rainfall over a 35-year period, taken from page 34 of the Atlas. In this instance, we decided not to attempt to draw contours around the rainfall data points but to represent them by

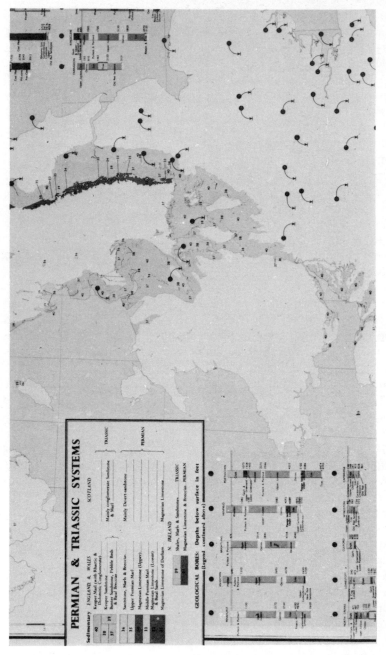

Figure 2   Geologic map showing extreme detail and use of coded boreholes. From page 13 of the Atlas of Britain. (Reproduced by permission of the Clarendon Press, Oxford.)

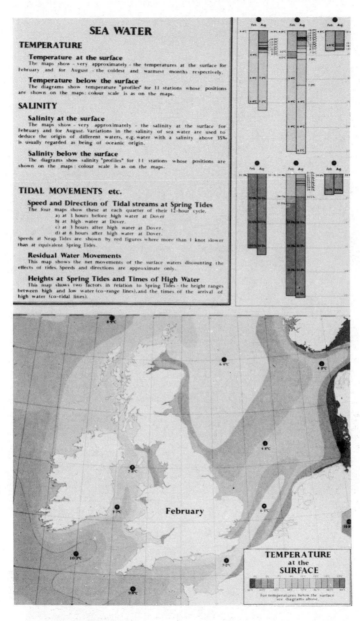

Figure 3 Part of a map showing temperature and salinity of the sea around Britain. Note surrounding profiles. From page 24 of the Atlas of Britain. (Reproduced by permission of the Clarendon Press, Oxford.)

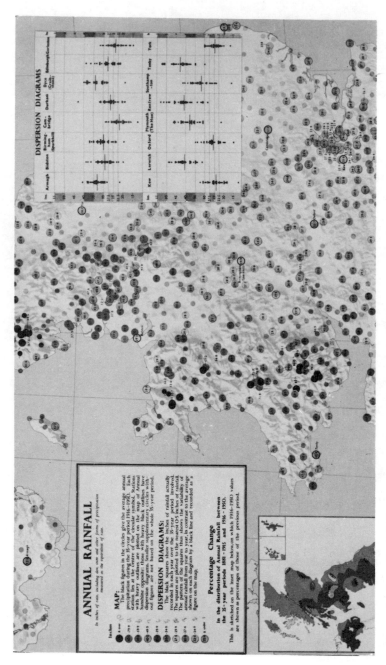

Figure 4 Annual rainfall map using color-coded dot symbols. Dispersion diagram inset has been moved from its location on original plate. From page 34 of the Atlas of Britain. (Reproduced by permission of the Clarendon Press, Oxford.)

figures inside circles and to underprint each circle with a distinct color code. I like to believe that at this scale, the eye can find its own patterns from this display. Of course, the relief pattern must also be borne in mind, though the hill shading which appears as the base of this map is, I think, inadequate.

Another point to which I wish to draw attention is the use of smaller, colored "blobs" to represent stations for which rainfall information for less than the total 35-year period was available. Finally, note the dispersion diagrams for some arbitrarily selected stations which are shown in the panel. Similar dispersion diagrams have been used on the monthly rainfall, temperature, and sunshine maps in the Atlas, and they impart some statistical gloss to the generalization of the maps. The irregularities of British weather and the improbability of repeating the average annual pattern in any one year is certainly underlined. This aspect of statistical reliability sometimes gets swept under the table in cartography, but it is an aspect in which the computer can help.

We now move on to page 43 of the Atlas, showing the distribution of a type of tree, the oak (Figure 5). This is one in a series of eight maps in which we attempted to analyze the wooded areas shown on the one-inch topographic map. However, the Forestry Commission survey of tree types was recorded on punched cards in terms of the sheet lines of the six inches to the mile series (roughly 10 by 10km). We laid down a grid of the six-inch maps of the country over a plot of the wooded areas, so that we could allot the statistics from the survey only to those areas which were wooded. We then mapped this data by distributing dots, each representing 100 acres of oak forest. This process would now be handled by "sieve" mapping from computer files, but the placing of the dots, if that graphic method were used, would still seem best done by hand.

Figure 6, taken from page 117, shows cotton spinning and cotton weaving and is one of a large series of industrial maps that were a feature of this Atlas. Although made manually, the maps were based on computer processed statistics from the Census of Production which is revised every four years. This census adopts its categories from the "Standard Industrial Classification". From manipulations of the Census of Production it was possible to identify for 1954 the numbers of workers in each town in each industry. One complication related to confidentiality. The information in the Census was collected on the reasonable understanding that it would not be transmitted in a form which might reveal vital information about the firms supplying it. For example, where there were only two factories of the same industry in the same town, the firms concerned had to be consulted before the information could be furnished for mapping. Some 30,000 firms were consulted, and 95 percent gave permission for the information to be mapped. "Confidentiality" remains a problem in computer mapping.

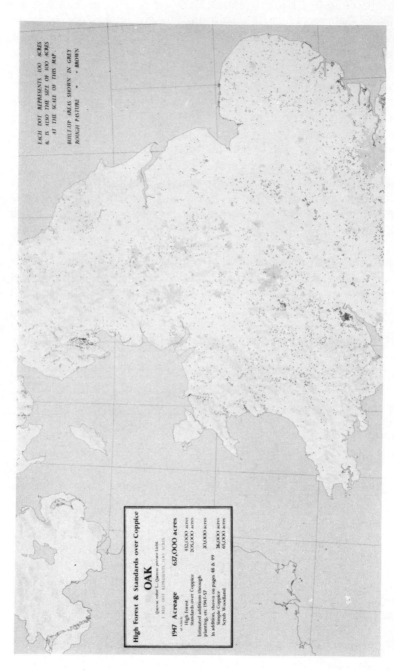

Figure 5 Dot map showing distribution of oak forest. From page 43 of the Atlas of Britain. (Reproduced by permission of the Clarendon Press, Oxford.)

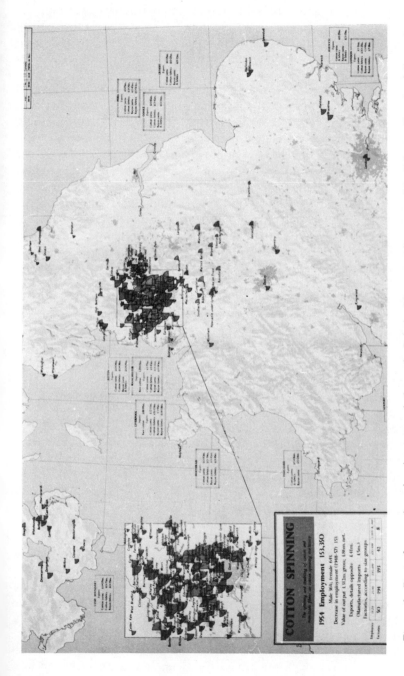

Figure 6 Part of map plate showing cotton industry in Britain. Note use of cartographic "blow-up" and small panels containing additional information. From page 117 of the Atlas of Britain. (Reproduced by permission of the Clarendon Press, Oxford.)

You will notice the geographical concentration of this particular industry and the cartographic method of a "blow-up". The symbol scale in these enlargements is identical to that of the main map, but the base scale has been increased by a factor of two. Computer cartography offers many possibilities for such variable-scaled maps.

I also want to draw your attention to one or two other trimmings around the main map. A good deal of attention was paid to setting each industry in its economic context by capsule information presented in the title panels. Note the comparability of different industries by output in financial terms, in contrast to the maps which show employment. Information about factory size-groupings is also shown. In addition it seemed important to try to show international trade relationships of each British industry, a factor upon which it is traditionally dependent, and it was also possible to obtain import and export statistics for individual industries in individual ports for the year 1954. To perform this type of collation of data in an entirely automated fashion may lie both beyond our ambitions as well as our purses in 1973.

The map shown in Figure 7 illustrates mortality. This map, from page 157 of the Atlas, is part of a series of sociological maps, and is based on circles whose size quantifies the population of each Local Authority. The coloring of these circles grades the special subject, in this case the death rate (a subject apparently of morbidly intense statistical interest). This seems an easy and quick candidate for computer mapping, apart from hidden-line removal where circles overlap (in this case, it is possibly cheaper to eliminate hidden lines by hand than by program). Note that graduated circles are quick symbols to draw by hand, while triangles and squares are drawn more quickly by automatic plotter.

Figure 8 is taken from page 168 and shows coastwise and inland shipping. Here was a subject for which data were very scarce. We finally located Lloyds Lists, which are published daily for each port and record the activities of individual ships. By diligent searching we were able to identify the movements of individual ships in the coastal trade from port to port and from day to day. On this basis it was possible to quantify these movements. The map also shows somewhat similar information from a different source, the records of the Post Office ship-to-shore radio service. Ships above a certain tonnage report their positions daily to this service; these records were analyzed in terms of tonnage, cargo, and direction for two particular days. The little ship symbols thus give a kind of photograph of the position of shipping on two particular days. A similar world map also appears in the Atlas. One can assume that shipping is a significant resource, but the data for mapping it are still not in digital form.

The Atlas contains several series of regional maps at 1:1M scale: these are an attempt to say the same thing over again at a larger scale and in a rather different way: redundancy is an important graphic device. Figure 9,

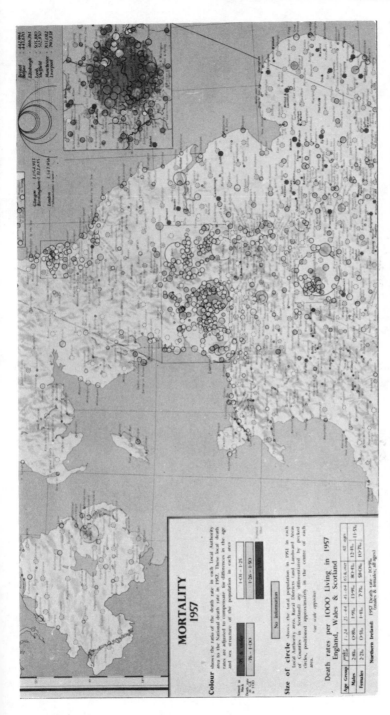

Figure 7   Mortality map for 1957, using coded circles to represent quantitative data. From page 157 of the Atlas of Britain. (Reproduced by permission of the Clarendon Press, Oxford.)

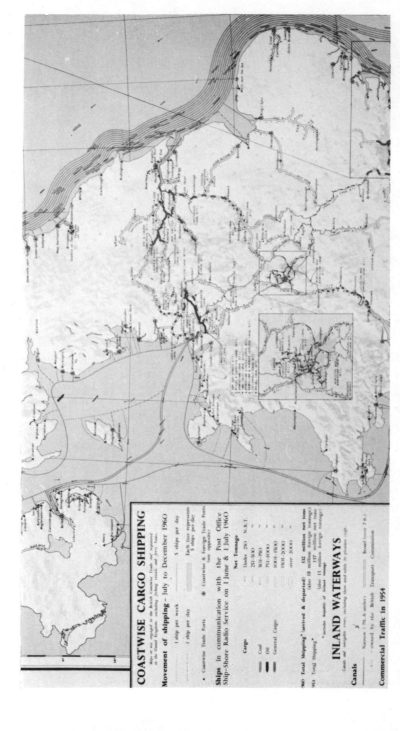

Figure 8 Map of coastal and inland shipping. Ship symbols show locations of ships on one specific day (June 1, 1960). From page 168 of the Atlas of Britain. (Reproduced by permission of the Clarendon Press, Oxford.)

Figure 9 Relief map of Wales and the Midlands having an overprinted grid for precise location of points. Original at a scale of 1:1M. From page 58 of the Atlas of Britain. (Reproduced by permission of the Clarendon Press, Oxford.)

for example, shows the region of Wales and the Midlands. This relief map appears on a double page spread alongside three others so it is possible for the user to move backwards and forwards between relief, vegetation, solid geology, and drift. If he wishes to ask a precise question about an exact point, he will make use of a grid printed over each map in an adequately recessive color. It is arguable that, if you had all this information neatly stacked and accessible in a computer file, you could retrieve whatever you wanted at a particular moment, with the added possibility that you could manipulate it as desired. Indeed, these are arguments that I have frequently used during the last five years. What is less clear is whether the computer bank version of this information would be cheaper and would be as concise and as precise (i.e. as high resolution) as it is in this graphic form. A computer bank would probably be more geared to answering some specific question *ad hoc* and perhaps less to provoking thought about what questions should be answered.

But to leave such generalizations, I would like you to notice on the relief map that height figures are sometimes accompanied by little black triangles; these cross-reference to the vegetation map shown as Figure 10. There, the same black triangles are accompanied by annual rainfall figures, hopefully a pertinent comment. On the vegetation map you may observe that we have accepted a basic topographical classification from the Ordnance Survey maps at one inch to the mile of "rough pasture", as distinct from the other land-use categories of woodland, open water, built-up areas, and farmland. Within the rough pasture category (whose boundaries have been surveyed), we have attempted a classification of the natural vegetation. Dividing lines between these vegetation categories are of quite a different order of reliability. I would also like to draw attention to a besetting problem of cartography, that of the minimum size of island that can be displayed and differentiated by color. These small areas of woodland and rough pasture have been taken directly from one-inch scale mapping. We believe that it is possible to push the resolving power of the eye to the point where this detail can be understood without complicating the issue by statistical generalization. At the same time, note a graphic point: the colors used would not be legible if each did not have a fine black bounding line around it. In theory, such a boundary seems likely to obscure and take away from the color or tone that is displayed. In practice, colored islands of this size fade into each other unless held apart by a black line. This problem of spatial generalization is one in which cartographers have some centuries of practical experience closely allied to printing technology. But, more work is needed, in particular with collaboration from perception psychologists and statisticians.

A similar series of 1:1M regional maps of industrial subjects was also included (Figure 11). Here we are dealing with point information. We identified (in two sets of maps for each region) 16 categories of industry, ranging from mining, engineering, precision, and jewelry making, in one set;

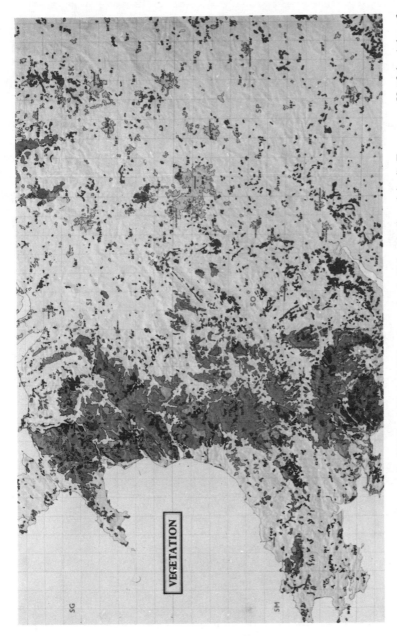

Figure 10 Vegetation map of Wales and the Midlands at the 1:1M scale (in original). From page 58 of the Atlas of Britain. (Reproduced by permission of the Clarendon Press, Oxford.)

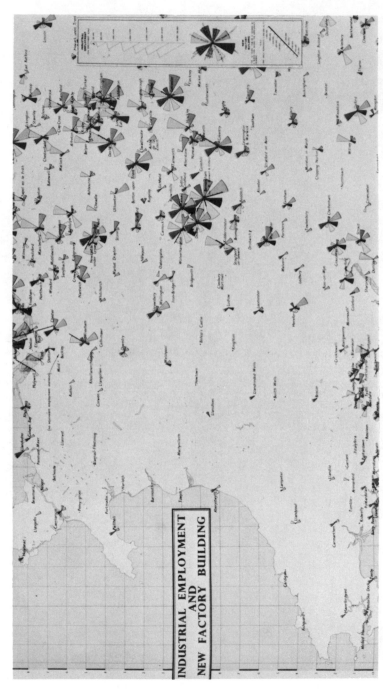

Figure 11   Employment map with trades indicated by "windmill" symbols. Note inset has been moved from original location on plate. From page 137 of the Atlas of Britain. (Reproduced by permission of the Clarendon Press, Oxford.)

to textiles, food and drink, paper and printing, and services such as gas, water, and electricity, in the other set. The data for the colored segments came from returns of the individual labor exchanges of the Department of Employment and are supplemented by details of new factory building over a decade, which are shown by the notched windmill arms alongside the segments. If you find these maps overpowering, and over condensed, bear in mind the pages and pages of statistics, or worst still, of computer tab sheets, which this map represents. The question is again one of generalization, and of how far quantitative graphics can be pressed in the interests of giving both a detailed and a synoptic view of a situation. I believe this to be a serious question so far as the computer graphic processing of data of this kind is concerned.

And now some *post hoc* comments. Although the maps that I have been describing are at scales of 1:2M and 1:1M, I believe they are valid illustrations of the problems of computer cartography or spatial data processing at any scale. In fact, "data reduction" and scale reduction are related requirements. In the computer case, there is the attractive, if theoretical, possibility of interrogating the original data file at any point, at speed, and hopefully at reasonable cost.

The illustrations have, I hope, suggested that it is often desirable to go to many different sources of data to be able to present a spatial problem in a wide circumstantial context. At present I would guess there is in Britain less than a one-in-five chance that spatial data that one may wish to use will be in digital form of any kind. There is less than a one-in-one hundred chance that it will be in a form which could be used directly without some major effort of pre-processing to make it compatible with the requirements of any system of automatic cartography. So there is, still, a major management problem in the compatibility of data sets.

One of the main criticisms of the Atlas of Britain in particular, and of cartography in general, is its slowness. The population distribution map, for example, was based on the Census of 1951 and the Atlas was published in 1963. The whole subject of cartography abounds with examples of data assiduously collected and lying unusable in a pipeline for such lengths of time as to erode much of the value that the data originally had. Recently the Experimental Cartography Unit was asked about mapping bathymetric and geophysical data as it was collected, quickly enough for the ship collecting it to return if necessary to particular areas for further surveying in greater detail. We should be considering carefully what it costs to speed up spatial data processing; also what is really being lost by our present slowness. "Instant maps" are essential in some subjects such as meteorology, for obvious reasons, but they can only be achieved by skillful structuring of data within the computer data file. At present, they rarely involve correlation between several different subjects.

The figures from the Atlas of Britain illustrate some of the graphic capabilities of high resolution manual cartography. Our experience with high accuracy flat bed plotters over the last five years convince us that computer cartography also has great potential elegance. Furthermore, it can achieve new graphic forms that are quite impractical by manual methods. It should be able to achieve these so rapidly that the designer could experiment with several different graphic forms and then decide which suits him best, in half the time that manual cartography would require to produce one form. The obstacles to a breakthrough in this area may lie less in the technology of graphics hardware than in the software of file stuctures and data management systems that will handle the data in a flexible way so as to encourage rather than discourage its interrogation.

I have sometimes felt that the Atlas of Britain is like a sleeping beauty frozen into paper and ink, quite inert. And of what map is this not true? But maps rank poorly as abstract art: their justification is that they are functional. If the map can claim to be the visual expression of a bank of information about a topic and an area, it should be permissible for the inquiring user to interrogate the information, to update bits of it, to ask for derivative information (such as slope maps from contours), to ask for the measurement of areas. Interactive graphics are a long way from even the standards of cartography of a decade ago in terms of costs, resolution, and graphic versatility; perhaps the ephemeral CRT map and the definitive printed one will always be natural complements to each other. One of the types of interrogation that is particularly beloved of planners is the ability to overlay. This business of spatial correlation (for example, between geology, pig farming, and mortality) has been conducted by geographers with tracing paper and ingenuity for generations. It is certainly an area of great interest in computer cartography. Some of my statistician friends, however, have suggested that to handle overlay exclusively by computer methods may be less economical and versatile than by the more graphical methods of "sieve" mapping (that is, superimposing color transparencies, perhaps themselves produced by a plotter).

Finally, the question of interrogating maps leads inevitably to the question of legibility. I propose as a postscript to cite two recent studies in this field which have produced some discouraging evidence on standards of map reading even among scientists. It is illogical, but a fact, that although large amounts of research and development effort are currently spent in examining cartographic and computer graphic techniques, very little is spent on evaluating the effectiveness of the map in terms of usability or legibility. In the past most cartographic "user" studies have been concerned with what information should be shown and not with the effectiveness with which the map is used. There has also been a tendency to record user's opinions, rather than their actual performance, as the assessment criteria.

A study by Hill (1973) was concerned with evaluation of half a dozen different versions of a 1:25,000 orthophoto map of a part of England, in comparison with the equivalent Ordnance Survey map of the same area. Although the experiments were carried out with military surveyors, they involved practical map reading tasks such as orientation and location identifications. In addition, the map users were asked to state both their confidence in and their preference for the form of map. Hill's results showed that neither confidence in the form of map nor preference for a map was reflected by the user's performance in answering factual questions with it. In other words, people's opinions about a map are a bad guide to how effectively they can actually use it.

Shaw (1972) reported three separate experiments on different tasks and different maps and two or three significant points emerge. One experiment was concerned with the effect of changes in map scale and color of background on the ability to read complex point symbols on geochemical maps. Test subjects had to identify and count certain specified symbols. Another experiment was concerned with interpolating information from contour maps. In this one, subjects were asked to estimate values for randomly selected points between contour lines or changes in layer tints. The third experiment was concerned with recognizing overall shapes and areas from contour maps. Subjects were given a simple shape-matching task to perform, using three types of cartographic representation; a contour line map, a contour layer map, and a contour line map with a closer contour interval (i.e., more information). Various groups of people were tested, varying in age, professional experience, and skill.

I do not want to go into the detailed statistical results of each of these experiments, but merely to draw your attention to some general conclusions from the results which are, I think, salutary. First, in all of the experiments, levels of map-reading accuracy were generally low. It is difficult to know precisely what is meant by this, but as a cartographer I think one assumes that the accuracy and precision used in putting information *into* the map will somehow be mirrored by the map user when he subsequently extracts information from the map. In the geochemical map experiment, for example, the subjects achieved an average success rate of less than 50 percent on the precise counting task. In the contour interpolation tests as many as 20 percent of the answers were not even within the right contour interval. Of the answers that were within the correct contour interval, a third were only accurate to within ± 25 percent. Is this level of performance adequate?

The second general point of interest which comes from these experiments is the effect, or rather the lack of effect, of age and experience. The tests were carried out with groups of 11-year olds in a grammar school, 16- to 18-year olds in a grammar school, cartography students at a technical college, "mature" students taking a geography degree course, practising cartographers, geologists, and scientific research workers. While it is true that all the test questions were intentionally simple and answerable directly from maps, in other words not depending on the user's general knowledge and past experience, it was surprising that there was so little difference between the different groups of subjects. Standards of accuracy were much the same from group to group. Age and experience, if it had any effect at all, was in speed rather than accuracy. There was in fact much greater difference within groups, say between one individual geologist and another, than between geologists and another group. There was also variation, or lack of consistency, within any one person's performance.

These experiments suggest that map reading is not a naturally acquired skill, and it should not be assumed that merely because someone uses a map as a professional tool, he will use it more accurately than anyone else. The use of maps is something that has to be taught, and perhaps taught at a much higher level than is the case at present. There may be an analogy here with ordinary reading skills. The assumption that a person has received all of the reading instruction he needs by the time he is taught to read at the age of seven or eight is now being challenged in relation to the alarming rates of adult illiteracy which are currently receiving attention. The same must be true of map reading, and to an even greater extent. The elementary map reading exercises given at the age of 11 or 12 are insufficient training for use of sophisticated cartographic displays later in life, especially as the cartographic language is extremely difficult to learn anyway, perhaps more analogous with Chinese than with western linguistic codes. And let us be aware of the natural tendency to design computer-graphic programs to imitate traditional cartographic conventions, in the mistaken belief that because they are traditional they are, *ipso facto*, legible.

It is a proper function of research to seek out the Achilles' heel, to identify weaknesses and inconsistencies in methods; and spatial data processing has a satisfactorily large number of them. Data are inadequate though voluminous, methods of processing are either too slow or too expensive, and results, in so far as they are comprehended, are either too much or too little biased. But to conclude a paper on the relevance of cartography in a volume on spatial data proceeding I would suggest three questions:

What spatial data can be processed economically now?

What are the aspects of a spatial problem that we should now be able to analyze more truthfully and circumstantially?

What can computer graphics communicate more readably now?

I would suggest there are no clear answers to these questions, and that for a decade or two we shall continue to need the skills of the cartographer and of the computer scientist as well as the ability to obtain the optimum from both. Each seems entirely relevant to the other.

References

Bickmore, D. P., and M. A. Shaw, eds., 1963, *The Atlas of Great Britain and Northern Ireland*: Clarendon Press, Oxford, 200 p.

Hill, A. R., 1973, *Orthophoto-map evaluation in the field*: presented at Annual Conference, British Cartographic Assoc., Cambridge.

Shaw, A., 1972, Objective evaluation of graphic displays of information: Social Science Research Council, *Final Rept.*, Project Rept. No. HR 976.

Compilation of Data for Computer-Assisted Relief Cartography

P. Yoeli

The geometric survey and description of the Earth's relief is used for the solution of the following problems:

(1) Creation of regular contour maps
(2) Creation of anaglyphic contour maps
(3) Determination of height differences between points
(4) Slope analysis
(5) Volume computations
(6) Intervisibility problems
(7) Creation of shadow pictures ("hill shading")
(8) Construction of axonometric, isometric, central-perspective, and panoramic drawings
(9) Construction of profiles
(10) Construction of three-dimensional relief models.

These problems can be treated by classical terrestrial surveys followed by preparation of topographical contour maps or by photogrammetric methods, through measurements on stereoscopic models of pairs of aerial or terrestrial photographs. Although most of them can be solved photogrammetrically without recourse to contour maps, it is customary to use these maps and reach the required solutions cartometrically (through measurements on the map).

In considering how best to use computers in topographical cartography, it is important to realize that contour maps are only a means to an end. Maps are an abstraction of reality and therefore a simplification. While the Earth's surface is a three-dimensional continuum [a function of two variables $z = f(x, y)$], contours are orthographic projections of parameter lines of this function ($z = $ constant) on the map plane, or representations of discrete values. The solid which would be outlined by these parameter lines if each of them was re-elevated to its own height is therefore only an approximation to the true surface; its accuracy depends on the scale of the map, the spatial accuracy of the contours, and their vertical spacing. Contours are a rigid three-dimensional measuring scale superimposed on the relief. All terrain details falling between the vertical intervals are lost. By contrast, stereoscopic models of a pair of aerial photographs are a continuous representation of the Earth's surface whose accuracy depends on the quality of the camera, the film, and the flying altitude.

In applying computers and their accessories to the solution of topographic problems, a computer-compatible description of the Earth's surface is required. If digital computers are used, this description naturally must be in digital form. This requires registration of the spatial coordinates of an array of points of the Earth's surface. Such an array is called a *Digital Terrain Model* (DTM). As with contours, the continuous surface is approximated by discrete values, the fundamental difference being that while the quantity of terrain information on a contour map depends on its scale, the point density of a DTM is, at least theoretically, optional. This means that its degree of approximation to the true surface can be regulated at will, provided the necessary source material is available. The accuracy of approximation depends on the source from which the spatial coordinates are measured, the density of the height points and their relative geometric situation. The denser the net, the more accurate the results and the greater the cost.

For most DTMs there are two stages of development: the initial stage comprising the input information with a relatively low density, and the second (interpolation) stage based on the points of the input data. For reasons of programming convenience, the second stage usually results in a dense regular grid. As the required point density depends on the type of topographical problem at hand, interpolation is usually effected in conjunction with the latter. Thus, a much denser grid is required for an analytical shadow picture (hill shading) than in intervisibility problems. If DTMs are used for interpolation of contours, the choice of density is influenced by the scale of the required map and the vertical interval chosen.

DTMs can be classified according to their source of initial input:

(1) Terrestrial surveys (leveling and tachymetry)
(2) Digitized contours (from either terrestrial or photogrammetric surveys)
(3) Photogrammetric measurements on stereoscopic models.

A second possible classification (Figure 1) refers to the pattern of point registration:

(1) Random points
(2) Semi-ordered points
(3) Ordered points.

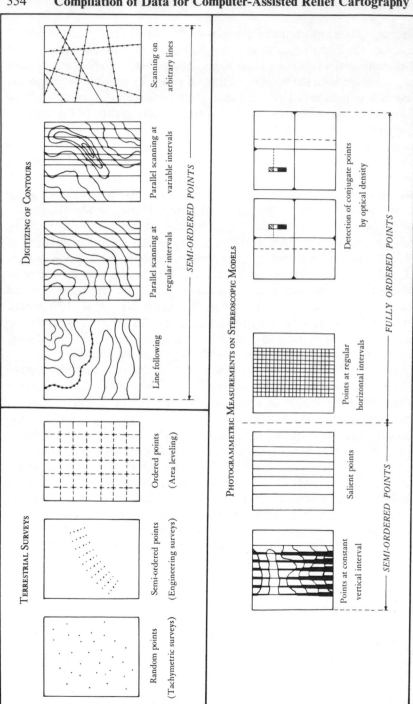

Figure 1 Sources of initial digital terrain models, from terrestrial surveys, by digitizing of contours on pre-existing maps, or from photogrammetric measurements on stereoscopic models.

The two classifications are closely related. Terrestrial surveys are usually carried out in a random point fashion. A pure random point distribution is characteristic of statistical surfaces. In professionally executed terrestrial surveys there is usually some logic in the point distribution because surveyors choose salient points such as extrema or those at which the terrain slope changes. Points also tend to be arranged along characteristic terrain lines such as ridges and valley lines. Surveys for engineering purposes are usually semi-ordered. Points from digitized contours are always semi-ordered. If digitizing is done by line following, the series of x, y coordinates along a definite contour corresponds to the same z coordinate. In scanning (registration of intersections of contours with profile lines) digitized points can have a varying degree of ordering, depending on the relation of the straight lines. They can be:

(1) Parallel to each other and equidistant
(2) Parallel to each other but not equidistant
(3) Non-parallel, with random directions and distances.

Photogrammetrically measured points used for relief mapping are usually semi-ordered or fully ordered. If the stereoscopic model is scanned along parallel straight lines at equal distances, the following modes of registration are possible:

(1) Salient points
(2) Points at regular vertical intervals
(3) Points at regular horizontal intervals.

Mode 2 resembles the scanning mode of contours along straight parallel lines and is, in fact, digital registration of what is known in orthophotoscopy as "dropped lines". Only mode 3 yields a fully ordered DTM in either a rectangular or a square grid format. It is also the only mode in which the second stage is superfluous, as the stereoscopic model can be scanned at much smaller horizontal intervals than needed for most cartographic purposes. In all other instances, interpolation is necessary if a dense regular DTM is to be created.

Digitizing of Contours

The method of creating DTMs through digitizing of contours has its drawbacks. The digital model does not approximate the Earth's true surface with any more accuracy than the contours themselves, and the process of digitizing actually introduces further inaccuracies. Moreover, the subsequent interpolation of a denser net of points may lead to additional "smoothing" and generalization of the relief and to further deviation from the original surface.

However, practical considerations may still dictate digitizing. The necessary aerial photographs and photogrammetric equipment are not always easily accessible, and existing topographic maps are often the most convenient source available. Digitizing is frequently resorted to with a view to generalized contours used on smaller-scale maps. Although in principle any degree of generalization can be achieved through regulation of the point density of the DTMs into which contours are interpolated, there are computer-assisted techniques which try to arrive at contours of derived smaller-scale maps by way of smoothing and generalization of the source map contours.

The decision to use contours as the source of a DTM may also be influenced by the degree of accuracy required in a specific topographical problem. The question of accuracy must be clarified, however, as the accuracy of the contour presentation can rarely be defined with certainty. For computer-assisted solution of all topographical problems on all possible scales, only photogrammetrically produced DTMs are recommended.

Principles of Digitizing

Digitizing of contours means conversion of contour lines into numerical values. This is accomplished by a "digitizer", which converts graphical data into a series of numerical definitions, usually five- or six-character data words in both the x- and y-axes.

Most digitizers consist of a level surface or digitizing table on which graphical data may be spread. The data on this surface can be scanned with a "cursor", which is connected to a data readout device which displays the x- and y-coordinates as the cursor is moved. The digital unit recording these coordinates serves as a link between the digitizer and a computer which handles the digitized data for further manipulation (Figure 2).

In order to describe the type of data digitized and to give it a locating address in the digital bank, additional data are provided by the operator.

According to their mode of action, digitizers can be classified as:

(1) Point digitizers
(2) Point and line digitizers by line following
(3) Scanners.

With type (1) the cursor is applied manually at a point and its coordinates are electronically measured and registered. The command for registration is given by the operator, who also adds the necessary "name" of the point. This method can be used for digitizing straight lines by registering their end-points.

The second mode is much faster and more versatile, as the cursor is made to follow lines. This movement is registered automatically at certain intervals in the form of absolute incremental rectangular coordinates.

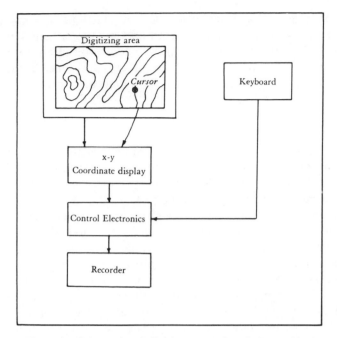

Figure 2 Schematic of digitizer operation. Information is obtained by automatically tracking movement of a cursor, or manually through a keyboard.

In scanning mode, the manuscript to be digitized is scanned in narrow strips parallel to one of the coordinate axes and every crossing point of the scan-line with lines or points on the manuscript is registered (Figure 3).

For contour digitizing, only the line following and scanning modes are practical. While the point digitizer can only be operated manually, line following digitizers may be operated both manually and semi- or fully

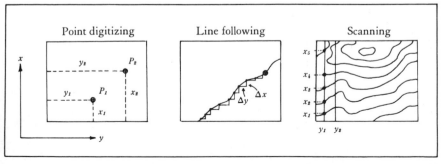

Figure 3 Three modes of digitizing by machine; point digitizing, line following, and scanning.

automatically. Scanners normally are fully automatic. In the semi-automatic mode, the map to be digitized is enlarged on a monitor screen together with the cursor, whose direction of movement is controlled electronically by the operator. In the fully automatic mode the cursor is positioned by the operator on the desired line, which it follows automatically under photoelectric control.

DTMs from Photographic Models

Relief cartography by photogrammetric models is to a large extent still "contour-oriented". The solution of topographical problems is mainly accomplished through the medium of contour maps produced with stereo-plotters. Compared with the tedious task of contour interpolation based on terrestrial tachymetric surveys of pre-photogrammetric times, this was a revolution which not only produced contours at an incredibly higher speed but also improved their accuracy to a standard previously unknown. With the advent of computer-assisted cartography and the possibility of computer processing of topographical data, including interpolation of the contours themselves into digital terrain models, the relationship between photogrammetry and cartography had to be readjusted. Computer-assisted topographical cartography requires digital data which is supplied mainly by digitizing graphic sources (contours or profiles) and delivered by photogrammetric methods. This intermediate step of graphic output delivered by photogrammetry, only to be digitized afterwards for cartographic data processing, seems to be an anachronism. The logical consequence of the latest developments in automated cartography is obviously the need for photogrammetric methods and equipment to supply DTMs directly. Being in possession of the most comprehensive data bank of the Earth's relief in the form of the stereo model, photogrammetry should produce DTMs free of the limitations inherent in contour descriptions of the Earth's surface. They should, in fact, be a computer-compatible record of the Earth's surface at an optimal degree of approximation.

Digitizing procedures are not new in photogrammetry. They were introduced for aerial triangulation work, for cadastral work, and for the creation of DTMs for engineering projects. As the points were measured individually, the process was slow and tedious. The advent of orthophotography gave the first impetus to a conceptual change. Recent developments in photogrammetric equipment, permitting manual or automatic production of dense regular DTMs from stereo models, actually opened new vistas in computer-assisted cartography.

Measurements of Fully Ordered DTMs

In the wake of the advent of orthophotography, photogrammetric equipment such as the Zeiss Ecomat 11 and Wild Stereocomat B-8 has been developed which can supply any kind of DTM required. With the Zeiss Ecomat 11, for example, the following operations can be done with stereo models:

(1) Registration of coordinates of single points
(2) Automatic registration of a sequence of points by constant adjustable increments x, y, and z ("distance mode")
(3) Automatic registration of points at constant adjustable time intervals ("time mode")
(4) Semi-automatic measurement and registration of fully ordered DTMs
(5) Fully automatic measurement and registration of fully ordered DTMs in conjunction with the Zeiss Planimat D2 and the Itek-correlator EC.

Registration can be done on a typewriter, paper tape, punched cards, or magnetic tape.

In the semi-automatic mode the operator scans the stereo model in parallel profiles identical to the process applied in orthophotography. However, instead of "dropped lines" (in graphical or digital form) the digitizer yields, in the distance mode, z-coordinates at distances ranging from 0.1 to 50mm. In the time-mode, z-coordinates can be registered at constant time intervals ranging from 0.1 to 9.9 seconds. The same range of intervals can be applied to the distances between the scan lines. A fully ordered DTM can be achieved only when scanning in the distance mode. In the time mode the number of points digitized depends on the speed of scanning. As this is influenced by the complexity of the terrain, fewer points are registered for slow and even slopes while the density of points increases in more mountainous terrain. It permits registration of salient points which in the distance mode might fall through the grid. It also economizes on the number of measured data points and facilitates the data storage problem. However, not being fully ordered, this mode of registration calls for interpolation of a fully ordered grid, if required for further cartographic processing.

The direction of the scan line is parallel to either the x or y machine coordinate. Options of the instrument include digitizing the relief in the form of contours. For the contours to portray the relief as precisely as a DTM based on a dense regular grid, they must be digitized at a very small vertical interval. They require much more data, continuous Δx and Δy, as compared to the constant increments for every grid line when digitizing in a regular grid. In addition, the stereoscopic model requires an absolute orientation.

Registration at regular horizontal intervals is the ideal mode for basic DTMs. A high density of measured points can be achieved economically. As the points are measured, *a priori*, in a regular grid, there is no need for further interpolation. This mode of registration may, however, prove too rigid and, if the constant Δx and Δy are chosen large in relation to the geomorphology of the terrain, certain characteristic features of the relief may be lost. To overcome this, the operator can manually digitize additional points. On the other hand, he can dispense with continuous registration of parts of the scanned profile, so the density of the DTM can be adjusted to the varying character of terrain even in the distance mode. This option, however, destroys the regularity of the grid and mathematical interpolation is needed before further use of the DTM can be made.

Scanning of Optical Densities and Identification of Homologous Points

With this method, the pair of overlapping photographs forming the photogrammetric model must first be digitized. This is done with a precision optical scanner which measures the densities of the photographic image, using a sampling process determined by the scanner spot size and the chosen number of optical gray levels. The results of the scanning are recorded in two large two-dimensional matrices representing the densities of elements making up the photographs. These matrices are called "digital photographs". The spot size of available scanners being approximately 0.1mm, the number of spots into which the overlap of a 18cm by 18cm photogrammetric model would be resolved is approximately $2 \cdot 10^6$.

The next step is to determine the transformation coefficients for the coordinates. (This is equivalent to the relative and absolute orientation procedure in analog-type photogrammetric instruments.) Data required for this computation are obtained by measuring the plate coordinates of at least six well-distributed points in the overlap. The terrain coordinates of at least three of these points must also be known.

The following step, the most difficult one, is to identify homologous points in the two photographs in order to be able to determine their heights from their parallax. There are various solutions to this problem; one consists of storing all known pairs of homologous points in the computer. In the beginning these are the points used for the relative and absolute orientation, which serve as centers around which additional homologous points are identified by comparison of the distribution of measured densities. The list of identified points grows continuously, each newly identified point serving in turn as a center for the detection of additional homologues. The last steps include the determination of the terrain coordinates of each point by means of those of the homologues in the digital photographs (Etrog, 1972).

Interpolation of Additional Points and DTMs

General Remarks and Accuracy of Interpolation

For computer-assisted solution of topographical problems, interpolation of fully ordered point grids is not absolutely necessary. Irregular or semi-ordered grids, usually comprising considerably fewer points than regular arrays, can even be advantageous, especially for small computers. It is, nevertheless, generally accepted that fully ordered DTMs are more convenient and easier to handle. Since dense regular arrays pose serious storage problems, the actual interpolation is best carried out in conjunction with solution of the specific problem at hand. The question of interpolation of additional points is extensively treated in literature, but usually in the context of contouring problems.

There are, in principle, two possibilities of arriving at a dense regular grid. These are:

(1)   By an analytical surface fit
(2)   By polyhedron or numerical approximation.

Techniques for surface fitting by computers are well established, such as least-square surface approximations. Others, like the "spline approximation", are based on a minimum curvature criterion. Some least-square approximations use trigonometric functions (Fourier series). The type of surface dealt with by topographic cartography is, however, so irregular as to defy any analytical definition. Moreover, many of the surface-fitting techniques have a "smoothing" effect, which is admissible only in the creation of *derived* cartographic products. In these circumstances, only a numerical method which seeks to order and increase the number of initial height points is practical.

The mode of interpolation of additional points depends on the character of the DTM initially measured. Referring to Figure 1, the following possibilities exist:

(1)   Random sample points
(2)   Digitized contours by line following
(3)   Parallel scan-lines of contours or photographs
(4)   Straight scan-lines in arbitrary directions.

Interpolation of Fully Ordered Point Grid Based on Random Sample Points

This mode of interpolation is typical of computer-assisted cartography of thematic maps, which deals extensively with statistical surfaces. The initial data very often consists of random sample points through which a surface must be interpolated. Random distribution of measured points occurs mainly in tachymetric terrestrial surveys. If the survey is carried out professionally, the points are not really random but rather salient points of the Earth's relief, chosen so that a linear interpolation in the direction of the gradient would usually result in a very close approximation.

Weighted Average. The main method used for interpolation of a regular grid from random arrays is based on computation of a weighted average of the

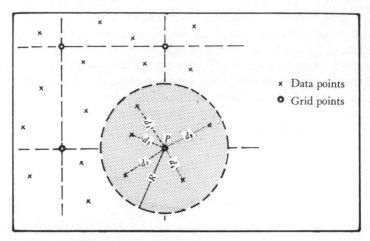

Figure 4   Calculation of mesh point P as a function of data points inside a neighborhood of radius R.

heights of a representative sample of n points in the vicinity of a grid node (Figure 4). If P(x, y) is a grid point, its height H_p is

$$H_p = \frac{\sum\limits_{i=1}^{i=n} H_i W_i(x, y)}{\sum\limits_{i=1}^{i=n} W_i(x, y)}$$

where i identifies any sample point, H_i is its height, and $W_i(x, y)$ is the weight of the sample point relative to P(x, y). The weighting function $W_i(x, y)$ must insure that the closer a data point is to a grid point, the higher is its weight. If a data point happens to coincide with a grid point, its height should be left unchanged. As only these points which lie in the near vicinity of the grid points have any significant relevance to its height, a maximum distance must be formulated so only points falling inside the circle are considered in the average.

Of the many possible weighting functions, the one described by Shepard (1968) and adopted by the Experimental Cartography Unit shall be mentioned here. The function is:

$$W_i = \frac{(1 - D_i)^2}{D_i^2} \qquad \text{for } D_i < 1$$

and

$$W_i = 0 \qquad \text{for } D_i > 1$$

where $D_i = d_i/R$, d_i being the distance between the point i and the grid point and R the radius of the sampling circle. The choice of R depends on the density of the data points and the character of the relief, but should be chosen so that the sampling circle includes at least four or five sample points. This method works well only if the data points are more or less evenly distributed, which is usually the case with topographical surveys. An interpolation method suitable for bridging gaps in random input data is described in IBM (1965).

Polyhedron Method. The polyhedron method approximates a surface by forming a system of triangular elements (Figure 5). Each element is a plane

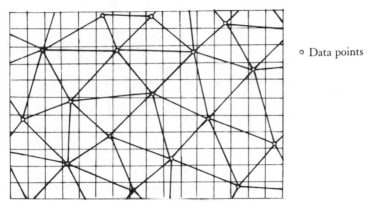

○ Data points

Figure 5 Construction of triangular net for estimation of contour locations by linear interpolation.

triangle with vertices defined by adjacent data points. No data point may lie inside a triangle. This presupposes that the surveyed points have been chosen in such a way that the assumption of a linear slope between two adjacent points is close enough to truth. In this system the intersections between sides of triangles and the superimposed regular grid are found by computer and their heights are determined by linear interpolation between the heights of the vertices.

The most difficult step is computer-executed formation of the triangles. According to one method described by Düppe and Gottschalk (1970), all possible lines connecting the given data points are computed and ordered according to length. The shortest line is chosen as the starting side and all lines crossing this side are excluded. Next, the shortest line among the others having a common vertex with the starting side is sorted out. This results in the first triangle. This process is repeated until all the triangles are found. Düppe and Gottschalk showed that the sum of the sides found is a minimum.

Interpolation of Fully Ordered Point Grid Based on Semi-Ordered Data Digitizing Contours by Line-Following. In contrast to most semi-ordered

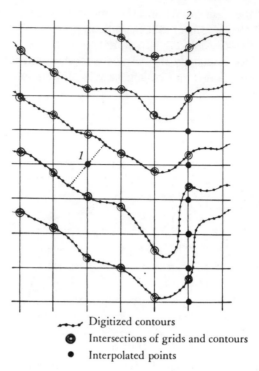

    Digitized contours

    Intersections of grids and contours

    Interpolated points

Figure 6 Contours digitized by line following, consisting of sequences of points of the same height.

configurations where data are arranged along straight lines, contours digitized by line following consist of sequences of points of the same height on which a rectangular grid is superimposed (Figure 6). Two possibilities for interpolating heights along the grid lines are:

(1) The intersection points of grid lines with contours are sought; a function of one variable is interpolated through these points and evaluated at the desired grid point (case 2 in Figure 6). This has the serious drawback that the accuracy of interpolation along grid lines depends on the relative directions of contours and grid lines, as this determines the number and density of intersection points.

(2) The most sensible method of interpolation seems to be to calculate, through the desired grid point, the shortest possible line connecting two contours between which the grid point is positioned (case 1 in Figure 6). The equation of this line at the desired grid point yields the required height. This is, in fact, the method by which a reader determines the height of any point on a contour map.

Interpolation Based on Semi-Ordered Points Along Parallel Profiles. Let us first consider the case of profile scanning with registration of data points at *constant vertical* intervals. This can be done on contour maps or on stereo models where it is usually accomplished as a byproduct of orthophotoscopy in the form of digital registration of "dropped lines" (Figure 7). Provided the

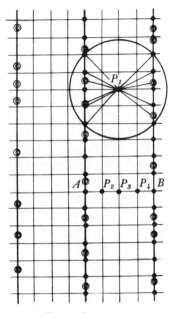

◎ Data points

● Interpolated points

Figure 7   Interpolation to a mesh from points digitized along two widely spaced profile scans.

spacing of the scan lines does not exceed that of points on contours digitized by line following, the two cases differ only in their mode of registration of the data points. With both, the initial DTM consists of sequences of points of equal height. Straightforward linear interpolation between pairs of adjacent points along the scan-line has the drawback that accuracy of the interpolation depends on relative directions of scan-lines and contours. It seems logical to determine heights of points to be interpolated as is done with contours digitized by line following. The only difference is that scan-lines can be assumed to be part of the grid, so ordering of the initial data points in one direction may be taken for granted.

The choice of density of the interpolated regular grid depends on the character of the topographical problem. If it happens that profile lines of the scan are farther apart than required, additional profiles have to be interpolated. This is a relatively minor problem if the initial input comes from contours digitized by line following. The spacing of points is so much smaller than the densest grid needed for any topographical problem that any required grid density can be interpolated. For example, points on contours of a $1:5000$ map digitized at an average resolution of 0.1mm lie in reality 0.5m apart. Topographical problems needing regular DTMs at this density are most improbable. The problem is different when input is from two widely spaced profile scans, from contour maps, or stereo models.

Additional profiles can be interpolated either by the weighted average method (P_1 in Figure 7) or by linear interpolation perpendicular to the scanned profiles (P_2, P_3, P_4 in Figure 7), using previously interpolated points A and B. The obvious option for interpolation based on profile scanning is in the direction of the scan-line. If this is done with too widely spaced scan-lines and data points registered at constant vertical intervals, the interpolated heights of additional points may prove to be of poor quality depending on the direction of scan-lines and the slope gradients. It is doubtful that nonlinear interpolation or surface-fitting techniques can improve the result significantly.

Much better results may be expected when data points along the profile are salient points, so the linearity of slopes between points is pre-established by the photogrammetric operator who supplies this type of initial DTM.

The need for computer-assisted interpolation of a denser grid into a height grid measured at *regular horizontal intervals* is an extremely rare contingency. Such grids are only encountered in area leveling, and the areas involved usually are too small to merit computerized work.

Digitizing of contour maps at constant *horizontal* intervals would make little sense. Rather than creating an initial DTM based on points lying on contours, it would consist of points graphically interpolated between them. Such arrays are obtainable only from photogrammetric sources. In fact, some of the most promising developments in photogrammetric equipment allow efficient measurement and registration of DTMs at regular horizontal intervals at such density as to make further interpolation superfluous.

These techniques produce a huge amount of input data and pose severe problems of storage and manipulation. Once these are solved, perhaps by on-line methods, they are the ideal combination of compiling photogrammetric data and computer-assisted solution of topographical problems.

References

Düppe, R. D., and H. J. Gottschalk, 1970, Automatische Interpolation von Isolinien bei willkürlich verteilten stützpunkten: *Allgemeine Vermessungsnachrichten*, v. 77, p. 423–426.

Etrog, U., 1972, Collecting and processing photogrammetric data by semi-automatic methods (in Hebrew): *Research Thesis Technion*, Dept. Civil Engineering, Israel Inst. Technology, Tel Aviv, 106 p. ·

IBM, 1965, *Numerical surface techniques and contour map plotting*: IBM Data Processing Application, White Plains, New York, 36 p.

Shepard, D., 1968, A two-dimensional interpolation function for irregularly spaced data: *Proc. 23rd Nat. Conference, Assoc. Computing Machinery*, p. 517–524.

Author Index

Subject Index